Prison Dog Programs

Mary Renck Jalongo
Editor

Prison Dog Programs

Renewal and Rehabilitation in Correctional Facilities

Springer

Editor
Mary Renck Jalongo
Emerita, Indiana University of Pennsylvania
Indiana, PA, USA

ISBN 978-3-030-25617-3 ISBN 978-3-030-25618-0 (eBook)
https://doi.org/10.1007/978-3-030-25618-0

This Springer imprint is published by the registered company Springer Nature Switzerland AG
The registered company address is: Gewerbestrasse 11, 6330 Cham, Switzerland

To those who are employed and volunteer in the justice field and remain committed to rehabilitation and restitution and second chances despite obstacles and disappointments.
Mary Renck Jalongo

Foreword

Introduction

The interdisciplinary group of scholars assembled for this volume have contributed to the development of an evidence-based understanding of canine training and rehabilitation programming in correctional institutions. As prison-based dog programs have grown in popularity, it is important to reflect on what is known about their development, implementation, successes, and opportunities, and always with an eye toward how they may continue to develop in the future. To set the stage for these discussions, this foreword will briefly survey the context of the American correctional system (in which most of the programs in this volume are set) and its goals, and the reasons for believing that canine programs have significant potential for shaping corrections—and society—positively.

"Pep" Goes to Prison

On the morning of Tuesday, August 12, 1924, many readers of the *Philadelphia Inquirer* newspaper were likely following the current "crime of the century" (Higdon 1999), the story of teens Nathan Leopold and Richard Loeb and their murder of neighbor Bobby Franks. Defended by legendary attorney Clarence Darrow, the case was front page news, above the fold, and on August 12, 1924, the *Inquirer* included a photograph and transcript from the trial as it was unfolding in Chicago ("Alienist says…," 1924).

Readers who continued through the paper to page 3 would find another criminal justice story, unique for its time and perhaps an early forbearer of the programs noted in this text, under the headline, "Gov. Pinchot's Dog Sentenced to 'Pen'." The article read, in part,

> The lovingest dog in Pennsylvania has been sent to the State's biggest prison for life because of his superhuman affection for humankind...Pep has done nothing wrong to bring upon him this sentence...He has an overwhelming love for everybody and he wants everybody to love him. Which explains why they are sending Pep to the Pen. The Governor, in his several visits to the great walled prison on what was once known as Cherry Hill, has found men who felt that they were abandoned of the world...No despairing man brooding in his cell can feel that he is forgotten by God and man, who will feel Pep's loving tongue caressing his languid hand. (Beamish 1924, p. 3)

This early effort with a canine "aid to the rehabilitation" of offenders (Beamish 1924, p. 3) was not an isolated case. The Pennsylvania Governor had reportedly been inspired by Governor Baxter of Maine, whose dog earned a full-page spread in the *Baltimore Sun*. Governor Baxter's dog was a collie eponymously named Governor and who was also sent to prison, with results reported by the institution's chaplain, Percy Clifford:

> There's an old lifer calls him Prince, and another calls him Jack. He's Carlo to some and Don to others. He's Duke and Rover and Buster and Master and Fido. They call him by the names of the dogs they used to have and they love him as they loved those pets of old. He brings back to them the dreams and memories of the days before they stepped off the path. And that's good for them...He has made life happier for all the men here, even the lifers, who have very little to be cheerful about ("The dog...," 1924).

While it is unknown how many such programs operated, or the extent to which inmates truly had interactions with prison dogs Pep and Governor as opposed to what was reported in news outlets (e.g., Dolan 2007), these stories remain an early indicator of recognition for the potential impact of the human–animal bond (for a historical overview, see Hines 2003) in correctional settings.

In particular, as more is known about the relationship between humans and dogs (e.g., Payne et al. 2015), perhaps it is only natural to consider how programming that draws upon this bond may be formally incorporated into correctional institutions. But what of the correctional context into which programs are incorporated? After a review of contemporary corrections—the environment into which the chapters of this volume are situated—discussion will return to the human–canine bond and its potential for correctional programming.

The Context of American Corrections

Corrections is a big business in the USA. Annual expenditures exceed $86 billion (Bronson 2018), and there are approximately 6.7 million adults under some form of correctional control—that is 2.6% of the adult population (Kaeble and Cowhig 2018). With the exception of approximately 482,000 persons held in jail while awaiting trial (Zeng 2018), having been denied or unable to afford bail or other pretrial releases (see Scott-Hayward and Fradella 2019), those supervised by correctional agencies have either pled guilty to or have been found guilty at trial of one or more criminal offenses.

However, there is a significant range in the severity and types of offenses and in the criminal histories, motivations, and backgrounds of offenders. For this reason, there is also a significant range in the types of criminal sanctions imposed through the correctional system. Sanctions can be thought of as existing along a continuum, ranging from less to more severe, with the criminal court system assigned the task of determining which sanction is most appropriate for which offense, committed by which offender. Of course, this is an inexact science.

At one end of the continuum is probation, a sentence in which offenders remain in the community with requirements to abide by the law and maintain contact with a probation officer, who not only monitors their behavior but also helps to identify areas of risk and need that may be addressed through programming. At the other end of the continuum is long-term incarceration in a state or federal prison, which may provide some measure of rehabilitative programming, but which is primarily focused on security both within and beyond the institution. In between are a range of other alternatives, such as drug courts, community service requirements, electronic monitoring, house arrest, day reporting centers, halfway houses, and more (see generally Owen et al. 2019).

As the focus of this book is on programs housed in correctional institutions, the balance of discussion of correctional context will focus on jail and prison facilities and approximately 2.1 million inmates (Kaeble and Cowhig 2018). It is, however, important to acknowledge one very important disclaimer, which is that it is very difficult to do more than draw broad generalities. This is because there is not one single correctional system in the USA; rather, there are multiple systems operated discretely from one another, resulting in significant variations in approach, organization, and focus.

There are three levels of correctional institutions in the USA. First, the federal government operates its own institutions, for persons who have violated federal law, through the Federal Bureau of Prisons (see Bosworth 2002). Second, each of the 50 states operates its own institutions, for persons who have violated state law, through their own departments of corrections. Federal and state institutions are classified as prisons, that is, institutions for the long-term confinement of offenders, usually those who have committed felonies and have been sentenced to a year or more of incarcerated time. Third, local governments operate jails, usually under the direction of a local sheriff or a regional jail authority, which generally house persons sentenced for misdemeanors, usually for less than one year of incarceration, as well as housing persons who were not released prior to their trials (see Cornelius 2008).

Further variation is evidenced when considering that, within the federal correctional system, fifty state systems, and multiple local systems, there are different types of institutions constructed for different purposes. This is generally reflected through security levels, which can be summarized as minimum, medium, and maximum, while recognizing that there is even variation among those and that there are also specialized housing units serving other purposes (e.g., medical units, protective custody, disciplinary custody, supermax). Minimum security facilities generally hold lower risk inmates and have fewer security features, security hardware and behavioral controls. Minimum security inmates may live in cells or in dormitory-style settings. Medium and maximum security facilities generally hold higher risk inmates and have more security features, security hardware and behavioral controls. The typical arrangement for a contemporary medium or maximum security facility is to have an open dayroom surrounded by individual or shared inmate cells (Owen 2016).

While this does indeed provide considerable variation in the types of correctional institutions and the practices within them, there are some broad perspectives that can shape an understanding of them. Significant among these are the waxing and waning of focus on one key correctional goal: rehabilitation.

Perspectives on Correctional Institutions and Rehabilitation

While probation is the most common sentence issued in American criminal justice, the USA has the world's highest incarceration rate (Walmsley 2018). This is not attributable to the level of crime in the USA as compared to other nations (Gottschalk 2006), but appears to be more directly related to politics and public policies promoting "get tough" approaches to issues of crime and justice (Clear 2007), such as the "War on Drugs" and the "War on Crime" that influenced criminal justice policy in the late twentieth century (see Beckett and Sasson 2004; for a thoughtful deconstruction of the "war on" metaphor, see Best 1999, Chap. 7). Others have suggested that contemporary corrections may be philosophically shaped by notions rooted in Foucault's (1977) *Discipline and Punish*, suggesting the use of the prison to exert total control and create "docile bodies" (p. 135). For instance, Garland (2001) suggests that corrections seeks "security, orderliness, and control, for the management of risk and the taming of chance" (p. 194). These sentiments also lean toward the use of incarceration as a dominant form of punishment, as it exerts the most substantial and direct control.

Historically, however, a high prevalence of incarceration has not always been the case. In fact, the incarceration rate in the USA was once substantially lower, with approximately 100 persons per 100,000 incarcerated in the nation's prisons and jails. With a small amount of variation, this rate was relatively stable between the mid-1920s (when data were initially available) and the mid-1970s. It was during the late 1970s and into the 1980s and 1990s when a surge in incarceration took hold of American corrections (Sourcebook of Criminal Justice Statistics 2013, Table 6.28. 2012), reaching a high point in both population and incarceration rates (1000 persons incarcerated per 100,000 in the population) in 2008, after which a slight decline has followed (Gramlich 2018).

This reflects changes in the goals of corrections, which in turn drive not only correctional policies, but also the types and extent of programming likely to be found in correctional institutions. Eastern State Penitentiary in Philadelphia—the same institution to which the dog Pep was sent as a gesture of hope from the

Governor to the inmates—is generally recognized as the first contemporary prison in the USA, and it was founded on a notion of rehabilitation. Of course, the notion of rehabilitation on which it was founded was one which emphasized total isolation from other human contacts, to encourage inmates to seek religious repentance (Friedman 1993). Charles Dickens visited the prison and assessed its rehabilitative scheme as follows in his *American Notes* (1842): "I believe that very few men are capable of estimating the immense amount of torture and agony which this dreadful punishment, prolonged for years, inflicts upon the sufferers" (p. 238). Even today, debates about the negative impacts of solitary confinement continue (e.g., Haney 2003) continue. The solitary program at Eastern State was discontinued, and rehabilitation was transformed over time into a more proactive and psychologically informed strategy.

With the Progressive Era and new understandings of the mind, rehabilitation became an accepted correctional goal in the late 1800s and into the 1900s. While an oversimplification of a more complex history, cracks in the rehabilitative veneer began to manifest in the mid-twentieth century, focused on concerns about how rehabilitative strategies were (or were not) implemented, the justice and equitability of a state correctional bureaucracy attempting to deliver rehabilitative behavioral treatments, a move toward getting tough in the wars on crime and drugs, and questions about the effectiveness of rehabilitative programs (see Cullen 2013). Regarding the latter point, in particular, a study by Robert Martinson (1974) was interpreted as suggesting that rehabilitation could not work, stating the finding that "with few and isolated exceptions, the rehabilitative efforts that have been reported so far have had no appreciable effect on recidivism" (p. 25). Granted, this was a sweeping and bold statement, and certainly one which did little to advance the rehabilitative cause.

It was at this time that the prison population in the USA began its dramatic increase. Without rehabilitation as a central focus of corrections, what was left? Criminologists Malcolm Feeley and Jonathan Simon (1992) observed that what was left might be classified as a new model, a "new penology," focused on simply warehousing offenders away from society in hopes that doing so would incapacitate their ability to commit further offenses. While Spelman (2006) found that the notable decline in crime—especially violent crime—that began in the 1990s was partially attributable to increases in incarceration, he was also quick to note that "other factors are responsible for the vast majority of the [crime] drop" (p. 123), and posed the unanswered question, perhaps as a value-based policy proposition, "whether the key to further reductions lies in further prison expansions, or (more likely) in…other factors" (p. 125).

Among those "other factors" may be a resurgence in rehabilitation. Research suggests that rehabilitation is supported by the public (e.g., Thielo et al. 2016), and empirical evidence indicates that it can indeed be effective. Weisburd and colleagues (2017) marshaled extensive evidence demonstrating that numerous rehabilitative interventions were effective, and went so far as to note that "Martinson's critique just 40 years ago and his conclusion that we should abandon the search for programmatic responses to crime and criminality are simply wrong" (p. 437).

Francis Cullen, one of the seminal researchers and leading advocates of rehabilitation programming, and his colleagues Daniel Mears, Cheryl Jonson, and Angela Thielo (2016) published an essay titled "Seven Ways to Make Prisons Work." Their recommendations included the use of reward structures to motivate inmate behavior, the use of the effective risk-need-responsivity (RNR) rehabilitative model, and ensuring that persons who interact with inmates—notably, correctional staff—are provided with sufficient training in the RNR model and other effective correctional practices, so their approach may be consistent with (rather than counter to) rehabilitative goals.

Cullen (2013) argues that the RNR model "has…developed into the dominant treatment paradigm" (p. 340). The full model is described by Bonta and Andrews (2017; at a minimum, Chap. 9 should be required reading for those engaged in correctional programming and rehabilitative efforts) and is comprised of 15 principles. While clearly a broad generalization of a complex but impactful theory, Cullen (2013) summarizes the model as follows:

> In summary, the RNR principles are legitimate precisely because they make sense. Thus, they recommend that correctional interventions focus on high-risk offenders, target empirically strong and malleable predictors of recidivism, and use treatments that are responsive to or capable of changing these dynamic risk factors. (p. 343)

Part of the very success of RNR is that it does not prescribe one treatment modality that is presumed to apply across all offenders; rather, it outlines a framework for developing and delivering rehabilitative programming in a validated, but individualized, manner, to maximize impacts. This helps to overcome the "panacea phenomenon" (Finckenauer and Gavin 1999, p. 13), in which a single preferred intervention is presumed to be the broadly applicable solution to crime. RNR helps us to understand that is not the case—there is no single panacea—but rather, successful endeavors result from matching the appropriate program, to the appropriate person, for the appropriate need, and ensuring that interventions demonstrate a "respect for the person" (Bonta and Andrews 2017, p. 177) with theoretical and empirical groundings.

Pep, Governor, and a Return to Dogs in Prison

Times have clearly changed since Pep and Governor made their entry to Pennsylvania and Maine prisons as a gesture of care toward the inmates. Contemporary correctional institutions, and the programming within them, cannot be viewed as a singular entity. At the same time, neither can—or should—prison canine programs be viewed as a singular entity, as different programs may serve different goals and different animal populations. Reflecting on the RNR perspective, the development of dog care and training programs must be carefully determined in order to ensure that the best fit possible is accomplished between program, institution, inmate, staff, and community participants. While a daunting task, it is also one where there is tremendous current potential. Consider the following forces that have come together in time:

- *Research on the human-animal bond has grown and, in particular, has significantly enhanced knowledge of human–dog attachments.* There is strong evidence of human-dog attachment (Payne et al. 2016), including physiological processes (Payne et al. 2015) and the ability of dogs to recognize emotions (Albuquerque et al. 2016). The bond may be conceptualized as dependent upon dyads, that is, the characteristics that each individual dog and human brings to a pairing, in turn increasing knowledge of how to enhance or maximize attachments (Rehn and Keeling 2016). New research is regularly being reported on the human–dog bond, and it is imperative that program coordinators maintain currency with it.
- *Multiple models for prison-based canine programs exist and have been empirically validated.* In the 2000s, there was a notable increase in the number of prison-based animal programs, many of which involved dogs as the animal subjects; correctional leaders tend to view such programs positively (Furst 2006). Programs with dogs, specifically, have been found to be beneficial for inmate participants, leading "to a safer and healthier prison environment in those pods and facilities where the programs are offered" (van Wormer et al. 2017, p. 537). In addition, research has found that dog programs provide "benefits to the participants (e.g., alleviated depression, improved self-control), the correctional facility (e.g., improved staff/inmate relations, a more hospitable environment), and to the community (e.g., providing training services, reducing recidivism)" (Cooke and Farrington 2016, pp. 871–872). Numerous case studies are available to shape the development of new or expanded programs (e.g., Antonio et al. 2017; Minton et al. 2015; Britton and Button 2005; Harkrader et al. 2004; and many others presented in this volume).
- *A renewed interest in rehabilitation may facilitate opportunities for new program development.* Further, the RNR model suggests the importance of matching the unique aspects of individual correctional institutions with the unique attributes of any given program, to best facilitate the ability of the resulting collaboration to meet institutional, inmate participant and community needs. While the RNR model does not prescribe one particular type of programming—animal-based or otherwise—its tenets can help to inform decisions and program planning, to ensure that they proceed in a deliberate and thoughtful manner.

The above triad of factors has led to the growth and establishment of dog programs in correctional institutions. The early years of Pep and Governor sought to use dogs to ameliorate the day-to-day hardships and conditions of incarceration as experienced by inmates (for the classic overview of prison conditions, see Sykes 1958). And, programming involving dogs may certainly still have this impact. However, the state of knowledge has increased to reflect that animal programs may also meet rehabilitative goals for offenders, may positively impact the correctional institution as a whole, and may provide a broader public service, whether by helping to train service animals for community members and by training animals that will be adopted through shelters, or through other prosocial activities. In this way, the role of animals in correctional facilities has moved from something ad hoc and novel to a series of empirically verified programs that contribute to multiple positive goals, and which are now established as part of the repertoire of American correctional programming. Accordingly, it is an excellent time to reflect on what is known about the effective operations of programs in correctional facilities and what their future may hold.

What's Ahead

The chapters in this volume bring many dynamic and provocative perspectives to the discussion of dog-related programs in correctional institutions, informed by both research and agency practice. The volume begins with Mary Renck Jalongo's overview in Chap. 1 of how prison dog programs fit within the context of human–animal interaction (HAI) studies, and how they meet important service animal and companion animal training needs. In Chap. 2, Gennifer Furst provides an overview of the research literature that establishes dog programs in correctional institutions as an evidence-based practice, surveying the interdisciplinary empirical work on program impacts and the nature of the human–dog bond. Recognizing that programs may take a variety of forms, in Chap. 3 Barbara J. Cooke provides an overview of the goals that programs may seek to accomplish—the most frequent are training service dogs and training dogs to be publicly adopted, but there are a number of additional specialized programs that some institutions offer. Taken together, these first three chapters demonstrate the need, positive impacts, and opportunities for dog training programs in correctional institutions.

The volume then moves to a discussion of some of the most significant planning issues that must be considered by new (or current) programs, offering perspectives for how to successfully navigate sometimes challenging tasks. In order to be effective, dog training programs in correctional institutions must represent a true partnership between the institution and one or more community agencies, which requires a close working relationship and ensuring that facilities, capacities, and capabilities are in place to effectively implement programs in a meaningful way. Chapter 4, by Mary Renck Jalongo, Mary Louden, and Lee Estock, addresses the importance of seeking, advocating, and receiving stakeholder support from a variety of audiences; the chapter also describes how change theory informs the steps necessary for establishing a program, from an initial need assessment, to the planning process, and then to implementation and outcome assessment. In addition, there must be a basic awareness of standards for animal care and what works in training. In Chap. 5, Amy Johnson and Laura Bruneau offer perspectives on animal welfare that must inform the adoption and implementation of any program, providing a set of recommended practices to help facilitate program operations. The concepts in these chapters are critical for the formative planning stages of a program, as gaining stakeholder support, understanding animal care, and determining how to best collaborate with community partners are essential to success in meeting program goals.

The next set of chapters move further into the specifics of program logistics and implementation, in terms of day-to-day considerations that shape program activities and outcomes. In Chap. 6, Leslie B. Hill and Benjamin Wright consider the unique environment of correctional institutions and their security needs, and how security considerations impact program delivery. Programs structured to function a particular way outside of prison walls may have to be modified to fit the environment within the walls, in order to be aligned with correctional agency regulation and protocols. Chapter 7, by Benjamin Wright, Mary Renck Jalongo, and Tonya Guy, provides guidance on the selection of inmate participants for dog training programs. This includes initial screening considerations and the types of training that may be included as part of the program, drawing upon examples from actual programs. In Chap. 8, Mary Renck Jalongo describes how theories of learning may be applied by inmate participants in dog training programs, including the role of knowledge, application of skills, dispositions, and feelings, and how each may be deliberately facilitated through curricula associated with the program. A reading of these chapters provides useful insights that are valuable in shaping program designs.

Correctional practices have increasingly moved toward evidence-based models, seeking to incorporate empirical evaluations and research findings in the development of effective programming. In Chap. 9, Angela Fournier and Lori Winston describes how program evaluation may be applied to dog training programs in correctional institutions, including both formative evaluations during the implementation of the program and summative evaluations measuring the outcomes of the program. Drawing upon actual examples, the chapter provides useful advice for constructing meaningful evaluations. James W. Conroy, Elizabeth Coppola, Charles S. Ferris, Nora L. Conroy, Steven J. Devlin, and Julie Boc share the results of a study of a dog program in the Philadelphia City Jail, including its impacts, in Chap. 10; the analysis demonstrates how the application of a multi-step strategy and effective presentation of data can, in turn, aid in advocating for further program development. In Chap. 11, Mary Renck Jalongo provides an overview of credentials that program participants may earn, which can serve as markers of accomplishment for individual participants in the program and for the program, itself. Thinking about program assessment through the lenses of evaluation research and credentialing can help programs not only to assess their outcomes, but also to serve as models for expansion of dog training programs in correctional institutions.

The human–dog bond is documented as a strong one. This offers much promise for programs in terms of their ability to yield positive outcomes. Chapter 12 brings a thoughtful analysis of the other side of the bond, as Mary Renck Jalongo and Mary-Ann Sontag-Bowman discuss how inmate trainers cope with loss that is inevitable when it is time for dogs to move forward from the program, out of the prison and into the community. It is critical to anticipate the psychological impact of what is simultaneously a program success coupled with a feeling of loss, and the chapter offers recommendations for doing so. Mary Renck Jalongo highlights the importance of personal narratives in Chap. 13, demonstrating that—consistent with findings grounded in neuroscience—the stories and lived experiences of program participants offer meaningful perspectives on prison dog programs, for researchers, program planners, program staff, and the public. In Chap. 14, Carmaleta Aufderheide and Mary Renck Jalongo turn the focus toward celebration, presenting examples of how to recognize the successes of the inmates who have participated in the program, and how to recognize the program and its contributions to the community. These issues, which are manifest during the actual implementation of programs, must be considered in the initial stages of program planning.

Finally, Appendix A provides an overview of selected programs, to illustrate the diversity in how they may be structured. Appendix A does not attempt to list all programs, which are now present in every US state and internationally (see Hill 2016), but is intended to offer a sampling of the variations that are present, in hopes that doing so may be useful for future research or programmatic development. Appendix B is a table that highlights the major reasons for bringing dogs into correctional facilities. It is designed to provide a concise overview of the different roles that dogs can fulfill in a corrections context.

Conclusions and a Path Forward

What follows is an exciting and dynamic volume. American corrections has taken many turns over time, each seeking a new (or sometimes rediscovered) means to address the issue of crime in society. Much has been made of rehabilitation, above, and the potential for dog training programs to contribute to that mission. But another goal that some hold for prisons and jails is to go beyond the notion of corrections per se, which through its etymology focuses on addressing individual offenders' actions, and instead to envision criminal justice as meeting restorative goals. In its most formal definition, restorative justice includes programming that seeks to restore the offender, the victim, and the community—all simultaneously—by addressing and repairing harms that have resulted from criminal offending (Cullen and Jonson 2012). Consider the potential that dog training programs in correctional institutions might have for doing so.

The rehabilitative effects and positive benefits to offenders and correctional institutions are certainly manifest, as noted above. At the same time, the benefits to the community can be construed as restorative efforts, through their effects. This can include positive tangible impacts, as each individual dog—whether working as a service animal to help others or being present as a companion animal along life's journey—is an expression of caring, delivered through the hard work and meaningful efforts of program participants. This can also include positive intangible impacts, as the value of the human–dog bond transcends cost-benefit analyses.

As such, perhaps programs such as those highlighted in this book represent a new turn in correctional programming. Joined with restorative justice are notions of humanism in correctional settings; humanistic or transforming corrections does not abandon an emphasis on offender accountability, but in working with offenders:

> is predicated upon the belief that no type of restorative or rehabilitative success can be achieved within a social context that continues to refuse to recognize the basic humanity of those individuals who find themselves in the criminal justice system. The inability to see the offender as a human being raises not only a variety of ethical concerns related to the project of criminal justice but also threatens any practical attempt to rehabilitate or restore these individuals to normal society, if, of course, the underlying purpose of incarceration is not simply to warehouse a specific segment of the population (Polizzi and Braswell 2009, p. 6).

Through the power of the human–dog bond, notions of restoration and transforming corrections are implicitly echoed through the chapters in this book, which demonstrate the remarkable impacts and collaborative successes—for inmates, staff, institutions, communities, and others—that dog training programs in correctional institutions may have. The insights yielded by each chapter have been shaped by tremendous voices of scholarship and experience, and will no doubt shape the next generation of program development. In turn, they may also shape the very enterprise of corrections.

Stephen S. Owen, Ph.D.
Professor, Department of Criminal Justice
Radford University
Radford, VA, USA
e-mail: ssowen@radford.edu

References

Albuquerque, N., Guo, K., Wilkinson, A., Savalli, C., Otta, E., & Mills, D. (2016). Dogs recognize dog and human emotions. *Biology Letters, 12*(1), 1–5. https://doi.org/10.1098/rsbl.2015.0883.

Alienist says Loeb lied by hiding facts. (1924, August 12). *Philadelphia Inquirer*, p. 1.

Antonio, M. E., Davis, R. G., & Shutt, S. R. (2017). Dog training programs in Pennsylvania's Department of Corrections: Perceived effectiveness for inmates and staff. *Society and Animals, 25*(5), 475–489. https://doi.org/10.1163/15685306-12341457.

Beamish, R. J. (1924, August 12). Gov. Pinchot's dog sentenced to "pen." *Philadelphia Inquirer*, p. 3.

Beckett, K., & Sasson, T. (2004). *The politics of injustice: Crime and punishment in America* (2nd ed.). Thousand Oaks, CA: Sage Publications.

Best, J. (1999). *Random violence: How we talk about new crimes and new victims*. Berkeley, CA: University of California Press.

Bonta, J., & Andrews, D. A. (2017). *The psychology of criminal conduct* (6th ed.). New York: Routledge.

Bosworth, M. (2002). *The U.S. federal prison system*. Thousand Oaks, CA: Sage Publications.

Britton, D. M., & Button, A. (2005). Prison pups: Assessing the effects of dog training programs in correctional facilities. *Journal of Family Social Work, 9*(4), 79–95. https://doi.org/10.1300/j039v09n04_06.

Bronson, J. (2018). *Justice expenditure and employment extracts, 2015—preliminary*. Bureau of Justice Statistics. Available at https://www.bjs.gov/index.cfm?ty=pbdetail&iid=6310.
Clear, T. R. (2007). *Imprisoning communities: How mass incarceration makes disadvantaged neighborhoods worse*. New York: Oxford University Press.
Cooke, B. J., & Farrington, D. P. (2016). The effectiveness of dog-training programs in prison: A systematic review and meta-analysis of the literature. *Prison Journal, 96*(6), 854–876. https://doi.org/10.1177/0032885516671919.
Cornelius, G. F. (2008). *The American jail: Cornerstone of modern corrections*. Upper Saddle River, NJ: Pearson Prentice Hall.
Cullen, F. T. (2013). Rehabilitation: Beyond nothing works. *Crime and Justice, 42*(1), 299–376. https://doi.org/10.1086/670395.
Cullen, F. T., & Jonson, C. L. (2012). *Correctional theory: Context and consequences*. Thousand Oaks, CA: Sage Publications.
Cullen, F. T., Mears, D. P., Jonson, C. L., & Thielo, A. J. (2016). Seven ways to make prisons work. In R. Matthews (Ed.), *What is to be done about crime and punishment? Towards a 'Public Criminology'* (pp. 159–196). London, UK: Palgrave Macmillan.
Dickens, C. (1842). *American notes for general circulation* (vol. 1). London, UK: Chapman and Hall.
Dolan, F. X. (2007). *Eastern state penitentiary: Images of America*. Charleston, SC: Arcadia Publishing.
Feeley, M. M., & Simon, J. (1992). The new penology: Notes on the emerging strategy of corrections and its implications. *Criminology, 30*, 449–474. https://doi.org/10.1111/j.1745-9125.1992.tb01112.x.
Finckenauer, J. O., & Gavin, P. W. (1999). *Scared straight: The panacea phenomenon revisited*. Prospect Heights, IL: Waveland Press.
Foucault, M. (1977). *Discipline and punish: The birth of the prison* (A. Sheridan, Trans.). New York: Vintage Books.
Friedman, L. M. (1993). *Crime and punishment in American history*. New York: Basic Books.
Furst, G. (2006). Prison-based animal programs: A national survey. *Prison Journal, 86*(4), 407–430. https://doi.org/10.1177/0032885506293242.
Garland, D. (2001). *The culture of control: Crime and social order in contemporary society*. Chicago: University of Chicago Press.
Gottschalk, M. (2006). *The prison and the gallows: The politics of mass incarceration in America*. New York: Cambridge University Press.
Gramlich, J. (2018, May 2). American's incarceration rate is at a two-decade low. *Factank: News in the numbers*, Pew Research Center. Available at http://www.pewresearch.org/fact-tank/2018/05/02/americas-incarceration-rate-is-at-a-two-decade-low/.
Haney, C. (2003). Mental health issues in long-term solitary and "supermax" confinement. *Crime and Delinquency, 49*(1), 124–156. https://doi.org/10.1177/0011128702239239.
Harkrader, T., Burke, T., & Owen, S. (2004, April). Pound puppies: The rehabilitative uses of dogs in correctional facilities. *Corrections Today* (pp. 74–79).
Higdon, H. (1999). *Leopold and loeb: The crime of the century*. Champaign, IL: University of Illinois Press.
Hill, L. B. (2016). *Becoming the person your dog things you are: An assessment of Florida prison-based dog training programs on prison misconduct, post-release employment and recidivism* (unpublished doctoral dissertation). Florida State University, Tallahassee, Florida.
Hines, L. M. (2003). Historical perspectives on the human-animal bond. *American Behavioral Scientist, 47*(1), 7–15. ahttps://doi.org/10.1177/0002764203255206.
Kaeble, D., & Cowhig, M. (2018). *Correctional populations in the United States, 2016*. Washington, DC: U.S. Department of Justice. Available at https://www.bjs.gov/content/pub/pdf/cpus16.pdf.
Martinson, R. (1974, Spring). What works? Questions and answers about prison reform. *Public Interest, 35*, 22–54.

Minton, C. A., Perez, P. R., & Miller, K. (2015). Voices from behind prison walls: The impact of training service dogs on women in prison. *Society and Animals, 23*(5), 484–501. https://doi.org/10.1163/15685306-12341379.

Owen, S. (2016). Prisons: Administration and organization. In W. Jennings, G. Higgins, M. Maldonado-Molina, & D. Khey (eds.), *Encyclopaedia of crime and punishment* (pp. 1030–1033). Hoboken, NJ: Wiley-Blackwell.

Owen, S., Fradella, H., Burke, T., & Joplin, J. (2019). *Foundations of criminal justice* (3rd ed.). New York: Oxford University Press.

Payne, E., Bennett, P. C., & McGreevy, P. D. (2015). Current perspectives on attachment and bonding in the dog-human dyad. *Psychology Research and Behavior Management, 8*, 71–79. https://doi.org/10.2147/prbm.s74972.

Payne, E., DeAraugo, J., Bennett, P., & McGreevy, P. (2016). Exploring the existence and potential underpinnings of dog-human and horse-human attachment bonds. *Behavioural Processes, 125*, 114–121. https://doi.org/10.1016/j.beproc.2015.10.004.

Polizzi, D., & Braswell, M. (2009). Introduction. In D. Polizzi & M. Braswell (Eds.), *Transforming corrections: Humanistic approaches to corrections and offender treatment* (pp. 3–12). Durham, NC: Carolina Academic Press.

Rehn, T., & Keeling, L. J. (2016). Measuring dog-owner relationships: Crossing boundaries between animal behaviour and human psychology. *Applied Animal Behaviour Science, 183*, 1–9. https://doi.org/10.1016/j.applanim.2016.07.003.

Scott-Hayward, C. S., & Fradella, H. F. (2019). *Punishing poverty: How bail and pretrial detention fuel inequalities in the criminal justice system*. Berkeley, CA: University of California Press.

Sourcebook of criminal justice statistics. (2013). Available at https://www.albany.edu/sourcebook/.

Spelman, W. (2006). The limited importance of prison expansion. In A. Blumstein & J. Wallman (Eds.), *The crime drop in America* (Rev. Ed., pp. 97–129). New York: Cambridge University Press.

Sykes, G. M. (1958). *The society of captives: A study of a maximum security prison*. Princeton, NJ: Princeton University Press.

The dog that went to jail for life. (1924, September 7). *Baltimore Sun* (p. 90).

Thielo, A. J., Cullen, F. T., Cohen, D. M., & Chouhy, C. (2016). Rehabilitation in a red state: Public support for correctional reform in Texas. *Criminology and Public Policy, 15*, 137–170. https://doi.org/10.1111/1745-9133.12182.

van Wormer, J., Kigerl, A., & Hamilton, Z. (2017). Digging deeper: Exploring the value of prison-based dog handler programs. *Prison Journal, 97*(4), 520–538. https://doi.org/10.1177/0032885517712481.

Walmsley, R. (2018). *World prison population list* (10th ed.). London, UK: International Centre for Prison Studies. Available at http://www.apcca.org/uploads/10th_Edition_2013.pdf.

Weisburd, D., Farrington, D. P., Gill, C., Ajzenstadt, M., Bennett, T., Bowers, K., et al. (2017). What works in crime prevention and rehabilitation: An assessment of systematic reviews. *Criminology and Public Policy, 16*(2), 415–449. https://doi.org/10.1111/1745-9133.12298.

Zeng, Z. (2018, February). *Jail inmates in 2016*. Washington, DC: Bureau of Justice Statistics. Available at https://www.bjs.gov/content/pub/pdf/ji16.pdf.

Acknowledgements

Special thanks are due to the administrators, staff, and inmate/handlers of the prison dog program at State Correctional Institution (SCI) Pine Grove. Kristen O'Hara from Extended Studies at Indiana University of Pennsylvania (IUP) has supported the program from the start. They have partnered with me over the past five years to design and offer a curriculum consisting of four courses for the inmate/handlers. I value the opportunity to teach classes in this program that leads to a certificate of completion in Humane Education and Dog Training from IUP.

The Pennsylvania Department of Corrections online newsletter, *All Paws on Deck,* was a valuable resource for those involved in prison dog programs. It is a source of pride that, at the time of this writing, every one of the state correctional facilities in the Commonwealth of Pennsylvania that houses inmates long term has some type of dog program in place. *All Paws on Deck* began in 2014 and is published biannually in June and December. It provides many excellent ideas on the successful implementation of prison dog programs, inmate testimonials, contributions from various staff members, the perspectives of the recipients of the dogs, and information about shelter or service dogs that are in training or already placed. All issues of the newsletter are available at: https://www.cor.pa.gov/About%20Us/Newsroom/Pages/Newsletters.aspx.

Lori Breece, Director of the Service Dogs Program for United Disabilities Services Foundation in Lancaster, Pennsylvania, graciously provided many of the photographs of service dogs trained by inmates at four different state or federal prisons.

Mary Louden, Founder and Director of Prison Greyhounds, in addition to sharing her insights on setting up a program, provided some of the photographs of the inmates and dogs.

A staff photographer of *The Indiana Gazette,* Jamie Empfield, provided photographs that enhance the quality of the book.

Thank you also to Melissa Peyton for applying her professional editing skills to reviewing the entire manuscript.

Contents

Chapter 1
Introduction: Building a Rationale for Prison Dog Programs

Mary Renck Jalongo

Background

The American criminal justice system holds more than 2.3 million people in prisons and other types of correctional facilities; in addition, there are nearly 3.7 million people on probation or parole (Wagner and Rauby 2017). According to U.S. Bureau of Justice Statistics, about 1 in 110 adults in the U.S. are incarcerated and 1 in 35 adults is under some sort of correctional supervision (Glaze and Herberman 2013). In the U.S., people of color, the disabled, the homeless, and the marginalized are over-represented in the prison population, a phenomenon called the "school-to-prison pipeline" (American Bar Association 2018). Internationally, there are some striking differences in approaches to working with individuals who are convicted of breaking the law. Some cultures view the purpose of imprisonment as a way to exact harsh punishment while others use incarceration to attempt to redress such things as neglect/abuse during childhood, social inequities, and lack of educational opportunity. While many enlightened professionals throughout history have regarded rehabilitation as the ideal outcome of incarceration, achieving it is far from the norm worldwide. In the United States Sentencing Commission's longitudinal study of 25,400 federal offenders, 49.3% had been arrested again within eight years of release or probation (Hunt and Dumville 2016). Bureau of Justice statistics for state correctional facilities are even more discouraging, with a 76.6% recidivism rate after five years. Little wonder, then, that America's prisons have been characterized as a revolving door (Pew Charitable Trusts 2011).

Interventions sufficiently powerful to effect changes in inmate behavior evidently are in short supply (Polaschek et al. 2019). In 2001, the United States Surgeon

M. R. Jalongo (✉)
Emerita, Indiana University of Pennsylvania, Indiana, PA, USA
e-mail: mjalongo@comcast.net

M. R. Jalongo (ed.), *Prison Dog Programs*,
https://doi.org/10.1007/978-3-030-25618-0_1

General concluded that nearly half of the violence prevention strategies were ineffectual at best or damaging at worst. There is little question that any strategy used to change inmates for the better needs to institute deep, rather than surface, levels of change. Both the duration and the intensity of the intervention matter. For instance, it would be rare for spending one hour per week in class over a few weeks' time to institute important changes in human behavior. Even interventions that might be otherwise effective sometimes fail inside prison, particularly if success depends on participants' willingness to reveal and discuss deeply felt emotions. Cultivating callousness can be a survival skill within prison cultures (Gupta 2008) and sharing personal or private feelings may be seen a weakness that increases vulnerability (Blazina and Kogan 2016).

Changing a habit can be difficult. Research in the field of psychology suggests that it requires, on average, 66 days of consistent practice to change an ordinary habit (e.g., making a commitment to exercise daily for 15 min). Some individuals change in as few as 18 days and while others take 254 days to meet their goal (Lally et al. 2010). Given that the psychological research investigates habits such as smoking cessation, it is not surprising if inmates—who are expected to change an entire lifestyle—fail to accomplish this goal. Freudian psychology identifies regression as a defense mechanism in human behavior and suggests that, when people are under stress, they tend to revert to more familiar behavioral repertoires. In the case of inmates, this typically would be a return to criminal activity. Current research in the field of neuroscience identifies three important influences on instituting behavioral change in human beings: (1) availability of an alternative habit, (2) strength of the motivation to change, and (3) the mental and physical resources to break the habit (Berkman 2017). Thus, the persistent challenge for those seeking to rehabilitate inmates becomes instituting programs that are sufficiently powerful to replace old habits with new ones as well as accomplish this with individuals who may be not only less well-equipped mentally and physically but also have fewer social supports than many other groups of people.

Human-Animal Interaction (HAI) as an Intervention

Increasingly, correctional institutions are turning to programs that involve the care and training of animals as a way to transform and educate inmates (Furst 2011). Care of and responsibility for animals as a treatment for people in desperate circumstances has a long history (Serpell 2015). For centuries now, the most enlightened social reformers have acknowledged that the human-animal bond can change people for the better. In the 1700s, the Quakers created a program for the mentally ill called The Retreat in which the residents cared for various types of animals. Rehabilitating animals features prominently in internationally recognized programs for youth with severe behavioral issues, such as Green Chimneys, a program that has been in existence since 1947 (Kaufmann et al. 2015). Today, human-animal interaction (HAI) is becoming the intervention of choice when individuals are resistant to change and need additional support, such as when children are reluctant readers (Levinson et al. 2017), nursing home residents are depressed and uncommunicative (Le Roux and Kemp 2009) and college students are homesick (Binfet and Passmore 2016). Likewise, programs that involve inmates in the care and training of animals are gradually becoming the intervention of choice in correctional facilities (Furst 2011). In the United States, some state correctional systems (e.g., Florida, Ohio, Pennsylvania) have set the goal of incorporating at least one animal care and training program at each of their facilities. Some correctional facilities, such as Fort Dodge Correctional Facility (FDCF) in Iowa that was featured in the 2011 documentary, *America's Toughest Prisons* were transformed by new leadership and dog programs. Under the direction of Warden J. McKinney, FDCF has one of the largest Leader Dogs for the Blind programs in operation, with as many as 50 dogs in training at one time and inmates requesting transfers to participate in that program (Aufderheide 2016). Of course, prison animal programs can include other animals, such as horses, cats, and other animals; however, the vast majority of these programs involve dogs and are referred to as prison dog programs (PDPs).

There are two major reasons that dogs predominate in the human-animal bond research. First of all, they are readily available—it is estimated that there are approximately 525 million dogs on the planet (Coren 2012) and there are 60.2 million households that include at least one dog and a total of 89.7 million owned dogs in the United States alone (American Pet Products Association, Inc. 2017). Dogs also do not require the amount of space that horses or other large domesticated animals need. In the majority of prison dog programs, the dogs are homeless, ill, injured, orphaned, or have behavioral issues and there is an ample supply of these animals at shelters and rescues. Where working and service dogs are concerned, dogs are the animal that is most important to the military, law enforcement, and citizens with disabilities. Prison dog programs can provide a steady supply of volunteers to raise and train puppies or adult canines to become assistance dogs.

Secondly, dogs have worked hard to earn their "best friend" status over the past 10,000 years of cohabitation with humans by becoming highly attuned to human emotions and uniquely well-suited for affiliation with human beings (Udell and Wynne 2008). Only apes can approach dogs' ability to study human faces, interpret social cues, and understand human pointing. Dogs also respond to distress—even when displayed by strangers—in empathic ways. For example, if a person pretends to cry, socialized dogs usually display "comfort offering" behaviors, such as placing their head in the person's lap, sitting close, and nuzzling (Custance and Mayer 2012). Dogs also respond in empathic-like ways when they hear the distress sounds of a human partner and levels of the stress hormone, cortisol, are more elevated with a familiar person than with a stranger who sounds distressed (Quervel-Chaumette et al. 2016).

Programs that house dogs in a correctional facility to achieve the dual purpose of rehabilitating inmates and helping dogs have been in existence since the 1980s (Bustad 1996). Most people credit Sister Pauline Quinn as the originator of prison-based dog training programs (Millman 2014). She instituted the Prison Pet Partnership, the first prison-based dog training program, at a women's correctional facility in the state of Washington in 1981 (Britton and Button 2006). Today, her project has been implemented throughout the world.

High-quality programs of this type meet the criteria for behavioral change. They demand a new focus and new behavioral repertoires from inmates over an extended period of time. They also entrust prisoners with responsibility for another living, dependent creature capable of receiving and giving affection. Working with dogs also gives inmates "permission" to show emotions and see themselves, other inmates, the staff and the institution differently (Blazina and Kogan 2016). As one inmate wrote in his journal, his 8-year-old daughter often referred to him as "my Dad who is in prison" but, after participating in the service dog training program, he had a new identity as "my Dad, the dog trainer." Inmates enrolled in dog care and training programs also report summoning new mental and physical abilities to institute more positive habits out of consideration for the animals in their care. They frequently discover new resources of patience, empathy, and determination when an animal is relying on them. An inmate who worked to rehabilitate a shelter dog with a history of abusive treatment said, "I just told her, 'no one's ever going to hurt you again'." His resolve to stay out of trouble was strengthened so that he could keep that promise and see her placed in a loving, permanent home. Many times, the work that the prisoners do with dogs represents a second chance for shelter dogs who are difficult to adopt or might otherwise be euthanized. Inmates often form a special bond with dogs who are "locked up" at a shelter and a sense of kinship with another living being who has poor impulse control, has made some bad decisions in the past, and has gotten into trouble.

Dog care and training programs also represent an opportunity for inmates to make a positive contribution to the outside while still on the inside. Instead of counting the days and imagining that they will make changes after they are released, they start making changes now. The photo below is of Deora, a 16-month-old Lab who spent her first year in a service dog training program housed in a correctional facility. Her two inmate handlers taught her skills that she used to help a person with a disability, and she became a highly successful and beloved service dog. An excerpt from an inmate dog trainer's journal captures the spirit of these projects. He wrote: "Deora changed my life for the better. She loves to please people. She will make somebody's life easier".

Deora, a service dog trained by inmates for United Disabilities Services, visits the Flight 93 National Memorial in Shanksville, PA. She was named after a young woman who was an animal rescuer and perished in the crash. *Photo Credit* Mary Renck Jalongo

Nevertheless, dog care and training programs in correctional facilities have been criticized for relying too heavily on anecdotal evidence as support for their existence and there has been a consistent call for more rigorous research methods (Mulcahy and McLaughlin 2013). There are three basic types of research that support these programs: (1) medical research, (2) surveys of prison administrators, and (3) self-report data gathered from the inmate participants. While there are calls for more experimental designs that use randomization and control groups, there are many impediments to conducting this type of research with vulnerable populations, such as inmates. Thus, and studies of this type are just beginning to emerge.

Research in Human Health

Dog training programs in correctional facilities require a substantial investment of time, effort and resources. Those who work in these programs are convinced that they are effective; however, personal commitment is not sufficient to sustain existing programs or persuade administrators to initiate new ones. What may be less well understood is the scientific evidence that supports these initiatives. There is a growing body of research on the physiological changes that take place during human-animal interaction in general and human-canine interaction more specifically (Beck 2014; Friedmann et al. 2015). For example, we now know that when people and dogs interact positively, it results in higher levels of oxytocin, the hormone that is attributed with feelings of "calm and connect" (Kikusui 2015; Miller et al. 2009; see Powell-Adam et al. 2019 for a review). At the same time, positive human-canine interactions frequently lead to reductions in cortisol, the hormone associated with stress in blood, urine, and saliva (Omert 2013). In their review of the research, Kaufmann et al. (2015) credit positive human-animal interactions with "increase of trust, positive social interaction and communication, and the reduction of depressiveness, anxiety, aggression and stress reactions" (p. 212). Planned, positive interactions between human and nonhuman animals can serve as an alternative or complementary therapeutic intervention for many people with a wide range of conditions, both physical and psychological (Fine and Weaver 2018). Interestingly, these changes are reciprocal and can be documented not only during dogs' interactions with a bonded human but also in shelter dogs who get attention and affection from a friendly stranger (Hennessy et al. 2006).

Survey Research

Another source of support comes from research in the field of corrections (Britton and Button 2006; Han et al. 2018; Hershman 2008; Hogle 2009). The practice of instituting HAI programs is widely supported by surveys with superintendents. In a national survey of prison administrators, 98.4% of the prison administrators completing the survey recommended a prison-based dog training program to others and, when asked to describe negatives, 60% indicated that there were no negatives (Furst 2006). The three top reasons that inmates gave for their decision to participate in these programs are: (1) love of dogs, (2) greater freedom, and (3) "giving back" to the community. Positive outcomes for inmates typically include: fewer disciplinary referrals, enhanced self-esteem, improved work habits, greater compassion for animals, and more acceptance of responsibility (Harbolt and Ward 2001; Moneymaker and Strimple 1991; Strimple 2003; Turner 2007). In addition, the practical skills acquired in working with dogs give inmates meaningful work to do while serving their sentence and often lead to job opportunities upon parole and reentry into society. Types of employment include dog training, dog grooming, work in animal shelters, or training as a veterinary assistant or technician. In fact, 33% of the correctional institution administrators in a national survey indicated that they were aware of former inmates who once participated in "cell dog" programs working in dog care and training services in the community upon their release (Furst 2006).

Self-report Measures with Inmates

A third way of studying the effects of these programs is to use self-report measures with inmates and analysis of the documents that they produce, such as journals.

A longitudinal outcomes study for the New Leash on Life program in Philadelphia, for example, provides numerous evaluation instruments that were used to assess the impact of the program on inmates (Conroy et al. 2012; see Chap. 10). In an interview study, inmates reported that working with the dogs resulted in them becoming more patient, less aggressive, and more receptive to helping other people; they also credited the program with modifying the corrections environment in positive ways (Turner 2007). Along similar lines, Cooke and Farrington (2016) interviewed incarcerated females and estimated that inmates' participation in dog programs reduced recidivism by approximately 30%. Findings from research with adjudicated youth have reported positive effects on behavior as well (Johnson and Bruneau 2016). As Levinson (1969), widely regarded as a pioneer in incorporating dogs into psychotherapy has written, animals can be "a half-way station on the road back to emotional well-being" (p. xiv).

Rationale for the Book and Major Trends

When professionals seek to begin, sustain, or evaluate dog care and training programs in correctional facilities, they frequently find that there is little in the way of published material to assist them. Many times, going online to review the websites of various correctional facilities or contacting different project supervisors directly are the only alternatives. The problem with this approach is that it tends to be based on personal experience with one program in a particular context rather than evidence-based and guided by multiple perspectives. Initiatives that bring animals into correctional facilities are complex, work intensive, require changes to the physical plant, and usually depend on financial support from outside the corrections systems. *Prison Dog Programs: Renewal and Rehabilitation in Correctional Facilities* is a way of addressing this gap in the literature. The book is, all at the same time, a *handbook* of practical guidance, a *literature review* that provides evidence-based recommendations, and a representation of *multiple stakeholders'* perspectives supplied by the diverse group of contributors represented across the edited volume.

One question that any effective book proposal needs to answer is, "Why this book at this time for this audience?" There are several trends that make this a particularly timely topic for an edited book.

International and Cross Disciplinary Research Evidence that now exists to support HAI has expanded, both in quantity and quality, and has gained wider acceptance as an initiative in correctional facilities (Ormerod 2008). To illustrate growth in the field, the first edition of Fine's *Handbook of Animal-Assisted therapy* was a small paperback; the fourth edition, published in 2015, is a large reference work. Currently there is an entire cross-disciplinary, international field of study emerging as reflected in the Human Animal Bond Research Institute (HABRI) that includes experts in medicine, psychology, sociology, education, corrections, veterinary medicine, animal welfare, and more (see Hoy-Gerlach and Wehman 2017 for a review). An organization called the International Association of Human-Animal Interaction Organizations (IAHAIO) has been formed. In addition, there are now two successful professional journals devoted entirely to the study of human-animal interaction (HAI): *Society and Animals* and *Anthrozoös*. The American Psychological Association not only has a division that focuses on human-animal interaction but also has published several books of research on the topic (Freund et al. 2016; McCardle et al. 2016).

Expansion in Roles for Service and Working Dogs Practically everyone is familiar with dogs used to guide the legally blind or assist people with mobility issues. The demand for these service dogs continues. However, new roles for working and service dogs are emerging. Just a few of them are hearing assistance dogs, seizure alert/response dogs, dogs for children on the autism spectrum, cardiac alert dogs, and dogs for military personnel with PTSD and/or physical injuries. Even within existing categories of working dogs, new and highly specialized roles have emerged, such as dogs trained to detect cell phones and computer storage devices, locate insect pests, alert to allergens (e.g., peanuts), identify certain types of cancer in small tissue samples, and detect underground gas leaks. Approximately 1/3 of dogs spontaneously respond to oncoming seizures (e.g., epilepsy, diabetes) and dogs are being trained to alert and respond (Hart and Yamamoto 2015). In many communities, specially trained dogs called "courthouse dogs" are being used by justice workers, social workers, and mental health professionals to provide emotional support to victims—particularly child victims—of crime, abuse and neglect during interviews and court testimony (Courthouse Dogs Foundation 2019).

Internationally, highly trained service dogs are in great demand, particularly as guide dogs for the blind. In the United States, the cost is prohibitive, ranging from $15,000 to $50,000. The wait list time is 1–3 years. The largest growth area appears to be for psychiatric service dogs, such as dogs for military veterans with Post-traumatic stress disorder (PTSD) or children on the autism spectrum (Froling 2009).

Empathy Development There is an emerging body of research in the corrections field to suggest that, when inmates interact with animals in positive ways and form a bond, increases in empathy often occur (Dawson 2016). This outcome is particularly important for the prison population. It is estimated that 50–77% of juvenile inmates have conduct disorders that are more prevalent in males, have a poorer diagnosis, and tend to show disregard for others and lack of prosocial emotions (American Psychiatric Association 2013). At the same time, research over the past 40 years suggests a link between gender role conflict and increases in depression, anxiety, substance usage, and interpersonal problems (O'Neil 2015). Working with dogs is widely regarded by psychotherapists as a valuable complement to other therapeutic interventions (Parish-Plass 2013), particularly for adolescents who are otherwise difficult to reach (Madden Ellsworth et al. 2016). Some countries have an extensive history with these programs, such as Canada (Challinor 2009; Taylor and Blanchette 2001) while other countries, notably Japan, are just beginning to incorporate dogs into their interventions with inmates (Koda et al. 2015).

The No-Kill Shelter Movement The American Society for the Prevention of Cruelty to Animals (ASPCA 2017) reported that 3.3 million dogs entered shelters. Only about half—1.6 million—of the shelter dogs were adopted while 670,000 were euthanized (ASPCA 2017). Although many people assume that these dogs are stray, homeless, rescued animals, over one million of them were voluntarily relinquished by their owners for a variety of reasons (ASPCA 2019). The reasons most often given for owner surrendered dogs are housing issues, time management problems, behavioral issues in the dogs, and financial insufficiency (Petfinder 2018). Documentaries that have exposed the abuses associated with factory farming of dogs or "puppy mills" have prompted more people to adopt from shelters or rescues. Yet even after dogs are placed in homes, they are sometimes returned to shelters or rescues and, according to one national study, 47% of the time, it is due to dogs' behavioral problems (Weiss et al. 2015). It is estimated that 96% of dogs relinquished to shelters have no obedience training (Kwan 2013). Now that many community shelters have moved away from euthanasia, this means that difficult-to-adopt animals may be housed for extended periods of time—perhaps their lifetimes—if they are not sufficiently rehabilitated to be adopted. However, almost none of these shelters have the resources to employ full-time dog trainers. Dog rehabilitation and training programs in correctional facilities are a major resource for addressing this issue. Many times, the training required is more along the lines of "house manners" than more serious problems, such as dog-on-dog aggression. When inmate/trainers prepare dogs for a smoother transition into homes, they are performing an important service to the community that benefits both humans and canines.

Unique Features of the Book

Another question that needs to be answered when proposing a book is, "How is this book different—and presumably better—than what is already available?" *Prison Dog Programs: Renewal and Rehabilitation in Correctional Facilities* differs from the other literature on the topic in the four important ways described below.

1. **Multidisciplinary perspective and multifaceted approach**. A search of Amazon and Barnes and Noble yielded only one book on the topic written from a corrections perspective (Furst 2011). This edited volume is both multidisciplinary and evidence-based, with perspectives not only from corrections personnel but also from curriculum experts, psychologists, veterinarians, animal welfare workers, and more. One advantage of an edited collection is that it can provide a chorus of opinion on a subject in a way that a single authored work cannot. This book reflects the viewpoints of an impressive group of professionals from different fields who play a role in the successful implementation of animal programs in prisons, including: justice workers, educators, veterinarians, dog trainers, program administrators, superintendents of correctional facilities,

counselors, psychologists, animal welfare workers, and researchers. This collaboration has served to enrich and enlarge viewpoints on animal rehabilitation and training programs housed in correctional facilities far beyond the local. To that end, we have drawn from the best that the relevant fields have to offer. If, for example, the focus is on collaboration with animal sheltering and rescue, we examined not only the programs themselves but also the relevant literature on effective collaboration, animal welfare, statistics on sheltering, research conducted in veterinary medicine, studies of canine behavior, and reports about prison dog programs throughout the world.

2. **Unifying theme**. A well conceptualized edited book is much more than a collection of individual contributions united only by the title page. Cohesiveness in an edited book can be accomplished partly by chapter format but, more importantly, by a basic premise for the work. The theme for this book emanates from the first dog training program in a correctional facility inaugurated by Sister Pauline, Pathways to Hope. The significance of hope—both for people and the other animals—is foundational to this work. In a study of 20 prisons worldwide, Dreisinger (2016) concludes:

   > Justice work is ultimately a grand redundancy, restlessly demanding more of itself: more labor, more movement, more struggle, more victories and losses. And that work is powered by the potent thing I strap on daily, like a life vest, the thing that buoys me and keeps my spirit alive with mission and meaning: hope (p. 306).

3. **Information on selected programs**. Dog care and training initiatives are in place at a wide variety of carceral institutions; however, if someone is seeking information, it will take an extraordinary time investment to review them online at the various websites. The Appendix of the book identifies 26 programs that have a presence in the professional literature as a way to support others responsible for inaugurating or sustaining a dog program in a correctional facility. This material offers insight on each program's origins, current operations, and achievements, thereby making it a valuable resource for those who are beginning or maintaining a prison dog program.
4. **Education and incentive programs for inmates**. In our view, taking these programs to the next level involves curriculum, instruction, and a tangible marker of the inmates' achievements. This book examines many different avenues for accomplishing this, including; collaborations with vocational education and training, alliances with postsecondary institutions, certificates issued by professional dog training groups, linkages with professional organizations, and reductions in time served for successful dog trainers. Making such credentials part of the inmates' experience holds the greatest promise as a re-entry tool. We see this as the next generation of more effective ways to set inmates on a positive, productive path.

Service dog puppies stand with their primary trainer for photo in a newspaper story. This photograph earned a national award. *Photo Credit* Jamie Empfield

Conclusion

When correctional facilities and shelter or service dog groups collaborate, many benefits are accrued. Those responsible for the dogs can rehabilitate/train dogs more affordably, the inmates acquire a marketable skill that they can pursue upon release or continue to practice while incarcerated, the community members seeking a well-mannered family dog are accommodated, people with disabilities in search of a service dog are supported, the correctional facility is perceived more positively out in the community, the dogs have the advantage of a trainer 24/7, and many animals become treasured family dogs or service dogs.

In a recent Facebook post from New Zealand, someone compared the treatment of the elderly in nursing homes to the treatment of prison inmates and suggested that the inmates fared far better with "a shower every day, video surveillance in case of problems, three meals a day, access to a library, TV, gym, doctors-on-site, and free medication if needed". Readers were invited to like and share if they agreed and many were quick to do so—without ever having been in a prison. As Larsen (2016) observes, "Forgiveness is a hard sell for most people in the United States, perhaps for most people in the West. Our trigger response is for vengeance, for punishment—getting even with those who harmed us" (unpaged). Yet international comparisons of correctional facilities suggest that countries and institutions with the best outcomes emphasize empathy, forgiveness and community support (Dreisinger 2016). The Nordic countries have the lowest recidivism rates in the world with only about 20% of offenders being convicted again upon release (Enders-Slegers et al. 2016). Their enlightened approach differs from the one taken by many societies in at least four important ways (Dreisinger 2016). First, punishment is not the prevailing goal. Secondly, prisons are small facilities that typically house fewer than 50 offenders. Third, linkages are forged out in the community so that the work and social services inside the facility are the same ones accessed upon release. Fourth, major funding is committed to rehabilitation efforts. Another country with very low recidivism rates is Australia (Fazel and Wolf 2016). Given the county's origins as a penal colony for Great Britain, there is an attitude of forgiveness toward convicts and work outside the institution in the community is the norm. International comparisons such as these illustrate the value of re-entry strategies that smooth the transition into society. As the impressive group of authors gathered for this volume would contend, it takes more humane, holistic approaches to succeed at inmate rehabilitation.

A review of the research on the effects of animals on human health illustrates this point. It describes a more expansive concept of health in which being healthy is much more than the absence of disease or injury; rather, human health is regarded as not only as physical health but also as psychological and social well-being (Friedmann et al. 2015). Collectively, these three components determine Quality of Life or QoL (Perea-Mediavilla and López-Cepero 2017) and there is an extensive body of research to document that interaction with animals—most often dogs—exerts a positive influence on QoL. Capitalizing on this potential is the crux of the matter for dog care, rehabilitation, and training programs in correctional facilities. These interventions hold great promise for instituting enduring and positive changes in the physical, psychological, and social behavior of inmates and therefore merit more in-depth and interdisciplinary study. As a psychologist who had worked in corrections for over 20 years observed, "I've seen and participated in many different interventions designed to change inmates, so I'm not easily snowed when somebody says they have changed. Those who participated in the dog training program really convinced me that they made positive changes in their attitudes and behavior."

When we embarked on this project, our goal was to produce the publication we wish had existed when we first got involved with prison dog programs. To that end, we offer to readers this edited book of theory, research, and practice in support of others who are initiating, maintaining, and evaluating dog programs in correctional facilities.

References

American Bar Association. (2018, September 24). *School-to-prison pipeline*. Retrieved March 1, 2019 from: https://www.americanbar.org/groups/child_law/resources/attorneys/school-to-prison-pipeline/.

American Pet Products Association, Inc. (2017). *2017–2018 APPA National Pet Owners Survey*. Greenwich, CT: Author.

American Psychiatric Association. (2013). *Diagnostic and statistical manual of mental disorders: DSM-5*. Washington, DC: Author.

American Society for the Prevention of Cruelty to Animals. (2019). *Animal homelessness*. Retrieved March 7, 2019 from: https://www.aspca.org/animal-homelessness.

American Society for the Prevention of Cruelty to Animals (ASPCA). (2015). *More than 1 million households forced to give up their beloved pet each year, ASPCA research reveals*. Retrieved March 7, 2019 from: https://www.aspca.org/about-us/press-releases/more-1-million-households-forced-give-their-beloved-pet-each-year-aspca.

American Society for the Prevention of Cruelty to Animals (ASPCA). (2017). *Pet statistics*. Retrieved April 27, 2017 from: https://www.aspca.org/animal-homelessness/shelter-intake-and-surrender/pet-statistics.

Aufderheide, C. (2016). *The application and effects of service dog training by inmates to self-perception and self-other overlap as a rehabilitative approach to incarceration*. (Unpublished master's thesis), University of Oregon, Eugene, Oregon.

Beck, A. M. (2014). The biology of the human–animal bond. *Animal Frontiers, 4*, 32–36.

Berkman, E.T. (2017). The neuroscience of self-control. In D. de Ridder, M. Adriaanse, & K. Fujita (Eds.), *Handbook of self-control in health and wellbeing*. Abingdon-on-Thames: Routledge. https://pdfs.semanticscholar.org/80d1/09294bd2ce6175e548d7974f79eec4a3456a.pdf.

Binfet, J. T., & Passmore, H. A. (2016). Hounds and homesickness: The effects of an animal-assisted therapeutic intervention for first-year university students. *Anthrozoös, 29*(3), 441–454.

Blazina, C., & Kogan, L. R. (2016). *Men and their dogs: A new understanding of man's best friend*. Switzerland: Springer.

Britton, D. M., & Button, A. (2006). Prison pups: Assessing the effects of dog training programs in correctional facilities. *Journal of Family Social Work, 9*(4), 79–95. Available: http://www.academia.edu/443498/Prison_Pups_Assessing_the_Effects_of_Dog_Training_Programs_In_Correctional_Facilities.

Bustad, L. (1996). *Compassion: Our last great hope* (2nd ed.). Bellevue, WA: Delta Society.

Challinor, L.A. (2009). *To study the educational and therapeutic benefits of using abandoned dogs in the rehabilitation of prisoners: USA, Canada*. The Winston Churchill Memorial Trust of Australia: Churchill Fellowship Report 2009.

Conroy, J. W., Ferris, C. S., Furdella, J. A., Vanni, C., & Conroy, N. L. (2012). *Canines in corrections: A qualitative analysis*. Retrieved November 1, 2014 from: http://www.eoutcome.org/Uploads/COAUploads/PdfUpload/NLOL-BriefReport2-Canines%20in%20Corrections-QualitativeAnalysis-Final%20_revised_%20December%202012.pdf.

Cooke, B. J., & Farrington, D. P. (2016). The effectiveness of dog-training programs in prison. *Prison Journal, 96*(6), 854–876.

Coren, S. (2012, September 19). *How many dogs are there in the world? Psychology Today blog*. Retrieved April 15, 2017 from https://www.psychologytoday.com/blog/canine-corner/201209/how-many-dogs-are-there-in-the-world.

Courthouse Dogs Foundation. (2019). Training people for successful partnerships with courthouse facility dogs. https://courthousedogs.org.

Custance, D., & Mayer, J. (2012). Empathic-like responding by domestic dogs (Canis familiaris) to distress in humans: An exploratory study. *Animal Cognition, 15*(5), 851–859. https://doi.org/10.1007/s10071-012-0510-1.

Dawson, J. (2016). Empathy through animals: Generating evidence-based outcomes for empathy development. *Juvenile and Family Court Journal, 67*(4), 43–54.

Dreisinger, B. (2016). *Incarceration nations: A journey to justice in prisons around the world*. New York: Other Press. Quoted in: https://www.counterpunch.org/2016/02/26/prisoner-rehabilitation-around-the-world/.

Enders-Slegers, M. J., Verheggen, T., & Eshuis, J. (2016). Awareness can change a society: The link between animal abuse and domestic violence in the Netherlands. In M. Pregowski (Ed.), *Companion animals in everyday life: Situating animal engagement within cultures* (pp. 251–265). New York: Palgrave Macmillan US.

Fazel, S., & Wolf, A. (2016). A systematic review of criminal recidivism rates worldwide: Current difficulties and recommendations for best practice. *PLoS One, 10*(6), e0130390. https://doi.org/10.1371/journal.pone.0130390.

Freund, L. S., McCune, S., Esposito, L., Gee, N. R., & McCardle, P. (2016). *The social neuroscience of human-animal interaction*. Washington, DC: American Psychological Association.

Friedmann, E., Son, H., & Saleem, M. (2015). The animal-human bond: Health and wellness. In A. H. Fine (Ed.), *Handbook on animal-assisted therapy: Foundations and guidelines for animal-assisted interventions* (4th ed., pp. 73–88). Waltham, MA: Academic Press.

Froling, J. (2009). *Service dog tasks for psychiatric disabilities*. Retrieved October 30, 2014 from: http://www.iaadp.org/psd_tasks.html.

Furst, G. (2006). Prison-based animal programs: A national survey. *The Prison Journal, 86*(4), 407–430.

Furst, G. (2011). *Animal programs in prison*. Boulder, CO: First Forum Press.

Glaze, L. E., & Herberman, E. J. (2013). Correctional populations in the U.S., 2012. *Bureau of Justice Bulletin,* 1–13. Retrieved November 18, 2014 from: http://www.bjs.gov/content/pub/pdf/cpus12.pdf.

Gupta, M. (2008). Functional links between intimate partner violence and animal abuse: Personality features and representations of aggression. *Society and Animals, 16,* 223–242.

Han, T. M., Flynn, E., Winchell, J., Gould, E., Gandenberger, J., Barattin, D., et al. (2018). *Prison-based dog training programs: Standard protocol*. Denver: Institute for Human-Animal Connection.

Harbolt, T., & Ward, T. (2001). Teaming incarcerated youth with shelter dogs for a second chance. *Society & Animals, 9*(2), 177–182. Retrieved January 2014 from: http://www.societyandanimalsforum.org/sa/sa9.2/harbolt.shtml.

Harkrader, T., Burke, T., & Owen, S. (2004). Pound puppies: The rehabilitative uses of dogs in correctional facilities. *Corrections Today, 62*(2), 74–80. Retrieved September 19, 2017 from: https://vadoc.virginia.gov/resources/events/aca-poundpuppies.pdf.

Hart, L. A., & Yamamoto, M. (2015). Recruiting psychosocial health effects of animals for families and communities: Transition to practice. In A. H. Fine (Ed.), *Handbook on animal-assisted therapy: Foundations and guidelines for animal-assisted interventions* (4th ed., pp. 53–72). Waltham, MA: Academic Press.

Hennessy, M. B., Morris, A., & Linden, F. (2006). Evaluation of the effects of a socialization program in a prison on behavior and pituitary-adrenal hormone levels of shelter dogs. *Applied Animal Behaviour Science, 99,* 157–171.

Hershman, C. L. (2008). Inaugural marine prison dog program assists wounded veterans. *Corrections Today, 70*(6), 46–48.

Hogle, P. S. (2009). Going to the dogs: Prison-based training programs are win-win. *Corrections Today, 71*(4), 69–72.

Hoy-Gerlach, J., & Wehman, S. (2017). *Human-animal interactions: A social work guide*. Washington, DC: National Association of Social Workers.

Hunt, K. S., & Dumville, R. (2016). *Recidivism among federal offenders: A comprehensive overview*. http://www.ussc.gov/sites/default/files/pdf/research-and-publications/research-publications/2016/recidivism_overview.pdf.

Johnson, A., & Bruneau, L. (2016). Healing bonds: Animal assisted interventions with adjudicated male youth. In C. Blazina & L. Kogan (Eds.), *Men and their dogs: A new understanding of man's best friend* (pp. 113–132). Switzerland: Springer International Publishing.

Kaufmann, M. E., Beetz, A., Kinoshita, M., & Ross, S., Jr. (2015). Enhancing special education environments with animal-assisted interventions at Green Chimneys: Opportunities and practical considerations. In A. H. Fine (Ed.), *Handbook on animal-assisted therapy: Foundations and guidelines for animal-assisted interventions* (4th ed., pp. 211–224). Waltham, MA: Academic Press.

Kikusui, T. (2015). Oxytocin-gaze positive loop and the coevolution of human–dog bonds. *Science, 348,* 333–336.

Koda, N., Miyaji, K., Kuniyoshi, M., Adachi, Y., Watababe, G., Miyaji, C., et al. (2015). Effects of a dog-assisted program in a Japanese prison. *Asian Journal of Criminology, 10*(3), 193–208.

Kwan J. Y. (2013). Owner attachment and problem behaviors related to relinquishment and training techniques of dogs, *Journal of Applied Animal Welfare Science, 16*(2), 168–183. doi: http://dx.doi.org/10.1080/10888705.2013.768923.

Lally, P., van Jaarsveld, C. H. M., Potts, H. W. W., & Wardle, J. (2010). How are habits formed: Modelling habit formation in the real world. *European Journal of Social Psychology, 40*(6), 998–1009. https://doi.org/10.1002/ejsp.674.

Larson, C. R. (2016). *Prisoner rehabilitation around the world.* Retrieved January 30, 2019 from: https://www.counterpunch.org/2016/02/26/prisoner-rehabilitation-around-the-world/.

Le Roux, M. C., & Kemp, R. (2009). Effect of a companion dog on depression and anxiety levels of elderly residents in a long-term care facility. *Psychogeriatrics, 9,* 23–26. https://doi.org/10.1111/j.1479-8301.2009.00268.x.

Levinson, B. (1969). *Pet-oriented child psychotherapy*. Springfield, IL: Charles C. Thomas.

Levinson, E. M., Barker, W. F., Van Zandt, P., Vogt, M., & Jalongo, M. R. (2017). Effects of reading with adult tutor/therapy dog teams on elementary students' reading achievement and attitudes. *Society and Animals, 25*(1), 38–56.

Madden Ellsworth, L., Tragesser, S., & Newberry, R. C. (2016). Interaction with shelter dogs reduces negative affect of adolescents in substance use disorder treatment. *Anthrozoös, 29*(2), 247–262.

McCardle, P., Gee, N., McCune, S., Esposito, L., & Freund, L. (2016). *The social neuroscience of human-animal interaction.* Washington, DC: American Psychological Association.

Miller, S. C., Kennedy, C., DeVoe, D., Hickey, M., Nelson, T., & Kogan, L. (2009). An examination of changes in oxytocin levels in men and women before and after interaction with a bonded dog. *Anthrozoös, 22*(1), 31–42.

Millman, J. (2014, March 18). Prisons give unruly rescue dogs a second chance. *The Wall Street Journal.* Retrieved April 28, 2017 from: https://www.wsj.com/articles/prisons-give-unruly-rescue-dogs-a-second-chance-1395195207?tesla=y.

Moneymaker, J., & Strimple, E. (1991). Animals and inmates: A sharing companionship behind bars. *Journal of Offender Rehabilitation, 16,* 133–152.

Mulcahy, C., & McLaughlin, D. (2013). Is the tail wagging the dog? A review of the evidence for prison animal programs. *Australian Psychologist, 48*(5), 370–378.

O'Neil, J. M. (2015). *Men's gender role conflict: Psychological costs, consequences, and an agenda for change*. Washington, DC: American Psychological Association.

Omert, M. (2013). *Made for each other*. New York: DeCapo Press.

Ormerod, E. (2008). Companion animals and offender rehabilitation—Experiences from a prison therapeutic community in Scotland. *Therapeutic Communities, 29*(3), 285–296.

Parish-Plass, N. (2013). *Animal-assisted psychotherapy: Theory, issues and practice*. Lafayette, IN: Purdue University Press.

Perea-Mediavilla, M. A., & López-Cepero, J. (2017). Expectations towards animal-assisted interventions and improvement on quality of life: Triangulating information from different actors and levels of analysis. In A. Maturo, S. Hošková-Mayerová, D. Soitu, & J. J. Kacprzyk (Eds.), *Recent trends in social systems: Quantitative theories and quantitative models* (pp. 399–406). Switzerland: Springer International Publishing.

Petfinder. (2018). *Why are pets given up*? Retrieved March 7, 2019 from: https://www.petfinder.com/pet-adoption/dog-adoption/pets-relinquished-shelters/.

Pew Charitable Trusts. (2011, April 11). *State of recidivism: The revolving door of prison.* Retrieved July 25, 2019 from: https://www.pewtrusts.org/en/research-and-analysis/reports/0001/01/01/state-of-recidivism.

Polaschek, D. L. L., Day, A., & Hollin, C. R. (2019). *The Wiley international book of correctional psychology*. New York: Wiley.

Powell-Adam, L., Guastella, J., McGreevy, P., Bauman, A., Edwards, K. M., & Stamatakis, E. (2019). The physiological function of oxytocin in humans and its acute response to human-dog interactions: A review of the literature. *Journal of Veterinary Behavior, 30,* 25–32.

Quervel-Chaumette, M., Faerber, V., Farago, T., Marshall-Pescini, S., & Range, F. (2016). Investigating empathy-like responding to conspecifics' distress in pet dogs. *PLoS One,* https://doi.org/10.1371/journal.pone.0152920.

Serpell, J. A. (2015). Animal-assisted interventions in historical perspective. In A. H. Fine (Ed.), *Handbook on animal-assisted therapy: Foundations and guidelines for animal-assisted interventions* (4th ed., pp. 11–19). Waltham, MA: Academic Press.

Sickmund, M. (2009). *Delinquency cases in juvenile court, 2005.* Washington, DC: Office of Juvenile Justice and Delinquency Prevention.

Strimple, E. O. (2003). A history of prison inmate-animal interaction programs. *The American Behavioral Scientist, 47*(1), 70–78.

Taylor, K., & Blanchette, K. (2001). *Results of an evaluation of the Pawsitive Directions Canine Program at Nova Institution for women.* Ottawa: Correctional Service of Canada.

Turner, W. G. (2007). The experiences of offenders in a prison canine program. *Federal Probation, 71*(1), 38–43.

Udell, M. A. R., & Wynne, C. D. L. (2008). A review of domestic dogs' (canis familiaris) human-like behaviors: Or why behavior analysts should stop worrying and love their dogs. *Journal of the Experimental Analysis of Behavior, 89,* 247–261.

Wagner, P., & Rauby, B. (2017, March 14). Mass incarceration: The whole pie 2017. *Prison Policy Initiative.* Retrieved April 31, 2017 https://www.prisonpolicy.org/reports/pie2017.html.

Weiss, E., Gramann, S., Spain, C. V., & Slater, M. (2015). Goodbye to a good friend: An exploration of the re-homing of cats and dogs in the U.S. *Open Journal of Animal Sciences, 5,* 435–456.

Chapter 2
The Empirical Evidence Supporting Dog Training Programs for Incarcerated People

Gennifer Furst

Introduction

Early research on prison-based animal programs examined the nature and extent of the proliferation that began in 2000 (Furst 2006). Today the literature is increasingly focused on prison dog training programs (DTPs). The programs take various forms—in some, incarcerated people raise puppies bred for specialized work and in others rescued shelter dogs are socialized to live as pets with some going on to specialized training. The extent of the interactions differ as well; in some programs participants take their dogs with them everywhere, while in others, the time spent with the dogs is more limited and focused on training. While the programs are designed to primarily aid the animals that are cared for and trained, research findings indicate the human participants experience a variety of therapeutic impacts. Indeed, the program effects can be seen in the staff and general populations who are not even directly involved with the programs. Both the plight of homeless shelter animals as well as the demand for service and working dogs are significant on-going social issues in the United States that can be positively impacted by these programs.

The positive impact of prison animal programs is rooted in the therapeutic nature of human-animal interactions (HAIs). Physicians and psychologists have long recommended companion animals for a variety of afflictions including physical impairments, recuperation from surgery, high blood pressure, substance use disorders and a range of disorders associated with aging (Serpell 2015). The effects have been used as effective interventions with those who have been physically or sexually abused, and people with chronic mental illness (ibid). Doctors have come to prescribe pets as good medicine. The idea that animals can benefit humans "has come to be accepted by mainstream psychological, educational, and medical

G. Furst (✉)
William Patterson University of New Jersey, Wayne, NJ, USA
e-mail: furstg@wpunj.edu

M. R. Jalongo (ed.), *Prison Dog Programs*,
https://doi.org/10.1007/978-3-030-25618-0_2

researchers and practitioners" (Coren 2015, p. xix). Companion animals offer a unique bonding experience for humans.

A nascent body of empirical research on the topic of prison DTPs continues to develop. The literature has grown from findings based largely on anecdotal reports and non-experimental studies with single-digit sample sizes to research that use more advanced scientific methodologies and complex statistical procedures. Recent research findings differentiate between both short term program effects, including lowering institutional violence and disciplinary charges, and long term goals such as increasing job opportunities that can positively impact reintegrative success. The growth in the body of research demonstrating the value of DTPs coincides with socio-political conditions that continue to increase demand for service and working dogs. The present chapter will examine the contemporary interdisciplinary literature that provides empirical evidence of the beneficial effects of prison dog programs.

Why Incarcerated People Need Programming Researchers increasingly refer to incarceration as criminogenic—that is, it encourages rather than discourages criminal behavior (e.g., Cullen et al. 2011; Duwe and Clark 2017; Walters 2016). In order to adapt to prison, people must often accept a code that rejects social norms and utilize criminal thinking; during the process of prisonization incarcerated people come to identify with the often violent carceral subculture (Clemmer 1940). Survival while incarcerated frequently requires men to demonstrate fearlessness and physical power (Fournier 2016). Fournier cites the work of Sabo et al. (2001) who describe maladaptive hegemonic masculinity as focused on "dominance, violence, and competition" or what Kupers (2005) labels toxic masculinity. Successful reintegration into free society, then, requires recovering "from the negative effects of incarceration prior to reentering society" (Fournier 2016, p. 176). With responsibility for a dog, incarcerated people can be vulnerable and express affection, not only verbally but physically as well. In carceral facilities, where touching another person can be a punishable act, the tactile comfort can be especially healing. The companionship that develops with an animal becomes a source of security in an adversarial environment. With animals, incarcerated people are given the opportunity to interact with a living being with no expectations or interest in their past actions or mistakes.

Not only must incarcerated people survive in oppressive and hostile environments, they often enter these facilities with a host of unmet needs. Most arrive having endured violence and social and economic instability; with limited resources they face a variety of struggles (Clear and Frost 2015; Travis et al. 2014; Wakefield and Uggen 2010). Incarcerated people are among society's most marginalized, with low levels of education, deficient employment histories, and limited social support. Academic, vocational, and therapeutic programming are especially important as they commonly face greater deficits than people in the general population (Travis et al. 2014). People serving prison sentences are disproportionately affected by mental health issues, including substance use disorders and trauma-related disorders (Allison and Ramaswamy 2016; Luciano et al. 2014). In general, incarcerated people suffer from a lack of general academic skills, and rates of illiteracy are high

(Lawrence et al. 2002). They also possess weak employment skills. Their work history and work skills are far below the national average (ibid). After incarceration they carry the stigma of having a criminal record. Frequently, these struggles are intergenerational—their parents and grandparents endured similar circumstances (Besemer et al. 2017). As a population vulnerable to "social isolation that leaves people without the social or family support they need during a…crisis" (Hart 2000, p. 60), the unconditional positive regard received from an animal can be of particular significance for incarcerated people.

Apart from unwanted animals there are few groups less revered than incarcerated people. According to law, both are property, albeit of little value, and have been caged and experimented on. Significantly, since help generally comes from above (i.e., we give to those less fortunate than ourselves), there are few opportunities for incarcerated people to help those worse off than themselves. But when given the opportunity, the results are powerful. Some could argue there is a certain irony that is created when a program pairs those whom society has judged as "bad" with others viewed as vulnerable or even helpless. The work they do can make it difficult to maintain reductive ideas about the villainous nature of incarcerated people. Incarcerated people who work with animals represent a group with a uniquely contradictory status. Adding to the social duality of prison DTPs program participants is how the work tends to violate traditional gender norms. Engaging in what is frequently nurturing work stands in stark contrast to the image of big, mean criminals sitting in cages—how the general public often characterizes incarcerated people. In fact, most program participants, like most incarcerated people, are male. Participating in a prison DTP can be an effective way to minimize the criminogenic effects of incarceration.

The Logic of Human-Animal Interactions

The therapeutic nature of animals has been used to ameliorate a wide range of human health issues for hundreds of years. Going back to the 9th century, animals were incorporated into the treatment of people with physical handicaps (Serpell 2000). The first documented use of animals for treating mental health disorders occurred at the York Retreat in 1796 in a facility overseen by Quakers who were horrified by the punitive conditions at the York Asylum (Shubert 2012). Rabbits and chickens were used to teach the patients self-control through positive reinforcement during their interactions with the animals that relied on them for care (Beck and Katcher 1996; Graham 2000; Morrison 2007). During the course of her work in the 1850s with men wounded in the Crimean War, the British nurse Florence Nightingale noted that "a small pet is often an excellent companion for the sick, for long chronic cases especially" (Nightingale 1860/1969, p. 103). In 1867 epileptics institutionalized at Bethel, in Germany, were treated with animal therapy (Beck and Katcher 1996; Morrison 2007). The first recorded use of animals in therapy in the United States was in the early 1940s at the Army Air Corps

Convalescent Hospital in Pawling, New York (Arkow 1998; Beck and Katcher 1996). Men recovering from service-related injuries worked with farm animals as part of a regimen of non-stressful activities.

Using animals to promote psychological health was formally introduced to practitioners in the 1960s by Boris Levinson, a child psychologist (Coren 2015). He reported making more progress in sessions where his dog joined him with difficult cases. Biographies of Sigmund Freud published around the same time documented the partnership he had with his dog, a Chow-chow. Freud found his patients were more comfortable and more willing to discuss their difficulties when his dog sat in. He theorized patients felt safe and accepted by the dog's lack of reaction (ibid). In the late 1970s Alan Beck and Aaron Katcher studied patients released from a cardiac care unit and found pet ownership best predicted who lived or died (Beck and Katcher 1996; Serpell 2015). After documenting the effects on heart disease, Beck and Katcher conducted an experiment designed to compare pet owners talking to a stranger with those talking to (and touching) animals, which is how most people interact with their pets. They found that participants' blood pressure was highest when talking to the researcher and lower when at rest, but lowest when the participants were talking to and petting their animals. And "since that first conclusion, that unlike talking to people, talking to animals reduces stress and blood pressure, the validity of the observation has been confirmed by many other investigators" (Beck and Katcher 1996, p. 81). (For more about the history of research on the health benefits of animals see Morrison 2007; Serpell 2015; Shubert 2012).

In addition to their long-recognized impact on physiological responses, animals have been identified as contributing to feelings of social support (Serpell 2015). Animals influence social status and increase social capital when they increase individuals' interactions with others; humans are often more communicative when animals are present. At the same time interactions with animals protect people from the risk of "criticism, rejection, evaluation, punishment, inattention, judgment, and unsolicited advice" which can come from other humans (Hamana et al. 2011, p. 1976). The intimacy that can be established between people and animals stems in part from the lack of language exchanged between them. "They ask no questions; they say no words that hurt; they offer no advice" (Arkow 1998, p. 93). They provide an alternative to the pressure to connect to people which can be especially difficult for people who have experienced traumatic events. Incarcerated people suffer from high rates of trauma (Wolff and Shi 2012); in fact, the vast majority of incarcerated females have histories of trauma (Green et al. 2005). Trauma negatively impacts a person's sense of safety, self-esteem, and self-efficacy, as well as the ability to develop trust. Because their trauma was caused by another human, victims may experience difficulty forging emotional bonds with other people (Yount et al. 2013). Interactions with animals can "stimulate a kind of love and caring that is not poisoned or inhibited by [their] experiences with people" (Beck and Katcher 1996, p. 153). Social isolation and persistent stress, inherent in prison life, make the unconditional positive regard from an animal particularly salient. Positive relationships such as these can "buffer or ameliorate the deleterious health effects of prolonged or chronic life stress" (Serpell 2015, p. 17).

In their discussion of an animal visitation program in a pediatric cardiology ward, Wu et al. (2002, p. 35) eloquently describe the profoundly unique nature of interactions with animals. They say

> a human-companion animal bond creates a relationship free of the stress and complexities of judgment and expectation. The exchange of affection between human and animal is not ambivalent, differing from human interpersonal relationships between family members and other loved ones, which are frequently charged with ambivalence and negative emotional states. Human love and comfort, if available at all, frequently must be earned through sacrifice and compromise, whereas pets offer a source of comfort that can be scheduled on demand of the owner in almost any quantity….The animal accepts without condition, loving without care of consideration, regardless of illness, deformity, or disability, offering security in that love and giving…a sense of empowerment in a sometimes overwhelming environment (pp. 354–355).

Given the inimitable power of animals to impact humans, it should be no surprise that HAIs between incarcerated people and dogs have a broad range of therapeutic psychological, physiological, social, and behavioral benefits.

Treatment Effects of HAI Interventions Just as animals are being used in a range of interventions with humans, the literature on why animals affect individuals as they do is "spread out over a number of journals and fields, constraining an integrative view" (Beetz et al. 2012, p. 234). The most current research adopts a biopsychosocial model of health that considers the relationships among biological, psychological, and social aspects of wellbeing (Friedmann and Son 2009). The mere presence of animals is able to alter individuals' perceptions, which in turn affects health; improved health results from experiencing increased psychosocial status and decreased stress response when with an animal (Friedmann and Son 2009). Positive interactions with animals subsequently impact interactions with other people. Researchers working with children with emotional, behavioral, social and learning challenges found an "increase of trust, positive social interaction and communication, and the reduction of depressiveness, anxiety, aggression and stress reactions" (Kaufmann et al. 2015, p. 212).

Much of the research conducted on HAI interventions has been descriptive, using case studies or small samples, and lacking control groups (Maujean et al. 2015). As a result, studies are often criticized for their weak designs, and researchers reiterate the call for additional research that uses more rigorous methodologies. Although the number of randomized experimental studies examining HAIs is not large, a small collection of high-quality, well-designed research exists and consistently reports positive results regarding treatment effects. Findings indicate evidence of positive impacts on psychosocial and physiological measures. Recent meta-analyses indicate HAI interventions can increase communication, interaction, and socialization with others (see Maujean et al. 2015; Nimer and Lundahl 2007; Rossetti and King 2010; Souter and Miller 2007). The researchers also found that patients with mood disorders better controlled their anger, experienced decreased depressive symptoms, distress, and anxiety (ibid). (A synthesis of these research studies and a discussion of oxytocin as a biological explanation for the findings can be found in Furst 2016.)

The prison DTPs examined here differ in several aspects from HAI interventions with other populations. Most importantly, the animal is not present specifically for the benefit of the program participant. The animals are not used in conjunction with clinical methods, such as psychoanalysis, in order to more effectively communicate with the patient or client (as in Animal-Assisted Therapy [AAT]). In prison, the programs do not have a medical or psychological counseling component. Participants undergo screening procedures that consider personal characteristics such as the nature of the individual's offense and prior institution behavioral record, but there is no regular program contact with a physician or therapist. Participants not only interact with animals (as in Animal-Assisted Interactions [AAIs]), but they work with or train them as well. Despite being unique from the types of HAI described above, the research regarding prison DTPs indicates their therapeutic impact on participants is similar. (A review of HAI in carceral facilities, including visitation programs and pet-keeping programs, can be found in Mulcahy and McLaughlin 2013).

HAI in Carceral Facilities The positive benefits of interacting with animals for people in emotionally stressful situations or those feeling lonely and isolated have seemingly obvious implications for the carceral environment. Incarcerated people face a variety of social and physical deprivations (Sykes 1958) and must find ways to cope with these conditions. It should be no surprise then that the first documented example of human-animal interaction in a carceral facility actually dates back to America's first modern prison—Eastern State Penitentiary in Philadelphia, opened in 1829. The British author Charles Dickens traveled from England to North America to visit the United States and learn about the young democracy. He toured Eastern State and published his reaction in his "American Notes" (1842/2004). He found the isolation the Quaker-designed institution depended on "cruel and wrong" and deemed the "slow and daily tampering with the mysteries of the brain to be immeasurably worse than any torture of the body" (1842/2004, p. 111). In this acutely oppressive facility, Dickens described coming upon a cell with "one man who was allowed, as an indulgence, to keep rabbits" (p. 115). Unfortunately any therapeutic impact of interacting with the animals was unable to prevent the man from appearing "as wan and unearthly as if he had been summoned from the grave" (ibid.). Formal programs in which incarcerated people worked with animals date back to the prison farms of the late 1800s (Furst 2011). However, raising livestock differs greatly from training and socializing domestic animals. In addition, the Black Codes were being used to send recently freed Black people back into forced labor—policies that made the farms de facto slave plantations. Coupled with the inevitable slaughter of the farm animals, they were not in any way therapeutic animal programs. The history of sanctioned therapeutic animal programs in carceral facilities, starting with the maximum-security psychiatric patients at Lima State Hospital in Ohio, can be found in a number of publications (see Deaton 2005; Furst 2011; Strimple 2003; Serpell 2015).

The first official prison DTP was implemented by Sister Pauline Quinn in 1981 at the Washington Corrections Center for Women, a maximum-security prison in Tacoma, Washington (see Quinn 2004). Through the Prison Pet Partnership program, incarcerated women participated in 11 weeks of courses taught through Tacoma Community College. In addition to the classroom instruction, they received hands-on lessons with local shelter dogs in training, grooming, and job-seeking skills (Hines, n.d). The shelter dogs became more adoptable and several were chosen for more advanced training to work with people with disabilities. Some administrators found participants more cooperative as a result of the program and others said the women learned self-control. Although some were initially apprehensive about the safety of the animals, the administrators reported that the program participants quickly become protective and concerned for the animals' welfare (Hines, n.d).

At the same time at Lorton Prison in Virginia, Leo Bustad, a veterinarian and founder of the Delta Society, today Pet Partners, established a program built around a prison chapter of the national People-Animals-Love group (Arkow 1998; Beck and Katcher 1996; Graham 2000; Hines, n.d.). In this pet adoption program, incarcerated people were paired with animals they could keep if transferred or released. In an evaluation conducted several years after it began, Moneymaker and Strimple (1991) found that participants reported significant reductions in feelings of isolation and frustration. Participants had fewer disciplinary infractions and demonstrated "considerable change in their outlook toward others and their sense of self-worth, as well as their sense of achieving a better goal in life" (p. 148). [More detailed histories of the first prison DTPs can be found in Deaton (2005) and Strimple (2003)].

One of the most unique aspects of DTPs is that they are not treatment programs in the traditional sense of prison programs (such as, for example, anger management or parenting programs). Prison DTPs do not administer education according to the conventional rehabilitation paradigm in which passive recipients learn about a topic and are expected to develop competence outside the classroom. Instead, while training, socializing, and caring for the dogs, participants develop prosocial reasoning, abilities, and behaviors (Furst 2007a). They are provided with the opportunity to use the skills they are learning and therefore experience, while still incarcerated, the benefits of these new ways. Rather than reading about decision making and taking on responsibility, participants make right decisions and demonstrate they are trustworthy by fulfilling high-level expectations every day. They do not passively receive information or lessons about how to be responsible and caring—*participants are responsible and caring.*

The Effects of Carceral Dog Training Programs

A growing body of research on carceral dog training programs has found a variety of benefits. Over time researchers have strengthened the methodologies of the studies they conduct. The literature began with anecdotes regarding success (e.g., Harbolt and Ward 2001) and descriptive studies based on self-reported effects and testimonies from program staff (e.g., Britton and Button 2005). Early research that examined disciplinary behavior and recidivism did so based on anecdotes and the working memories of program staff members, not official records (e.g., Furst 2007b). Since the first scholarly article that reported the treatment effects of carceral DTPs published over 20 years ago (Walsh and Mertin 1994), the body of empirical evaluative research has grown to approximately 30 studies. A number of quasi-experimental quantitative and mixed methods studies in which researchers administered validated survey instruments and examined disciplinary records have been published (e.g., Fournier et al. 2007). More recent work utilizes stronger methodological approaches such as control groups to collect data (e.g., van Wormer et al. 2017). A point to note: the treatment effects of carceral DTPs reported in the latest studies are aligned with those from earlier research.

Given the repeatedly similar findings over time, the results are arguably reliable: we see great overlap in the qualitative themes revealed in the interview and survey responses. In their review of Australian programs Humby and Barclay (2018) categorized the responses they received regarding the benefits of the programs as: physiological, psychological, socialization, vocational/educational, environmental, behavioral, and recidivism. van Wormer et al. (2017) grouped the outcome variables into four categories: recidivism, disciplinary behavior, emotional/psychological effects, and socio-behavioral effects in one of the largest studies to date. In a nearly comprehensive review of all published studies, Cooke and Farrington (2016) divided treatment effects into categories they label as externalizing (recidivism, behavioral infractions, and self-control) and as internalizing (mental health and well-being, depression, self-esteem, and self-efficacy). Leonardi et al. (2017) identified seven themes in interviews with 70 participants of a DTP at a Scottish facility for young male offenders: positive effects, motivation, charitable work, self-efficacy, improved skills, impulsivity control, and emotional management.

In one of the first peer reviewed articles to formally document the dynamics of the programs that have been repeatedly found by researchers, Britton and Button (2005) conducted qualitative interviews with 38 incarcerated men who trained puppies in basic obedience commands for future work as service dogs. In addition to identifying motivations to join, participants described a number of challenges they experienced in the program. They reported the hyper-surveillance they faced as a result of the dogs, from both staff and other incarcerated people; they were noticed wherever they went in the facility. Non-participants were also potential sources of conflict as the handlers would have to prevent others from giving their dog snacks or otherwise interfere with training. Some reacted negatively to the dog, due to fear or dislike of dogs and the handlers made sure to avoid those people. The final challenge they faced was giving up their dog when training was complete (see Chap. 12). Benefits of the program included changes in attitudes and emotions, such as increased patience and decreased anger; an improved institutional climate that was calmer and more normalized; and the opportunity to participate in restitution as a link to the community.

Furst (2006) reported similar results in the written responses to a self-administered national survey of prison staff. According to the 36 surveys, the sense of responsibility and accomplishment; opportunity for meaningful work and resulting job skills;

patience/anger management, and improved social relations were commonly identified as positive aspects of the programs. The researcher found that staff resistance to implementing the programs was the most commonly identified negative aspect of the programs. The following year Furst (2007a, b) reported findings from interviews with 15 incarcerated females who raised puppies for future advanced training as service and working dogs. In addition to the self-identified therapeutic effects identified above, several women reported physical health benefits including losing weight, gaining control over diabetes, and sleeping better. Ten years later Antonio et al. (2017) studied the perceived effects of DTPs in Pennsylvania. Their self-administered questionnaire was answered by 62 program participants and 29 staff members in six State Correctional Institutions (SCIs)—two female and 4 male facilities. Women more than men reported greater belief in the programs' ability to impact recidivism, decrease non-violent misconduct, and create a sense of community. Participants reported greater belief than staff that the programs reduced recidivism and provided marketable skills.

In a study of six incarcerated males who worked in a DTP, Turner (2007) identified seven themes from the in-depth, qualitative interviews she conducted: patience, parenting skills, helping others, increased self-esteem, improved socialization skills, normalizing environment, and calmer environment. Similar findings came from Williams and Metz (2014) who used a photovoice method to examine the benefits of participating in a shelter DTP for at-risk adolescent males (ages were not provided). Five participants were given cameras for a month and asked to take pictures that related to two research questions: "What does training the dog mean to you?" and "How is your life different now that you are training animals that need you?" Researchers met with the participants and asked them to narrate their photos. Six themes emerged from the conversations. Respondents reported that their work with the dogs helped them increase their patience. They also discussed their attachment to the dogs and the bond they formed with the dogs they trained, as well as the sadness they experienced when the program ended. The young men reported they wanted to make better decisions so they could remain free and continue to achieve goals. They enjoyed being able to help others and reduce their focus on themselves; they wanted to serve as role models for other young people who would come into the program. They were also proud of the commands they taught their dogs. Finally, the respondents reported identifying with the dogs who, like them, were locked up.

In the most methodologically sound research of the time, Fournier et al. (2007) conducted a quasi-experimental between-subjects study with 48 incarcerated males living in the facility's Therapeutic Community (TC). Half of the sample participated in the DTP and half did not. According to official records, the treatment group was associated with fewer institutional infractions and greater progress in the substance abuse-related TC treatment; according to a validated survey instrument, the group also showed improved social skills. The researchers found statistically significant improvements in these dependent measures compared to the control group.

Minton et al. (2015) conducted 30 semi-structured interviews with incarcerated females participating in a service dog training program. Participants reported positive effects in the areas of emotional and physical health, self-concept, goal-directed behaviors, empathy, and self-control. They had improved positive interactions with others, both other incarcerated women and facility security staff. Similar to other research findings, the women reported facing challenges in interactions with those who did not support the program. Several women mentioned having been on a waiting list to get into the program and their willingness to make any necessary sacrifices to stay in the program. Respondents noted improvements in their physical health including weight loss and better control over diabetes and high blood pressure. The dog contributed to feelings of having a unique identity, different from the hundreds of other incarcerated women who all wear the same uniform and are permitted only limited personal items. Having positive goals and responsibilities contributed to improved self-identity and self-discipline. Making restitution also influenced their ability to move beyond continued "purposeless and self-blame" for past harms and mistakes (p. 493).

Cooke and Farrington (2015) collected qualitative data from interviews with 12 adult female program participants, 8 juvenile female program participants, and 2 program coordinators and 5 staff members (N = 27). The incarcerated adult females were housed in a work camp and trained both service and shelter dogs; juvenile females trained shelter dogs in 8-week classes. The findings indicated that participation in a DTP helped to alleviate the pains of imprisonment which females experience more strongly than males (Collica-Cox 2010). The program participants reported their psychological and emotional health were positively impacted by the program in the form of stress relief and comfort. They experienced a "healing effect" that enabled participants to "deal with psychological and emotional problems that ranged from general fears and worrying to more severe conditions like depression and PTSD" (Cooke and Farrington 2015, p. 206).

Similar to the national population of incarcerated adult females, most of the program participants were mothers. For mothers separated from their children, one of the most intensely experienced pains of imprisonment, the dogs served as a replacement for the desire to nurture a living being and show physical affection through touching and kissing. The responsibility the women took on through their participation also helped restore their relationships with their children who were proud of their mothers' hard work and restitution. A lack of employment skills and resulting economic instability also contributes to poor self-image. Successfully training dogs improved self-efficacy and empowered the participants to have confidence in their ability to accomplish their goals.

The dorms where the program participants and dogs were housed had no violence, compared to other parts of the institution. The sense of physical security benefited not only the participants, but also their family members and staff who worked in the units. The ability to trust, uncommon in the prison setting, was fostered by the program. The participants felt they could trust each other with their dogs (and their possessions) and the security staff trusted them more than the general population, not only because they fulfilled their responsibilities with the dogs, but also because participants want to remain in the program and avoid infractions. The women also noted they felt trusted by the dogs who were reliant on them for care. They reported that they learned more from the DTP than from other programs they had participated in previously. The staff at the facility for the juvenile program noted that the program made the experience of incarceration more proactive and complemented other programs in which the girls were enrolled. The overall sense of altruism the participants experienced from giving back to both society and the recipients of the dogs enabled them to view their sentences differently. It alleviated some of the guilt they felt. [See Toch (2000) for a discussion of altruistic activities as a beneficial form of carceral treatment].

The following year the same authors (Cooke and Farrington 2016) conducted two meta-analyses of 10 studies with a total of 310 program participants and 514 control group members. The researchers divided the treatment outcomes into two categories: internalizing (mental health and well-being, depression, self-esteem, and self-efficacy) and externalizing (recidivism, behavioral infractions, and self-control). Using sophisticated statistical procedures, they found DTPs have a positive effect on recidivism, mental health, self-perception, and the experience of imprisonment, and social skills. Their systematic qualitative analysis of the prison DTP literature found similar results that included benefits to the participants (e.g., alleviated depression, improved self-control), to the facility (e.g., improved staff/inmate relations, a more hospitable environment), and to the community (e.g., providing training services, reducing recidivism).

Fournier (2016) analyzed 102 applications from men in the general population of a prison who applied to participate in a prison DTP. She found the most common theme focused on the ability of the program to help cope with incarceration by reducing stress and enabling positive moods. In a second theme the men described the attributes they would bring to the program including their previous experience with dogs and their existing patience and kindness. Respondents also referred to committing to caring for the dogs as they would their children and family members. Another theme included comments regarding restitution and giving back—by helping the dogs as well as the adoptive families. The final theme indicated the men identified with the shelter dogs who had been rejected and mistreated, and need a second chance.

Fifteen of the 102 applicants participated in a focus group and the themes that emerged in the open forum echoed those they wrote about individually on the applications. They sought responsibility and a sense of accomplishment from training dogs as well as the accompanying therapeutic effects of stress reduction and increased patience. Fournier contextualizes these findings as reflecting healthy, rather than toxic, masculinity; the "open expression of emotions is counter to the stoicism expected in typical prison settings" (2016, p. 186). They also described how having dogs in prison normalized the environment, making it more home-like. She found program participants were "more nurturing than aggressive, more expressive than stoic, and more cooperative than competitive" (p. 188). In short, the program participants were able to transcend the norms of the prison environment.

Leonardi et al. (2017) conducted semi-structured interviews with 70 young male offenders (16–21 years old) in a Scottish prison. Nine key themes about the therapeutic effects of the program emerged: feelings about the dogs; positive effects on mood and the facility environment; commitment to the responsibility and motivation from the rewarding experience; charitable aspect; self-efficacy and achievement; improved skills for employment and learning; the positive social impact on improved relationships; reduced impulsivity and increased self-control; and increased emotional management of patience and anger. Unlike the vast majority of programs studied, participants in this program were not limited by their offense type or institutional records.

In the largest study to date van Wormer et al. (2017) used a matched sample (based on 40 variables) of 484 treatment group members, and 517 control group members from WA state prisons, most of which have a DTP. The researcher conducted an outcome evaluation using institutional records they examined for fewer infractions, fewer grievances, and improved behavior. They found participants had significantly fewer serious infractions (aggressive behavior such as destruction of property or possession of a weapon), fewer violent infractions, and filed fewer grievances. They found the programs reduced serious infractions and grievances by over 10%; however, the number of sanctions received was not impacted by participation. The authors argue that "given the rigorous methods used to collect and analyze the data…, it would be difficult to argue that the provision of this program is anything but a promising practice" (p. 534). Because the program is offered when participants have a significant amount of time left on their sentences, to ensure their ability to complete the dog's training, it is a good alternative to the more common "backload" approach in which programs are offered just before release.

In the latest research to examine DTPs outside the U.S. Humby and Barclay (2018) conducted a national survey in Australia and found 23 prisons in six Australian states offer the programs. Results from self-administered surveys of program staff (18 animal welfare organization representatives and 8 correctional staff) identified four themes: engaging in altruistic activity by helping dogs and giving back to society; personal development skills from an increased sense of responsibility and greater confidence/self-esteem; improved social skills and relationships among incarcerated people and with staff members; and vocational skills development.

Recently Grommon et al. (2018) examined the effects of a DTP on juveniles in a county detention facility. They utilized a pretest-posttest experimental design with a population drawn from eligible youth; the treatment group was comprised of 177 participants and the control group 133. The researchers found no differences between the groups using scales they created to measure self-esteem, empathy, optimism, pessimism, compassion, and social competence. Despite the strength of their methodology, they warn their results are not generalizable due to the short-term low dose of the intervention which consisted of five one-hour sessions with the dogs. They suggest the programs, as low cost activities that are not less effective than standard practices and provide participants with opportunities to give back to the community, are still viable options for carceral managers.

The most common criticism of the work conducted on the treatment effects of carceral DTPs is the lack of research regarding the impact on recidivism. The majority of outcomes studied in the literature are intermediate, such as improved social skills or increased morale, rather than long-term, such as recidivism (van Wormer et al. 2017). In the first study to do so, Hill (2018) found participants had a statistically decreased likelihood of re-arrest for any reason (including technical violations, which are not criminal offenses) and re-arrest for a new crime within one year of release. Hers was a quasi-experimental retroactive design that used a matched sample of 728 (390 program participants and 338 control group members). Although her study provides evidence to the nay-sayers that carceral DTPs do, in fact, "work" we should ask ourselves if we want to rely on recidivism as a measurement of success.

Traditionally, program effectiveness has been determined by the single outcome of recidivism, defined simplistically as a return to incarceration; however, recidivism is a complex phenomenon based on a number of factors and therefore should not be blamed on ineffective programming. Recidivism is the result of any of several actions on the part of the offender, law enforcement, or parole officer. As such, researchers (e.g., Lawrence et al. 2002; Mears et al. 2002; Travis and Petersilia 2001) recommend utilizing a broader definition of benefits that includes not only reduced recidivism, but more long-term goals including improved health and family relationships that can also lead to greater public safety. When programs are "held to the sole criterion of reduced recidivism, many programs, in fact, may not be effective. Other measures…may be more appropriate for assessing their effectiveness" (Mears et al. 2002, p. 68).

In a March 2018 report from researchers at the Harvard Kennedy School Program in Criminal Justice Policy and Management they argue "recidivism is not a robust measure of effectiveness" as it "misleads policymakers and the public, encourages inappropriate comparisons of dissimilar populations, and focuses policy on negative rather than positive outcomes" (Butts and Schiraldi 2018, p. 1). They "encourage the development and use of more suitable measures—namely, positive outcomes related to the complex process of criminal desistance" (p. 2). Given the criminogenic nature of incarceration we must ask if it is reasonable to expect any one program can prevent recidivism. Outcome measures related to the ability of formerly incarcerated people to socially integrate and those "focused on social development and community-wellbeing are more useful for evaluating the effects of justice interventions" according to these experts (p. 2). Using these criteria to evaluate carceral DTPs, the programs are clearly successful.

Limitations of Research The quasi-experimental nature of the vast majority of prison research is an ongoing challenge for this area. True random selection, whereby anyone in a prison facility could be chosen to participate in a dog training program is generally not feasible. Incarcerated people with extensive disciplinary records are typically not eligible for participation. Concern for the dogs' safety and the access to increased freedoms and privileges creates risks most facility and dog program administrators are unwilling to take. Fournier et al. (2007) suggest a group-randomized trial in which prison facilities are randomly assigned to have a program. Another option might be comparing dog training program participants to those in different strengths-based programs such as participants in college programs, those permitted to work outside prison walls in maintenance or grounds crews, or as program aides in which they assist civilian program directors. Incarcerated people who work in positions in which they are entrusted with higher- level responsibilities may allow for research that avoids the ceiling effect. As Fournier (2016) points out, it can be difficult to know whether positive treatment effects are due to participation in the program or "if they are just a reflection of the healthiest inmates rising to the top" (2016, p. 191). For example, eligibility for these programs often relies on, in part, a clean disciplinary record, making analysis of participants' institutional infractions compared to the general population superfluous.

In Mulcahy and McLaughlin's (2013) review of the literature they note "there are few good quality studies to support the growing popularity of PAPs" (p. 375). Like others (e.g., Cooke and Farrington 2016; Humby and Barclay 2018), they point out small sample sizes, insufficiently described methodologies and limited demographic information threaten the validity of the studies. However, in the years since their publication we have seen a number of methodologically sophisticated studies with large samples published (e.g., Hill 2018; van Wormer et al. 2017). The research is, however, still limited by self-selection bias; the programs attract specific types of people who are then screened according to explicit parameters. They recommend future research consider whether incarcerated people with greater needs (i.e., lower functioning) could more greatly benefit from program participation. They also suggest collecting baseline data on key variables and formally evaluating institutional climate using both qualitative and quantitative methodologies. The literature lacks research on whether infractions and violence at the facility and unit or dormitory levels are impacted by the presence of the dogs.

What We Still Need

Despite our increased knowledge regarding carceral DTPs, we have more to do. Programs are still being justified as primarily beneficial to the dogs and the recipients of the dogs, yet we lack research about those who receive the dogs. In one of the few studies to examine the effects of carceral training on dogs, Hennessy et al. (2006) found dogs socialized by incarcerated males exhibited significant improvement in compliance with commands and were calmer in an unfamiliar situation in the posttest compared to the pretest. No research has been conducted regarding the quality of the trained canines. We also need additional longitudinal research on program participants. We do not know if the skills learned in the program lead to increased employment opportunities or if participants go on to gain employment in animal-related positions.

One of the largest pieces missing from the research on DTPs is a theoretical understanding of why the programs work. For example, why do participants violate the so-called convict code of not working with the administration, not showing emotion, and acting tough (Fournier 2016)? Why do the programs appear to protect participants from the brutalization effect of incarceration (see Haney 2006; Hill 2018)? In his discussion of the construct validity of animal-assisted therapy and activities, Marino (2012) identifies what he terms construct confounding which can occur when the treatment includes more than one active component. In DTPs the dog "is a complex stimulus that has potentially a number of therapeutic features, such as being soft to the touch or making eye contact" (p. 143). Dismantling procedures can combat the effect by exposing the control group to similar stimuli except for key components of the treatment. However, devising a comparable, active control for carceral DTPs remains a challenge.

Research has found participating in a prison dog training program can contribute to the creation of a positive self-identity and bring about the transformation Maruna (2001) theorizes is necessary for criminal desistance (see Furst 2007a). People who adopt "valued social roles" and who "learned new, or organized existing skills to support the new role, surrounded themselves with people who reinforced the new role, and rewrote their life narrative to tell a story of strength and resilience instead of hopeless victimization" are able to more successfully desist from crime (Veysey 2008, p. 3). A person will believe s/he can successfully change when those around him believe s/he can. When a person engages in pro-social activities and develops social bonds, s/he accrues social capital. Not only does s/he accept conventional society as part of the process of desistance, "but conventional society must accept that this person has changed as well" (Maruna and LeBel 2010, p. 76). Positive outcomes fundamental for change are likely to result from carceral programs that recognize the possibility of "recovering, reclaiming, and transforming one's sense of self, of expanding the capabilities to affect others, to be affected, and to experience a continual metamorphosis" as a human being (Arrigo and Milovanovic 2009, p. 6).

Nearly two decades ago Hans Toch argued that transformation in self is encouraged by participating in what he called "altruistic activity" or "activity designed not for profit or gain but to assist some underprivileged people who stand in manifest need of assistance" (2000, p. 270). Similarly, the strengths-based approach to corrections outlined by Maruna et al. (2004) refers to this idea as generative activity which allows "convicts and ex-convicts to make amends, demonstrate their value and potential, and experience success in support and leadership roles" (p. 140). Participating in these types of activities can provide "a sense of purpose and meaning, allowing them to redeem themselves from their past mistakes, and legitimizing the person's claim to having changed" (p. 133). The resulting growth can lead the individual to reject his "past offender identity" and adopt "a new identity and a new self and a new set of goals" (Toch 2000, p. 276). Maruna et al. (2004) found desisters often adopted a role as a wounded healer, having experienced "the transformation of identity from victim to survivor to helper" (p. 142).

Maruna's earlier research has been supported by more recent research from Australia. Researchers there studied offenders' belief in their redeemability, or ability to "reintegrate and lead genuinely good, crime free lives" (O'Sullivan et al. 2018, p. 1318). They found three themes that predicted desistance in the personal narratives of offenders: (1) belonging, (2) agency, and (3) optimism. The first, belonging, referred to the idea that a person feels connected to a larger community and has a place in it. A sense of agency is reflected in a sense of control over desistance and the third theme was optimism when they believed they could successfully desist from crime and reintegrate into society (ibid). Thus, when offenders tell their recovery stories or narratives and indicate they believe they can make a contribution to and play a role in society, and are optimistic about their ability to do so, they are likely to successfully desist from crime.

Conclusion

Carceral DTPs continue to demonstrate their value for participants, other incarcerated people, facility staff, and the dogs and their recipients. The flexibility of the program models, their relatively low cost to implement, and the continually growing body of evidence regarding their success make them a worthwhile initiative. Given the acknowledgement of incarceration's criminogenic nature, implementing reliable and effective treatment programs is crucial. We have evidence that DTP participants experience the transformation that often precedes successful desistance from crime (see Maruna 2001; Maruna et al. 2004; Veysey 2008). Distinguished criminal justice scholar Doris Layton MacKenzie has pointed out that "a focus on individual change is critical to our understanding of what works in corrections" (2006, p. 337).

Participants of carceral DTPs make a contribution to larger social issues when the program is designed to rescue unwanted animals that would otherwise be destroyed. The rising demand for work dogs and perpetual unmet need for service dogs creates a market where the large blocks of time had by incarcerated people make them ideal candidates to conduct the intensive and time-consuming training required for animals to go on to specialized service work (see Furst 2015). Program participants can engage in noble work that serves the community and fills a need. Having incarcerated people and animals help each other in a symbiotic relationship is uniquely therapeutic on an individual level as well as beneficial on an aggregate level.

References

Allison, M., & Ramaswamy, M. (2016). Adapting animal-assisted therapy trials to prison-based animal programs. *Public Health Nursing, 33*(5), 472–480.

Antonio, M. E., Davis, R. G., & Shutt, S. (2017). Dog training programs in Pennsylvania's Department of Corrections: Perceived effectiveness for inmates and staff. *Animals & Society, 25*, 475–489.

Arkow, P. (1998). *Pet therapy: A study and resource guide for the use of companion animals in selected therapies* (8th ed.). Stratford, NJ: Author.

Arrigo, B., & Milovanovic, D. (2009). *Revolution in penology: Rethinking the society of captives.* Lanham, MD: Rowman & Littlefield.

Beck, A., & Katcher, A. (1996). *Between pets and people: The importance of animal companionship.* West Lafayette, IN: Purdue University Press.

Beetz, A., Uvnas-Moberg, K., Julius, H., & Kotrschal, K. (2012). Psychosocial and psychophysiological effects of human–animal interactions: The possible role of oxytocin. *Frontiers in Psychology, 3,* 234–245.

Besemer, S., Ahmad, S. I., Hinshawa, S. P., & Farrington, D. P. (2017). A systematic review and meta-analysis of the intergenerational transmission of criminal behavior. *Aggression and Violent Behavior, 37,* 161–178.

Britton, D. M., & Button, A. (2005). Prison pups: Assessing the effects of dog training programs in correctional facilities. *Journal of Family Social Work, 9*(4), 79–95.

Butts, J., & Schirladi V. (2018, March). *Recidivism reconsidered: Preserving the community justice mission of community corrections.* Boston, MA: Program in Criminal Justice Policy and Management, Harvard Kennedy School.

Clear, T. R., & Frost, N. A. (2015). *The punishment imperative: The rise and failure of mass incarceration in America.* New York: NYU Press.

Clemmer, D. (1940). *The prison community.* New York: Holt, Rinehart, and Winston.

Collica, K. (2010). Surviving incarceration: HIV prison-based peer programs build communities of support for female offenders. *Deviant Behavior, 31*(4), 303–313.

Cooke, B., & Farrington, D. P. (2015). The effects of dog-training programs: Experiences of incarcerated females. *Women & Criminal Justice, 25,* 201–214.

Cooke, B., & Farrington, D. P. (2016). The effectiveness of dog-training programs in prison: A systematic review and meta-analysis of the literature. *The Prison Journal, 96*(6), 854–876.

Coren, S. (2015). Foreword. In A. H. Fine (Ed.). *Handbook on animal-assisted therapy: Foundations and guidelines for animal-assisted interventions* (4th ed.) (pp. xix–xxii). Waltham, MA: Academic Press.

Cullen, F., Johnson, C., & Nagin, D. (2011). Prisons do not reduce recidivism: The high cost of ignoring science. *The Prison Journal, 91*(3), 48–65.

Deaton, C. (2005). Humanizing prisons with animals: A closer look at "Cell Dogs" and horse programs in correctional institutions. *The Journal of Correctional Education, 56*(1), 46–62.

Dickens, C. (1842/2004). *American notes.* London, England: Penguin Books.

Duwe, G., & Clark, V. (2017). The rehabilitative ideal versus the criminogenic reality: The consequences of warehousing prisoners. *Corrections: Policy, Practice, and Research, 2*(1), 41–69.

Fournier, A. (2016). Pen pals: An examination of human-animal interaction as an outlet for healthy masculinity in prison. In C. Blazina & L. R. Kogan (Eds.), *Men and their dogs* (pp. 175–194). Switzerland: Springer International Publishing.

Fournier, A., Geller, E. S., & Fortney, E. (2007). Human-animal interaction in a prison setting: Impact on criminal behavior, treatment progress, and social skills. *Behavior and Social Issues, 16,* 89–105.

Friedmann, E., & Son, H. (2009). The human-companion animal bond: How humans benefit. *Veterinary Clinics of North America: Small Animal Practice, 39,* 239–326.

Furst, G. (2006). Prison-based animal programs: A national survey. *The Prison Journal, 86,* 407–430.

Furst, G. (2007a). Prison-based animal programs: Self-reported effects of participation and implications for desistance. *Prison Service Journal, 172,* 38–44.

Furst, G. (2007b). Without words to get in the way: Symbolic interaction in prison-based animal programs. *Qualitative Sociology Review, 3,* 96–109.

Furst, G. (2011). *Prison-based animal programs: A comprehensive assessment.* Boulder, CO: FirstForum.

Furst, G. (2015). Prisoners, pups and PTSD: The grassroots response to veterans with PTSD. *Contemporary Justice Review, 18,* 449–466.

Furst, G. (2016). Helping war veterans with posttraumatic stress disorder: Incarcerated individuals' role in therapeutic animal programs. *Journal of Psychosocial Nursing and Mental Health Services, 54,* 49–57.

Graham, B. (2000). *Creature comfort: Animals that heal.* Amherst, NY: Prometheus Books.

Green, B., Miranda, J., Daroowalla, A., & Siddique, J. (2005). Trauma exposure, mental health functioning, and program needs of women in jail. *Crime & Delinquency, 51,* 133–151.

Grommon, E., Carson, D., & Kenney, L. (2018). An experimental trial of a dog-training program in a juvenile detention center. *Journal of Experimental Criminology*, 1–11.

Hamana, L., Hamana-Raz, Y., Dagan, K., Greenfeld, H., Rubinstein, C., & BenEzra, M. (2011). A preliminary study of group intervention along with basic canine training among traumatized teenagers: A 3-month longitudinal study. *Children and Youth Services Review, 33,* 1975–1980.

Haney, C. (2006). *Reforming punishment: Psychological limits to the pains of imprisonment.* Washington, DC: American Psychological Association.

Harbolt, T., & Ward, T. (2001). Teaming incarcerated youth with shelter dogs for a second chance. *Society & Animals, 9*(2), 177–182.

Hart, L. (2000). Psychosocial benefits of animal companionship. In A. Fine (Ed.), *Handbook on animal-assisted therapy: Theoretical foundations and guidelines for practice* (pp. 59–78). San Diego, CA: Academic Press.

Hennessy, M. B., Morris, A., & Linden, F. (2006). Evaluation of the effects of a socialization program in a prison on the behavior and pituitary-adrenal hormone levels of shelter dogs. *Applied Animal Behavior Science, 99*(1–2), 157–171. https://doi.org/10.1080/23774657.2018.1433564.

Hill, L. (2018). Becoming the person your dog thinks you are: An assessment of Florida prison-based dog training programs on postrelease recidivism. *Corrections: Policy, Practice, and Research.* https://doi.org/10.1080/23774657.2018.1433564

Hines, L. (1998). Overview of animals in correctional facilities. In Delta Society (Ed.), *Animals in institutions.* Renton, WA: Delta Society.

Humby, L., & Barclay, E. (2018). Pawsitive solutions: An overview of prison dog programs in Australia. *The Prison Journal, 98*(5), 580–603.

Kaufmann, M. E., Beetz, A., Kinoshita, M., & Ross, S., Jr. (2015). Enhancing special education environments with animal-assisted interventions at Green Chimneys: Opportunities and practical considerations. In A. H. Fine (Ed.), *Handbook on animal-assisted therapy: Foundations and guidelines for animal-assisted interventions* (4th ed., pp. 211–224). Waltham, MA: Academic Press.

Kupers, T. (2005). Toxic masculinity as a barrier to mental health treatment in prison. *Journal of Clinical Psychology, 61*(6), 713–724.

Lawrence, S., Mears, D., Dubin, G., & Travis, J. (2002, May). *The practice and promise of prison programming*. Washington, DC: The Urban Institute.

Leonardi, R., Buchanan-Smith, H. M., McIver, G., & Vick, S. (2017). "You think you're helping them, but they're helping you too": Experiences of Scottish male young offenders participating in a dog training program. *International Journal of Environmental Research and Public Health, 14,* 945–972.

Luciano, A., Belstock, J., Malmberg, P., McHugo, G., Drake, R., Xie, H., et al. (2014). What predicts incarceration among urban adults with co-occurring severe mental illness and substance use disorders? *Psychiatric Services, 65*(11), 1325–1331.

MacKenzie, D. L. (2006). *What works in corrections: Reducing the criminal activities of offenders and delinquents.* Cambridge, England: Cambridge University Press.

Marino, L. (2012). Construct validity of animal-assisted therapy and activities: How important is the animal in AAT? *Anthrozoös, 25*(Supplement 1), 139–151.

Maruna, S. (2001). *Making good: How ex-convicts reform and rebuild their lives.* Washington, DC: American Psychological Association.

Maruna, S., & LeBel, T. (2010). The desistance paradigm in correctional practice: From programs to lives. In F. McNeill, P. Raynor, & C. Trotter (Eds.), *Offender supervision: New directions in theory, research and practice* (pp. 65–89). New York: Routledge.

Maruna, S., LeBel, T. P., & Lanier, C. S. (2004). Generativity behind bars: Some "redemptive truth" about prison society. In E. De St. Aubin, D. P. McAdams, & T. C. Kim (Eds.), *The Society* (pp. 131–151). Washington, DC: American Psychological Association.
Maujean, A., Pepping, C. A., & Kendall, E. (2015). A systematic review of randomized controlled trials of animal-assisted therapy on psychosocial outcomes. *Anthrozoös, 28*(1), 23–36.
Mears, D. P., Lawrence, S., Soloman, A. L., & Waul, M. (2002). Prison-based programming: Why it's needed and what it can do. *Journal of Mundane Behavior, 64*(2), 66–71.
Minton, C. A., Perez, P. R., & Miller, K. (2015). Voices from behind prison walls. *Society & Animals, 23*(5), 484–501.
Moneymaker, J., & Strimple, E. (1991). Animals and inmates: A sharing companionship behind bars. *Journal of Offender Rehabilitation, 16,* 133–152.
Morrison, M. L. (2007). Health benefits of animal-assisted interventions. *Complementary Health Practice Review, 12*(1), 51–62.
Mulcahy, C., & McLaughlin, D. (2013). Is the tail wagging the dog? A review of the evidence for prison animal programs. *Australian Psychologist, 48*(5), 370–378.
Nightingale, F. (1860/1969). *Notes on nursing*. New York: Dover.
Nimer, J., & Lundahl, B. (2007). Animal-assisted therapy: A meta-analysis. *Anthrozoös, 20*(3), 225–238.
O'Sullivan, K., Williams, R., Hong, X., Bright, D., & Kemp, R. (2018). Measuring offenders' belief in the possibility of desistance. *International Journal of Offender Therapy and Comparative Criminology, 62*(5), 1317–1330.
Quinn, P. (2004). *Paws for love*. Exeter, NH: Townsend.
Rossetti, J., & King, C. (2010). Use of animal-assisted therapy with psychiatric patients: A literature review. *Journal of Psychosocial Nursing and Mental Health Services, 48*(11), 44–48.
Sabo, D., Kupers, T. A., & London, W. (2001). Gender and the politics of punishment. In D. Sabo, T. A. Kupers, & W. London (Eds.), *Prison masculinities* (pp. 3–18). Philadelphia, PA: Temple University Press.
Serpell, J. A. (2000). Creatures of the unconscious: Companion animals as mediators. In A. L. Podberscek, E. S. Paul, & J. A. Serpell (Eds.), *Companion animals and us* (pp. 108–121). Cambridge: Cambridge University Press.
Serpell, J. A. (2015). Animal-assisted interventions in historical perspective. In A. Fine (Ed.), *Handbook on animal-assisted therapy: Foundations and guidelines for animal-assisted interventions* (4th ed., pp. 11–19). Amsterdam: Academic Press.
Shubert, J. (2012, April-June) Dogs and human health/mental health: From the pleasure of their company to the benefits of their assistance. *U.S. Army Medical Department Journal*, 21–29.
Souter, M. A., & Miller, M. D. (2007). Do animal-assisted activities effectively treat depression? *A meta-analysis. Anthrozoös, 20*(2), 167–180.
Strimple, E. (2003). A history of prison inmate-animal interaction programs. *The American Behavioral Scientist, 47*(1), 70–78.
Sykes, G. M. (1958). *The society of captives: A study of a maximum security prison*. Princeton, NJ: Princeton University Press.
Toch, H. (2000). Altruistic activity as correctional treatment. *International Journal of Offender Therapy and Comparative Criminology, 44,* 270–278.
Travis, J., & Petersilia, J. (2001). Reentry reconsidered: A new look at an old question. *Crime & Delinquency, 47*(3), 291–313.
Travis, J., Western, B., & Redburn, F. S. (2014). *The growth of incarceration in the United States: Exploring causes and consequences*. Washington, DC: The National Academies Press. Available from: https://www.nap.edu/download/18613.
Turner, W. G. (2007). The experiences of offenders in a prison canine program. *Federal Probation, 71*(1), 38–43.
van Wormer, J., Kigerl, A., & Hamilton, Z. (2017). Digging deeper: Exploring the value of prison-based dog handler programs. *The Prison Journal, 97*(4), 520–538.
Veysey, B. (2008, May/June). Rethinking reentry. *The Criminologist, 33*(1), 3–5.

Wakefield, S., & Uggen, C. (2010). Incarceration and stratification. *Annual Review of Sociology, 36,* 387–406.

Walsh, P., & Mertin, P. (1994). The training of pets as therapy dogs in a women's prison: A Pilot study. *Anthrozoös, 7*(2), 124–128.

Walters, G. D. (2016). From prison to the streets: Can importation work in reverse? *Law and Human Behavior, 40*(6), 660–669.

Williams, R. L., & Metz, A. E. (2014). Examining the meaning of training animals: A photovoice study with at-risk youth. *Occupational Therapy in Mental Health, 30*(4), 337–357.

Wolff, N., & Shi, J. (2012). Childhood and adult trauma experiences of incarcerated persons and their relationship to adult behavioral health problems and treatment. *International Journal of Environmental Research and Public Health, 9*(5), 1908–1926.

Wu, A., Niedra, R., Pendergast, L., & McCrindle, B. (2002). Acceptability and impact of pet visitation on a pediatric cardiology inpatient unit. *Journal of Pediatric Nursing, 17,* 354–355.

Yount, R., Ritchie, E. C., Laurent, M. S., Chumley, P., & Olmert, M. D. (2013). The role of service dog training in the treatment of combat-related PTSD. *Psychiatric Annals, 43*(6), 292–295.

Chapter 3
Exploring Types of Programs: *Dog Rescue, Rehabilitation and Training*

Barbara J. Cooke

Introduction

> *As we all know time moves forward, but what is interesting to look at is the connection between this locomotion time has and the innate yearning we have to move forward. From childhood we learn to crawl forward, then eventually walk forward, actions lying in the physical realm of our psychological awareness, we not only move forward with time, but use it as a tool and set timelines for aspirations, goals, dreams, and challenges. Unfortunately, as life tends to happen, a harsh turn of events, a bad choice can separate us from our forward motion with time, instead to a world where we stay stagnant, waiting for time, alone, to move forward. Most grow accustomed and eventually relish in their idleness; having everything taken care of for them, thus relinquishing goals that take time to achieve. With the mundane life that most prison jobs offer, who can blame them for waiting on time to move itself, without them, till the moment of freedom and life begins again. But this program, as I see it, and, as it has done for me, offers a calling to displace the idle life of prison, and render an outcome that can only be obtained, by once again working with people and time, moving forward and achieving a goal.*
>
> *With that said, there is a distinct line between an inmate and a K-9 caretaker, handler, or trainer. You see men where suddenly their backward looking emptiness has changed its direction and its essence.*
>
> *Now they work together;*
>
> *And now they look ahead.*
>
> Adam, D.A.W.G.S. participant.

Over the last 30 years, innovative and alternative forms of correctional programming have developed and grown in popularity. Some of the most popular forms of alternative programming are prison animal programs, especially dog care and training programs. Over 330 correctional institutions in the United States and

B. J. Cooke (✉)
Texas A&M University—Kingsville, Kingsville, TX, USA
e-mail: barbara.cooke@tamuk.edu

M. R. Jalongo (ed.), *Prison Dog Programs*,
https://doi.org/10.1007/978-3-030-25618-0_3

globally have implemented such programs. There are several types of dog care and training programs. In dog-training programs (DTPs), offenders train shelter dogs for adoption or train dogs to work as service animals. There are also more specialized dog care and rehabilitation programs that include grooming, private training for owned dogs, fostering, and veterinary medical care. As Adam, a program participant in Florida, recounts in the quotation that begins this chapter, dog programs can provide a different rehabilitative experience for offenders. Anecdotal reports (see Cooke and Farrington 2014) suggest that their growth in popularity stems from both the service that the programs provide to the community, as well as their rehabilitative outcomes. This chapter will explore the different types of dog care and training programs found in correctional facilities, how their structure and implementation vary, and the extent of their implementation.

This chapter begins by examining the history of animals in United States corrections and in what capacity they are currently found in correctional facilities. This leads into a discussion of the most common types of dog care and training programs. DTPs are far more common than the other forms of programs and will be the primary focus of the remainder of the chapter. DTPs vary in structure and implication; this chapter describes these variations and how widely they are implemented. This chapter also discusses the intended purposes of dog care and training programs; some programs focus primarily on the outcomes of the dogs (e.g., their training success), while others stress the importance of offender outcomes. All of these variations in program implementation and mission have implications for dog program researchers and practitioners and this chapter will conclude with a discussion of these implications.

Animals in American Prisons

Animals have been found on the campuses of American correctional facilities for well over a century. Historically, animals have primarily served utilitarian purposes in prisons; dogs have been widely used as guard animals and to track the scent of escaped prisoners. Until recently, in the criminal justice system, dogs have primarily been used as tools of law enforcement rather than tools of rehabilitation (Furst 2011).

This utilitarian use of animals in correctional facilities extends to prison farms, which have held a place of historical significance in American corrections. This history is traced back to the slave plantations in the South. In fact, Louisiana State Penitentiary, commonly known as Angola, was originally a plantation and has had an active prison farm on its premises since its inception. The prison farms at Angola and at Mississippi State Penitentiary were historically the largest and most controversial[1] prison farms in the country and both of these prison farms are still in use today (Winters 2013).

Many prison farm programs in the United States were dismantled in the 1970s because the manual labor of prisoners could not compete with the technological developments of agribusiness in terms of moderating food costs (Winters 2013). However, in the mid-1990s, farms became popular again in some prisons for their ability to "occupy prisoner time", act as a source of revenue for the prison or to cut food costs, and for their psychological benefits (Currie 2008, p. 1). Today, prison farms are still popular throughout the American South and in many other states (Winters 2013), but now these farms include nontraditional agricultural industries like fish farming. In fact, many of these prison industries are a form of prison animal program.

While animals have been used in a variety of therapeutic settings, it was not until the early twentieth-century that dogs first began to be used therapeutically in prisons. As previously mentioned, the utilitarian usage of animals in prison (e.g., guard dogs, prison farms) has had a strong and controversial presence in America's penal history, but the recognition of the therapeutic benefits of implementing prison pet programs has been a relatively recent development (Furst 2011; Strimple 2003). The first and most well known instance of an inmate caring for animals or other creatures is the case of Robert Stroud, the Birdman of Alcatraz, an inmate who raised canaries at Leavenworth Federal Prison (not during his time at Alcatraz, despite the nickname) (Furst 2011; Strimple 2003).

Subsequently, during World War II, German POWs who were incarcerated in New Hampshire were allowed to work with horses and other animals. Unlike the inmates who worked with animals on prison farms, these inmates were allowed to interact with and care for animals specifically because of the therapeutic benefits of such interactions. This progressive focus strengthened the morale of the prisoners and fostered a positive relationship between the facility and the community (Strimple 2003).

Towards the latter half of the twentieth century, the therapeutic effect that animals had on offenders became a primary reason for their presence in institutions. In 1975, David Lee, a psychiatric social worker at Lima State Hospital for the Criminally Insane in Ohio, took notice of hospital patients caring for an injured bird and the subsequent effects that caring for the bird had on the inmates. Lee implemented a larger pet program in the hospital. Lee reported that having the pets in the hospital ward resulted in a lower necessity for medication, fewer instances of violence, and eliminated instances of suicide (Furst 2011; Lai 1998; Strimple 2003).

In the 1970s, a new type of program developed that combined both the therapeutic elements of human-animal interaction and the utilitarian purpose of having inmates work with animals. In partnership with the Bureau of Land Management, Dr. Ron Zaidlicz of the National Organization for Wild American Horses

[1]Angola in particular has received a lot of criticism for its prison farm and harsh conditions (Center for Land Use Interpretation, n.d.).

established the first horse program at the Colorado State Penitentiary in Cañon City. The goal of the program was to train inmates in equine husbandry so that they could in turn train wild mustangs. The prison could then sell these tamed and trained horses as a source of revenue (Bachi 2013; Deaton 2005; Furst 2011; Strimple 2003). As will be discussed below, this model prison program is still in use today.

In 1982, cats and other animals at the Central Facility of the District of Columbia Department of Corrections in Lorton, Virginia were cared for by the inmates. This program was revolutionary in that it also introduced, in an official capacity, the use of pet programs to teach marketable skills. Although horse programs and traditional prison farming taught practical skills like equine husbandry, the program at Lorton was the first to offer an Assistant Laboratory Animal Technician course that enabled participants to leave the correctional facility with an official certification (Strimple 2003).

In 1981, the first prison-based dog-training program was founded at the Washington Corrections Center for Women in Gig Harbor, Washington by Sister Pauline Quinn and Dr. Leo Bustad, the latter being a pioneer of human-animal interaction research (Strimple 2003). The establishment of the program (now called the *Prison Pet Partnership Program*) at the Washington Corrections Center for Women was revolutionary for three reasons: (1) it was the first prison-based dog-training program; (2) it was a rehabilitation-aimed program that was founded in a women's prison, unlike most prison programs which are founded in men's prisons and only subsequently adapted for women's prisons (Button 2007); and (3) its anecdotal success spurred the proliferation of more DTPs throughout the United States and worldwide.

Common Types of Prison Animal Programs

As discussed above, animal programs in correctional settings have grown in popularity and have taken several different forms. In this section, we will discuss the most common forms of animal programs. By far, the most common type of program are DTPs. Other types of Animal Assisted Activity or Intervention programs have also grown in popularity. These activities include therapy animal visitation, rehabilitation, fostering, and animal care, such as boarding and grooming. While the focus of this chapter is on dog care and training programs, there are many programs with other animals, like cats and horses. These animal training and care programs look and operate differently. First, we will discuss the basics of DTPs and then we will look at other types of animal care programs.

Dog-Training Programs

In dog-training programs, offender participants train domestic dogs to either work as service dogs (e.g., seeing-eye dogs, search and rescue dogs, assistance dogs) or to increase the adoptability of shelter dogs. In the United States, there are currently over 330 correctional facilities across all 50 states and worldwide that have implemented prison dog programs. These programs are found in male and female facilities at the adult and juvenile levels.

As will be discussed later, DTPs vary in implementation structure and practice. They also source their dogs from a variety of venues; some programs (e.g., *Pawsitive Approach*) use specially bred Labrador puppies while others (e.g., *PAWS*) use "death row dogs" who are likely to be destroyed at a local animal shelter. Another, less common type of rescue DTP are those that are breed specific, like the *Greyhound Friends Prison Foster Program.*

DTPs vary in their admittance criteria, which can include any combination of interviews, psychological tests, criminal history, history with animals, length of sentence remaining, and behavior records. Participation in DTPs is not always limited to the most well-behaved and least risky offenders; for example, a DTP in Susanville, California uses offenders with behavior problems, with the aim of encouraging prosocial behavior and *Project Second Chance* in New Mexico sometimes uses juveniles who have histories of animal abuse or dog-fighting (Lai 1998).

The oversupply and low demand for bully breeds and mixes often makes them the focus of prison dog programs that partner with shelters. *Photo Credit* Mary Renck Jalongo

These variations can be an obstacle in evaluating these programs (see Cooke and Farrington 2016), but it is possibly the flexibility of DTPs that makes them popular. It is unlikely that many prisons establish DTPs with the sole aim of promoting wellbeing or desistance, but rather because of the inherently altruistic nature of the programs; DTPs promote a positive image of corrections activities and provide a meaningful service to the communities in which they are located.

On the surface, DTPs appear to have qualities that appease both rehabilitative and retributive climates. The offenders learn a valuable trade, may benefit from interacting with the dogs, and, by training service dogs and saving the lives of shelter dogs, the offenders provide a valuable service to the community.

Animal Care Programs in Prisons

A variety of animals can be found in correctional facilities. They can serve utilitarian purposes, act as pets, or be part of an animal program. The most common types of prison animal programs are DTPs, equine programs, and cat programs (Furst 2011). Prison industry operations and wildlife rehabilitation programs are comparatively less common or not necessarily animal assisted therapies, but will also be discussed.

Horse Programs As previously discussed, horse programs, also known as equine programs, have been established in American prisons since the 1970s. Though wild horse programs still remain popular, not all equine programs train wild horses. Horse programs have inmates care for, gentle (domesticate), and sometimes train horses. The horses are often wild mustangs, retired racing horses, or rescued abused horses. In these programs, the participants generally visit the stables on a daily or regular basis to train and care for the horses (Bachi 2013). The general activities do depend on the type of horse program.

One of the oldest programs is the *Wild Horse Inmate Program* (*WHIP*), which is a partnership with the Bureau of Land Management (BLM). *WHIP* is currently run in five states. Another popular form of horse program is the rehabilitation of retired thoroughbred racing horses (e.g., *TRF Second Chances Program*). Programs like *Last Chance Ranch* rehabilitate neglected and abused horses. Like the *TRF Second Chances Program*, horses are rehabilitated and then adopted out into the community. Inmates in these programs care and sometimes train the horses. While there is a therapeutic avenue for horse programs (Bachi 2013), compared to dog programs, they do present a feasibility obstacle for many correctional facilities. They require a lot of geographic space and stables, as well as a dependable supply of horses. Also, because of the size of the animals and their untamed status, they can present more risk of serious injury to participants than dog programs.

Cat Programs As previously mentioned, cat programs have also had a history in prison, but were originally focused on inmates having pets or caring for feral cats who happened to live on the prison grounds. In today's cat programs, the participants generally care for and socialize kittens (e.g., like *Inmates Nursing Kittens* (*INK*) and *Jail Cats*) and cats from animal shelters. Unlike dog programs, there is no real training component. Some of the adult cat programs, like *Women Inmate Social Kitty Retreat* (*WISKR*), foster cats with behavioral and health issues. When the cats are rehabilitated, they can be adopted out either through the cat program or the partnering animal shelter. The most common form of cat program is the Trap-Neuter-Return (TNR)[2] format, like *Alley Cat Allies*. In these programs, inmates work with a local shelter and their TNR efforts. The cats generally stay in the cells with the participants and the participants are responsible for their wellbeing around the clock. More than 25 correctional facilities in the United States have implemented some form of cat program.

Animal Therapy While the programs discussed above largely focus on the help and assistance that the inmates can give to animals, another type of animal program focuses on the help and assistance that animals can give inmates. There are a number of animal-assisted therapy (AAT) programs in correctional facilities. The two most common animals used in AATs in prison are horses, like the *Stable Pathways* program, and dogs, like the *Parenting, Prison, and Pups*[3] program. In these programs, inmates are generally visited by therapy teams (a handler and therapy animal) on a periodic basis. The inmates do not train or care for the animals, but instead only interact with the animals and experience the therapeutic benefits of these interactions (Beetz et al. 2012; Jasperson 2010; Fawcett and Gullone 2001).

Prison Industries Animals have been a part of prison industries since before the Civil War. As previously mentioned, prison farms have had a long history in American Corrections and they remain a common form of animal program in prisons. In the prison farm type of prison industries, inmates operate dairy farms, cattle farms, rear livestock, and raise chickens. Texas and Louisiana operate a large number of these ventures. More unique forms of prison industry operations include bee keeping, fish farming, goat dairy farming. In these programs, inmates are like farm employees rather than program participants. There are industries related to dogs, as well. Carpentry programs have included manufacturing of dog beds and houses. Prison industries do turn a profit for the correctional facilities, but they do also teach inmates employable skills. There is potential for therapeutic benefit as well (see Moeller et al. 2018).

Wildlife Rehabilitation Wildlife rehabilitation programs are a relatively rare form of prison animal program, but their status as a unique combination of altruistic activity and animal program warrants a discussion. Oregon and Washington have seen a number of these programs implemented in partnership with conservation and sustainability agencies. Inmates have helped rear and release endangered species like spotted frogs and Western Pond Turtles. El Dorado Correctional Facility in Kansas used to operate a Wildlife Rehabilitation Center that cared for injured

---

[2]TNR programs aim to help reduce the number of feral cats in a community by trapping them, neutering/spaying them, and returning them to their original environments. In some TNR programs, when a cat is deemed adoptable, they are adopted into the community instead of returned back to their environment.

[3]The *Parenting, Prison, and Pups* program is a multi-modal program that also incorporates parenting skills training alongside therapy dogs.

wildlife. The animals in these types of programs are not domesticated and necessarily affectionate; therefore, they may not reap the same benefits of Human-Animal Interaction as dog programs (see Fawcett and Gullone 2001; Cooke and Farrington 2014), for example, inmates could benefit from engaging in altruistic activity in the form of conservation (see Cooke 2017). An obstacle for correctional facilities in implementing these programs is the potential for the transmission of contagious diseases and injury, particularly for large wild animals.

Other Animal Programs Though the above types of prison animal programs are the most common forms, there are other, less common types of programs, too. The *Sheriff's Animal Farm* in Key West, Florida is a petting zoo with injured animals, or those otherwise ineligible for release into the wild, that have been rehabilitated. There are also veterinary clinics, like the one at the Wynne Unit in Texas and programs in which inmates earn their veterinary technician certification. There are also programs, like those operated by the Georgia Department of Corrections and the *Prison Pet Partnership*, in which inmates groom dogs and/or earn grooming certification. The *Prison Pet Partnership* and other programs also operate kennels and offer dog boarding services. There are also programs, like the *K9 Companion Program*, that offer dog training services for private citizens.

All of these varieties of prison animal programs discussed in this section offer potential avenues for therapeutic and rehabilitative outcomes and provide valuable services for the community. DTPs have been the most widely implemented and researched. They also vary widely in format and implementation (Table 3.1).

Table 3.1 The most common types of prison animal programs

Type of program	Animals involved	Types of activities	Extent of programming
Shelter Dog-Training Programs	Dogs from an animal shelter that has a partnership with the program	Routine training sessions to increase adoptability. Dogs stay with inmates or in separate kennels and are cared for by inmates	Over 280 correctional facilities in the United States
Service Dog-Training Programs	Dogs specially bred to be service dogs or from an animal shelter that has a partnership with the program	Basic or advanced training for a range of services. Dogs stay with inmates or in separate kennels and are cared for by inmates	Over 45 correctional facilities in the United States
Wild Horse Programs	Wild horses from the Bureau of Land Management	Gentling of horses. Inmates visit the stables regularly to care for and train horses	7+ correctional facilities in the United States
Retired Thoroughbred Rehabilitation	Retired race horses	Inmates visit the stables regularly to care for and train horses	10+ correctional facilities in the United States

(continued)

Table 3.1 (continued)

Type of program	Animals involved	Types of activities	Extent of programming
Cat Fostering	Kittens and cats from partnering animal shelters. Some come from TNR programs	The kittens or cats stay with inmates or in separate kennels and are cared for by inmates. They are socialized and rehabilitated if there are behavioral or health issues	Over 26 correctional facilities in the United States
Prison Industry	Dairy cows, cattle, goats, swine, horses, chicken, bees, and other farm animals	Industrial farming, herding, and breeding, depending on the species. Inmates work at the facility	Over 42 correctional facilities in the United States
Wildlife Rehabilitation	Frogs, turtles, sheep, butterflies, and other injured and endangered species	Breeding, caring for, rehabilitating, and releasing wildlife	7+ correctional facilities in the United States

Sources Furst (2011), Cooke and Farrington (2016) and Cooke's database

Program Implementation Variation

Dog-training programs vary in structure and implementation and tend to do so in accordance with the demographics and needs of their canine and human participants as well as according to the structure and ethos of the correctional facility in question. There is no specific manual or program structure that DTP coordinators or correctional facilities must follow in order for the program to be labeled as a DTP, but some programs, like *PAWS* in Texas, have developed a manual for the facilities that implement their program. DTPs are flexible and able to develop their own standards of implementation and several programs (e.g., *Puppies Behind Bars*, *National Education for Assistance Dog Services*) use these standards to implement their program in more than one correctional facility.

The relative flexibility in the implementation of DTPs is arguably an advantage over other intervention programs that might require program coordinators and practitioners to follow a manual because DTPs allow the program coordinators and correctional facility administration to adapt the program for their own specific needs. However, an advantage of having a manual for programs that are demonstrated to be effective is that adherence to the manual should improve the fidelity of implementation.

Broadly speaking, there are two types of DTPs: those that train shelter dogs for adoption and those that train dogs to work as service animals. Within these categories, DTPs differ in implementation structure and practice on a program-by-program basis. DTPs acquire their dogs from various sources. Some programs use purebred dogs, generally Golden Retrievers or Labradors, who are specially bred for qualities that make them good service dogs (e.g., *Puppies Behind Bars*). Other DTPs (both service and shelter dog programs) use "death row dogs," homeless dogs who are scheduled to be destroyed at an animal shelter (e.g., *D.A.W.G.S.*). Programs like *Prison Greyhounds,* that are breed specific work with purebred dog rescue groups. *Prison Greyhounds* helps retired racing greyhounds adjust to life off the track and prepares them for adoption.

As a result of their different backgrounds, dogs in DTPs vary in demeanor and training and care needs. The puppies that are specially selected to become assistance dogs will require a different type of training from those rescued from shelters. Shelter dogs sometimes have a history of dog-fighting or exhibit problematic behavior issues, which require special care and training. Some programs actually specialize in rehabilitating dogs with behavior problems and histories of abuse or dog-fighting.

DTPs also vary by participant admittance criteria; interviews, psychological tests, criminal history, history with animals, length of sentence remaining, and behavior records while incarcerated may all be used to screen program participants (discussed in Chap. 7). Some programs have an application procedure in place whereby inmates can elect to join the program and apply (e.g., *D.A.W.G.S.*). Other programs automatically place participants in the program if they meet a certain list of criteria (e.g., *WOOF*). Some DTPs use a combination of the two models (e.g., *Paws on Parole*). Furthermore, participation in DTPs is not necessarily limited to the most well-behaved and least risky offenders (e.g., *Project Second Chance, D.A.W.G.S.*).

Beyond the selection of offenders and dogs, the DTPs often operate in different ways. Some programs, like the now defunct *Prison Pup* program, require offender handlers to take classes in animal husbandry and dog training before they are allowed to handle or train a dog in the program. Course and certification requirements are not limited to animal husbandry and related coursework. Several programs require program participants to have either their high school diploma or G.E.D. (General Educational Development diploma) before they can join the program. This requirement is more common at facilities that also have G.E.D. programs onsite.

Once in the program, dogs and inmates are paired in different ways. Sometimes the program coordinator assigns the dogs to inmates based on the personalities of the dog and inmate (e.g., *Operation Second Chance*). After the offenders have been assigned dogs (or, in some cases, like the aforementioned *Prison Pup* program, request to care for a specific dog), the caring of the animal is handled in various ways.

In some programs, there are two or more inmate handlers per dog (e.g., *U.T.O.P.I.A.*) and the dogs live in the cell with the primary handler(s). In this case, there is generally a primary handler and other handlers in the team have other responsibilities that are specific to that particular program. These duties may include feeding, walking, and bathing the dog, or acting as an apprentice to the more experienced primary handler. It is common in this DTP structure that new program participants enter at the lowest rank in the program hierarchy and work their way towards becoming a primary handler. In other programs, there is only one program participant per dog (e.g., *Blue Ribbon Program*) and that participant is responsible for all aspects of the dog's care and training.

As alluded to above, the dog may or may not be housed with program participants. It is common for the dog program as a whole to be housed in its own unit, wing, annex, or dormitory. In this case, the dogs are generally housed in the cell with their (primary) trainer. Sometimes, the dormitory is shared with other inmates who are not in the program. In other DTPs, the dogs are housed in a kennel that is separate from the residential facilities at the correctional facility (e.g., *Project POOCH*).

In addition to and as a result of the two types of training (adoption versus service), the length, structure, and focus of DTPs vary. Some programs run in cycles where the training of a single dog or "class"/cohort of dogs is treated as a cycle. These programs run for a specific time period that generally lasts between three weeks and 24 months (Furst 2011; Harbolt and Ward 2001). Other DTPs, like *Operation Second Chance*, do not run in specific cycles and instead the dogs remain with the handlers for as long as it takes for them to be adopted. In other programs, participants meet monthly for a few hours to train the dogs (Grommon et al. 2018). The infrequency of contact with dogs of such programs could reduce the therapeutic outcomes of dog programs.

Program participants stay in DTPs from 3 to 26 months, with an average stay of 10.8 months (Furst 2006). DTPs also vary in participant numbers and participant demographic make-up in terms of age, gender, ethnicity, and offense type (Furst 2011). Some DTPs focus primarily on the dogs, making their training the priority of the program, while others stress the importance of rehabilitating the inmates and providing them with educational and vocational resources. Finally, some DTPs include certification programs that certify offenders (or prepare offenders for future certification) in a variety of enterprises (Currie 2008; Furst 2006; Strimple 2003). These include dog training, grooming, and kennel management (e.g., *Prison Pet Partnership*). Other programs either directly or indirectly (through correspondence courses) offer veterinarian technician certification (e.g., *New Leash on Life*) and small animal husbandry certificates (e.g., *PAWS*).

The extent of these variations is fairly unique to correctional programming. However, the flexibility can be an asset to the prison and community by meeting their needs and implementation ability. As most of the shelter DTPs do not rely on taxpayer money (Cooke and Farrington 2016). In comparison to other possible interventions, they are relatively inexpensive to operate they are also comparatively inexpensive. All of these features have contributed to their growth in popularity over the last 30 years.

Extent of Programming

Over 330 correctional facilities and several prevention programs throughout the U.S. have implemented various types of PDPs and they are growing increasingly popular worldwide. DTPs can also be found in England, Canada, Australia, New Zealand, South Africa, Austria, Italy, Poland, Spain, and Scotland. Several programs have caught the attention of the media and researchers, making their work well known in the animal welfare community, corrections, and among the general public. One such popularly recognized program is *Project POOCH*, founded in 1993 by Joan Dalton at McLaren Juvenile Correctional Facility in Oregon. This DTP was the first of such programs for juvenile offenders. Unlike many adult programs, in *Project POOCH* the dogs do not reside with the offenders; instead the offenders are considered employees of the onsite kennel in which they care for and prepare the dogs for adoption (Davis 2007).

Another early program is *Puppies Behind Bars*, which was founded in 1997 in New York state by Gloria Gilbert Stoga. This program has proven to be a particularly effective training resource for service dogs. The program reports that 87% of the dogs are successfully trained as service dogs compared to 50% of dogs trained by civilians (Puppies Behind Bars, n.d.). This program has been featured in various popular culture mediums such as Good Housekeeping magazine and The Oprah Winfrey Show.

Another, even less researched, form of DTP has arisen outside prison walls; programs like the *High-Schooled Assistance Dog Program* and *Tender Loving Compassion* program use at-risk youths, youths with a history of dog-fighting or animal abuse, or juvenile offenders who are not incarcerated to train and/or care for dogs. Presumably, any benefits found in prison-based DTPs may similarly apply to community-based prevention DTPs allowing them to prevent future criminal activity. However, as programs outside of correctional facilities are not the focus of this research, they will not be discussed in depth.

While all 50 states have implemented at least one DTP, Ohio, North Carolina, and Florida have implemented the most DTPs. Ohio has implemented DTPs in all its 32 correctional facilities, making it the state with the largest implementation of DTPs (Ohio Department of Rehabilitation and Correction 2013). Twenty-three of Pennsylvania's 24 state correctional institutions have a dog program of some type (All Paws on Deck) North Carolina has implemented 21 DTPs in 69 of its correctional facilities (North Carolina Department of Public Safety 2013). Florida has implemented 24 DTPs in its 68 correctional facilities, though their DTPs are primarily implemented in their work camps, which are annexes of their correctional institutions (Florida Department of Corrections 2013).

When resources are stretched thin, it is important that they are allotted to programs that are not only beneficial on paper, but also beneficial in practice. As states struggle in a poor economic climate, prisons and programs are routinely closed; consequently, it has been difficult to maintain an accurate count of the DTPs that are currently running. Nonetheless, programs have continued to sprout up across the United States and the world. At least 126 correctional facilities have implemented new DTPs in the last ten years alone. It is essential that we continue to research these programs to better understand the potential participant outcomes and impact on prisons and the community that they have.

This program manager takes a pup to a local restaurant to support his service dog training. *Photo Credit* Mary Renck Jalongo

Key Takeaways

Prison animal programs have become an increasingly popular form of correctional programming. Animals have a long history of use in American prisons, but their therapeutic use is relatively recent. By far, the most common form is dog training programs that have inmates care for and train shelter and assistance dogs. Other popular types of animal programs include horse programs, cat programs, animal therapy, prison industries, and wildlife rehabilitation. Programs vary in their implementation and structure. This flexibility has allowed prisons to adapt programs to their needs.

References

Bachi, K. (2013). Equine-facilitated prison-based programs within the context of prison-based animal programs: State of the science review. *Journal of Offender Rehabilitation, 52*(1), 46–74.

Beetz, A., Uvnäs-Moberg, K., Julius, H., & Kotrschal, K. (2012). Psychosocial and psychophysiological effects of human-animal interactions: The possible role of oxytocin. *Frontiers in Psychology, 3,* 1–15.

Button, A. (2007). *"Freedom from themselves": Gendered mechanisms of control, power, and resistance in prison dog training programs*. Unpublished doctoral dissertation, Kansas State University.

Cooke, B. J. (2017). Altruism prison programmes in America: A platform for transformation. In E. van Ginneken & E. Hart (Eds.), *New perspectives on desistance theoretical and empirical developments* (pp. 139–162). London: Palgrave.

Cooke, B. J., & Farrington, D. P. (2014). The perceived effects of dog-training programmes in correctional settings. *The Journal of Forensic Practice, 16*(3), 171–183.

Cooke, B. J., & Farrington, D. P. (2016). A systematic review and meta-analyses on the effects of prison-based dog-training programs on recidivism and psychological factors. *The Prison Journal, 96*(6), 854–876.

Currie, N. (2008). *A case study of incarcerated males participating in a canine training program*. Unpublished master's thesis, Kansas State University.

Davis, K. (2007). *Perspectives of youth in an animal-centered correctional vocational program: A qualitative evaluation of Project Pooch*. Unpublished master's thesis, Portland State University.

Deaton, C. (2005). Humanizing prisons with animals: A closer look at "cell dogs" and horse programs in correctional institutions. *Journal of Correctional Education*, 46–62.

Fawcett, N., & Gullone, E. (2001). Cute and cuddly and a whole lot more? A call for empirical investigation into the therapeutic benefits of human–animal interaction for children. *Behaviour Change, 18*(02), 124–133.

Florida Department of Corrections. (2013). *Want to Know More About Our Inmate Dog Training Programs?* Retrieved December 10, 2013 from http://www.dc.state.fl.us/apps/utopia/learn.html

Furst, G. (2006). Prison-based animal programs: A national survey. *The Prison Journal, 86*(4), 407–430. Retrieved July 28, 2019 from: https://www.csc-scc.gc.ca/publications/fsw/pet/pet-eng.shtml

Furst, G. (2011). *Animals programs in prison: A comprehensive assessment*. Boulder, CO: Lynne Reinner Publishers.

Grommon, E., Carson, D. C., & Kenney, L. (2018). An experimental trial of a dog-training program in a juvenile detention center. *Journal of Experimental Criminology*, 1–11. http://doi.org/10.1007/s11292-018-9346-2

Harbolt, T., & Ward, T. H. (2001). Teaming incarcerated youth with shelter dogs for a second chance. *Society and Animals, 9*(2), 177–182.

Jasperson, R. A. (2010). Animal-assisted therapy with female inmates with mental illness: A case example from a pilot program. *Journal of Offender Rehabilitation, 49*(6), 417–433.

Lai, J. (1998). *Pet facilitated therapy in correctional institutions*. Ottawa: Correctional Service of Canada, Office of the Deputy Commissioner for Women. Retrieved July 28, 2019 from: https://www.csc-scc.gc.ca/publications/fsw/pet/pet-eng.shtml

Moeller, C., King, N., Burr, V., Gibbs, G. R., & Gomersall, T. (2018). Nature-based interventions in institutional and organisational settings: A scoping review. *International Journal of Environmental Health Research, 28*(3), 293–305.

North Carolina Department of Public Safety. (2013). *North Carolina Department of Public Safety, Prisons Facility Listings by Region*. Retrieved March 1, 2019 from http://www.doc.state.nc.us/dop/OfficialDOP.RegionMap.pdf.

Ohio Department of Rehabilitation and Correction. (2013). *Field Operations*. Retrieved December 10, 2013 from: http://www.drc.ohio.gov/web/prisprog.htm

Puppies Behind Bars. (n.d.). *Puppies behind bars: Puppies behind bars trains inmates to raise puppies to become service dogs for the disabled and explosive detection canines for law enforcement*. Retrieved March 10, 2019 from http://www.puppiesbehindbars.com/

Strimple, E. O. (2003). A history of prison inmate-animal interaction programs. *American Behavioral Scientist, 47*(1), 70–78.

Winters, R. (2013). Evaluating the effectiveness of prison farm programs. *Corrections.com*. Retrieved from http://www.corrections.com/news/article/33907-evaluating-the-effectiveness-of-prison-farm-programs.

Chapter 4
Planning and Implementing a Prison Dog Program

Mary Renck Jalongo, Mary Louden and Lee Estock

Introduction

Individuals who are convicted of criminal behavior in contemporary U.S. society may encounter various types of dogs as they go through the justice system. An offender may have come into contact with police dogs used to apprehend a perpetrator or for crowd control. When inmates go to court, they may see courthouse dogs—registered and insured therapy dogs that are specially trained to support victims of neglect, abuse, and violence during interviews or court testimony (Courthouse Dogs Foundation 2019). Once inside, inmates are apt to see—and some may possibly resent–scent detection dogs that are used to locate drugs, cell phones, and other contraband. If the jail or prison works with a humane or rescue organization, a wide array of dogs of different breeds, mixes, colors, shapes, sizes, and temperaments will be short-term residents as inmates teach the dogs skills that will make them more appealing as family dogs or perhaps as assistance dogs. In some instances, the shelter itself has been relocated inside the prison and is operated by the inmates, as in the Pen Pals, Inc. program. It was first set up in response to the large number of homeless dogs after hurricane Katrina in Louisiana; now the program is focused on rescuing meat market dogs from South Korea (Skene 2019; Smith and Unti 2016). Some correctional facilities have partnered with a school of veterinary medicine and inmates may be responsible for bottle feeding orphaned puppies or caring for ill and injured dogs throughout the animals' rehabilitation. When a correctional facility offers a service dog program, puppies as young as 10 weeks old may be there for 12–

M. R. Jalongo (✉)
Emerita, Indiana University of Pennsylvania, Indiana, PA, USA
e-mail: mjalongo@comcast.net

M. Louden
Prison Greyhounds, Indianapolis, IN, USA

L. Estock
SCI Pine Grove, Indiana, PA, USA

M. R. Jalongo (ed.), *Prison Dog Programs*,
https://doi.org/10.1007/978-3-030-25618-0_4

18 months or, in the case of guide dogs for the blind, perhaps two years. For facilities that provide dog training to the public or that offer grooming services or operate boarding kennels, many different family dogs will be on site for short periods of time as inmates acquire the requisite vocational skills to work in those roles. There may be an employee with a service dog, an innovative program that permits visiting therapy dogs, or a dog that a counselor incorporates into professional treatment plans. Thus, what once was viewed as a veritable apparition—seeing dogs in prison—is gradually becoming more commonplace.

A document that should be required reading for everyone responsible for prison dog programs is *Prison-Based Dog Training Programs: Standard Protocol* (Han et al. 2018). A research team from the University of Denver's Institute for Human-Animal Connection (IHAC) conducted interviews with 20 different prison dog program administrators and reviewed the literature. The project was co-sponsored by the Humane Society of the United States (HSUS). The document is available for free download at https://animalstudiesrepository.org/cgi/viewcontent.cgi?article=1001&context=anitobe. It provides clear guidance on the following:

- Establishing policies and procedures when operating in a corrections context
- Identifying key personnel from different fields
- Funding strategies that enhance sustainability
- Securing the necessary materials to deliver a PDP
- Evaluating physical spaces
- Supervising and monitoring the progress of the dogs and the trainers
- Implementing practices that promote health and safety of participants
- Emphasizing animal welfare
- Recognizing the importance of planning, staffing, communication, internal support, and training curriculum in successful program implementation
- Selecting and training inmate/handlers
- Understanding the potential benefits of PDPs for dogs, humans, prisons, local communities, and society as a whole.

Reviewing this document provides a general orientation to PDPs. The first step in program development is to establish the need for the initiative.

Needs Assessment

Any program that brings people and dogs together must place the safety, health, and well-being needs of humans and animals as the top priority. Concerns are apt to be raised when dogs enter the workplace. In a thorough review of the literature Foreman et al. (2017) discuss health, safety and well-being issues in considerable detail. The ground rules they set are:

- Know and abide by the law, whether it is federal (e.g. Americans with Disabilities Act), state (e.g. dog bite law), and local (e.g., county dog licensing requirements).
- Investigate insurance and liability issues prior to instituting a dog program to get appropriate coverage.
- Educate all stakeholders about the program's purpose.
- Work with knowledgeable experts when establishing policies and procedures.
- Involve human resource personnel.
- Ask legal counsel to review documents outlining policies and procedures before the dogs arrive.

Human Responses to Dogs in the Workplace

Not everyone will be in favor of bringing dogs into a jail or prison. Thus, it is important to anticipate objections to dogs' presence in the workplace and have a strategy for responding to each concern. Table 4.1 summarizes common issues surrounding dogs and strategies for responding to each one.

The demand for service dogs has increased exponentially in the United States. This is the "Class of 2019" at State Correctional Facility Pine Grove in Pennsylvania. *Photo Credit* Jamie Empfield

Table 4.1 Objections to dogs in the workplace

Objection	Issue	Ways of addressing concern
Fears and Phobias	About 11% of people report that they are afraid of dogs, an estimated 3.3–7% have phobias—an irrational fear of dogs	Give people an opportunity to privately disclose fears and phobias. Create a "Dog Committee" consisting of different stakeholders so that issues can be brought to them for resolution. Decide when the problem is sufficiently severe to limit dogs' access to certain areas or the facility
Allergies	About 15–30% of people with allergies are allergic to dogs and cats. Allergic reactions vary in intensity from irritated eyes and throat to anaphylactic shock	Survey personnel to determine existing allergies and their severity. Limit exposure of those who are allergic and designate "dog free" zones. Dander typically is the allergen and it is less potent when dispersed; therefore, a person who wants the dog program but is allergic might be able to interact with a dog outside without having a reaction. In more closed spaces, air cleaners with high-efficiency particulate arrestance (HEPA) filters may work. Some individuals may be willing to take medication in order to interact with dogs. Determine if personal protective equipment (e.g., disposable gloves) followed by hand washing is effective. Bathe dogs regularly and use anti-dander wipes
Animal-borne diseases (zoonotic)	Disease can be transmitted from canine to human through internal/external parasites; contact with feces, urine, skin, or respiratory secretions from dogs; or contaminated food and water. Immunocompromised individuals are at greatest risk	All resident and visiting dogs must be dewormed, vaccinated, and on flea/tick preventatives. Dog feces in the yard must be picked up and disposed of properly. Indoor flooring and the dogs' bedding should be cleaned regularly. Dogs with bandages, respiratory disease, or gastrointestinal disease should be barred from entering or removed from the facility until the medical problem is resolved. The single most effective measure against spreading worms, viruses, bacteria, and fungi is thorough hand washing (Brodie et al. 2002). Antibacterial pumps and wipes are less effective but still useful

(continued)

Table 4.1 (continued)

Objection	Issue	Ways of addressing concern
Slip, trip, and fall hazards	Most of the injuries to people in the U.S. from slip, trip and fall incidents are to seniors. People who are less steady on their feet, such as individuals with balance issues or toddlers, can be easily knocked down by a boisterous dog	Train dogs not to pull on leashes or jump up on people. Teach them as soon as possible to sit when they meet a person. Educate personnel to avoid stepping over dogs, to wipe up spills, and pick up toys. Be particularly careful if dogs are in places other than their living quarters—such as in the visitor's room. Prevent situations where a leash can create a tripping hazard. Teach dogs to stay underneath a table or chair until invited out. Consult with legal counsel about policies and procedures
Dog bites	Because there are over 70 million dogs in the U.S. alone, dogs are the leading cause of bites to humans. Only about 18% of bites are severe enough to require medical attention	Get thorough and expert temperament evaluations of any dogs—particularly shelter dogs—before they are brought into the facility (Grace 2016). Require any visiting/therapy dogs to have training and to have passed tests, such as the American Kennel Club's Canine Good Citizen Test or the therapy dog tests of widely respected organizations. Require evidence that dogs claimed to be service animals have completed training. Know the dog bite law in your state (https://injury.findlaw.com/torts-and-personal-injuries/dog-bite-laws-by-state.html). There may be mandatory reporting of any dog bite that requires medical treatment. Establish a reporting procedure that makes the nature of the injury clear. If the skin is broken, there is risk of infection, so the wound should be cleaned and disinfected
Fights between dogs	Injuries to dogs as well as to people who attempt to separate them are common	Get a professional to assess dog-to-dog interactions in adult animals prior to bringing them into the facility. Teach program participants to be observant and to interpret canine behavior using photographs and videos. Implement strict on-leash guidelines and keep dogs separated from one another,

(continued)

Table 4.1 (continued)

Objection	Issue	Ways of addressing concern
		especially when they first arrive. Avoid face-to-face encounters between dogs as these are most likely to be perceived as a threat and generate a reaction. Give dogs time to walk alongside one another at a distance at first, then closer until everyone seems relaxed. Consult with expert trainers, handlers, and/or an applied animal behaviorist for site-specific recommendations before permitting multiple dogs to come into the facility. Always supervise play outdoors and intercede if it becomes too rough
Cultural differences	In some parts of the U.S. and throughout the world, there are so many stray and diseased dogs roaming around that they are viewed as pests. Not everyone has a culture of pet keeping; they may tolerate dogs only because they will protect property and would never consider bringing them indoors. For some people, dogs are viewed as competition for scare food resources or as carriers of disease and parasites.	Consider evaluating employees' acceptance of dogs' presence in the workplace using a confidential survey. Rely on volunteers and make accommodations in a respectful manner for employees who do not want contact with dogs. Use a "dogs in the workplace" committee to review policies, practices, and concerns that surface. Employers and human resource managers will need to determine at what point the objections of one or more employees to the inclusion of dogs are sufficient to limit or exclude dogs from the workplace

Columns 1 and 2 adapted from Foreman et al. (2017)

Identifying Needs of Stakeholders

Before embarking on a project, it makes sense to demonstrate that there is a need for the innovation. Providing this rationale is important when attempting to persuade others about the value of the initiative and drafting a proposal. Table 4.2 identifies needs of the institution, the inmates, and the dogs in the community.

Table 4.2 Needs assessment of stakeholders in prison dog programs

Correctional facilities need…
Interventions capable of transforming thinking and habits in positive directions
Work assignments that function as a reward system for inmates
Cost-effective strategies to promote rehabilitation
Evidence-based initiatives that reduce recidivism
Programs that support successful reentry upon release
Tangible evidence of contributions to the larger community that counteract stereotypes
Inmates need…
Opportunities to discover talents, acquire marketable skill sets, and advance learning
Job assignments that contribute to the formation of new identities
More occasions for positive interactions with corrections administrators and staff
Collaboration with dedicated and altruistic community members consistent with organizational missions
Validation and support from professionals outside the penal system
Recognition of excellence in accomplished work
Families and people with disabilities need…
Expert advice on matching a dog to the family's lifestyle
Dogs that are socialized, well-behaved and reliably trained
In the case of a person with a disability, a dog individually trained to assist with specific tasks that would increase independence
Guidance in continuing with the dog's training and being consistent
Someone on the outside to contact if issues arise
Support if the dog does not work out and it has to be rehomed
Dogs in the community need…
Treatment consistent with enlightened views of animal welfare
Major investments of time, attention, patience, and care from humans
Lives lived in loving homes and, in some cases, second or subsequent chances at homes
Socialization and training that reflects enlightened, evidence-based practices
Kinds and amounts of training matched to dogs' strengths that and allow them to realize their full potential
Thoughtful preparation for future roles, placement with people, and follow-ups on progress

Needs of the Dogs

Whenever someone in the community thanks the staff at our local shelter for their work, they typically respond with, "We do it all for the animals". To quote the motto of the American Society for the Prevention of Cruelty to Animals, "We are their voice." It is critically important to consider the dogs' welfare. Although this is discussed in considerable depth in Chap. 5 of this volume, it is sufficiently important to be addressed here as well. First and foremost, responsible owners/handlers/trainers of dogs are obligated to be animal guardians. This includes paying attention to signs of distress, removing dogs from stressful environments, providing sufficient time to "just be a dog", and knowing when to intervene and remove a dog from a training program. Each time that a dog is lost to negligence or abuse on the

Table 4.3 Standards of care from key professional organizations

Organizations	URL
Association of Shelter Veterinarians (ASV) and American Society for the Prevention of Cruelty to Animals (ASPCA)	Shelter checklists based on the ASV guidelines www.aspcapro.org/resource/shelter-checklists-based-asv-guidelines
Assistance Dogs International	Assistance dog standards https://assistancedogsinternational.org/standards/adi-standards/
Human Animal Bond Resources Central (HABRI) Purdue University	The use of dogs in hospital settings https://habricentral.org/resources/54871/download/hc_brief_dogsinhospitals20160115Access.pdf
Delta Society	Pet partners program standards (for therapy animals) https://petpartners.org/standards/

part of staff or inmates, it is a public relations nightmare that goes viral on social media. A single incident often results in immediate disciplinary action and sometimes leads to dismantling a very worthwhile program that has operated successfully for many years. There have been media reports about a shelter dog that attacked a visitor at a prison and a highly trained police dog that perished after his handler foolishly left the dog in a hot car. People may worry that dogs in the program will receive substandard care, be neglected, or even abused by inmates, so making the commitment to animal welfare clear at the outset is important when seeking support for the program.

One widely cited way of beginning conversations about the most basic rights of animals is "The Five Freedoms", a list generated in 1965 in the United Kingdom. Even though these standards had farm animals and agricultural contexts in mind, they do provide a foundation. The five freedoms are: (1) freedom from hunger or thirst; (2) freedom from discomfort; (3) freedom from pain, injury or disease; (4) freedom to express (most) normal behavior; and (5) freedom from fear and distress. The work of several other groups can be helpful in reflecting on what dogs need from their care-givers and trainers. These include the organizations and online documents in Table 4.3.

Planning and Implementing the Program

Initiating a dog program will require some important changes in behavior, so it is helpful to first consider how people—particularly the inmates—might respond to the proposed innovation. One way of conceptualizing responses to innovation is to consider the concerns that tend to dominate as people progress to an acceptance of change. People who are in the earlier stages of a change process generally have more self-focused concerns. For inmates new to a PDP, self-concerns may include wondering who their dog training partner will be or whether they will be "good at" dog training. As individuals become more comfortable with and skilled in participating in an innovation, their concerns shift to focus on broader impacts, such as how their efforts will affect working relationships with others or the outcomes for the recipients of a dog they've trained. Contemporary change theory identifies seven stages of concern which we apply to prison dog programs in Table 4.4.

Table 4.4 Stages of concern applied to dog programs

Stage of concern	Inmate concerns	Staff concerns
0: Unconcerned	"I know there's a dog program here but don't know anything about it."	"We don't have a dog program here."
1: Informational	"I ran into a service dog in training at the barber shop. I've had dogs before and I'd like to know how they got it to mind so well."	"I saw the puppies coming in and I wonder how they selected the inmates and how this program operates, exactly."
2: Personal	"If I get accepted into the program, how is that going to change my routine? I heard some of the guys saying that the puppies had diarrhea and they were up and down with them all night."	"Maybe this is a better assignment than what I'm doing currently. What would I have to do to qualify?"
3: Management	"I'm wondering how long it will take me to learn how to be a dog trainer."	"Won't there be some safety and security risks associated with bringing dogs in here? How are they going to take the dogs outside without risking escape? Some of the tools they use could become weapons."
4: Consequence	"This kind of dog training is new to me and I wonder how my puppy will respond."	"They are having an orientation for staff who are willing to take the dogs on an outing or home for the weekend. I want to support the program, so I plan to go."
5: Collaboration	"My dog got scared by a food cart so I need to talk with the guys and the trainers about how to help him get over it."	"I went through some training to learn how to handle the service dogs. Now I am assigned to the gate of that pod."
6: Refocusing	"Now that I have trained three service dog puppies, I have more ideas about what to do if a dog has a behavior problem. When I get out, I want to volunteer at the humane society and see if I can help more difficult dogs."	"Our new Superintendent is a big supporter of dog programs and worked with a few different ones before coming here. I am going to put in a request to travel to the service dog provider's facility and complete all of the work to become a service dog trainer."

Source for stages: American Institutes for Research (2017), Hall and Hord (2015)

Initiatives to begin a dog care and training program can come from within the institution or outside. In either case, it is important to provide a sound rationale that is geared to the particular institution. Mary Louden is the director of Prison Greyhounds, a project that is used to help former racing greyhounds transition to life as family dogs. When people hear "retired racing greyhound", they sometimes assume that the dogs are elderly. Usually, this is not the case. Because they are athletes, most retire rather young unless they were so successful on the track that they were used for breeding. The typical "retired racer" is between 1 and 4 years old. Prison Greyhounds began when Mary adopted a greyhound that "graduated" from Lorain Prison. She sought to start a non-profit 501c program based in Indianapolis that would bring greyhounds from Florida to a local prison and teach the dogs "house manners" so that they could become family dogs. The program was three years in the planning phase and started with three greyhounds in 2012. Since then, over 130 retired racers in 35 different groups have been fostered through the Putnamville Correctional Facility in Greencastle, Indiana. She outlined her planning and implementation process at a conference using the talking points in Table 4.5.

Inmate/handlers with Prison Greyhounds are pictured here with the retired racing dogs they prepared for life in a home with a family. *Photo credit* Mary Louden

About this program, one inmate who struggled with literacy tasks yet was a very skilled dog handler wrote:

> he's not a racer, he's a heart chaser and a vary loving an cuddling dog he reminds me of my dog out home which I lost to distemper yeh sad but Zack's helping me coupe with it. It was a sign cause I lost my othe dog befor they arrived here. He's a great dog an who ever adopted him are vary luckey to have him as there new BF.

The inmates get to know the dogs well, so they participate in writing the dogs' stories to share with adopters, as Box 4.1 (p. 71) illustrates (Table 4.6).

See Lai (1998) for another resource that provides very detailed lists of what is necessary to deliver a dog program.

Table 4.5 The planning and implementation strategy for Prison Greyhounds Mary Louden

1. **Getting Prison Greyhounds started** • Incorporated in 2009, built infrastructure of volunteers, talking with prisons, raising funds. This took three years of patience and persistence! • 2010—We acquired our 501c3 nonprofit status through Legal Zoom ($600)—a major cost savings over legal fees • The first group of three greyhounds arrived at Putnamville in 2012 • We registered our logo/trademark name • We are not a chapter or affiliate of another group; rather, we operate independently to manage adoptions and run the prison program • Our goal is to stay local: local leadership, community, volunteers, and donors. We are "small by design" and will not place or adopt dogs outside our area • Special insurance is required for this program; many groups that consider starting a program do not realize they will need a new insurance company • Before the first greyhounds were placed in the prison, we held Greyhound Orientation for handlers, staff. We brought 4 of our own adopted greyhounds inside to do this
2. **Selecting which prison to partner with** • Ask yourselves: How far are your key prison team volunteers willing to drive on weekly basis, to check on greyhounds, coach the inmate-handlers, and deliver supplies? • We sent letters to all prison superintendents that were within a reasonable driving range to gauge their interest in partnering with our program • If they already had a dog program they were happy with, they answered "No—Not now". Most felt it would cause confusion to have two different dog programs • We ultimately partnered with a Level 2 medium security men's facility. Be flexible. Any PDP has to be adapted to each corrections context initially and then modified as things change • The number of dogs depends on the prison. Influences such as fluctuating populations, construction, the flu, etc. can impact the number of available inmate/handlers • The major challenge was that everything was provisional at first. We approached the prison with: "*If* we raise the final funding we need, would you be willing bring this program to your facility?" At the same time, we had to approach potential donors with: "*If* we get a prison on board with the project, would you be willing to support it?"
3. **The set up** • We decided to place 4–8 dogs in a dorm of 135 offenders. Placement is affected by the physical plant • We questioned the maturity level of some juvenile offenders to properly care for the dogs, so we decided to work with adults • There are no assurances of how long a handler will be with you. Inmates can transfer out at any time, even in the middle of a dog's session. So, we decided on two handlers for each dog. Although one trainer is experienced and the other is "learning the ropes" they share equal responsibility for the dogs • We insisted the dogs reside at the facility, sleeping right alongside the handlers and their bunks, not in a kennel off site. This is particularly important for Greyhounds because they already have kennel experience and need to transition to home life • The goal is a successful transition to house pet rather than obedience, canine good citizenship, or therapy training. Most Greyhounds, for example, have never walked on stairs and need to learn this. Mainly, the inmates teach "house manners" so that former track dogs are more adoptable • Security cameras provide extra reassurance to us that the dogs are well treated • Retired racers are noted for being calm and gentle; they are accustomed to being handled and they usually love and trust people. This helps to create a bond with their inmate/handlers

(continued)

Table 4.5 (continued)

• Handlers are responsible for monitoring and protecting dogs from the other offenders around them who want to feed the dogs people food • Only handlers, dogs and staff can use the dog yard. Handlers are responsible for cleaning up after dogs, indoors and out • Dogs go everywhere in the prison except to chow and the medical building. Visiting such places as the chapel, classes, and recreation yard furthers their socialization
4. **Finances** • We cover all program costs through donations and rely on an all-volunteer staff • Some items that need to be budgeted for include: routine and emergency veterinary services, dog items (e.g., food, dishes, crates, treats, toys, collars, leashes, muzzles, flea/tick/worm treatments, winter coats); and learning materials (books, blank paper, folders, copying)
5. **Emergency plans to consider** • There should be a canine first-aid kit on site • What vet will the prison use? Some are willing to give the program reduced prices. Choosing this individual can be an area of disagreement within the organization • Guidelines for identifying what constitutes an emergency are necessary. Staff need to know who to call and when • Authorization forms for veterinary services need to set up in advance. Our policy is to pre-authorize up to $600 if necessary at the emergency vet • A volunteer from Prison Greyhounds will pick up a dog requiring medical treatment unless it absolutely should not wait. If time is of the essence, then the staff take the dog
The Participants
6. **Handlers: we do not choose inmate-handlers** • We do not accept offenders with: a history of spousal, child, or animal abuse; violent crimes or sex offenses; or membership in gangs • We do not interview them; they are selected by staff and they show up at our meeting. However, we can fire them for any behavior that violates their agreement with us and these rules are made clear from the start • Many of the inmate/handlers do not have strong literacy skills, so we keep print materials at a newspaper reading level • We prefer handlers with at least one year remaining on their sentences so that they can complete the program • Prior experience with formal dog training is not a requirement. Over time, we have concluded that some offenders with previous dog training experience can be resistant to change—something that is reported in the research (see Zazie 2018)
7. **Dogs: we do not choose the greyhounds for the program** • The group in Florida selects our dogs. They talk to kennel workers and racing trainers to identify suitable prison fosters. The dogs will be housed in a dorm, so temperament suited to easy adjustment in a crowd of people is the primary consideration. They strive to identify dogs that are confident, friendly, outgoing, and "bomb proof" • Each track dog is fully vetted and has already recovered from spay/neuter surgery prior to arrival at the prison • Retired racers are, in many ways, the perfect prison dogs. They are: highly socialized to people and other dogs, trained athletes with gentle ways, accustomed to being handled for grooming purposes, on a turn out schedule for their elimination, and are spirited but not high energy

(continued)

Table 4.5 (continued)

8. **Volunteers, adopters and staff: we do select our Prison Greyhound team (very carefully)** • Volunteers are required to complete two orientations—one with our greyhound group and one with prison personnel • Volunteers participate in a debriefing after each delivery of dogs on New Dog Days
9. **Establish healthy barriers between offenders and the volunteers and adopters** • No contact is permitted outside of the official meetings–no individual interactions, no correspondence, and no gifts • Handlers are anonymous on our social media (Facebook, website) • Families of handlers following our Facebook page are welcome, but they cannot identify handlers by name or relationship • If volunteers, adopters, or inmates' families want to support the program, they can give a donation on behalf of the dog and the inmates are notified about it • Inmate/handlers only get vague descriptions of families who have adopted the dogs they worked with • If a volunteer ever gets contact from an offender or his/her family while still incarcerated or after-parole, this must be reported. Our only contact with these offenders is while they remain in our program • Potential adopters cannot meet dogs after they have entered the prison program because it is an imposition on staff to supervise public coming in • In preparation for Dog Adoption Day the handler prepares an anonymous letter about the dog to the adopter. These letters are posted anonymously on Facebook as well
10. **Staff: working with staff** • We find it works best to have one staff contact person and one greyhound group contact person • The greyhound group contact sends the prison staff contact a weekly gate release for those who will be present • Every time the greyhound group volunteers go in, they have an escort from the prison staff. Realize that every state is different and each prison in each state differs as well • Remain flexible and remember that the dog program is a guest at the facility
The Curriculum
11. **Reading material** • We developed our own *Inmate-Handlers Manual*. It is a Word document that is easily revised and printed out at home • We use *Retired Racing Greyhounds for Dummies* (Livingood 2000) as the primary text; Branigan's (2003) *Adopting the Racing Greyhound* is used as extra reading. We also use an article on sleep startle. Books remain with the program rather than being kept by the inmates
12. **Weekly dog reports** • Handlers are given blank forms to complete • Volunteers collect them each week • Reports are the property of Prison Greyhounds and are not shared with adopters. The program director screens the reports for questionable content (e.g., dog mislabeled aggressive or shy, complaint about corrections staff) • Social media team uses the screened material, program director's notes, and dogs' racing records to create posts

(continued)

Table 4.5 (continued)

13. **Weekly dog meetings** • Meetings are scheduled with staff members' availability in mind. A team of at least two volunteers attends each meeting. The group convenes in an available space (e.g., visiting room, library, chapel, dog yard) • The Handler Application and Liability Waiver are distributed and submitted by inmates in person at their first meeting • Handlers store their materials in a vinyl pocket folder • Dogs are evaluated physically and emotionally on a weekly basis. We also use the process of delivering items (e.g., food, treats) to inspect the dorms (e.g., check to see that water is clean/available to dogs, make sure crates are clean and comfortable) • Group discussions give the offenders an opportunity to interact with community members
Implementation
14. **New dog day** • We have a "drop site" away from the prison where volunteers and pre-approved adopters greet the trailer that delivers the new hounds. The dogs are there for about an hour to stretch their legs, meet potential adopters, and have a potty break before we drive them an hour away to the prison • If a pre-approved adopter selects a dog, it still has to complete the prison program. The adopters never meet or communicate with the inmates during that time (about 8 weeks), but they can follow the dog's progress on Facebook • The adopters and the volunteers at the "drop site" do not travel to the prison. Instead, a different group of 6-8 people on our prison volunteer team drive the dogs to the facility. The greyhounds arrive as a group on the same day • When the dogs arrive at the prison from the track, 6-8 volunteers walk 4-8 greyhounds, take them to the dog yard, trim their nails, escort them to the inmates' dorms. After the volunteers and greyhounds arrive at the dorms, each offender gives the greyhound assigned to him a bath as a way to get to know one another and begin establishing a bond. The volunteers stay with the inmate/handlers during the baths while they do this and help to get the dogs settled in their new environment for the night
15. **Dog graduation day (scheduled at weekly dog meeting time)** • This date is determined entirely by when the next greyhounds can arrive • We emphasize that it is the dogs who graduate, not the handlers • We print out certificates of program completion on card stock and distribute them • A group photo is taken to commemorate the event
16. **Dog adoption day** • All prison dogs leave on the same day; usually, this occurs about two days before the new dogs arrive • Dogs go directly from prison to their forever homes—they are ready! • Neither the handler nor the handler's family can adopt a dog • Although it is difficult for handlers to give up a dog, it is also character building. Most of our handlers had a substance abuse issue. It is an unselfish act to train a dog for someone else. They know they are "giving back" and that is a good thing

As dog racing tracks in the U.S. continue to close, the future of retired racers is uncertain. However, the insights here are applicable to many other types of prison dog programs.

Lee Estock is a Superintendent with 20 years in the corrections field who has worked with five different dog programs, both those that train shelter dogs and those that train service dogs. He offers the following recommendations on initiating a prison dog program.

Table 4.6 Implementing a prison dog program: A guide for superintendents

Instituting a dog program requires some important considerations prior to introducing any dogs into a correctional setting. Safety and security are at the top of the list. The following is an overview of varied experiences with dog programs within State Correctional Institutions. The outline begins prior to introducing dogs and progresses through issues that we encountered during implementation
Developing and selling the idea to staff. Begin with staff buy-in and a basic understanding of the program. Everyone—even those who are not participating directly–needs to understand the reputation of the different partners and the purpose of the program. After a basic understanding of the program is established and both staff and inmates have buy-in then you can set the rules of the program. Most people are very accepting of dogs and puppies, so a hard sell approach usually is not necessary
1. Safety a. Staff—Some people are not comfortable with dogs and do not want them around. Others may accept dogs on principle but have allergic reactions that force them to avoid contact with canines. Where the inmates are concerned, you will want to consider the animals' welfare and place them in a housing unit where employees are supportive of the program's mission. Dogs are sensitive to feelings of other animals as well as the people they interact with. The easiest way to ensure you have the right people is by asking for volunteers. You can further test employees' dedication by offering an orientation to the dog training program that will allow them to take a dog home temporarily for the purpose of socializing the animal and reinforcing its training. If it is the first time dogs are present at the facility, training staff and inmates to identify signs of fear or aggression in dogs is recommended. This may be particularly important for programs that bring in adult shelter or rescue dogs b. Inmates—Inmates may initially volunteer for the program because they care about dogs and want important/interesting work to do. Obviously, their criminal record has an effect on the selection process (see Chap. 7). The mission of the partner organization bears consideration. For example, if the dogs are going to be placed as comfort dogs for domestic violence victims, inmates convicted of that crime should be excluded. Length of time at the facility matters as well; non-violent offenders need to undergo a period of adjustment before they can take on a huge commitment such as becoming a lead trainer in a service dog program. Inmates may not fully appreciate that dog care and training is a 24/7 commitment and not like other, more traditional jobs. There may be some physical abilities required, such as sufficient strength to lift a dog into a tub for bathing or pick up a large bag of dog food. Psychological health, such as the ability to manage frustration and remain calm while working with a dog are important traits. There is also some pressure on the inmate/trainers for their dogs to succeed (Dreschel and Entendencia 2013) and some may not be able to cope with it. Select carefully from among the volunteers but also make it easy for the inmates to remove themselves from the program if it is not for them. Stress on the inmates can be detrimental to the safety of the dogs and the trainers. Reduce the possibility that a dog will be "trainerless" by having two inmate/trainers assigned to each dog. Plan for down time from the demanding schedule too. This is a key part of the program not only for the trainers but also for the dogs c. Dogs—Puppies often are the easier choice where the safety of staff and inmates is concerned. Programs for adult shelter dogs can be successful; however, the people responsible for evaluating the dogs' temperament need to be particularly skilled. Some recognized dog

(continued)

Table 4.6 (continued)

training groups that adhere to the "least invasive minimally aversive" or LIMA principles are the Association for Professional Dog Trainers (APDT) and Certification Council for Professional Dog Trainers (CCPDT). Problem behaviors associated with fear and aggression are more likely to be manifested in homeless dogs, particularly those who have been neglected or mistreated. If the facility does decide to work with shelter/rescue animals, it is critically important to provide additional training to staff and inmates on dealing with abused dogs. It is gratifying to see dogs turn around with attention and training and be adopted successfully. Despite everyone's best efforts, some dogs may not succeed as family pets or as service dogs. Pay attention and document the dog's behavior to ensure that no one is being put at risk. The process for removing a dog from the program should be clearly stated in a memorandum of understanding (MOU) between the shelter/rescue or service dog provider and the correctional facility
2. Security a. Contraband—When it comes to the successful operation of a correctional facility, nothing trumps security. It is possible for dogs to become a way of introducing contraband into the institution. To prevent this, continue to rely on universal precautions. If, for example, a dog is returning to the facility after going on an outing with a staff member, make sure the animal is put through the same search procedures as any other visitor or staff member. Many assistance dogs wear vests identifying them as working dogs or service dogs and for convenience, the vests have small pockets to carry items. Institutional policy should include searching of the vests and leashes. Inmates also may use the pockets to transport drugs or weapons within the facility. Conduct random pat searches of the dogs. Inmates may think they are targeted for a drug search and even try to use a dog as a drug mule by getting the dog to ingest drugs and carry until them until the dog has a bowel movement. Designate specific areas for the dogs' elimination, monitor those spaces with a video camera, and do random checks of the dogs' outdoor space. Realize that an inmate/trainer may not want to participate in offenses such as these but might be coerced by someone else. Inmates not participating in the program may try to present themselves as dog handlers to gain access to an outdoor area. Many programs have a special photo ID for inmates in the program and post photos of the trainers and their dogs outside the cell to avoid confusion b. Operational changes—From the earliest days of their professional training, prison administrators are taught that sticking to routines helps to avoid incidents. When dogs are introduced into the mix, they have different ideas. They get sick, they have accidents in their cells and have to get out to eliminate. Usually this is not a problem but it can be a way to manipulate the schedule and in-cell time during lockdowns. Inmates are most secured when they are confined to their cells; however, dogs need access to the outdoors which inherently creates a risk. It is helpful to get the dogs on a regular turnout schedule so that there are fewer disruptions to routines, but this is less feasible for puppies. Make certain that there is adequate security monitoring and that taking the dogs out is recorded in the operational schedule. Communicate this to both staff and inmate/trainers. Another important issue with a prison dog program is transportation of the dogs to regular and emergency veterinary services. This needs to be spelled out in the policies and procedures c. Changes to the physical plant-At the very least, dogs are going to need sufficient space to rest at night, training space, and an outdoor exercise area. When deciding about the indoor space, it may be necessary to move some inmates around to create an area dedicated to the program. One facility with small cells raised the inmates' beds higher off the floor to provide a space underneath that was sufficient to accommodate a normal sized dog. Ideally, a large outdoor area for training and another one for elimination would be available. If not, there may be ways to work around it. An urban facility in another state had no outdoor space to speak of but wanted a dog program, so they partnered with a rescue that specialized in small dogs, taught the dogs to

(continued)

Table 4.6 (continued)

use indoor potty pads, and advertised these dogs as ideal for people who could not otherwise have a dog, such as seniors with limited mobility, apartment dwellers, and those who work long hours
3. Agreements or Contracts a. Most service dog programs have a standard agreement made up but this should be reviewed and approved through the organization's legal department. It is helpful to see examples, so contact other, well-established programs that are similar and review these documents. Clarify who is paying for what and how the payment will be processed. If, for example, the staff need to make some purchases of incidentals, what is the agreed upon process for reimbursement? More potentially costly issues surface and need to be planned for as well, such as veterinary bills or emergency services for a dog. Clarify what veterinary care each dog will have prior to its arrival, how routine care will be managed, and the policies/procedures related to emergency care. Respect the rights of the dog group and spell out under what conditions the dog will be removed. Agreements and contracts are essential when problems surface. They also prevent a situation where a dog in crisis has to wait for someone's approval before getting treatment b. Organizations have forms of documentation that they need to submit to maintain their reputations, licenses, insurance coverage, and so forth. Make sure that both staff and inmates understand their responsibility for providing documentation. To illustrate, when we partnered with a university, the director of non-credit educational offerings for community members required all instructors for the courses to submit an application and, after the classes began, the instructors had to submit lesson plans (as PowerPoint presentations) for each class meeting throughout the first year. Depending on the purpose of the program, there also will be a process in place for deciding who is eligible to become the trained dog's owner. Adopting a shelter dog typically is accomplished through an application process. For service dogs with nearly two years of training, much more will be required, including medical documentation of the disability and some training in how to work with the dog. These practices need to be understood by all partners to avoid misunderstandings out in the community c. Most of the time, effective communication and clear expectations for all stakeholders are the surest ways to prevent a problem. Issues such as transportation procedures, emergency protocols, cleaning practices, areas the dogs are not permitted to visit, and procedures for removing a handler or dog from the program all need to be agreed upon in advance of an issue
4. Funding a. One source of appeal for prison dog programs is that they frequently are more affordable than many other types of interventions. In collaborations with animal rescues and shelters and service dog providers, those organizations typically contribute the staff and the materials/services necessary to take care of the dogs. To increase sustainability, those responsible for programs need to diversify their funding streams. Some ways of generating financial support might include: working with a local veterinary hospital to get services at a reduced cost; sponsoring a dog and/or paying for the privilege of getting to name a service dog; charging higher adoption fees for shelter dogs who have passed the American Kennel Club's Canine Good Citizen test; grant proposals to nonprofit organizations; using online platforms such as GoFundMe to solicit donations, working with university students to organize a fund raiser (e.g., 5 K race, dinner, car wash); connecting with a pet supply store to get discounts/donations; establishing an emergency medical fund; enlisting the support of other inmates to support the program (e.g., design a dog grooming area); creating a print or online "wish list" (e.g., on Amazon); and providing grooming, boarding, or dog training services to the community for a fee. Conduct an analysis of all possible funding sources

(continued)

Table 4.6 (continued)

b. The work hours of the inmate/trainers extend well beyond those of a typical job so, if inmates are paid a small wage for work in the system, consider looking into paying the inmates in the prison dog program at the highest rate c. Basic materials that need to be purchased and replenished for the dogs include: training aids (e.g., collars, leashes, harnesses, treats and treat bags, orthopedic equipment for training service dogs); toys and chews (approved by the dog group and veterinarian); clothing (e.g., vests for service dogs, coats or boots as needed/recommended, color-coded bandanas for therapy dogs); food and feeding supplies, kennels, crates and bedding; grooming supplies (e.g., brushes, shampoo, towels, toothbrushes/paste); cleaning materials (e.g., waste bags, disinfectant, paper towels); medicines (e.g., flea/tick preventative, heartworm treatment, prescriptions, over the counter meds as recommended by the veterinarian)
5. Potential Benefits a. The presence of dogs can exert a positive influence on the culture of the institution. In their review of the literature, Han et al. (2018) note that PDPs can enhance communication, improve interpersonal relationships, and decrease infraction rates or other misconduct. "Within institutions, PDPs break down barriers between correctional officers and inmates by providing opportunities for communication and by humanizing inmates in the eyes of correctional officers, which promotes a more pleasant environment. In addition, the presence of the dogs serves to calm housing units and improves the mood of other inmates, which creates a safer prison environment (Han et al. 2018, p. 16) b. Inmates—It teaches inmates responsibility, patience, and discipline. It instils a sense of pride in their accomplishments which builds confidence. After the dogs leave to become family pets or complete the next step in their preparation as service dogs, the inmates smile when they hear positive reports about the dogs they trained. This gives them a purpose and they learn sacrifice through letting that dog go to a higher purpose. Many times, inmates' families are supportive of the dog program. Our local inmate advocacy group, for example, raised $5000 that was donated to the program. Inmates also acquire a skill set that can be translated into a job upon their release from prison c. Staff—Dog programs increase morale and camaraderie. Communication improves as staff ask questions about the dogs and come to appreciate the hard work that the inmate/trainers are putting in. Staff who want to support the program further by taking the dogs to various events or home for the weekend complete a training. It includes such things as the commands to use with the dogs, making introductions between the dogs and the family (human and animal), practices that ensure the dogs' safety while traveling, how to deal with common puppy behaviors, and ideas about dog-friendly places the dogs can visit. When the dog returns, the staff member shares notes on what the dog learned with the inmate/trainer. d. Community—Well-trained dogs make a contribution to the community that is respected, recognized and valued. In general, the public is supportive of a prison dog program. Among all the different possible interventions, it is one of the most powerful in terms of attracting support and demonstrating, as one inmate put it, that "something good can come out of here."

Box 4.1 Sample Posting for Greyhound Adoption

Barry (Barry Sanders)
Male
Red
75A-66405
Born 7/10/15
75#
1/23/19- Barry is 3. 75#. Confident, friendly, outgoing. Graduated from the prison program. No cats! A survivor of Hurricane Michael! Barry listens and responds well. Gets along well with everyone, enjoys the interaction. He responds well to "leave it" and "kennel up". Loves being brushed. Rain does not bother him. Very playful! Collects toys into his kennel. He has mastered stair climbing. Walks well on leash, sometimes pulls a little. Rarely barks. Barry's ears are very expressive and fun to watch on a walk. It is almost like they have their own mind and move in every direction and shape imaginable! Loves food! Chosen for the prison program! Comfortable around a lot of people. Likes squeaky toys. Likes to confiscate the offender-handlers' socks in the prison!

Outputs and Outcomes

Evaluation strategies may be broadly defined as formative (i.e., ongoing), or summative (i.e., or conducted at an endpoint of the program). Chapters 9 and 10 provide an in-depth discussion of evaluation strategies. In this section, we highlight the strategy of building formative, "along the way", methods of evaluation into the program. There are at least three advantages to doing this:

- Increasingly, private grants programs are requiring applicants to include a plan for evaluating outcomes.
- Evaluation data can assist program designers/developers in making mid-course adjustments that enhance the quality of the program.
- Gathering evaluation data while the program is in operation provides evidence to support a program's continuation if it is in jeopardy of being discontinued.
- Different stakeholders and different methods of evaluation (e.g., interviews, self-administered surveys, descriptive statistics) build a stronger argument that the program is beneficial.
- Formative evaluation data can be shared with various stakeholders as a route to continuous program improvement.

We highly recommend using what is referred to as a logic model of evaluation (The Corporation for National and Community Service 2019). These models are favored because they can communicate the entire evaluation plan in a visual manner. While there are many different logic models, a basic logic model has the following four columns:

1. Inputs—the human, financial, organizational, community and material resources available or required to deliver the program. Some examples for a dog program would include the on-site supervisors, the source(s) of funding for the dogs' care, the groups participating in the program, possible donors for the program, and changes to the physical plant.
2. Activities—the processes, tools, events, and actions necessary to fulfill the program's mission and achieve stated goals. For example, some corrections staff members will need training to supervise the inmate/trainers. A process for selecting and dismissing inmate/trainers has to be identified. Partners in the program need to agree upon their roles and responsibilities.
3. Outputs—direct products of the program activities. These frequently are stated as numbers. Referring back to item 2 above, outputs would be number of corrections staff members who completed the training, number of inmate/trainers chosen, and the different signed agreements/contracts in force amongst the partners.
4. Outcomes—expected changes *in the populations served* that result from the activities. These differ from outputs because they focus on changes in

knowledge, attitudes, behaviors, or conditions. An outcome for inmates might be a comparison of scores on a measure of empathy before and after program completion. For a program that trains homeless dogs to become family dogs, survey or telephone interview data about the dogs gathered from the families who adopted them would be an outcome. For the corrections staff, Likert-scale questionnaires (i.e. Strongly Agree, Agree, Undecided, Disagree, Strongly Disagree) in response to a series of statements could provide an outcomes measure. This would be particularly useful if the first questionnaire were administered prior to starting the dog program and the second survey were administered after the program has been in operation for a period of time. Another type of outcome could be documented through a series of qualitative interviews (Seidman 2019) with administrative personnel from each partner institution.

See the University of Wisconsin-Madison's (2019) Program Evaluation and Development site for additional information on developing logic models.

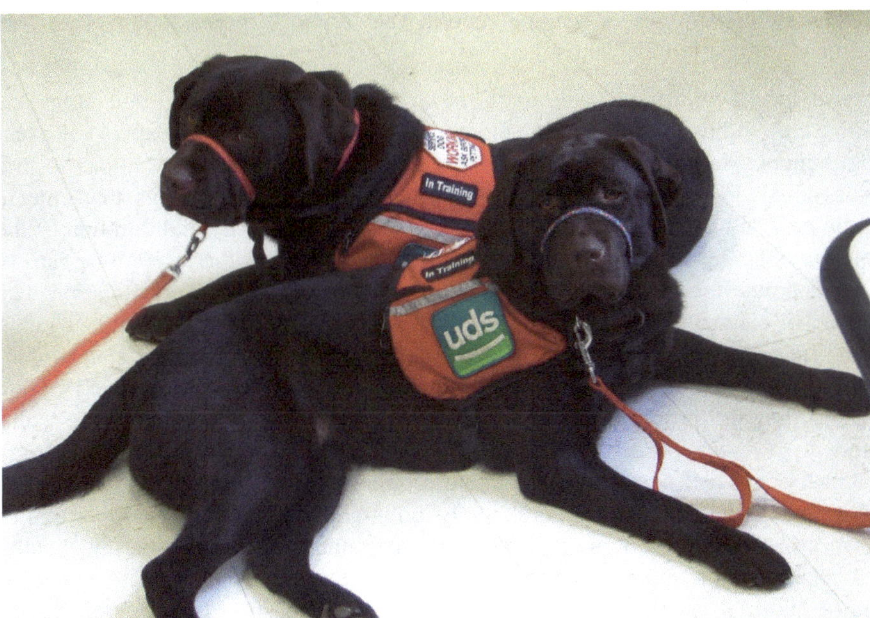

Milton and Deora. These littermates were part of the first group of service dogs trained by inmates through a partnership between United Disabilities Services Foundation and State Correctional Institution Pine Grove. *Photo credit* Lori Breece

Conclusion

As organizations plan and implement prison dog programs, it is helpful to consider what distinguishes these initiatives from many other types of interventions.

Attachments Formed For centuries, dogs have been recognized noted for their ability to form strong bonds with humans and become loyal companions (Miklosi 2018). The literature on the strength of the bond between humans and dogs suggests that the time invested is an important influence on attachment. This helps to explain why a bond with a dog that lives outside in a kennel usually is weaker than a bond with a dog that is brought into the home and seen as part of the family (Jalongo 2018). Inmate/trainers make a huge investment in the dogs in their care and are in one another's company many more hours per day than the dogs kept by adults who are working and children who are attending school. Furst (2006) found that inmates assigned a human-like identity to the animals they worked with. Particularly for inmates who have had disturbed or disappointing attachments with humans, a secure bond with a dog can be an important form of social support (Serpell 2017). Unlike people, canines are unfazed by a person's physical attractiveness, social class, academic abilities, or criminal record. They do not criticize, judge, or ridicule and they are nearly always available.

Intensity and Duration of Program Most shelters operate on a tight budget and do not have the funds to hire dog trainers nor do they have a cadre of expert volunteer dog trainers. Many service dog providers are non-profit and cannot afford to hire professional dog trainers for all phases of the dogs' training. Dogs that enter a prison program have access to extensive training. The intensity and duration of the program is longer for the inmates as well. Unlike other jobs that use a time card to log in and out of work, dog care and training is an all day, every day obligation. The number of contact hours between an inmate/trainer and others is not limited to "in class" time. There are more frequent interactions with other inmates, staff, volunteers, and instructors because the inmate/trainers usually are accompanied by the dogs as they go through their daily routines. The duration of their inmates' commitment to a dog program also extends over a longer period of time. A study conducted in Israel of various vocational programs for the incarcerated concluded that the most effective ones offer relatively long training that: provides opportunities to work in the field while incarcerated, considers the prisoners' needs holistically, and corresponds to demands of the labor market (Shoham et al. 2017). It could be argued that high-quality prison dog programs address each of these components.

Affordability In their meta-analysis of educational programs for inmates, Fogarty and Giles (2017) noted that cost-effectiveness is one of the most important considerations in choice of interventions. Prison dog programs typically are supported by shelters, rescues, service dog providers, volunteers and donations. As a result, many times they can be implemented, even by correctional facilities with few financial resources. Generally speaking, prison dog programs are an affordable alternative in a corrections context.

Normalization of the Environment In the human-animal bond literature, dogs' presence in different settings (e.g., nursing homes, hospitals, courthouses) is viewed as counteracting a cold or clinical environment (McCardle et al. 2011; Mulcahy and McLaughlin 2013). One of the themes that emerged from Turner's (2007) interview study with inmates was that dogs made the institution more home-like in some ways and there are many anecdotal accounts of inmates who were very moved by the sight of a dog at a correctional institution. For a person who truly cares about dogs, watching joyful puppies at play or getting an affectionate response from an adult dog elicits feelings of calm, contentment, and joy.

Prosocial Behaviors Many of the skills acquired in conjunction with dog training are applicable to other important roles in life and in work. Skills such as empathy, dealing with others, and forming positive relationships with family and peers are difficult to teach in a classroom but interactions within a dog program may function as a sort of "booster" that increases responsivity (van Wormer et al. 2015). In interviews with inmates, they often mention the effects of participation in dog programs on their interactions with family members noting, for instance, that many of the skills they are learning—such as patience, consistency, and empathy—have enabled them to become better parents (Antonio et al. 2017).

Fidelity of Implementation When a family volunteers to be puppy raisers for a service dog, it is difficult to ensure that everyone adheres to the rules. For example, service dogs are not permitted on beds and are not allowed people food but a dog trainer might be appalled to visit a home and see a young child sharing his bed and chocolate candy (which is dangerous to dogs) with a service dog puppy. In a correctional facility, there is video surveillance as well as monitoring by staff. Inmates know that violating the rules is likely to signal the end of their participation in the program. Many service dog providers prefer PDPs because the training protocols are followed more faithfully and are associated with a significant uptick in the performance of service dogs.

Holistic Development Both the United Nations and the Council of Europe have argued that prisoners have educational rights that are aimed at the full development of the human personality (Costelloe and Warner 2014). In Humby and Barclay's (2018) survey of 23 prisons in six Australian states, they documented a wide range of influences on inmates' development associated with participation in canine prison programs. These included: opportunities to become dog trainers, give back to society, gain a sense of responsibility, improve self-confidence and social skills, and acquire vocational qualifications to improve job opportunities post-release.

Identity Incarcerated individuals who participate in dog programs have an opportunity to forge a very different identity than the one in their criminal records. Staff and community members can see the dedication and hard work required in dog care and training and this can result in a new reputation for the inmates. As a participant gains credibility within a high-quality program, it is possible for them to name some people who believe in them, treat them with respect, and value the work that they are doing. It is this type of transformation that is the cornerstone of rehabilitation (Veysey et al. 2009).

Selectivity Some critics of positive results from prison dog programs have argued that they focus on the "cream of the crop" amongst the incarcerated and that the reported outcomes are the product of selection bias rather than attributable to program effects. Comparatively few inmates are involved. Out of consideration for the animals, these programs do need to be and will continue to be selective. For example, few people realize that all military working dogs (MWDs) for all branches of service are prepared at a single location: Lackland Air Force Base in San Antonio, Texas. At any given time, this 3350 acre facility has over 60 trainers working with more than 400 dogs. Becoming a MWD handler is one of the most highly sought and prized assignments. However, only those who are at the top of their class are given this important responsibility. The fact that not everyone who wants to work with an MWD is permitted to do so does not diminish in any way the contributions that handlers and dogs make. The prison dog program community needs to adopt a similar stance rather than apologize because sample sizes are small and inmates are not randomly selected or assigned. Working with the dogs is a privilege reserved for inmates with a sincere commitment to helping dogs and other people.

In a review published by the Heritage Foundation, Larkin (2016) notes that there is a tendency to hold prison dog programs to a higher standard:

> Federal and state programs that use convicted offenders to train homeless dogs bring together two groups of creatures whom society has often thrown away and does not want to see or be concerned about. Yet those creatures seem to be able to help, support, and rehabilitate each other. We should not fail to take advantage of the reformative potential of prisoners and dogs just because we cannot *prove* that by working together they will necessarily improve the prospects for each other in every case. That is too tall an obstacle to ask someone to hurdle. No program run by people should be expected to work 100 percent of the time. That is asking for perfection.

Prison dog programs are not perfect but they certainly do qualify as a promising practice. Planning and implementing them thoughtfully offers the best chance to reap the maximum benefits from programs that bring inmates and canines together to achieve goals that are consistent with the missions of each partner institution.

References

American Institutes for Research. (2017). *Stages of concern*. Retrieved August 4, 2017 from: http://www.sedl.org/cbam/levels_of_use.html.

Antonio, M. E., Davis, R. G., & Shutt, S. R. (2017). Dog training programs in Pennsylvania's Department of Corrections: Effectiveness for inmates and staff. *Society & Animals, 25*(5), 475–489.

Branigan, C. A. (2003). *Adopting the racing greyhound*. New York: Howell Book House.

Brodie, S. J., Biley, F. C., & Shewring, M. (2002). An exploration of the potential risks with using pet therapy in healthcare settings. *Journal of Clinical Nursing, 11*(4), 444–456. https://doi.org/10.1046/j.1365-2702.2002.00628.x.

Corporation for National and Community Service. (2019). *Logic models*. (https://www.nationalservice.gov/sites/default/files/upload/OpAC%20Logic%20Model%20draft%20in%20progress.pdf).

Costelloe, A., & Warner, K. (2014). Prison education across Europe: Policy, practice politics. *London Review of Education, 12*(2), 175–183.

Courthouse Dogs Foundation. (2019). *Training people for successful partnerships with courthouse facility dogs*. Retrieved March 10, 2019 from: https://courthousedogs.org/.

Dreschel, N. A., & Entendencia, K. (2013). Stress during certification testing in prison drug detection dogs and their handlers. *Journal of Veterinary Behavior: Clinical Applications and Research, 8*(4), e28.

Fogarty, J., & Giles, M. (2017). Recidivism and education revisited: Evidence for the USA. *Research in Agriculture and Applied Economics, 16*(2), 511–514.

Foreman, A. M., Glenn, M. K., Meade, B. J., & Wirth, O. (2017). Dogs in the workplace: A review of the benefits and potential challenges. *International Journal of Environmental Research and Public Health, 14*(5), 498. Retrieved February 20, 2019 from: https://www.animalsandsociety.org/new-research/dogs-workplace-review-benefits-potential-challenges/.

Furst, G. (2006). Prison-based animal programs: A national survey. *The Prison Journal, 86*(4), 407–430.

Furst, G. (2007). Without words to get in the way: Symbolic interaction in prison-based animal programs. *Qualitative Sociology Review, 3*(1), 96–109. Retrieved February 28, 2019 from: http://www.qualitativesociologyreview.org/ENG/Volume6/QSR_3_1_Furst.pdf.

Grace, K. (2016, March 16). *Evaluating service dog candidates at the shelter: Five traits to look for*. Retrieved February 25, 2019 from: https://www.anythingpawsable.com/service-dog-candidates-shelter-traits/.

Hall, G. E., & Hord, S. M. (2015). *Implementing change: Patterns, principles and potholes* (4th ed.). Upper Saddle River, NJ: Pearson.

Han, T. M., Flynn, E., Winchell, J., Gould, E., Gandenberger, J., Barattin, D., Tedeschi, P., & Morris, K. N. (2018). *Prison-based dog training programs: Standard protocol*. Denver: Institute for Human-Animal Connection. Retrieved February 28, 2019 from: https://animalstudiesrepository.org/cgi/viewcontent.cgi?article=1001&context=anitobe.

Humby, L., & Barclay, E. (2018). Pawsitive solutions: An overview of prison dog programs in Australia. *Prison Journal, 98*(5), 58–603.

Jalongo, M. R. (Ed.). (2018). *Children, dogs and education: Caring for, learning alongside, and gaining support from canine companions*. New York: Springer International Publishing.

Johnson, A., & Bruneau, L. (in press). Prison populations and pet loss. In L. R. Kogan & P. Erdman (Eds). *Pet loss, grief, and therapeutic interventions: Practitioners navigating the human-animal bond.* New York: Routledge.

Lai, J. (1998, April). *Pet facilitated therapy in correctional facilities*. Paper prepared for Correctional Services of Canada by Office of the Deputy Commissioner for Women. Retrieved July 28, 2019 from: https://www.csc-scc.gc.ca/publications/fsw/pet/pet-eng.shtml.

Larkin, P. J. (2016). *Prisoners, dogs, training and rehabilitation*. Retrieved February 26, 2019 from: https://www.heritage.org/crime-and-justice/report/prisoners-dogs-training-and-rehabilitation.

Livingood, L. (2000). *Retired racers for dummies*. New York: IDS.

McCardle, P., McCune, S., Griffin, J. A., Esposito, L., & Freund, L. S. (Eds.). (2011). *Animals in our lives: Human-animal interaction in family, community, and therapeutic settings*. Baltimore, MD: Paul H. Brookes Publishing Co.

Miklosi, A. (2018). *The dog: A natural history*. Princeton, NJ: Princeton University Press.

Mulcahy, C., & McLaughlin, D. (2013). Is the tail wagging the dog? A review of the evidence for prison animal programs. *The Australian Psychologist, 48,* 369–378.

Seidman, I. (2019). *Interviewing as qualitative research: A guide for researchers in education and the social sciences* (5th ed.). New York: Teachers College Press.
Serpell, J. (Ed.). (2017). *The domestic dog: Its evolution, behavior and interactions with people* (2nd ed.). New York: Cambridge University Press.
Shoham, E., Zelig, A., Hesisi, B., Weisburd, D., & Haviv, N. (2017). The "black box" behind prison-based vocational training. *European Scientific Journal, 20*(1), 106–132. https://doi.org/10.1002/9781118845387.wbeoc261.
Skene, L. (2019, January 28). Dogs bred for dinner table in South Korea get a second chance at Dixon Correctional's shelter program. *The Advocate.* Retrieved March 5, 209 from: https://www.theadvocate.com/baton_rouge/news/article_4f26b958-232e-11e9-bddc-6fd45a6b9344.html.
Smith, J., & Unti, B. (2016). Second chances: Pen Pals Inc, the Dixon Correctional Institute, and Louisiana's Post-Katrina Animal Rescue Legacy. *Corrections Today, 79*(1), 40–44.
Turner, W. G. (2007). The experiences of prisoners in a prison canine program. *Federal Probation, 71*(1), 38–43.
University of Wisconsin-Madison. (2019). *Program evaluation and development.* Retrieved February 24, 2019 from: https://fyi.extension.wisc.edu/programdevelopment/logic-models/.
Van Wormer, J., Kigerl, S., & Hamilton, Z. (2015). *Digging deeper: Exploring the value of prison-dog programs.* Retrieved February 24, 2019 from http://sustainabilityinprisons.org/wp-content/uploads/2015/04/WADOC-Dog-Program-Manuscript-for-WADOC.pdf.
Veysey, B. M., Christian, J., & Martinez, D. (Eds.). (2009). *How offenders transform their lives.* Cullompton, Devon: Willan Publishing.
Zazie, T. (2018). Barriers to the adoption of humane dog training methods. *Journal of Veterinary Behavior: Clinical Applications and Research, 25,* 28. https://doi.org/10.1016/j.jveb.2018.03.004.

Chapter 5
Caring for and About Dogs: Animal Welfare Considerations

Amy Johnson and Laura Bruneau

Introduction

Frank G has a successful dog walking and dog sitting business in Chicago, Illinois. He is also a Puppy Counselor with the Leader Dogs for the Blind with 20 volunteers under his supervision. Long before that, Frank was an inmate in an Iowa prison. While in the program, Frank participated in a prison dog program, successfully raising and training raising four dogs to become working dogs. Now, Frank continues to raise puppies and is currently training his twelfth puppy. He credits his current good life with the Puppy Raising program and the staff from Leader Dogs who supported his journey. "In this program, we all just wanted similar things, to do good for society," said Frank. "This program doesn't just help one person, the visually impaired person, but the inmate as well. That sense of accomplishment makes you want to raise another puppy. It feels good." At the time of this writing, Frank will soon be working with EDK9 scent detection dogs with Leader Dogs, which is an exciting next step for him. Frank believes people who may have made poor decisions in the past can find themselves again and move forward with purpose and meaning. Indeed, Frank is a living example of this.

This story illustrates the potential impact of integrating animals into correctional facilities, with multiple purposes for the betterment of the inmate, animal, and society. The American Veterinary Medical Association's statement on the human–animal bond provides a foundation for understanding the symbiotic relationship between people and animals—"the human–animal bond is a mutually beneficial and dynamic relationship between people and animals that is influenced by behaviors

A. Johnson (✉)
Center for Human Animal Interventions, School of Nursing, Oakland University, Rochester, MI, USA
e-mail: johnsona@oakland.edu

L. Bruneau
Adams State University, Alamosa, CO, USA

M. R. Jalongo (ed.), *Prison Dog Programs*,
https://doi.org/10.1007/978-3-030-25618-0_5

that are essential to the health and well-being of both" (AMVA 2019). Building upon this concept, correctional facilities have implemented programs which serve the dual purpose of training dogs and rehabilitating prisoners over the past four decades. As these programs are becoming increasingly popular, it is imperative to address animal welfare considerations within this book. In essence, prison-based animal programs (PAPs) should mutually benefit both the humans and animals participating.

Human–Animal Interactions Within Correctional Facilities

Humans have long held a fascination with animals. Based upon our "innate interest in living things" and a "predisposition to attune to animal life" (Melson and Fine 2015, p. 218), animals help humans feel connected through the unique human–animal relationship. The biophilia hypothesis is an important theoretical foundation for the human–animal bond and subsequently, the success of human–animal interventions. Wanting to discover the core of human relationships with the natural world, Wilson (1984) hypothesized that all humans make connections with other life forms, in addition to the natural environment. In particular, this connection can be best explained through survival, in that humans are attuned to nature so they can accurately assess threats to safety. More succinctly, the biophilia hypothesis asserts there is a need to bond with nature.

Similarly, attention-seeking behavior is evident in both humans and other social animals, such as dogs. *Attentionis egens* (Odendaal 2000), which is Latin for needing attention, describes the motivation behind interspecies social bonding, stemming from our mutual capacity to give and receive affection and comfort (Lindsay 2005). Recent brain studies even show that neurons in the amygdala on the right side of the brain react differently to animal images as opposed to human images, landmarks, or known objects; even infants have a distinct preference for images of animals rather than toys or other objects (Serpell et al. 2017). Because humans and dogs are social animals with the need to interact, in most cases, this is effectively attainable by positive human–animal interactions (Odendaal 2000). Indeed, humans need reciprocal, social relationships (Baumeister and Leary 1995) just as they need oxygen, food, and shelter (Johnson and Bruneau, in press). Boris Levison, the father of Animal-Assisted Therapy, once posited that feelings of alienation in the human world compel a man to seek connections in nature (Hines 2003).

People who belong to a vulnerable population, such as inmates, often feel socially isolated or de-humanized. However, it is possible for interspecies relationships to provide a sense of belonging and companionship, as well as meet existential needs (Johnson and Bruneau, in press; Pachana et al. 2011). Having meaning or a purpose in life is at the very core of inmate rehabilitation models which integrate PAPs (Furst 2006). Through these innovative and increasingly popular programs, inmates care for and train animals, as well as contribute positively to society (Furst 2011).

Origins of Prison-Based Animal Programs

Animals included in programing for rehabilitative purposes started many centuries ago (Deaton 2005). A more thorough review of the topic can be found in Chap. 3. For the purposes of this chapter, those instances that include dogs are addressed. In Washington, DC in 1919, the Government Hospital for the Insane (later named St. Elizabeth Hospital) was asked by the Secretary of Interior, Franklin K. Lane, to add dogs into the facility where the inmates could interact and befriend them (Strimple 2003). William Alanson White, M.D., was the superintendent of the institution and agreed to test such interactions (Strimple 2003). Later, in 1944, the Army Air Force Convalescent Center in Pawling, New York brought in dogs, horses, and farm animals as a diversion during the patients' intensive therapy (Beck 2006). In 1947, the Ross family opened a home and school for emotionally and mentally impaired children, called Green Chimneys in Brewster, New York. Green Chimneys, which is known internationally for providing innovative human–animal interventions with children (Friesen 2010), is still in operation today.

In 1979, a dog trainer named Sister Pauline (formerly Kathy Quinn) brought dogs to the Washington Correction Center for Women (WCCW). In partnership with Dr. Leo Bustad, founder of Pet Partners (2019), Sister Pauline was integral in the implementation of prison dog programs in many facilities in the Washington state area (Deaton 2005; Strimple 2003). Since then, there has been an influx of innovative programs designed for correctional facilities that incorporate animals into the milieu, including dogs, horses, farm animals, wildlife, fish, bird, rabbits, guinea pigs, gerbils, and cats (Cushing and Williams 1995).

Today, there are PAPs in all 50 states of the U.S. as well as in many other nations (Hill 2016). The most common types of programs are community service/ pet adoption programs, service animal training programs, vocational programs, visitation programs, livestock care programs, and wildlife rehabilitation programs (Furst 2011). This chapter will focus on service animal training and adoption programs.

Benefits of Prison-Based Animal Programs for Inmates

Regarding the treatment of inmates and recidivism rates, a commonly accepted belief is that "nothing works" (Koldstad 1996, p. 324). Unfortunately, this perception persists today. Typically, the public and judicial systems do not value rewarding prisoners with therapeutic or educational interventions (Furst 2011; Strimple 2003) and prefer a punitive environment (Deaton 2005), which only furthers marginalization. Rehabilitation programs can provide the social skills necessary to alter self-image as a criminal, which in turn may keep inmates from re-offending (Koldstad 1996). Further, developing empathy in inmates decreases the likelihood of committing crimes in the future.

Fortunately, methods of rehabilitation that include animals have been steadily increasing. PAPs typically require that inmates care for and train animals to improve their lives, while also allowing for restitution to society—a true win-win-win scenario. The success and popularity of PAPs have meant an increase in the number of programs offered around the country, particularly over the past two decades (Britton and Button 2005; McCulcahy and McLaughlin 2013). Fortunately, the empirical evidence for PAPs is also growing (see Chap. 1 for a full review of this literature). For example, a meta-analysis of ten studies indicated significant mean effect sizes on outcomes of dog training program participation (Cooke and Farrington 2016). Further, involvement in PAPs can lead to lower rates of recidivism (Hill 2016). Through these programs, inmates learn employable skills which help in securing jobs outside of prison related to animal care (Humby and Barclay 2018).

Generally, PAPs have been found to positively impact the prison system, lessening the frequency of behavioral infractions and increasing adherence to policies (Britton and Button 2005; Furst 2011; Hill 2016), as well as reinforcing relationship building and decreasing feelings of isolation (McCulcahy and McLaughlin 2013; van Wormer et al. 2017). From a systemic perspective, PAPs increase morale, keep the inmates busy which results in fewer conflicts, and help to bridge connections between staff and inmates (Beseres 2017). For example, inmates notice that staff and corrections officers sometimes treat them more kindly because of interactions between trainers and their animals. One inmate expressed, "The COs treat us differently because we're doing something special and worthwhile" (Furst 2011, p. 128). Practicing prosocial skills with animals can provide a bridge to these same experiences with humans. This promotion of humanity within prison programming allows others to view offenders as better citizens rather than better criminals (Furst 2011).

Additionally, research findings suggest PAPs can lead to personal improvements for inmates in the areas of self-esteem, patience, empathy, compassion, anger management, and responsibility in adults (Cooke and Farrington 2016; Furst 2011; McCulcahy and McLaughlin 2013; van Wormer et al. 2017). Inmates who have witnessed positive changes in the dogs' behaviors are motivated to review and alter their behavior (Britton and Button 2005). Also, inmates who had difficulty in childhood may have learned to repress feelings of fear and vulnerability, thereby hindering their ability to attune to others. Dogs, in particular, are noted for their attunement to the feelings of humans, so they can function as models of responsiveness (Schoen 2002). Through interaction with animals, inmates can "give themselves permission" to display emotions (Lasher 1998). As prisoners often feel disconnected and isolated both physically and psychologically, animals provide a sense of belonging and unconditional love, enhancing the existential need for purpose and meaning (Pachana et al. 2011).

Benefits of Prison-Based Animal Programs for Animals

Research related to the benefits for inmates is easy to locate within the PAP literature, although there is still much more to be learned. Yet PAPs are not, nor should they be, solely about human participants. As there are other sentient beings involved in the process, questions arise as to their welfare. Indeed, another essential aspect to learn more about is the benefit to the animals in these programs. Much of the focus on PAPs within the research literature has been on the benefit to the inmates, rather than on the health and welfare needs of the animals (Moran 2015). For example, Beseres (2017) recently completed a comparative analysis of six PAPs across the United States. The benefits of these programs were primarily advertised as benefits to the inmates (e.g., psychological and social improvements, vocational gains, providing inmates with a sense of a purposeful life) in addition to benefits to the greater community.

Yet, dogs benefit by participating in high-quality PAPs. For example, dogs who are brought in from animal shelters for training are more likely to be adopted, and are more likely to remain in their new homes permanently. Or consider the useful skills that shelter dogs gain through training to become service dogs or perform search and rescue; these programs benefit dogs, who without the chance to work with the trainers, may have been euthanized (Deaton 2005). Service dog trainees who work with the inmates can also benefit by receiving quality socialization during the critical puppyhood stages in order to be placed with other loving humans as they grow older.

However, we argue that the literature on PAPs is limited in regards to the practical application of ensuring the welfare of dogs. This lack of inclusion becomes not only a moral issue, but also an ethical issue—potentially putting inmates, facilitators, and dogs at risk. Because dogs cannot verbally advocate for themselves, they must be viewed as more vulnerable and powerless than the inmates. Indeed, Anderson (2011) proposed a definition of powerless as "those who are without a voice in, or ability to influence, the political process except by proxy (that is, someone who will act on their behalf for altruistic reasons" (p. 6).

Animal Welfare in Correctional Facilities

Any discussion about the potential powerlessness of animals in correctional facilities must at least take a look at the welfare of animals who have participated in other types of PAPs. As a comparison, consider the history of prison farms, and the obvious link between slavery and prison labor exploitation (Browne 2010; Furst 2011). In fact, many former slave plantations are now prison farms that inmates work on for little to no pay and are also used for the breeding and slaughter of animals (Furst 2011). The quality of these prison farms is also in question, per the reporting of an inmate inside the Texas prison systems (Washington 2017). Many of the animals kept in prison are kept in abhorrent living conditions that harm the physical and psychological well-being of chickens and pigs, among other animals (Washington 2017). These examples raise the question—if other PAPs lack standards for ensuring optimal welfare, what about the well-being for dogs who participate in prison dog programs?

For example, there is a potential risk of abuse to the animals. Abuse or neglect has occurred within detention programs, though the full extent is not known (Britton and Button 2005). In a review by Meers et al. (2010) of prisons and rehabilitation facilities in Belgium, 79% of the reporting facilities offer AAIs, including caring for shelter and residential animals. Six, or 25%, of the facilities, reported negative incidents related to animal welfare, including management problems, negligence with feeding procedures, breeding without permission, bite incidents, stress signals from the animals, and animals running away or hiding. There are also reports of health-related issues due to being overworked (Montalvan and Witter 2012). In other instances, families who were not fully prepared to take on the responsibility of a pet returned trained dogs to the shelter, causing confusion and additional stress to the animals (Montalvan and Witter 2012).

Further, very recently, an Ohio inmate was indicted for the death of the dog he was training for community adoption. The dog, a 4-year old named Evie, died of blunt force trauma to the abdomen (Associated Press 2019). Authorities believe there was ongoing abuse to the dog, and the inmate currently faces a 1-year sentence for the dog's death. While this is an extreme and rare event, a lack of appropriate handling may lead to animals experiencing harm (Zamir 2006). For example, people may feed animals too much, overwork them, or fail to provide them with enough rest time. Inappropriate or inconsistent training methods may be used, resulting in potential tension between inmates. For example, in one facility which used choke collars and aversive training methods, some of the non-participating inmates got angry and confronted the trainers (Britton and Button 2005). It is noteworthy that, in this example, the conflict occurred as a response to protecting the dogs. Indeed, while negative incidents can happen, the majority of research, in addition to anecdotal evidence, suggests that these dogs are safe (Ormerod 2008), and truly loved and cared for by the inmates and staff.

Research on Benefits to Dogs in Prison-Based Animal Programs

Within the field of Human–Animal Interactions, several studies have reviewed dog welfare with inconsistent results (Ng et al. 2014). These inconsistencies are partly due to small sample sizes, and having too many intervening factors (e.g., the age of the dog, previous experiences, temperament, conditions of the room, clients in the room, etc). We do have reason to believe that prison dog programs do have some other direct benefits to dogs. Studies related to stress reduction within the shelter environment have shown positive results such as more frequent social interactions with humans. These interactions are beneficial because all the dogs learn to act confidently around humans and respond to cues that are intended to keep the dogs safe—such as reliably returning to the owner when the dog's name is combined with the "come" command. Being well-behaved helps with adoptability and decreases stress-induced responses, both behaviorally and physiologically (Hennessy et al. 2006).

In one example, a recent study in Japan examined stress on dogs and their handlers during an AAI program in the prison, utilizing a questionnaire and measurement of dogs' saliva cortisol concentrations before and after the therapy sessions (Koda et al. 2015). The dogs mostly did not show significant signs of stress, which was confirmed by the subjective ratings of the handlers. And, more importantly, the dog's saliva cortisol values typically decreased after participating in the session (Koda et al. 2015). In another study on the effects of training on dogs in prisons, Hennessy et al. (2006) identified that dogs showed significant improvement in following commands and were calmer in unfamiliar situations.

When implemented and monitored appropriately, prison dog programs that bring in dogs from local shelters for training can be helpful to dogs because life in shelter environments is stressful (Hennessy et al. 2006; Protopopova 2016). The sensory overload experienced in shelters can be overwhelming to even the most well-adjusted dog and much more so for a dog who is already stressed, nervous, or skittish. Being confined to a small, narrow kennel does not allow a dog to move comfortably nor interact with other dogs, and dogs spend more time in flight or fight mode (Protopopova 2016). This chronic stress impacts their immune systems, leaving them compromised for a variety of health issues typical in shelters and a lower life expectancy (Hennessy et al. 2006; Protopopova 2016). In contrast, in prisons, many dogs are with their trainers 24/7, which not only helps them to excel at training but provides consistency and a sense of companionship (Deaton 2005).

The screening processes also help to ensure safety for the dogs. Program facilitators often credit the lack of harm to animals to the rigorous application process. Usually, inmates have to earn their way into these programs (see Chap. 7 for an in-depth review on this topic), and these inmates relish the chance to do something meaningful and life-changing for the dogs and individuals/families who receive them (R. Handeline, personal communication, February 19, 2019). The next section describes the two most common types of prison dog programs, including shelter dog training/adoption and service and assistance dog training while highlighting practices to ensure the safety of the dogs.

Shelter Dog and Assistance Dog Programs

Not all prisons or programs can accommodate dogs residing with inmates for an extended period. For example, in juvenile detention facilities, organizations often bring hard-to-adopt rescue dogs to the facilities for training with the adjudicated youth. These programs may integrate an educational or therapeutic component in addition to the training piece. Throughout the training curriculum, the youth trainers learn both "hard" skills (i.e., teaching the dog to "sit" or how to walk nicely on a leash) and "soft" skills (i.e., how to work with others or listening), and in some cases, curriculum to improve the likelihood of finding a job in animal care upon release (Humby and Barclay 2018). Facilitators will bring dogs to the facility or take the youth to a dog shelter two or three days a week. An example of this type of program is Teacher's Pet: Dogs and Kids Learning Together in Michigan, which pairs hard-to-adopt shelter dogs with youth in detention facilities. A recent study on this program with 138 youth who completed the 10-week program, indicated that the inmates described a sense of hope, as well as a desire to contribute to the community (Seivert et al. 2016).

In these types of programs, goals for the inmates include promoting traits such as empathy, perspective taking, and patience (Seivert et al. 2016), while goals for the dogs include basic obedience or passing the AKC's Canine Good Citizen test. Dogs who are selected for the program range in age from puppyhood to adulthood and often have behavioral challenges, but typically a sound temperament (Seivert et al. 2016). Before acceptance into the prison dog program, facilitators screen and evaluate the youth. Prior violent crimes or harm to animals do not necessarily preclude an inmate from participation; some programs specifically want to work with inmates who have behavioral problems or a history of animal abuse so that inmates learn the proper care of animals (Hill 2016), and to build empathy (Evans and Gray 2012). Yet, during programming, caution and vigilance are warranted (Hatch 2007). Facilitators and volunteers accompany the dogs to ensure their protection and welfare. Such programs are commonly run by, or in collaboration with dog trainers.

In contrast, training service and assistance dogs is a more time-intensive program. The high cost of training service and assistance dogs makes these types of prison dog programs very appealing. On average, training a service or assistance dog costs about $20,000 and may take 18–24 months to complete. Dogs are trained, based on their suitability, to work with persons who are visually impaired, hearing impaired, have a seizure disorder, or have a severe post-traumatic stress disorder (Garcia 2014). These types of prison dog programs work well; for example, dogs trained using the prison program models learn faster than other dogs trained by full-time puppy raisers (Garcia 2014). Within these programs, puppies come from breeders of trait-specific dogs or from rescue organizations after an evaluation to determine suitability.

The inmates are with the dogs at all times, except weekends when the dogs leave with foster parents who provide the dog's exposure to environments not found within prison settings (e.g., parks, public spaces, streets; Drew et al. 2013). While in their charge, it is the responsibility of the inmate trainers to maintain the welfare of the dogs. An example of this type of program is Leader Dogs for the Blind, which runs programs in 11 facilities in Michigan, Iowa, and Minnesota, and adheres to the standards set by Assistance Dogs International (2019). According to the Vice President of Leader Dogs, it is easy to monitor the safety and welfare of the dogs with the inmates because of the lack of privacy that the inmates have (R. Handeline, personal communication, February 19, 2019). Staff and administrators are vigilant about observing behavior for the safety of inmates and the welfare of the dogs.

Because inmates are so thankful for the opportunity to raise puppies and give back to a community in need, the inmates are often the dog's best advocate. There have been a few accusations made against inmates about pain or injury inflicted upon the dog. However, those rare accusations are investigated quickly and most often turn out to be a disgruntled prisoner attempting to "get back" at another by getting them removed from the program (R. Handeline, personal communication). Service and assistance dog training programs require a formal process for recruiting inmates which usually begins with interviews and reviewing documented behavior. Further, inmate trainers who have trained multiple dogs often act as mentors to the newer trainers.

Critics to this type of programming question the protection of the puppies from abuse; however, most inmates find this program a privilege and do not want to be removed from the program (Drew et al. 2013). Furthermore, due to the security measures taken within penitentiaries, all inmates are continuously watched by commanding officers, administrators, and other inmates, making any aggressive behaviors or violent activities visible (G. Furst, personal communication, February 19, 2019). Modern correctional facilities also have extensive video monitoring in place.

However, the discussion on service or assistance dog training leads to a bigger conversation about animal welfare for service dogs in particular (Beck 2006). Highly trained service dogs, for example, are asked to perform stressful activities every day that are unnatural for dogs without regard to their emotional health (Beck 2006). Just because the dogs carry heavy bags or walk through crowded areas per their training, does not mean that they enjoy it or are comfortable doing it. Or, the dogs' inability to interact with other humans or dogs may cause boredom and apathy. Dogs are sentient creatures (Furst 2011), but are not able to communicate their choices to humans in obvious ways to the untrained eye.

Further, dogs in training may not feel like training every day. The dogs may be uncomfortable around a specific person or another dog. Former inmate and Leader Dog trainer Frank G expressed during an interview with one of the authors that the inmates were taught to be attuned to the dogs' signs of stress or discomfort (e.g., excessive yawning or pacing). If these behaviors were observed, the inmate/handlers were able to take the dog back to their cells to rest or go for a walk within the facility. This example brings up a critical point for animal welfare considerations in prison dog programs—training.

Dog Training

Dog training is controversial, but a necessary topic for animal welfare. If dog training produces fear and insecurity commonly associated with coercive training methods, this could lead to psychological issues, or fracture the relationship with the trainer. Rather than working from a bonding perspective, responding to cues may be done out of fear. Stressed humans often have difficulty learning and retaining new information, and stressed dogs may have similar experiences. Also, the use of coercion in dog training may reinforce the same harsh methods inmates saw or used on the outside, or even while in prison. Rather, methods of training and engagement should foster trust, without subjecting the dog to unnecessary pain, fear, or coercion. Indeed, this type of training may vicariously benefit inmates in learning positive strategies for getting their needs met with humans in their lives.

Studies of aversive training versus reward-based and force-free training have demonstrated that confrontational methods like "alpha rolls," staring down a dog, or grabbing and shaking the dog has resulted in dogs responding with aggressive behaviors (Herron et al. 2009). Additionally, harsh punishment affects dogs' behaviors negatively, hindering ability to learn—while conversely, dogs' ability to learn and playfulness both increase when non-confrontational methods are used (Rooney and Cowan 2011). Aside from the goal for inmates to be less aggressive, using force-free training techniques provides alternative methods for obtaining desired results. Aversive dog training might lead the dog to develop fears of people, making it harder for them to be adopted.

Stress in Dogs

A key aspect of dog training is learning canine communication. In stressful situations, dogs behaviorally and physiologically attempt to adapt through calming signals, displacement signals, or self-soothing (Ng et al. 2014). Examples of these behaviors include lip licking, scratching, shaking, jumping, moving head repetitively, paw raising, yawning, tongue flicking, closing mouth, panting when not hot, licking self or objects, and self-grooming (Glenk et al. 2013; Glenk 2017; McConnell and Fine 2015). Lip licking occurs far more frequently than other stress signals (Glenk et al. 2013; Glenk 2017; McConnell and Fine 2015). Body shaking (when a dog is not wet) has been shown to have the effect of decreasing the stress hormone, cortisol. Therefore, body shaking may be indicative of the dog attempting to cope with stress (Glenk et al. 2013; Glenk 2017). All facilitators, trainers, and participants need to know the baseline behaviors of the species, breed, and individual dogs (Stewart et al. 2016) with whom they work, and recognize and respond to stressors as soon as they occur, including when the dogs become agitated or disinterested.

Asking an animal to continue when they are displaying signs of stress does not meet optimal welfare (Glenk et al. 2013). For example, a dog in training in prison may be intimidated by the yelling of other inmates. Or, the sensory overload is too much, as is often the case within the prison environment. However, this does not mean that a nervous or uncomfortable dog should automatically be disqualified from participation as the dog can gain confidence over time and with the appropriate interaction and environment. Another example is if the dog is being restrained or petted when specific stress signals are present. In this case, the dog's emotional and physical needs are not met, nor is animal welfare (Broom 2010).

With this recognition and knowledge, the inmate may learn insights that apply to other relationships with peers, family, and the community at large.

Within human animal interventions, research by Ng et al. (2014) has demonstrated that in unpredictable social interactions, the dog has to continuously adapt to these situations, resulting in stress and fatigue. Indeed, not knowing what to expect can be anxiety-provoking for both humans and dogs (Ng et al. 2014) and these unfamiliar and unpredictable interactions can be the biggest stressors dogs face (McEwen and Wingfield 2003; Ng et al. 2014). For this reason, dogs living with the same person, or visiting the same location with the same individuals on a regular schedule, can provide that sense of predictability that dogs need.

Additional stressors for dogs involved in human–animal interactions in the prison setting include being hugged by strangers; being patted on their heads, paws, tail, or muzzle; being on-lead, being in an environment that is too warm, or has textured floors; and working extensive hours (Glenk 2017; Houpt et al. 2007; Ng et al. 2014). Further, long-term exposure to stress can lead to detrimental effects on dogs (Evans and Gray 2012), and in one study, a program was suspended when the therapy dog was diagnosed with a disease in which the suspected cause was high, consistent stress (Glenk 2017).

In a recent article interviewing trainers at several prison dog programs (Miller 2016), typically positive training methods (e.g., food, toys, and praise) were used, in conjunction with extensive education and testing. For example, inmates had to progress through coursework, which could include up to seven different books and videos at each level, in addition to writing reports, taking tests, and passing skill assessments. Coursework included information on basic animal health, pet first aid and CPR, dog body language, and canine communication (Miller 2016).

Indeed, in reviewing various prison dog programs for this chapter, the authors identified that inmates were typically gaining the necessary information on canine communication, and signs of stress in dogs. Further, it appears that inmates recognize that dogs are sentient creatures and can also identify and attend to potentially stressful situations. Having an educated and competent person provide oversight to training programs is critical, as inadvertent harm may occur. This chapter now turns to an essential discussion on the moral issues inherent in human–animal interactions.

Moral Implications of Human–Animal Interactions

On a macro level, the animal rights movement operates under a "no-use" tenet when it comes to animals benefiting humans, raising important ethical and moral questions about PAPs (Furst 2006). For example, in animal-assisted therapy, best practices put animal welfare as a top priority, e.g. never forcing the therapy animal to travel, perform tasks they hesitate to perform, and to provide quiet time between sessions (Zamir 2006). Liberationists challenge such interactions to ensure a high quality life and whether or not the benefits of participating in human–animal interaction programs provides a suitable life (Zamir 2006).

As described previously, the American Veterinary Medical Association's statement on the human–animal bond provides a foundation for understanding the symbiotic relationship between people and animals; yet, little attention is given to the well-being of the animal (Ng et al. 2015). While the stories of human growth in prison dog programs are powerful and humbling, if we don't observe the well-being of the dogs, these programs risk exploitation of the animals, which sends an unintentional message to the inmates. Even some of the terminology within the scholarly literature, such as stating that dogs "serve as therapeutic tools" (Mercer et al. 2015, p. 43), may imply that the needs of the human being are placed far above the needs of the animal. When does "using" an animal in animal-assisted interactions cross the line and become exploitation (Zamir 2006)?

Rooted in the biophilia hypothesis introduced at the beginning of the chapter, is also the idea that our evolutionary ties to non-human animals have not always worked out for the benefit of non-human animals (Katcher and Wilkins 1993). Non-human animals continue to provide a source of food, clothing, and labor for humans. Indeed, from a legal perspective, animals have few rights, and often have little value (Furst 2011). Furthermore, Rooney and Bradshaw (2014) questioned the notion of "what's good for us, is good for them" (p. 242). These misconceptions of animal welfare can form through anthropomorphism, or assigning human qualities to animals. Or, the misconceptions of animal welfare can develop though anthropocentrism, which is assuming the animal sees the world through human senses versus their own (Rooney and Bradshaw 2014). Indeed, sacrificing the experience of the animal for the sake of the human is considered exploitation (Zamir 2006).

Welfare refers to an animal's ability to adapt or cope in its environment at the physiological, behavioral, and medical level (Broom 2010; Broom and Fraser 2015; Glenk et al. 2013; Glenk 2017). Determining welfare is difficult as it's often based on the subjective and value-based evaluation of the observer (Ng et al. 2015). Animal welfare needs to be assessed as often as possible from the animals' perspective, but behavior-based assessments may be useful in evaluating a dog's well-being (Fine et al. 2013). Research that uses measures of physiological changes (Rooney and Bradshaw 2014) such as salivary or urinary cortisol tests, is another way to document stress in dogs. Further, the World Organisation of Animal Health (OIE 2019) defined animal welfare as "the state in which an animal is coping with the conditions in which it lives." Therefore, dynamic and ongoing assessments are critical in any human–animal interaction programming.

Five Freedoms and Characteristics of a True Bond

Most animal welfare literature references the Five Freedoms (Brambell 1965) to evaluate animal welfare for those under human control. Mainly written for agricultural production, shelters and animal welfare organizations have taken on the Five Freedoms as the basic standards of welfare. The Five Freedoms include (a) Freedom from Hunger and Thirst, (b) Freedom from Discomfort, (c) Freedom from Pain, Injury or Disease, (d) Freedom to Express Normal Behavior, and (e) Freedom from Fear and Distress.

However, like others before us, we argue that the Five Freedoms is not enough. The Five Freedoms set a minimum standard and focus more on removing something negative, e.g. pain or discomfort, rather than adding or promoting something positive (e.g., well-being). In a classic work, Iannuzzi and Rowan (1991) posited the addition of Tannenbaum's (1989) Characteristics of a True Bond to the Five Freedoms when working with therapy and service animals. In reviewing the Characteristics for a True Bond, it is easy to see how prison dog programs can fit this model, as both the dog and the inmate are benefiting from the relationship. The characteristics include the following (Tannenbaum 1989):

1. A continuous, ongoing relationship rather than one that is sporadic or accidental
2. Produce not just a benefit but a significant benefit to both, and that benefit must be a central aspect of the lives of each
3. Involve a relationship that is, in some sense, voluntary
4. Relationship must be bidirectional
5. Entitle each being in the bond to respect and benefit in their own right rather than simply a means to an end.

Building upon this list, Yeates and Main (2007) argued to consider the potential feelings of the animals, (e.g., to include what they like and what they want within training and in human–animal interactions). And, Mellor (2016) takes this one step further, arguing for Quality of Life (QoL) rather than just looking at survival strategies. The QoL scale contains five categories (two positive, two negative and a neutral point of reference). The positive categories include (a) a good life, where the balance of positive and negative experiences is mostly positive and operating beyond minimum requirements; and (b) a life worth living where the balance of positive and negative experiences leans more towards the positive and the minimum requirements are maintained with occasional instances to promote more positive. The neutral category is the point of balance where both positive and negative experiences are equal. The negative categories are (a) a life worth avoiding where the negative experiences outweigh the positive experience but can be addressed quickly through veterinary care or modified husbandry practice, and (b) a life not worth living, where the animals' experiences are mostly negative without quick remediation and euthanasia is the most humane option (Mellor 2016).

While much of the QoL scale points to livestock, zoos, aquariums, and animals in the home, Mellor (2016) affirms that anyone accountable for the care and welfare of animals ought to use the latest, up-to-date information available to implement any size change that is required not only to ameliorate negative experiences, but also to foster positive ones. Because of our knowledge, skills, attitudes, and familiarity with the animals, humans have the strongest influence in animal welfare, e.g. the ability to recognize and address negative welfare issues. Continuous exposure to positive interactions is essential when promoting the human–animal bond to animals are under human control (Mellor 2016).

Thus, integrating the Five Freedoms, the Characteristics of a Bond, and the Quality of Life Scale to prison dog programs means that dogs can, *at a minimum:* (a) move freely (excluding times when being on a lead provides safety), (b) have access to food and water when they need it, (c) have breaks when needed in a bed that they desire, (d) have more predictable than unpredictable interactions, (e) experience a sense of control, and (f) ultimately, be able to be a dog. Ideally, prison dog programs should also focus on ways to enhance the human–animal bond, for both the inmate and the dog.

Best Practices for Animal Welfare in Correctional Facilities

According to Furst (2011), an ideal PAP should include an educational component for inmates to learn about the animals with whom they work. Also, a PAP has inmates working to rehabilitate animals to improve the animals' life circumstances and involves humane and compassionate care with animals. A PAP must meet these standards to provide the foundation for animal welfare. We propose several best practice recommendations for any prison dog program, as grouped by various roles (Table 5.1).

Table 5.1 Best practices in prison dog programs

Program Administrators	Program Facilitators	Inmates
• Work collaboratively with facilitators to minimize any risk of injury or disease • Assess environmental conditions best suited for safe housing and training, in addition to space for play for the dogs • Provide dogs with immediate veterinary care when needed • Collect data on what happens to dogs after adoption, to further assess for animal welfare issues • Acknowledge that other animals may be "rescued" by inmates (e.g., wild animals, rats, bugs), but PAP programs should be controlled and regulated • Evaluate programs in pairing dogs with more high-risk populations, under careful supervision	• Possess dog behavior training background and extensive experience • Regularly screen and evaluate animals for participation in the program • Be able to connect with the inmates, in addition to the animals • Develop screening protocols for the selection of inmates for the program • Promote the mutuality in the human-animal relationship, to strengthen the bond • Use appropriate terminology including not saying "use animals." or referring to them as "tools" • Bring in people with human-animal interaction experiences to talk to inmates	• Recognize and respond appropriately to signs of stress, animal fatigue, and burnout • Provide dogs with freedom from persistent interaction with humans • Halt, or modify training if the dog is not comfortable Provide enrichment, play and rest for the dogs • Help dogs achieve Canine Good Citizen status • Consider social and cultural values when working with animals • Develop prosocial skills, including empathy and patience • Engage in humane and compassionate care for the animal

Ethics

Overall, the field of Human–Animal Interactions lacks standardized guidelines for the ethics of these human–animal relationships, in addition to the criteria that would help to safeguard the animals' welfare (Ng et al. 2015). However, the ethical principle of mental health providers and physicians, "First, do no harm," which applies to many allied health and human service providers, is of particular importance and it should extend to the animals involved in the interventions (Stewart et al. 2016) to avoid exploitation, whether deliberate or inadvertent. In research, there are guidelines in place through Institutional Board Review committees to protect human and animal research subjects at institutional levels. At universities, animals can only be handled in a manner that was set by the ethics committee. The Institutional Animal Care and Use Committee (IACUC) also observes the ethical treatment of animals in research (Ng et al. 2018). Having guidelines and standards in place that emphasize the welfare of animals in prison-based animal programs are also necessary.

Up until the last 25 years, welfare standards for animals participating in AAIs were scarce (Beck 2006). Several agencies developed policies and procedures specific to their organizations that are applicable to PDPs. These include the aforementioned, Green Chimneys, who published *People and Animals: A Therapeutic Animal-Assisted Activities Manual* (Senter 1993) for programs within residential facilities with attention to logistics such as space, maintenance, animal health, and funding. Also, Pet Partners developed guidelines for volunteers and professionals participating in the program, particularly with the elderly entitled *Guidelines: Animals in Nursing Homes,* to establish program parameters and evaluate programming (Beck 2006). These standards were quite thorough and effective related to animal welfare; however, they were written—or at least interpreted—as program-specific guidelines, rather than overarching standards.

All professions must have a set of standards to run effectively and with intentionality. For example, Pet Partners recently developed and endorsed a set of core competencies specific to the knowledge, skills, and attitudes related to animal welfare for volunteers involved in AAIs (Stewart 2016). These competencies were developed in conjunction with the competencies endorsed through the American Counseling Association for Animal-Assisted Therapy in Counseling (Stewart et al. 2016). Competencies include knowledge of species-specific body language and signs of stress specific to the species, breed, and individual animals. For example, having owned dogs in the past, currently owning a dog, or volunteering with dogs does not constitute sufficient knowledge (Stewart et al. 2016). Indeed, prior experience can sometimes cause inmates to think that they already know everything about dogs when many of their assumptions concerning dog training methods would be at odds with accepted practices of professionals in the field. The applications of inmates seeking to work with dogs sometimes refer to other questionable practices as well, such as backyard dog breeding operations or keeping dogs tethered outside constantly, which is now illegal in many states. Inmates may view these situations as completely acceptable because their families "have always done it this way". When poorly implemented prison dog programs fail to build a solid foundation of understanding the communication patterns of the dogs, they put the dogs' well-being at risk.

Since the field of PAPs is still relatively new, an umbrella organization with a specific code of ethics does not yet exist. Having professionals with the educational background and experience in canine communication can help prevent unwanted or chronic stress in dogs as well as deter any inclination towards abuse or neglect. The trainers, however, are not always within the facility, often leaving inmates alone with the dogs they are training. For example, residential dogs living in a mental health unit might reside in the facility, but without one specific person to look out for the dog, it is easy to assume others are caring for the animal, leaving the dog ultimately unattended and neglected (Iannuzzi and Rowan 1991). Indeed, without a formalized set of ethical codes or competencies, dogs frequently are put in harm's way. At the very least, those responsible for supervising prison dog programs need to follow best practice recommendations to offer minimum standards that ensure the protection and welfare of the animals.

Conclusion

The field of animal welfare has expanded significantly over the last couple of decades. The Animal Behavior and Welfare Group at Michigan State University, for example, offers undergraduate as well as graduate courses geared towards training individuals to assess animal welfare and animal behavior. What started as a grassroots phenomenon (Furst 2015), has become an international focus, e.g., One Welfare (Pinillos et al. 2017). Building off the One Health movement, the One Welfare framework acknowledges the strong link between human well-being and animal welfare. This model works well when conceptualizing the needs of inmates and animals in PAPs, as it doesn't make sense to look at the benefits in isolation. Ultimately, no prison dog program can make a claim to quality without making the welfare of the dogs a priority.

References

American Veterinary Medical Association (AMVA). (2019). *Human-animal bond.* Retrieved May 1, 2019 from: https://www.avma.org/KB/Resources/Reference/human-animal-bond/Pages/Human-Animal-Bond-AVMA.aspx.

Anderson, J. L. (2011). Protection for the powerless: Political economy lessons for the animal welfare movement. *Stanford Journal of Animal Law & Policy, 4,* 1–63.

Assistance Dogs International. (2019). *Assistance Dogs International homepage.* Retrieved March 15, 2019 from: https://assistancedogsinternational.org/.

Associated Press. (2019, January 3). *Ohio inmate indicted in death of prison foster dog*. Retrieved from https://fox8.com/2019/01/03/ohio-inmate-indicted-in-death-of-prison-foster-dog/.

Baumeister, R. F., & Leary, M. R. (1995). The need to belong: Desire for interpersonal attachments as a fundamental human motivation. *Psychological Bulletin, 117*(3), 497–529.

Beck, A. (2006). The use of animals to benefit humans: Animal-assisted therapy. In A. Fine (Ed.), *Handbook on animal-assisted therapy* (pp. 21–40). San Francisco, CA: Academic Press.

Beseres, M. (2017). *Unintended rehabilitation: A comparative analysis of prison animal programs*. Retrieved from Sophia, the St. Catherine University repository website: https://sophia.stkate.edu/msw_papers/713.

Brambell, F. W. R. (1965). *Report of the technical committee to enquire into the welfare of animals kept under intensive livestock husbandry systems*. Cmnd 2836, London: HMSO.

Britton, D. M., & Button, A. (2005). Prison pups: Assessing the effects of dog training programs in correctional facilities. *Journal of Family Social Work, 9*(4), 79–95.

Broom, D. M. (2010). Cognitive ability and awareness in domestic animals and decisions about obligations to animals. *Applied Animal Behavior Science, 126*, 1–11.

Broom, D. M., & Fraser, A. F. (2015). *Domestic animal behaviour and welfare* (5th ed.). Boston, MA: CABI.

Browne, J. (2010, Spring). Rooted in slavery: Prison labor exploitation. *Race, Poverty, and the Environment*, 78–80.

Cooke, B. J., & Farrington, D. P. (2016). The effectiveness of dog-training programs in prison: A systematic review and meta-analysis of the literature. *The Prison Journal, 96*(6), 854–876.

Cushing, J. L., & Williams, J. D. (1995). The wild mustang program: A case study in facilitated inmate therapy. *Journal of Offender Rehabilitation, 22*(3/4), 95–112.

Deaton, C. (2005). Humanizing prisons with animals: A closer look at "cell dogs" and horse programs in correctional institutions. *Journal of Correctional Education, 56*(1), 46–62.

Drew, J. D., Dearborn, C., Evans, M., Gagne, A., McBean, D., Saville, F., & Silliman, T. (2013). The power of prison pups: The impact of the NEADS program on inmate dog trainers, MCI/Framingham, and the community. *Laselle College*, 1–51.

Evans, N., & Gray, C. (2012). The practice and ethics of animal-assisted therapy with young people: Is it enough that we don't eat our co-workers? *British Journal of Social Work, 42*, 600–617.

Fine, A. H., Peralta, J., & Colver, P. (2013). The development of the pet assisted therapy welfare assessment tool. In *Paper Presented at the 2013 IAHAIO Conference, Chicago, Illinois, July 20–22*.

Friesen, L. (2010). Exploring animal-assisted programs with children in school and therapeutic contexts. *Early Childhood Education Journal, 37*(4), 261–267.

Furst, G. (2006). Prison-based animal programs: A national survey. *The Prison Journal, 86*(4), 407–430.

Furst, G. (2011). *Animal programs in prisons: A comprehensive assessment*. Boulder, CO: First Forum Press.

Furst, G. (2015). Prisoners, pups, and PTSD: The grassroots response to veterans with PTSD. *Contemporary Justice Review, 18*(4), 446–449.

Garcia, K. (2014). Prisons and pups: An examination of service dog training and their weekend families. *In BSU Honors Program Theses and Projects*. Item 58. Available at: https://vc.bridgew.edu/honors_proj/58/.

Glenk, L. M. (2017). Current perspectives on therapy dog welfare in animal-assisted interventions. *Animals, 7*(2), 1–17.

Glenk, L. M., Kothgassner, O. D., Stetina, B. U., Palme, R., Kepplinger, B., & Baran, H. (2013). Therapy dogs' salivary cortisol levels vary during animal-assisted interventions. *Animal Welfare, 22*(3), 369–378.

Hatch, A. (2007). The view from all fours: A look at an animal-assisted activity program from the animals' perspective. *Anthrozoös, 20*(1), 37–50.

Hennessy, M. B., Morris, A., & Linden, F. (2006). Evaluation of the effects of a socialization program in a prison on behavior and pituitary-adrenal hormone levels of shelter dogs. *Applied Animal Behaviour Science, 99*(1), 157–171.

Herron, M. E., Shofer, F. S., & Reisner, I. R. (2009). Survey of the use and outcome of confrontational and non-confrontational training methods in client owned dog showing undesired behaviors. *Applied Animal Behaviour Science, 117*(1–2), 47–54.

Hill, L. B. (2016). *Becoming the person your dog thinks you are: An assessment of Florida prison-based dog training programs on prison misconduct, post release employment and recidivism.* Retrieved April 15, 2019 from http://purl.flvc.org/fsu/fd/FSU_2016SP_Hill_fsu_0071E_13183.

Hines, L. M. (2003). Historical perspectives on the human-animal bond. *American Behavioral Scientist, 47*(1), 7–15.

Houpt, K. A., Goodwin, D., Uchida, Y., Baranyiová, E., Fatjó, J., & Kakuma, Y. (2007). Proceedings of a workshop to identify dog welfare issues in the US, Japan, Czech Republic, Spain and the UK. *Applied Animal Behaviour Science, 106*(4), 221–233.

Humby, L., & Barclay, E. (2018). Pawsitive solutions: An overview of prison dog programs in Australia. *The Prison Journal, 98*(5), 580–603.

Iannuzzi, D., & Rowan, A. N. (1991). Ethical issues in animal-assisted therapy programs. *Anthrozoös, 4*(3), 154–163.

Johnson, A., & Bruneau, L. (in press). Prison populations and pet loss. In L. R. Kogan, & P. Erdman (Eds). *Pet loss and mental health care providers.* New York: Routledge.

Katcher, A., & Wilkins, G. (1993). Dialogue with animals: Its nature and culture. In S. Kellert & E. O. Wilson (Eds.), *The biophilia hypothesis* (pp. 173–197). Washington, DC: Island Press.

Koda, N., Watanabe, G., Miyaji, Y., Ishida, A., & Miyaji, C. (2015). Stress levels in dogs, and its recognition by their handlers, during animal-assisted therapy in a prison. *Animal Welfare, 4*(2), 203–209.

Koldstad, A. (1996). Imprisonment as rehabilitation: Offenders' assessment of why it does not work. *Journal of Criminal Justice, 24*(4), 323–335.

Lasher, M. (1998). A relational approach to the human-animal bond. *Anthrozoös, 11*(3), 130–133.

Lindsay, S. R. (2005). *Handbook of applied dog behavior and training: Procedures and protocols.* Ames, IA: Blackwell Publishing.

McConnell, P., & Fine, A. H. (2015). Understanding the other end of the leash: What therapists need to understand about their co-therapists. *Handbook on Animal-Assisted Therapy* (pp. 103–113). New York: Academic Press.

McCulcahy, C., & McLaughlin, D. (2013). Is the tail wagging the dog? A review of the evidence for prison animal programs. *Australian Psychologist, 48,* 369–378.

McEwen, B. S., & Wingfield, J. C. (2003). The concept of allostasis in biology and biomedicine. *Hormones and Behavior, 43*(1), 2–15.

Meers, L. L., Stefanini, C., Sofie, D., Normando, S., Samuels, W. E., Kalmar, I. D., et al. (2010). Is it wise to involve animals in prisons and rehabilitation programs? A study conducted in Flanders (Belgium). *Journal of Veterinary Behavior, 51*(1), 50.

Mellor, D. J. (2016). Updating animal welfare thinking: Moving beyond the "Five Freedoms" towards "a life worth living". *Animals, 6*(3), 21.

Melson, G. F., & Fine, A. H. (2015). Animals in the lives of children. In A. H. Fine (Ed.), *Handbook on animal-assisted therapy: Foundations and guidelines for animal-assisted interventions* (pp. 179–194). San Diego, CA: Academic Press.

Mercer, J., Gibson, K., & Clayton, D. (2015). The therapeutic potential of a prison based animal programme in the UK. *Journal of Forensic Practice, 17*(1), 43–54.

Miller, P. (2016, May). Jail house dogs. *The Whole-Dog Journal,* 15–19.

Montalvan, L. C., & Witter, B. (2012). *Until Tuesday: A wounded warrior and the golden retriever who saved him.* New York: Hyperion.

Moran, D. (2015). Budgie smuggling or doing bird? Human-animal interactions in carceral space: Prison(er) animals as abject and subject. *Social and Cultural Geography, 16*(6), 634–653.

Ng, Z., Albright, J., Fine, A. H., & Peralta, J. (2015). Our ethical and moral responsibility: Ensuring the welfare of therapy animals. In A. H. Fine (Ed.), *Handbook on animal-assisted therapy: Foundations and guidelines for animal-assisted interventions* (pp. 357–376). San Diego, CA: Academic Press.

Ng, Z., Morse, L., Albright, J., Viera, A., & Souza, M. (2018). Describing the use of animals in animal-assisted intervention research. *Journal of Applied Animal Welfare Science*, 1–13.

Ng, Z. Y., Pierce, B. J., Otto, C. M., Buechner-Maxwell, V. A., Siracusa, C., & Werre, S. R. (2014). The effect of dog–human interaction on cortisol and behavior in registered animal-assisted activity dogs. *Applied Animal Behaviour Science, 159,* 69–81.

Odendaal, J. (2000). Animal-assisted therapy—magic or medicine? *Journal of Psychosomatic Research, 49,* 275–280.

Ormerod, E. (2008, Autumn). Companion animals and offender rehabilitation experience from a prison therapeutic community in Scotland. *Therapeutic Communities, 29*(3), 285–296.

Pachana, N., Massavelli, B., & Robleda-Gomez, S. (2011). A developmental psychological perspective on the human-animal bond. In C. Blazina, G. Boyraz, & D. N. Shen-Miller (Eds.), *The psychology of the human-animal bond* (pp. 151–165). New York: Springer.

Pet Partners (2019). *About pet partners.* Retrieved from https://petpartners.org/about-us.

Pinillos, R. G., Appleby, M., Manteca, X., Scott- Park, F., Smith, C., & Velarde, A. (2017). Consultation to define a One Welfare framework. *Veterinary Record, 180*(7), 1–7.

Protopopova, A. (2016). Effects of sheltering on physiology, immune function, behavior and the welfare of dogs. *Physiology & Behavior, 159,* 95–103.

Rooney, N. & Bradshaw, K. (2014). Canine welfare science: An antidote to sentiment and myth. In A. Horowitz (Ed.). *Domestic dog cognition and behavior* (pp. 241–274). Berlin: Springer-Verlag.

Rooney, N. J., & Cowan, S. (2011). Training methods and owner–dog interactions: Links with dog behaviour and learning ability. *Applied Animal Behaviour Science, 132*(3–4), 169–177.

Schoen, A. M. (2002). *Kindred spirits: How the remarkable bond between humans and animals can change the way we live.* London: Souvenir Press.

Seivert, N. P., Cano, A., Casey, R. J., Johnson, A., & May, D. K. (2016). Animal assisted therapy for incarcerated youth: A randomized controlled trial. *Applied Developmental Science, 22*(2), 139–153.

Senter, S. (Ed.). (1993). *People and animals: A therapeutic animal-assisted activities manual for schools, agencies and recreational centers.* Brewster, NY: Green Chimneys Press.

Serpell, J., McCune, S., Gee, N., & Griffin, J. (2017). Current challenges to research on animal-assisted interventions. *Applied Developmental Science, 21*(3), 223–233.

Stewart, L. A. (2016). *Animal-assisted interventions competencies.* Retrieved from https://petpartners.org/wp-content/uploads/2014/12/Tiered-AAI-Competencies_2016.pdf

Stewart, L. A., Chang, C. Y., Parker, L. K., & Grubbs, N. (2016). *Animal-assisted therapy in counseling competencies.* Alexandria, VA: American Counseling Association, Animal-Assisted Therapy in Mental Health Interest Network.

Strimple, E. O. (2003). A history of prison inmate-animal interaction programs. *American Behavioral Scientists, 47*(1), 70–78.

Tannenbaum, J. (1989). *Veterinary ethics.* Baltimore, MD: Williams and Wilkins.

van Wormer, J., Kigerl, A., & Hamilton, Z. (2017). Digging deeper: Exploring the value of prison-based dog handler programs. *The Prison Journal, 97*(4), 520–538.

Washington, K. M. (2017, Fall). Horrible conditions for livestock animals in Texas Prisons exposed. *Earth First! Journal, 3,* 44–45.

Wilson, E. O. (1984). *Biophilia.* Cambridge, MA: Harvard University Press.

World Organisation for Animal Health (OIE). (2019). *Animal welfare at a glance.* Retrieved from http://www.oie.int/en/animal-welfare/animal-welfare-at-a-glance/.

Yeates, J. W., & Main, D. C. J. (2007). Assessment of positive welfare: A review. *The Veterinarian Journal, 175,* 293–300.

Zamir, T. (2006). The moral basis of animal-assisted therapy. *Society and Animals, 14*(2), 179–199.

Chapter 6
Considering the Correctional Context: *Security Issues in Prison-Based Dog Training Programs*

Leslie B. Hill and Benjamin Wright

Introduction

As noted throughout this book, the introduction of dogs in a correctional environment has numerous benefits. Despite the positive anecdotal and empirical evidence regarding dog programs in correctional facilities, such programs do not come without security concerns. The mission of a prison is twofold: to create a safe and secure environment for the inmates and staff and to offer programs to the inmates to aid them in their rehabilitation (Seiter 2011; Josi and Sechrest 1996). Neither of these missions allow for simple solutions and those in charge of overseeing an institution often walk the line between these two seemingly contradictory tasks. The two dominant themes that emerge from these missions are custody and treatment (Seiter 2011). Seiter (2011) explains that custody entails the control of inmate movement and activities within a prison, with the intent of preventing escape or violence. On the other hand, treatment requires implementing rehabilitation programs that creates a more restorative environment, while allowing the inmates to better themselves in preparation for re-entry. Those in charge of an institution have the difficult task of accomplishing these two missions, a feat which is not easily achieved due to the appearance of mutual exclusion, and thus requires careful planning and strong leadership (Hunsicker 2008).

To successfully implement rehabilitation programs into an institution, one must first consider the safety and security of the institution, the inmates and the staff (Josi and Sechrest 1996). The implementation dog training programs into an institution as a form of rehabilitation is no different, despite their recent rise in popularity. They are now present in all 50 states and many other countries (Cooke and Farrington 2014). Despite their widespread growth, they still present many concerns for those in charge of a

L. B. Hill (✉)
The Citadel, Charleston, SC, USA
e-mail: lhill4@citadel.edu

B. Wright
Radford University, Radford, VA, USA

M. R. Jalongo (ed.), *Prison Dog Programs*,
https://doi.org/10.1007/978-3-030-25618-0_6

prison–most notably, security—and thus require careful planning. Safety in an institution requires predictability and uniformity in day-to-day activities (Josi and Sechrest, 1996) and introducing animals into the institution clearly violates both of those requirements. Wardens and other institutional staff have to oversee the continuous movement of the animals in, out and around the institution, all of which can increase the introduction of and movement of contraband throughout the facility. Furthermore, many of the tools and medications needed for the dogs can be abused by the inmates. This chapter will cover many of the chief concerns regarding the addition of a dog training program into an institution, while simultaneously discussing the impact dog training programs may have on each of these concerns. The information gathered for this chapter comes from the personal experiences of a former Treatment Program Supervisor and Warden at several prisons, including a minimum security male Virginia Correctional Institution (Lunenburg Correctional Center) with a dog training program, correspondence with other prison based dog training program supervisors, as well as an ongoing multi-modal research project regarding prison animal programs in three South Carolina Department of Corrections (SCDC) facilities. As mentioned above, the Virginia correctional institution is a minimum security facility (Lunenburg Correctional Center), while two of the South Carolina Institutions (Allendale C.I. and Camille Graham C.I.) are medium security facilities, serving males and females respectively, and one (Perry C.I.) is a maximum security institution for male inmates. Examining experiences with prison based dog training programs from different custody levels, across different states, and serving different genders allows for a comprehensive comparison of security protocols. Despite the benefits that dog programs may have in the correctional environment, the custody and control of inmates must prevail, even at the cost of program effectiveness (Furst 2006). However, as this chapter will demonstrate, correctional facilities have been able to successfully incorporate dog training programs into their facilities, regardless of the many security challenges that these programs present.

Policies Regarding Perimeter Security of the Prison

One of the most pressing concerns an institutional administrator has to consider when implementing a dog training program is how to address perimeter security concerns. Seiter (2012) explains that "perimeter security" refers to the physical barrier that keeps inmates within an institution in the form of fencing, usually with barbed wire on the top or woven throughout the fence. An additional component of perimeter security is keeping unwanted contraband out of the facility. Recent additions to perimeter security include wire nets that extend vertically several hundred feet upwards or horizontally over the top of the institution, with the intention of reducing the ability for drones to drop contraband over the walls (Grohs 2017). For example, Perry C.I. (maximum security) uses these vertical wire nets as well as gun towers. Their Associate Warden explained that the wire netting makes it a lot easier for correctional staff to see the drones before they drop contraband over the fence. Most of the other South Carolina Institutions also rely on "Rovers", i.e., officers in mobile vehicles patrol the outside of the prison both to deter and intercept escapes or contraband.

When it comes to perimeter security, the dog training programs present a few concerns that require assessment and planning before program implementation. The first issue is that the introduction of dogs into the facility affords handlers the opportunity to get too close to the perimeter when taking dogs outside for exercise or elimination. Facilities must establish protocols that allow for such access while having a negligible impact on facility movement and security. The South Carolina Department of Corrections allows each institution to determine their own strategy for dealing with this concern. The Assistant Deputy Director of Programs and Services said "they know their house better than anyone at Headquarters will," thus they allow them to deal with it on an institutional level. For instance, Camille Graham C.I. (medium security) created an area of the yard specifically for the animals. However, the Associate Warden (AW) indicated that the dog area was originally near the fence line and prison administrators were concerned that civilians would throw contraband over the fence allowing the inmates in the dog training program to easily retrieve it because the dog area was so close to the fence line. At first, the AW merely had the Rover check that area more frequently, but eventually decided to move the dog area closer to the interior of the institution. She clarified that there were no incidents that caused the movement of the dog area, but they were wary and wanted to prevent any potential problems. Furthermore, the facility requires that the dogs be escorted by inmates, on leashes at all times to prevent them from running too close to the perimeter which would require an inmate to go retrieve them near the perimeter. The Lieutenant at Allendale C.I. who oversees their dog training program echoed the concerns at Camille Graham C.I. and indicated that, while there was no specific dog area, the dog handlers were merely told to keep the animals on leashes and close to the interior.

On the other hand, Perry C.I. does it slightly differently. Their institution only has two dogs that have been there for several years, both of which were trained to go out the back door of the dorm, use the bathroom and come back. The dogs are housed in the character dorm[1] and the inmates merely have to ask a CO to unlock the back door so the dog can go out and come back, after which the back door is locked again. Before the dog is trained to come back, the inmates escort them outside and bring them back. While there is no designated dog area, the inmates that escort the untrained dogs know to stay clear of the fence. All the inmates in the program expressed concern about getting too close to the fence due to the gun towers. As one inmate explained, "we wear bright orange! We're a big target for them to shoot! I'm not getting anywhere near that fence!" Occasionally, the dogs sometimes get too close to the fence line (while off-leash), but as described above,

[1]Many facilities at SCDC implement a character dorm which is usually the best behaved unit in the yard. The inmates have to participate in a cognitive retraining program and sign a behavior contract to be allowed in the dorm. However, Allendale C.I. is a character *institution*, meaning all the inmates must behave or risk being sent to a higher custody level.

the inmates never follow them. At this institution, the prison administrators were less concerned about keeping the dogs away from the fence line because they have gun towers and wire nets, both of which make it much harder for the inmates close to the perimeter to receive contraband.

Dogs require access to outside areas for exercise, elimination of waste, and training. *Photo Credit* Sherry Bratcher Sasin

Control of Inmate Movement and Accountability

On February 12, 2006, John Manard, a convicted murderer serving a life sentence for first-degree murder, aggravated robbery, and possession of firearms for the 1996 killing of a man during a carjacking, escaped from the Lansing Correctional Facility in Lansing, Kansas. Ms. Young, a volunteer at the facility, had established the Safe Harbor Prison Dog program in August of 2004 and inmate Manard had been a dog handler in the program for approximately one year. Inmate Manard was able to escape the facility after Ms. Young secreted him inside of a dog crate, loaded him into her van, and drove away from the facility. Fortunately, inmate Manard and Ms. Young were captured within two weeks of escape. A review of this incident revealed that security staff failed to properly search Ms. Young's van prior to exiting the facility. She was eventually sentenced to 21 months in prison for her role in the escape.

Security breaches that lead to the escape of an inmate tend to produce a swift response from corrections administrators. Much of the time, the reaction is to terminate the program. Fortunately, in the case of the Lansing facility, staff recognized the overall benefit of the program and continued it after the escape.

Assuring the secure custody of inmates is the chief goal of the prison. Historically, the United States is particularly good at preventing escapes from custody and thus escapes are quite rare in modern prisons. Understandably, correctional administrators have been hesitant to implement programs that may adversely impact the custody and control of the inmate population. Despite the rarity of escapes, security concerns require that staff are aware of the location of offenders at all times. Offenders will often times seek locations within the facility where illegal activities such as drug use, gambling, and sexual conduct may occur. Therefore, it is vital that corrections staff who are implementing a dog program account for the movement of offenders within and outside of the facility.

Prison rules and regulations typically enforce strict offender movement control. However, inmates involved in dog training programs typically are afforded greater freedom to move throughout the facility. In fact, greater freedom of movement has been cited by inmate dog handlers as one of the primary benefits of program involvement (Britton and Button 2005). Flexibility is necessary to maintain the health of the dog and simultaneously monitor the location of the inmates. In a correctional facility, controlling the movement of the inmates is an integral part of the security of the institution. One method of accounting for offender location is through an institutional count. During an institutional count, all activities at the facility cease. Count occurs several times per day so that correctional officers can verify the location of all offenders. Although institutional counts are an essential function to facility security, such activities may be hindered by dog programs. Thus, it is important that institutions determine specific protocol about what to do with the animals during the count. For instance, all three South Carolina institutions allow the animals to be present during the count or simply allow the animals to be in the inmates' cells while they report to the designated area for the count.

The presence of dogs during mass movement may cause distractions and interrupt facility movement. Therefore another strategy is the creation of a daily schedule that limits the ability for the inmates to move about the institution, making monitoring their movements much easier and more predictable (Seiter 2012). Most facilities develop some type of movement protocol or schedule. Prior to implementation of a dog program, a facility must evaluate their movement schedule to address the needs of the dog and the movement required for dog training and/or programming. This allows for inmate accountability, in that the daily schedule allows those that oversee them to know exactly where they should be at all times. When creating the daily schedule, many facilities restrict the number of handlers that may be released during times of mass movement, such as meal time, to ensure proper care for the dogs during such activities. Therefore, facilities may require that a limited number of handlers be released during movement so that other handlers are available to monitor the dogs in the housing unit. Another concern with regard to offender movement is the identification of handlers. Staff must be able to identify handlers to ensure they are authorized to escort dogs. Offenders who have not been designated as dog handlers may falsely present themselves as a handler in order to move more freely throughout the facility or access equipment. Most programs maintain an accurate listing of dog handlers to prevent such an occurrence. Additionally, some programs issue inmates designated as dog handlers special identification cards or specialized clothing so they may be easily recognized.

Housing Dogs in a Controlled Setting

Understandably, the incorporation of animals into an institution will disturb the daily schedule of the inmates for a number of reasons. For instance, the dogs need bathroom breaks and need to exit the facility if they need veterinary services. In addition, the institution has to consider where and how to house dogs when the inmates are busy, such as during chow, if the handler has another job, or if the handler participates in another program or class. Regarding bathroom breaks, all of those in charge of the dog programs at SCDC recommend scheduling at least one CO per shift (in the dog dorms) be a "dog person." Both of the women in charge of overseeing the dog programs in the medium security prisons were concerned that the inmates were trying to take their dogs out more than necessary for nefarious reasons or to simply break up the monotony of the day. A CO who understands dogs and their schedules reduces the opportunity for the inmates to take the dogs out more than necessary, thus controlling their movements. However, this was explicitly contrasted by the inmates in the dog program at Camille Graham C.I. who indicated that they were often denied the ability to take their dogs out when they needed to go to the bathroom. Consequently, there were several accidents indoors, which created a chain reaction of sorts. The inmates explained, when one dog would go to the bathroom inside, the other dogs would try to "mark" on top of it, thus creating more indoor accidents. As a result, the Associate Warden at Camille Graham C.I. created a schedule for the dogs' bathroom breaks that could be incorporated into the daily schedule. She then wrote a memo for all the COs so that they knew the schedule and she is very strict about making sure they stick to the schedule.

While the Associate Warden at Perry C.I. also indicated it was important for at least one CO per shift in a dog dorm be a dog person, it was for a different reason. She had to make it clear to the COs that the "dogs aren't inmates" and that they need to go outside. Given that they work in a maximum security institution, those COs were more wary of allowing the inmates to break with the daily schedule and allow them to take their dogs out. Other institutions require that anytime an offender is allowed access to a yard at night that tower officers or observation (yard) officers are notified. Additionally, facilities typically specify that yards be only utilized for bathroom breaks from dusk to dawn. Additionally, they usually require that correctional staff log the times that offenders enter and leave the yard with their dogs.

Another concern regarding the daily schedule is the removal of a dog should it fall ill. In most cases, vet visits can be coordinated in advance. However, that is not always possible and to accommodate emergency medical visits, facilities should maintain all medical records for the dogs in an area accessible to supervisory staff, after hours. Such protocols allow for staff to quickly remove an ill dog while ensuring that necessary records are transported with the dog. Each SCDC institution had a similar protocol for that situation: if a dog is sick, the inmates are to inform a CO on duty, who will then radio the liaison. The liaison will then contact the affiliation that provides the dogs to come pick up the animal and transport it to a veterinarian. Each facility identifies a liaison who is able to contact the affiliate for any number of dog-related emergencies. In the event that an animal falls sick while the liaison is not on site, each shift supervisor has the phone number of the liaison.

Depending on the institutional protocol regarding housing the dogs, the staff member(s) in charge of the program have to coordinate the inmates' movements, while accounting for the institution's policy about leaving the dogs alone. At Camille Graham C.I., their policy is to never leave the dogs alone and each of the dog handlers have at least one job or program to go to per day. As a result, the Associate Warden has them work together in teams of two so that the dogs are never left by themselves to roam around the dorm. Inmates may be allowed to bring their dogs into their jobs/classes but some areas of the facility—such as the medical area—are a no dog zone. Therefore, the Associate Warden has to be cognizant of whether animals are allowed in jobs/classes when carefully choosing which inmates need to be paired together. Additionally, this is also something she has to consider when selecting which inmates can participate in the program. Inmates that have assignments that allow animals makes scheduling much easier. When we last spoke, the Associate Warden was considering expanding the dog handlers to groups of three because the inmates were so busy with their other commitments.

On the other hand, the dog dorms at Allendale C.I. and Perry C.I. are structured as "pods" with cells facing a common area. The animals can reside in their cells or in the dayroom when the inmates are busy elsewhere. However, the program at Allendale C.I. is structured so that the inmate handlers rely on and support one another, so the dog handlers can request that another inmate handler take their dog outside during the scheduled bathroom breaks, if they will be unavailable at that time. The dog program at Perry C.I. identifies alternates, who are tasked with taking care of the dog, should the handler be unavailable. The use of alternates is a very popular option for dog training programs, as many other institutions also frequently use alternates (Furst 2007). It is also a way for inmates who are interested in the dog program to get some on-the-job training prior to becoming dog trainers. Other institutions simply crate the animals when they need to be left alone, therefore making the creation of inmate daily schedules even easier.

Control of Contraband

Contraband is an issue in every correctional facility in the United States (Cox 2016) and thus the elimination of contraband is always at the forefront of prison administrators' and other staff members' minds. The control of contraband is a never-ending task for those who work in an institution; shrewd inmates can find a way to hide contraband almost anywhere (Grohs 2017). Correctional institutions spend a great deal of time both creating procedures to prevent the introduction of contraband and searching for it once it has come inside the facility (Grommon 2017). Contraband is separated into one of two categories. One source of contraband in a correctional setting is tools. Tools are separated into one of two categories. Class A tools should never be used without direct staff supervision these tools are stored in a secure area when not being used (Seiter 2012). These include sharp objects such as knives or blades or anything that could aid in an escape, like bolt cutters, ropes or ladders. On the other hand, Class B tools, such as pliers and power cords, still need to be inventoried but may be stored and given out under less stringent conditions (Seiter 2012). Class B tools still have to be stored and accounted for but may be utilized by inmates in less stringent conditions.

The addition of a dog training program has the potential to allow the introduction of contraband into an institution as the transference of the supplies needed for the animals into the facility creates a "non-traditional" point of entry (Guerico 2017). As a result, it is imperative that institutions anticipate ways in which contraband can be introduced into the facility when implementing a dog training program and update their procedures accordingly. Pro-active control methods are one of the ways to effectively reduce the introduction of contraband into a facility (Cox 2016) and thus, most institutions utilize standardized entry searches and screen practices (Grommon 2017). Usually the facility designates a staff member to coordinate items coming inside of the facility for dog programs. For example, the Florida Department of Corrections has a member of security staff designated as the Program Coordinator at each correctional facility with a dog program (S. Achen, personal communication, May 14 2018). The Program Manager is responsible for controlling the flow of supplies and coordinating activities of the program. By designating a member of security staff as the Program Manager, each facility ensures that items are inspected by security staff prior to coming inside the secure facility. To prevent the introduction of contraband, facilities also typically require that items, such as dog food, are in factory sealed containers or brought in containers that are easily searched such as clear plastic bags or storage bins.

Each of the South Carolina Department of Corrections facilities has its own procedures for bringing anything into the institution, including dog supplies; however, many of the policies and procedures are quite similar. For instance, when Allendale C.I. was interested in starting a dog program, they modeled their policy for bringing dog supplies into the institution after Perry C.I's thorough procedure. First, the liaison from the shelter sends an email to the Warden listing every single item she will be brining into the prison. The Warden will then approve or disapprove the items and then forwards the list of approved items to the contraband unit. The contraband unit then systematically checks every item coming into the prison and compares it to the list of approved items.

From there, each SCDC institution has different policies regarding the storage and inventory of the dog supplies. At Allendale C.I., once the contraband unit checks all the supplies, they are then transported to the supply room in the dog dorm. At that point, it is inventoried by the inmates. One inmate, the "medical designee" is in charge of keeping track of all the medications that come into the facility. He counts every single pill and notes that on the inventory form. The medical designee also creates a file for each dog that comes into Allendale C.I.; should a dog become ill, the medical designee fills out a medicine form in which he keeps track of any medications, including the dosage and date any medication is given to the dog. This form is then double-checked against the inventory by correctional staff at random intervals. The medications are kept in a locked cabinet and the medical designee and the Lieutenant that oversees the program are the only two with the key. Most of the medications for the dogs are for worms or bacterial infections, "things that won't get an inmate high," as clarified by the Associate Warden of Perry C.I., so most administrators aren't particularly worried about the inmates abusing the medications. When dogs need post-surgical pain medications, these are controlled even more stringently.

Inside a correctional facility, tools are typically stored on a shadow board; a board with fasteners to hold tools and often includes outlines of the tools that are stored on the board. When a tool is issued to an offender, a record of the item that was issued to the inmate is recorded. Staff typically also place a "chit" on the board to identify which offender was given the tool. A chit is a small round metal tag which contains a unique identifier which is associated with a particular offender or staff member. This system of shadow boards and chits allow staff to quickly identify tools that are currently in use or may be missing. At the end of each shift, staff are required to account for all tools in their work area. Most institutions also keep track of the tools needed for the dogs by keeping stringent records. At Allendale C.I., one inmate is in charge of inventorying anything non-medical: collars, leashes, dog bowls, cotton balls, laundry detergent pods, dog food, etc. Both he and the medical designee submit their inventories to a third inmate who enters it into a computer database. Once a month, they generate a report and send it to the program liaison and the Lieutenant. In addition to the daily security checks completed by the Lieutenant, occasionally the contraband team will do spot checks during which they select random items and days to make sure everything is as it should be. The following lists provide examples of inventories of items required to run a dog program. As you can see from the list below, there are a number of items that must be accounted for because of the potential for abuse.

Indiana's Prison Greyhound Program:

1—Crate (next to the handler's bunk)
1—Pillow with pad
1—Martingale Collar (to be worn at all times)
1—ea.—Food/Water Bowl
Treats/Rawhide (when available)
1—Rubber Finger Tipped Toothbrush
1—Raincoat
1—Glove
1—Dog Toy
1—Muzzle
1—Rubber Hound Brush (Glove)

1–4' to 6' lead
1—Waterproof Reversible Winter Coat
Bread Bags for Waste
Canine First Aid Kit (secured in a designated location in the housing unit)

Most of the tools needed to care for dogs are classified as Class B tools: collars, leashes, metal dog bowls, nail clippers, scissors, and medicine for the animals. The inmates are permitted to use them without direct supervision; however, each institution keeps an inventory of each of them and checks the inventory regularly, as described above. Regarding the basic supplies, none of the administrators are overly concerned about collars, leashes and bowls because as the Associate Warden of Perry C.I. explains, "there are much better weapons in here." The Lieutenant that oversees the program at Allendale C.I. was likewise unconcerned with those tools, she stated that cellphones are a much more serious issue; a view that is supported in the corrections literature (Grommon 2017).

All three SCDC administrators indicated that none of the dog supplies or medicines had gone missing during their tenure. The only incident involved a group of inmates at Allendale C.I. "selling" bleach to other inmates who wanted to clean their cells and clothing. Now the Unit Manager keeps the bleach in her office. Additionally, none of the prison administrators had experienced violence in their prison involving the dog supplies. The only incident involved a leash and it was of a sexual nature. Two COs were doing their daily walk through when they found two female inmates together in a compromising position. One of the inmates had been choking the other with the leash during a sexual encounter. The latter had passed out and the former was trying to wake her up when the COs interrupted her. She was promptly given medical attention and removed from the program permanently.

Another concern of all the prison administrators was the use of the dogs' supplies to aid in the movement of contraband. While it did occur from time to time, overall all the administrators indicated it was a rare occurrence. The most common way to transport contraband was in the dogs' poop bags. At Perry C.I., after a former gang member was allowed into the program, he was caught transporting drugs and tobacco in a poop bag. Interestingly, the other inmates in the program informed the administration of his scheme and they caught him in the act. At Camille Graham C.I., they have a trashcan that is specifically designated for the poop bags. However, one of the COs recalled an instance in which she saw a dog handler with a poop bag heading to a non-dog trashcan. As soon as the inmate deposited the bag, the CO pulled the trash just in case the inmate was attempting to transfer contraband. The Associate Warden and the CO agreed that in future, they'd like to have a poop chute with trashcan on the other side of the fence to avoid such problems. They both also suggested that another way to avoid the inmates using the dogs to transfer contraband would be to have a designated fenced in dog area, in which other inmates were not allowed. At Allendale C.I. there were two occurrences of inmates using the poop bags to transport ice and additional food back to their dorm. They were given a warning but not expelled from the program. Less common is the movement of contraband in the dogs' food and toys. There was only one incident of this; the CO's found scissors in the dog food at Camille Graham C. I., and they were promptly confiscated.

The introduction of dog programs involve additional supplies and equipment that could be abused by inmates. *Photo Credit* Sherry Bratcher Sasin

Potential for Conflict

The introduction of dogs in a controlled and cramped correctional environment, where offenders have little input into deciding who they associate with, may cause tensions. In their study of male and female correctional facilities in Kansas, Britton and Button (2005) found challenges with increased visibility and the potential for conflict. The researchers found that many participants in dog care and training programs feel a sense of hyper-surveillance from offenders and staff. Such surveillance could lead to potential conflicts as dog handlers become frustrated by perceived offender and staff interference. For instance, although fairly uncommon, some offenders will attempt to interfere with training programs (Britton and Button 2005). Such meddling is usually related to jealousy because he or she is not involved in the program.

Within the correctional environment, offenders will often utilize "snitch" notes to inform the administration of security issues with regards to an offender involved in a job or program to potentially create an opening. For example, one of the inmates in charge of the animal programs at Allendale C.I. had to be placed in solitary confinement while institutional staff investigated false claims against him by jealous inmates. The false charges against him ranged from an illicit affair with the affiliation liaison to a child pornography ring. In a somewhat similar situation at Perry CI., a jealous inmate (who was denied entry into the program) began reporting to the Associate Warden that the inmates in the program were rubbing peanut butter on their genitals and letting the dogs lick it off. When she dismissed his many complaints, he began writing multiple letters to the senator about this alleged "abuse." Therefore, administrators must remain cognizant of inmates' intentions when addressing "snitch" notes. The Associate Warden who oversees the dog program at Perry C.I. says that it's important to keep your ear to the ground in order to determine the legitimacy of complaints. A few trustworthy individuals can let her know if what she's hearing from the other inmates is true and requires a warning, suspension or removal. But she said it's just as important to watch both the way the inmate interacts with the dogs and watch the dog, because "they'll tell you if something is wrong." She said there was one instance where an inmate was too affectionate with the dog and she removed him from the program because she didn't like the way he interacted with the dog. She clarified "if one guy gives you the creeps, trust your gut and take him out…this is prison."

Conflict may also arise between inmates due to ignorance of program guidelines or training techniques. For instance, inmate dog trainers must ensure that they are following program guidelines that may restrict the interactions dogs have with others. At times offenders and staff may fail to respect these guidelines (i.e. feeding the dog, petting the dog without permission) which has the potential to cause conflict (Britton and Button 2005). Many of the offenders participating in Britton and Button's (2005) study felt a personal obligation to protect their dogs, a sentiment that might or might not extend to their fellow offenders. Therefore, inmates involved in the dog program might lash out at offenders whom they see as disrespecting or harming their dog. Staff members have to be prepared to intercede when these misunderstandings occur.

On the other hand, conflict between inmates may arise when those inmates not in the program sometimes misinterpret proper training techniques as "animal abuse." The allegations of abuse may especially be problematic for service programs that employ the techniques of leash training in which dogs are trained using gentle leader or head harnesses (Britton and Button 2005). Others may view these training tools as muzzles that harm the dog and restrict its breathing, eating, or drinking. Inmates that are not trained in this technique often misinterpret this as animal abuse and either confront the inmate themselves or complain to their superiors. For example, one inmate at Allendale C.I. filed multiple complaints about an inmate that used his leg to block a dog from leaving his cell. The inmate who filed the complaint claimed the inmate handler kicked the dog. Therefore, facilities have to be prepared to deal with an influx of complaints regarding misinformed or jealous inmates. Given that other inmates may react with such negativity toward potential abuse of dogs by inmate handlers, it appears that violence seems to surface when inmates are protecting the dogs rather than being directed toward the animal (Furst 2006).

Nevertheless, the potential for the animals to be abused by the inmates cannot be overlooked. While this is an extremely rare occurrence, there are few documented instances where inmates have mistreated animals (Furst 2006). Recently, a dog was killed by an inmate at Warren Correctional Institution in Ohio. The dog training program at the prison was dissolved after a necropsy revealed that the dog died of blunt force trauma (Farber 2018). Then again, one could argue that the potential for abuse in a prison environment is much lower than in the community. As mentioned previously, offenders who participate in dog therapy or training programs typically face close scrutiny from staff and offenders at the facility (Britton and Button 2005). There are also a number of safeguards not present in a community setting that mitigate the likelihood of animal abuse in a correctional setting. For instance, dogs within correctional facilities have regular contact with facility staff and in most instances, the affiliates that provide the dogs. Issues of abuse with the dog could easily be detected, as many of these individuals are trained to detect signs of abuse. Additionally, the correctional environment has multiple cameras which reduces the opportunity for abuse. Lastly, an offender's mistreatment of an animal in a correctional environment may be met with harsh consequences as offenders typically adopt internal rules among themselves to protect the animals (Korten 2007). Violation of such informal agreements in the correctional environment are often met with severe sanctions. For example, an inmate at a maximum security prison was murdered after he spat soda on another inmate's cat (Cusack 2015).

Issues with Dog Aggression and the Spread of Disease

If not vetted properly, both in terms of aggression or illness, the dogs themselves could endanger others (see Chap. 4 for a discussion of health and safety issues related to dogs in the workplace). Dogs have the potential to injure inmates, staff, or visitors either unintentionally or as an act of aggression. As a result, most correctional agencies require that dogs be temperament tested by a volunteer or qualified individual prior to entering a correctional facility. In addition, many institutions have specific policies in place regarding vaccines and precautions to take to prevent the spread of disease.

Supplementary precautions may be undertaken to minimize the risk of harm to others while inside of the correctional facility. The South Carolina Department of Corrections excludes dogs of specific breeds that have a history of aggressive behavior (SCDC 2016). Other programs merely require a minimum age prior to participation in a training program. Some states or individual institutions implement dog restraint policies. For example, the Florida Department of Corrections requires that dogs be kept on a leash at all times and the leash will be in the hand of an inmate assigned to the program unless: (a) released into an enclosed canine exercise yard; (b) incorporated as a part of the training program; or (c) the animal is crated

(Florida Department of Corrections 2018). Similarly, the Prison Greyhound Program in Indiana and Greyhound Pets of America in South Carolina, require that the greyhounds be muzzled and leashed whenever they are outside of the housing unit (Putnam Correctional Facility 2012). The Associate Warden of Camille Graham C.I. clarified that the dogs needed to be leashed and muzzled out of consideration of inmates with fears and phobias of dogs. She was worried that, if the dogs got loose, these inmates might get too close to the fence and/or injure themselves in an attempt to get away from the dogs. However, the few times the dogs did get loose, nothing happened.

An additional precaution can be found at Washington Department of Corrections facilities. Their programs take measures to ensure that others are aware of the dogs' current level of training in order to assist in quickly identifying the dog's level of predictability. Interestingly, dogs being trained in Washington state facilities wear colored collars or bandanas to indicate their current level of training. Details of these designations are noted below:

a. Red: The dog is new to training and may be unpredictable. Only the dog's handler and trainer should touch the dog. The dog must be crated while the offender is sleeping or not present in the dorm/cell.

b. Yellow: The dog has received some training, and his/her behavior has been shown to be fairly predictable. The handler should remind the requester that the dog is not fully trained.

c. Green: The dog willfully follows directions and is in the final stage to complete the AKC's Canine Good Citizen test. The handler will pay attention to the dog's behavior, looking for clues that indicate the dog is displeased, and act accordingly (Washington Department of Corrections 2016)

Another concern which cannot be overlooked is the potential for the spread of disease. Tens of thousands of people annually contract zoonotic diseases, which are infectious diseases that are spread from animals to humans (Zoonotic Diseases 2018). A variety of illnesses can result from these harmful germs such as viruses, bacterial, parasites, and fungi germs and the results can range from mild sickness to death (Zoonotic Diseases 2018). It is estimated that more than 6 out of every 10 known infectious diseases in people are spread from animals, and 3 out of every 4 new or emerging infectious diseases in people are spread from animals (Zoonotic Diseases 2018). Dogs can appear healthy even when they are carrying germs that can make people sick. Due to these concerns, facilities must also take additional precautions to ensure that dogs entering prison-based dog training programs are healthy and will not adversely impact the health of others. The South Carolina Department of Corrections specifies that the vaccines necessary to be included in a dog program are: rabies vaccination, parvo, distemper, and Bordetella (kennel cough) (SCDC 2016). Similarly, the state of Washington requires the following of each animal entering a correctional facility: (1) all dogs and cats must be free of parasites and current on all required vaccinations, documentation included and (2) dogs and cats with special needs must be approved in advance by the Program Coordinator (Washington Department of Corrections 2016).

Staffing Concerns

When implementing any program into a correctional facility, it is important to address any and all concerns of those who work in the facility. Many of the correctional officers have security-related concerns that have the potential to lead to clashes between themselves and treatment staff, which can undermine the efficiency of the institution (Hunsicker 2008). Often, treatment staff or volunteers from the animal organizations are more focused on rehabilitation and do not consider custody and control issues (Hunsicker 2008). Therefore, it is important to assess the staff support of dog programs and address their security concerns regarding the introduction of treatment volunteers and their equipment into a correctional environment. Furthermore, these security concerns need to be shared with the affiliates so that they understand the ramifications of disregarding security protocol.

Staff buy-in is essential to the success of any program in a correctional setting. Not only is this vital for program integrity, it is also necessary to ensure safety and security issues are addressed in a timely, efficient manner. While it is undeniable that some correctional staff are reluctant to afford inmates the opportunity to interact with dogs in a prison environment, contrary to stereotypes, many correctional staff are committed to the human services role of their employment. Those staff that recognize this role are often able to either maintain positive relationships, or improve their relationships with offenders and are less fearful than those who remain distant. The adversarial nature of the officer's relationship with offenders and the bureaucratic routines of the correctional facility are often the main sources of stress for correctional officers. Establishment of communication between offenders and staff is essential to any program's success. Therefore, it is imperative that the staff not only understand the need for dog programs, but also support them. The Associate Warden at Camille Graham C.I. recommends holding a staff briefing prior to the implementation of a dog program with the explicit purpose of discussing animals in an institution. She indicated that during this briefing, it is imperative to make sure the staff are ok with animals in the institution and to determine if any of them are allergic to or afraid of dogs. But more importantly, she stressed that it is essential to use the staff briefing to make sure the staff understand the need for the program. She explained that this program is extremely important for the inmates, and the staff need to understand that in order to reduce the potential for conflict between inmates and staff who think the inmates shouldn't have dogs. An additional staffing concern for correctional administrators is the influence of correctional officer unions on prison policy procedure (Furst 2006). Any changes that are made to the conditions of the work environment must be approved by the union prior to implementation (Furst 2006).

Another important aspect of dog programs is the use of external agencies and animal service organization staff associated with the program. Staff and volunteers from external agencies and organizations must typically meet the eligibility criteria of volunteers. Such participants must undergo a thorough background check to ensure individuals who may negatively impact security are not allowed admission.

Despite these efforts, sometimes individuals will become involved in an inappropriate relationship with offenders. It is important for correctional staff to monitor interactions between program volunteers and inmates to ensure professional boundaries are maintained. For example, Florida Department of Corrections policy requires that volunteers remain within 'sight and sound' supervision of a Department certified staff member at all times (Florida Department of Corrections 2018). This policy helps to ensure the protection of the volunteer as well as observe the interaction of the volunteer with the inmates. Efforts must be made to ensure all staff associated with a dog program do not over sympathize with program participants. For instance, an orientation conducted by staff for volunteers and dog program partners needs to alert them to offender manipulation techniques and how to maintain professional boundaries. Additionally, facilities may utilize technology such as cameras or tracking devices to monitor the location of volunteers and staff. These devices may also include panic alarms to alert staff in cases where a volunteer or staff member feels threatened.

The failure to maintain professional boundaries is not limited to volunteers and staff from visiting organizations. Furst (2006) noted that a correctional officer thanked an animal program participant by providing a hamburger after a speaking engagement for school children. The correctional officer with over 25 years of experience was reprimanded and subsequently resigned. The community volunteers and trainers associated with the program were so disappointed in the actions taken against the officer that they were no longer willing to work with the facility. As a result, the animal program dissolved. Correctional administrators must take minor transgressions seriously to prevent further fraternization and security concerns. It is therefore imperative that contracted agencies and volunteers are aware of the seriousness of fraternization and the possible security breaches that may result.

Multidisciplinary Team

One way to address many of the staffing concerns mentioned above is the creation of a multidisciplinary team to address potential security and safety concerns prior to implementation. For example, a multidisciplinary team in a correctional facility may consist of staff from security, medical, safety, treatment, maintenance, psychology, and administrators such as Unit Managers. Multidisciplinary teams may also include representatives from contracted agencies that are a part of the dog program (i.e. shelters, veterinary clinics, etc.). Some facilities may also include inmate representatives on such teams so that concerns are communicated both from and to the inmate population. The creation of a multidisciplinary team allows dialogue to address safety and security concerns before they arise and enhances communication with staff and inmates at the facility. Addressing these issues before they arise will enhance staff and inmate investment in the program. This is important because it establishes a network where safety and security issues are addressed either prior to or immediately after implementation. If staff and inmates do not feel invested in the program, they will not feel empowered to communicate and address concerns that arise. If such concerns are not addressed, serious security issues may result. The established multidisciplinary team could also research similar programs to determine "best practices" for implementation (See the Appendix at the end of this volume for an annotated list of programs).

The establishment of a multidisciplinary team could also effectively address stakeholder concerns and educate staff and offenders regarding the benefits of dog programs. Staff and inmates may be suspicious of any program that is different from routine intervention. Dog programs are no exception and prison staff historically have been hesitant to introduce dogs into the prison environment. Dog programs were first questioned as a threat to security but are now viewed as an innovative way to approach rehabilitation. The commitment of staff and offenders is necessary for any progressive program. The multidisciplinary team could serve to educate stakeholders regarding the benefits of such programming. Such dialogue creates the opportunity for staff and inmate flexibility as the program is implemented. Facilities that lack some degree of flexibility will not be well suited for a dog program.

Figure 6.1 provides an example of how a multidisciplinary team may be constituted when planning for and maintaining a dog training program in a correctional facility.

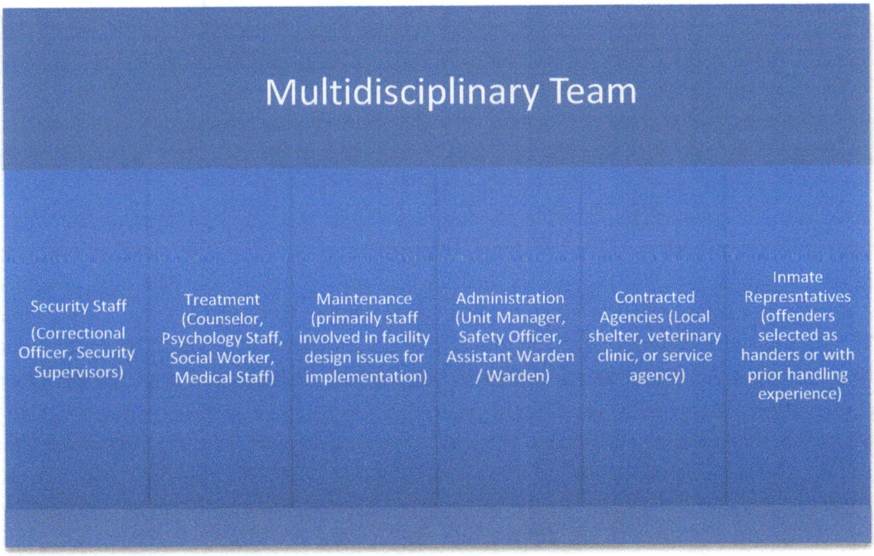

Good Treatment is Good Security

Fig. 6.1 Multidisciplinary Teaming in Prison Dog Programs

Good Treatment Is Good Security

There is an abundance of research that concludes that participation in prison-based treatment programs helps to reduce institutional misconduct (Dietz et al. 2003; Langan and Pelissier 2001; Gussak 2004). In a corrections context where security threats are ever present, high-quality interventions that reduce institutional misconduct should be encouraged. Thus far, the limited research available indicates that dog training programs are no different; both Fournier et al. (2007) and Hill (2016) found that those inmates who participated in dog training programs had statistically significantly fewer institutional infractions compared to a control group. Furthermore, there is evidence that dog training programs make participants more willing to comply with the institutional regulations and authority (Fournier et al. 2007; Richardson-Taylor and Blanchette 2001; Office of the Deputy Commissioner for Women 1998). Like any other desired correctional treatment program, inmates are more likely to curb their antisocial behavior both to become eligible to participate or to continue participation. However, the dog programs seem to improve the environment of a correctional facility more so than traditional rehabilitation programs, in that the presence of dogs in a prison relaxes both inmates and correctional officers alike, often creating a more therapeutic environment and raising morale (Bachi 2013; Deaton 2005; Furst 2011; Strimple 2003; Turner 2007). Additionally, there is evidence that these programs improve the relationship between inmates (Currie 2008; Davis 2007; Ormerrod 2008) which can reduce the likelihood of fights (both physical and verbal) and lead to more positive interactions between inmates and correctional staff (Currie 2008; Davis 2007; Furst 2006; Lai 1998; Richardson-Taylor and Blanchette 2001; Strimple 2003; Turner 2007).

The dog programs seem to increase the morale of the entire institution, which then enhances the security of the facility. Despite the initial skepticism of staff at Bland Correctional Center in Virginia, correctional officers and administrators quickly began to see the benefits for the entire facility. The staff at the Bland Correctional Center echoed prior researchers by indicating the program increased the morale of offenders and employees (Harkrader et al. 2004). All three women in charge of the programs in South Carolina prisons indicated that the dog program increased optimism among the inmates. At Camille Graham C.I., the Associate Warden and the Warden both indicated that the inmates seemed happier. The Associate Warden also noted that even the inmates who weren't in the program seemed more cheerful because they got to pet the dogs. The unit manager for the dog dorm at Allendale C.I. said seeing and being around the animals made her happier and the inmates were much easier to oversee. She noticed the inmates were kinder to one another and it seemed like a totally different environment, seeing the inmates interact with one another while discussing the dogs. At Perry C.I., the Associate Warden indicated that the dogs helped with the inmates' depression and anxiety. Multiple inmates at each of the three South Carolina correctional facilities corroborated this and indicated that they either no longer needed or now required a smaller dosage of their medications as a result of the dog program. One female inmate at Camille Graham C.I. was removed from the mental health unit and placed in the dog program as a part of her treatment and now she no longer needs her medication. It is common knowledge that inmates with mental illnesses are often difficult to manage in a correctional setting (James and Glaze 2006; Butler et al. 2014), so high-quality programs that reduce the need for their medication is something that is highly desirable.

All of the inmates in the South Carolina dog programs validated the program coordinators' observations. The inmates at Perry C.I. noted that the addition of the dogs instantly changed the environment for the better; they felt like entire yard was more relaxed with the dogs around. In fact, they said there was no comparison and it didn't feel like prison, much less a maximum security prison. Many of the inmates at Allendale C.I. ruminated about the experiences they've had at other prisons without animals, prisons they referred to as "thunder domes." They said the environment of Allendale C.I. was so much more therapeutic compared to the thunder domes that it couldn't even be placed in the same category. They clarified that the dogs helped to relieve the pressure of the daily stresses of incarceration; when they've had a bad day, being around the dogs just melted their tension away.

In addition to the improved environment at the Bland Correctional Center, the staff also confirmed other researchers' findings, noting that the offenders participating in the program had improved teamwork, better social skills, and developed a new sense of responsibility (Cooke and Farrington 2016; Furst 2006; Harkrader et al. 2004; Mulcahy and McLaughlin 2013). The program coordinator at Camille Graham C.I. said that the animals created more cohesion in the unit and she felt the inmates got along better because of the animals. Likewise, the inmates at all three South Carolina institutions corroborated the correctional staff members' observations and indicated that they were getting along better with the other inmates. The inmates at Allendale C.I. noticed that the dogs help to reduce the number of altercations (verbal and physical) and they joked that the animals get in more fights than they do. The females at Camille Graham C.I. echoed these thoughts as well but indicated that they noticed that the dogs responded to their moods and thus kept a grip on their temper to avoid fighting with someone because they didn't want to upset their dog. They recalled a unique instance when two women were about to get into a fight and one of the dogs walked over and put his head on one woman's lap which caused her to instantly stop arguing. Additionally, all the SCDC inmates noted that the dogs helped their communication skills, the dogs made them more sociable towards other inmates and made talking to each other easier. Similarly, they found themselves interacting with other inmates more positively when inmates they didn't know would approach them and ask to pet their dog. One inmate at Perry C.I. said he used to have no friends because of the way he spoke to others but now that he's got a dog, socializing has become much easier for him and he has a few friends. Other researchers have noted this as well and refer to animals as "social lubricant" that enables positive social interaction between individuals who have trouble interacting with others (Wood et al. 2007; Brooks et al. 2012).

Researchers have also noted that dog programs often diminish the adversarial relationship between staff and offenders and seem to bridge the gap between the two (Hogle 2009; Harkrader et al. 2004; Katcher et al. 1989), perhaps contributing to the improved environment noted above. For instance, these programs offer staff and offenders an opportunity to discuss something positive and reduce tension and violence facility-wide (Britton and Button 2005; Cooke and Farrington 2016; Cusack 2015; Furst 2006; Mulcahy and McLaughlin 2013; Strimple 2003). All three program coordinators in South Carolina indicated that the introduction of the dogs helped with the interaction between the inmates and the correctional staff. For instance, the Associate Warden at Perry C.I. noted that she saw more interaction between the correctional staff and the inmates as a direct result of the dogs. Additionally, the program coordinators at all three SCDC prisons noted that it is quite common for the correctional staff to adopt one of the dogs from the program, which creates common ground between the inmate handler and the staff member. This creates an opportunity for positive communication because the correctional staff often share updates about their dog and ask for continued training advice from the inmate handler who trained and/or socialized their dog.

Likewise, the SCDC inmates all indicated that the dogs improved their relationship with most of the correctional staff. An inmate at Perry C.I. in the dog program said it was the first time in 30 years that a CO had treated him with respect and trust. In the same way, one inmate at Camille Graham C.I. said that she felt the COs treated her with more respect, especially when she remembers which COs don't like dogs and made an effort to keep her dog away from them. An inmate at Allendale C.I. recalled a time when he was called to the Warden's office and was worried he was in trouble the whole walk there, only to have the Warden ask him advice on how to keep his dog from jumping on him. Furthermore, when the correctional staff adopt one of the dogs, it becomes easier for the inmates to see the correctional staff in a new light and they are often thankful that the correctional staff gave their dog a good home. The inmates confirmed the program coordinators' observations and said that the dogs provide a shared frame of reference for inmates and staff; it also helps offenders to see that the COs are human too. One inmate at Perry CI said that his improved relationship with the COs is a comfort to his family when they come to visit. He said it puts them more at ease when the CO says hi and is friendly to him in front of his family.

Dogs can bring out the best in people and often create a calmer, more therapeutic environment in a prison. *Photo credt* Sherry Sasin

Conclusion

This chapter discussed many of the security challenges faced when implementing a dog training program into a correctional environment. The degree of these challenges is dependent upon a number of factors such as the physical layout of the facility, security level of the offender population, available space, and the attitudes of the staff and offender populations toward such programming. Prison-based programming that utilizes animals appears to the lead the way in prison administrators' acceptance of new and innovative programs (Furst 2006). Although many remain reluctant to bring canines into correctional contexts, the increasing popularity and growing evidence base for prison dog programs suggests that they will exist in many forms in many different penal institutions both in the U.S. and internationally.

Some of the challenges noted by prison administrators were staff resistance, peoples' fear of animals, the mess and noise dogs can create, lack of resources such as staff and space, and resentment from non-participating inmates. Interestingly, no administrators listed security issues as a major obstacle to prison animal programs (Furst 2006) and, as described in this chapter, the additional security concerns are manageable with forethought and close monitoring.

Furthermore, rehabilitation programs are crucial to the success of any correctional institution. As discussed above, correctional administrators will readily admit that one way to enhance security at a correctional facility is to keep offenders engaged in productive and meaningful programming. As one prison superintendent who has worked with four different dog programs in his career expressed it, "There is almost no downside to the initiatives." Although careful thought is needed when considering the logistics of a dog program, addressing the issues noted in this chapter will go a long way in reducing potential security breaches. From the evidenced success of dog programs and the benefits discussed in this chapter, it appears that the implementation of a successful dog training program enhances institutional security rather than threatens it.

References

Achen, S. (2018, May 14). *Personal telephone interview.*

Bachi, K. (2013). Equine-facilitated prison-based programs within the context of prison-based animal programs: State of the science review. *Journal of Offender Rehabilitation, 52,* 46–74.

Britton, D. M., & Button, A. (2005). Prison Pups: Assessing the effects of dog training programs in correctional facilities. *Journal of Family Social Work, 9*(4), 79–95.

Brooks, H. L., Rogers, A., Kapadia, D., Pilgrim, J., Reevers, D., & Vassilev, I. (2012). Creature comforts: Personal communities, pets, and the work of managing a long term condition. *Chronic Illness, 9,* 87–102.

Butler, H. D., Johnson, W. W., & Griffin, O. H. (2014). The treatment of mentally ill supermax: An evaluation of state supermax policies. *Criminal Justice and Behavior, 41*(11), 1338–1353.

Cooke, B. J., & Farrington, D. P. (2014). Perceived effects of dog-training programmes in correctional Settings. *Journal of Forensic Practice, 16*(3), 171–183.

Cooke, B. J., & Farrington, D. P. (2016). The effectiveness of dog-training programs in prison. *Prison Journal, 96*(6), 854–876.

Cox, A. (2016). Watch, listen and learn: Contraband prevention plans. *American Jails,* (3), 8–12.

Currie, N. (2008). *A case study of incarcerated males participating in a canine training program* (Unpublished doctoral dissertation). Kansas State University, Manhattan, Kansas.

Cusack, C. M. (2015). *Animals and criminal justice.* New York: Routledge.

Davis, K. (2007). *Perspectives of youth in an animal-centered correctional vocational program: A qualitive evaluation of Project Pooch (Unpublished research monograph).* Portland State University, Portland, Oregon.

Deaton, C. (2005). Humanizing prisons with animals: A closer look at "Cell Dogs" and horse programs in correctional institutions. *Journal of Correctional Education, 56,* 46–62.

Dietz, E. F., O'Connell, D. J., & Scarpitti, F. R. (2003). Therapeutic communities and prison management: An examination of the effects of operating an in-prison therapeutic community on levels of institutional disorder. *International Journal of Offender Therapy and Comparative Criminology, 47,* 210–223.

Farber, M. (2018, September 3). Ohio animal rescue center claims inmates with prison program killed dog: 'We are absolutely heartbroken.' *Fox News.* Retrieved November 27, 2018 from: https://www.foxnews.com/us/ohio-animal-rescue-center-claims-inmates-with-prison-program-killed-dog-we-are-absolutely-heartbroken.

Florida Department of Corrections. (2018). February 13). *Service dog training and canine obedience training for canine adoptions, Procedure, 506,* 102.

Fournier, A., Geller, E., & Fortney, E. (2007). Human-animal interaction in prison setting: Impact on criminal behavior, treatment progress and social skills. *Behavior and Social Issues, 16,* 89–105.

Furst, G. (2006). Prison-based animal programs: A national survey. *The Prison Journal, 86*(4), 407–430.

Furst, G. (2007). Without words to get in the way: Symbolic interaction in prison-based animal programs. *Qualitative Sociology Review, 3*(1), 96–109.

Furst, G. (2011). *Animal programs in prison: A comprehensive assessment.* Boulder, CO: Lynne Rienner Publishers.

Grohs, M. (2017). *Contraband frustration* (pp. 12–18). July/August: Corrections Forum.

Grommon, E. (2017). Managed access technology to combat contraband cell phones in prison: Findings from a process evaluation. *Evaluation and Program Planning, 66,* 39–47.

Guerico, G. F. (2017). *Layers of security optimize contraband detection* (pp. 34–40). March/April: Corrections Forum.

Gussak, D. (2004). A pilot research study on the efficacy of art therapy with prison inmates. *The Arts in Psychotherapy, 31*(245–25), 9.

Harkrader, T., Burke, T. W., & Owen, S. S. (2004). Pound puppies: The rehabilitative uses of dogs in correctional facilities. *Corrections Today, 66*(2), 74–79.

Hill, L. (2016). *Becoming the person your dog thinks you are: An assessment of Florida prison-based dog training programs on prison misconduct, post-release employment and recidivism*. Florida State University. Retrieved March 1, 2018 from: http://purl.flvc.org/fsu/fd/FSU_2016SP_Hill_fsu_0071E_13183.

Hogle, P. S. (2009). Going to the dogs: Prison-based training programs are win-win. *Corrections Today, 71*(4), 69–72.

Hunsicker, L. (2008). *Security and treatment collaboration. Corrections today, 70*(5), 26–27.

James, D., & Glaze, L. (2006). *Mental health problems of prison and jail inmates*. Washington, DC: Bureau of Justice Statistics Special Report.

Josi, D., & Sechrest, D. (1996). Treatment versus security. *Journal of Offender Rehabilitation, 23* (1–2), 167–184.

Katcher, A., Beck, A., & Levine, D. (1989). Evaluation of a pet program in prison—The Pal Project at Lorton. *Anthrozoös, 2*(3), 175.

Korten, D. (2007, May 31). Indiana State Prison, Michigan City, Indiana: A Better Place for Everyone, Cat Odyssey. Retrieved from: http://catodyssey.blogspot.com/2007/05/indiana-state-prison-michigan-city.html.

Lai, J. (1998). *Literature review: Pet facilitated therapy in correctional institutions*. Ottawa, Ontario: Correctional Services of Canada. Office of the Deputy Commissioner for Women Correctional.

Langan, N. P., & Pelissier, B. M. (2001). Gender differences among prisoners in drug treatment. *Journal of Substance Abuse, 13,* 291–301.

Mulcahy, C., & McLaughlin, D. (2013). Is the tail wagging the dog? A review of the evidence for prison animal programs. *Australian Psychologist, 48*(5), 370–378.

Office of the Deputy Commissioner for Women. (1998). *Literature review: Pet facilitated therapy in correctional institutions*. Ottawa, Canada: Correctional Service Canada.

Ormerod, E. (2008). Companion animals and offender rehabilitation: Experiences from a prison therapeutic community in Scotland. *Therapeutic Communities, 29,* 285–296.

Putnam Correctional Facility. (2012, January 25). *Prison Greyhound Program*. Facility Directive ISF 108.

Richardson-Taylor, K., & Blanchette, K. (2001). *Results of an evaluation of the Pawsitive Directions Canine Program at Nova Institution for Women*. Ottawa, Ontario: Correctional Service of Canada.

Seiter, R. (2011). *Corrections: An introduction*. Upper Saddle River, NJ.: Pearson Education.

Seiter, R. (2012). *Correctional administration: Integrating theory and practice*. Upper Saddle River, NJ.: Pearson Education.

South Carolina Department of Corrections. (2016, June 17). *Animal based programs*. Policy PS-10.16.

Strimple, E. O. (2003). A history of prison inmate-animal interaction programs. *American Behavioral Scientist, 47*(1), 70–78.

Turner, W. (2007). The experiences of offenders in a prison canine program. *Federal Probation, 71*(1), 38–43.

Washington Department of Corrections. (2016, January 1). *Offender dog/cat programs*. Policy DOC 700.350.

Wood, L., Giles-Corti, B., Bulsara, M., & Bosch, D. (2007). More than a furry companion; The Ripple Effect of companion animals on neighborhood interactions and sense of community. *Society and Animals, 15,* 43–56.

Zoonotic Diseases. (2018, August 9). Centers for Disease Control and Prevention. Retrieved October 1, 2018 from: https://www.cdc.gov/onehealth/basics/zoonotic-diseases.htm.

Chapter 7
Screening and Selecting Inmates for Program Participation

Benjamin Wright, Mary Renck Jalongo and Tonya Guy

Introduction

Which inmates are suited for the important responsibility of caring for and training dogs? A collaboration between the Institute for Human-Animal Connections at University of Denver and the Humane Society of the United States yielded a standard protocol for prison dog programs. In it, they summarized the traits sought in inmates selected for participation in these initiatives as follows:

> Staff often look for handlers who have a love of animals, as this relates to their motivation for participating in the program. Being a handler is not an easy task. Staff routinely state that handlers train their dogs 24/7, so having the appropriate motivation not only helps handlers stay committed but also encourages them to behave accordingly to remain in the program …Generally, compassion, empathy, and a positive attitude are key attributes of successful handlers. Other handler qualities that support successful training are the ability to encourage and praise the dogs and to remain calm when interacting with the dogs… handlers must be able to work as a team and to communicate effectively with others…[and] demonstrate appropriate anger management and conflict resolution skills that support their ability to work with their dogs and others. (Han et al. 2018, pp. 32–33)

This chapter will look at the various criteria utilized by correctional facilities in determining inmate eligibility to participate in a dog care and training program. Although there are a number of similarities between program eligibility criteria, there are some notable differences that are specific to the particular context.

B. Wright
Special Services Faculty, Radford University, Radford, VA, USA
e-mail: bwright59@radford.edu

M. R. Jalongo (✉)
Emerita, Indiana University of Pennsylvania, Indiana, PA, USA
e-mail: mjalongo@comcast.net

T. Guy
Canine Partners for Life, Cochranville, USA

M. R. Jalongo (ed.), *Prison Dog Programs*,
https://doi.org/10.1007/978-3-030-25618-0_7

Additionally, this chapter will provide examples of program eligibility criteria for a number of successful dog programs.

Initial Selection Criteria for Inmates

Identifying handlers who meet these entrance criteria relies on a rigorous selection process for inmates seeking participation in the program. Program administrators must balance the goals of effecting change in the inmate and improving the situation for the dogs. Most facilities exclude inmates from participating in dog programs if they have a history of domestic violence, child abuse, or violence against animals. Other criteria utilized in the selection of program participants include institutional conduct such as the absence of disciplinary infractions and having a solid work history. Some facilities require the input of staff who are familiar with the inmate. Additional considerations include the inmate's mental health which can be assessed through psychological evaluations or mental health record reviews. In order to properly evaluate inmate eligibility and suitability for a dog program, some facilities will pair prospective handlers with experienced handlers. In an effort to reduce recidivism and provide transferrable skills upon release from incarceration, many dog programs have an application process, a letter stating the inmate's goals, and/or an interview process. For programs that require the training of service dogs, the time remaining to serve on the inmate's sentence usually is considered. Table 7.1 is an example of the standards used to select participants for the Indiana Canine Assistant Network (ICAN) Program that trains companion and disability assistance dogs.

Programs that include a vocational education component or continuing education in affiliation with a postsecondary institution typically require a high school diploma or General Education Diploma (GED). Depending upon the expected outcomes for the dogs, (e.g., passing the American Kennel Club's Canine Good Citizen, therapy dog programs, or a Public Access Certification Test), inmates also may be required to demonstrate familiarity with the rules of the therapy dog group, the specific training procedures for a service dog, and the items on the test as a precondition for admission to the program.

The opportunity to work with dogs inside of a correctional facility is a privilege that is reserved for inmates who demonstrate a desire to commit to the goals of the program and make significant changes. Perhaps the most difficult task in selecting inmate participants is understanding their motivation for being involved in the program. First and foremost, inmates must demonstrate compassion and/or positive attitudes toward the dogs. In a study of men's and women's correctional facilities in Kansas, Britton and Button (2006) found that the most common impetus for becoming involved in a dog program is the love for dogs. The next most common motivation found among program participants in Britton and Button's (2006) study was the freedom that being involved in the dog program provided them. The final most significant motivation for program participants was their ability to give back

Table 7.1 Eligibility criteria for ICAN program

Facility Directive 172—Pendleton Correctional Facility (11/14/17)
To be eligible for an ICAN Handler position, applicants: • Must be able to participate in the program for a minimum of 36 months • Must not have a documented record of cruelty to animals • Must not have a psychiatric diagnosis that would negatively influence performance or mood stability • Must be 12 months clear of any A or B Conduct Reports and 6 months clear of any C or D Conduct Reports within the facility. If the individual has transferred from another facility and conduct records from that facility for the previous year are available, these may be considered suitable at the discretion of ICAN staff and Facility Coordinator • Must have an education level of GED or above • Must have the physical ability and stamina to perform tasks of lifting (up to 80 lbs), bending and walking • Must have presented himself as a responsible adult throughout the facility; this includes complying with work and education assignments, housing rules, and medical orders • Although not required, prior experience with dogs will be considered a plus in most cases • Applicants who meet the above criteria may be invited to participate in an interview with an ICAN staff member and the IDOC Facility Coordinator. Input from others within the facility may be solicited • Applicants who are selected for handler positions undergo a 12-week probationary period. During this time handlers follow a structured program of reading and hands-on work with other handlers, ICAN staff and dogs. Probationary handlers are expected to pass tests (with 80% or above). These tests include written and hands on components

to the community. Inmates saw their participation in the program as an opportunity to repair some of the harms their criminal actions had on society (Britton and Button 2006). Additionally, inmates may see participation in a dog training program as an opportunity to gain vocational skills that will assist in their transition to the community. Prison inmates have an abundance of time, something that is an important advantage over community members "on the outside". They may be more motivated to work than some community members as a way to counteract the tedium of prison life or to earn the menial wage offered so that they can purchase food or basic items offered for sale in the facility (Weiss 2001). Some PDPs programs pay inmate/trainers at a higher rate than for other jobs completed in the corrections context, which can be another way to incentivize participation.

Equally important to the selection of inmates to participate in dog programs is the monitoring of participants who are involved in the program. Prior to beginning a dog training program, most facilities require inmates to sign a contract that clearly outlines their responsibilities as well as ground rules for dismissal from the program. Such contracts typically require not only adherence to institutional rules and regulations but also compliance with regulations that are specific to the training program. Table 7.2 is an example of the apprenticeship agreement used in Indiana's Animals Depending on Prison Time (ADOPT) program. The program also provides for reductions in time served for outstanding inmate/trainers. ADOPT offers a U.S. Department of Labor internship where inmates become certified in Animal Training and team with a local shelter to train dogs who might not otherwise be adopted.

Interview and Testing

The majority of dog programs have some type of interview process to select participants for the program. Furst (2006) found in her national survey of prison animal programs that only 11.3% of the respondents do not have an interview as a part of the selection process. Although the interview process varies from institution to institution, Furst (2006) found that the most common participants in the interviews were, in rank order, program staff, followed by other prison staff or administrators, and finally, representatives of the affiliated non-profit agencies. Some facilities also perform a review of psychological evaluations or administer psychological survey instruments as a part of the selection process and/or a medical screening to ensure that inmates accepted into the program are physically capable of performing their duties.

In order to maintain positive relationships with contracted agencies, it is important that these partners with the correctional facility are involved with the selection process. Some ways to achieve this include having agency representation on the interview panel or consulting with the nonprofit group when establishing or revising admissions criteria for inmates seeking to join the program. Additionally, some facilities involve inmates currently involved with the dog program in the selection process. For example, part of the interview process for the selection of inmates in the ICAN program in Indiana is the input from current handlers through an inmate committee (Pendleton Correctional Facility 2017). Involving inmates in the selection process provides a number of benefits but also may have negative consequences. Given the popularity of dog programs, staff must be cognizant of the fact that inmates may attempt to involve other inmates that are their friends or associates without consideration of their qualifications or motivations for entering the program. Additionally, the inmate population should not perceive program membership as being biased toward inmates who associate with handlers. However, involving inmates in the selection process does provide transparency in the selection process. An additional benefit of involving inmates in the selection process is that program administrators will receive more information to aid in the screening of inmates. In the prison environment, inmates may be more informed regarding the motivations or behaviors of inmates who are looking to become involved in the program.

Table 7.2 A.D.O.P.T. Apprenticeship Agreement

As a participant in the Rockville A.D.O.P.T. Apprenticeship Program:

1. I will follow all R.C.F. policies and procedures for programs and jobs
2. I will follow all guidelines established for the successful completion of the program
3. I will cooperate with the program directors and my trainer
4. I will remain free of an A or B conduct violations/excessive C or D reports during my apprenticeship
5. I will perform all duties assigned to me by my trainer
6. I will conduct myself in a professional manner at all times

I understand that I will:

1. Be required to honestly complete all documentation concerning my training
2. Be responsible for keeping an accurate and detailed log of my work experiences and having the log approved by my trainer
3. Be responsible for the safe keeping of the Monthly Work Experiences Log until the apprenticeship is completed
4. Need to remain infraction free of any A or B conduct violations/excessive C or D violations or I will be rmoved from the program
5. Be responsible for working with my trainer to assure that I get the opportunity to complete all the varied work experiences
6. Serve a probationary period of not less than 90 days and during this probationary period either the apprentice or the sponsor may terminate the Apprenticeship Agreement

I also understand that the Apprenticeship Program requires 3600 hours of on-the-job work experience completed in a two year time frame as well as 288 hours of related training.

I understand that after successfully completing this Apprenticeship Program I am eligible for 183 days reduction in sentence per policy #01-04-101.

________________________________ ________________

Apprentice Signature and DOC # Date

________________________________ ________________

Trainer Signature Date

Perhaps the greatest benefit of a screening and/or interview process is the evaluation of inmate motivation for program involvement. Inmates may wish to enter the dog program for the wrong reasons. Some inmates may become involved in dog programs strictly to be viewed by correctional staff, parole officers, and others as changed individuals or as a route to impressing the parole board more favorably (Moneymaker and Strimple 1991). Further, it is not uncommon for inmates to underestimate the amount of work entailed in dog training. Even successful program participants often mention that there was a disconnect between their initial expectations and the realities of the job, as the following comment from an inmate/service dog trainer suggests:

> Raising pups may seem like a lot of fun, but it is a great deal of work. The pups live in the rooms with us, and we are there for every part of their day…from food, treats and water, to bathing, brushing, combing, trimming hair and nails, brushing teeth and cleaning ears. We even have to pick up their 'output.' Since they go everywhere with us, we often have to clean 'everywhere' off their paws. I'm talking to YOU, snow, salt, mud and grass. As the pup handlers say, MUST LOVE DOGS. (Anonymous inmate handler 2015, p. 23)

There is little question that program participants must demonstrate a responsibility and commitment toward program goals. Table 7.3 describes the entrance requirements and interview procedures for Prison Paws, a dog training program offered at women's prisons in Montana. The program features basic obedience training as well as boarding and grooming services. Inmates are trained as groomers and receive training regarding dog health and wellness. One form of financial support for the program is to offer boarding, grooming, and training services to private individuals as an industry.

Table 7.3 Prison Paws guidelines for consideration for employment, January 2018

Classification and disciplinary history
• Custody Classification must be Medium or lower • Applicant must have been in the facility for a minimum of 120 days *(applications will be accepted after 90 days)* • Applicant must have clear conduct for a minimum of 90 days before interview • Applicant must not have a Major write-up for a minimum of 120 days • All past disciplinary actions may be taken into account. This includes but is not limited to: theft, property offences, fighting, threatening and insolence • Applicant must be programming compliant • Applicant must not have been terminated from another work position in the last 90 days • Applicants must have a high school diploma, a GED or be actively working on their GED/Hi-Set
Application process
• Employment applications are available on each pod or through Inmate Services • All applications should be sent to the Prison Paws Supervisor via MWP facility mail • Employment application must be completed • Incomplete applications WILL NOT be considered. Employment history must include ALL positions held in this facility • Applications will be reviewed for completeness, accuracy and spelling

(continued)

Table 7.3 (continued)

***Initial screening of applications for employment is based on classification, disciplinary history, program compliance, application, references from case workers/supervisors and work history**
Post-interview process
• Once you have been interviewed, you will receive a memo via facility mail that either offers you employment with Prison Paws, or declines you, based on the other candidates being interviewed • If you are offered employment, you will be placed on the waiting list until another Prison Paws inmate position becomes available • Since we do not always know in advance when an inmate worker will be leaving our employment, we have no estimate as to how long a newly hired inmate will be on the waiting list • If you are hired for Prison Paws and are currently working somewhere else, you do not need to give your two-week notice until you are actually moved down to start work in the Prison Paws program on G-Pod

To demonstrate an inmate's willingness to adhere to program goals, many programs require inmates to complete a probationary period. The PAL program which was researched by Moneymaker and Strimple (1991), for example, requires inmates to complete a 90-day probation period to determine the characteristics that PAL members are looking for in a dog handler.

As mentioned previously, some programs include a review of mental health records or completion of psychological screening instrument as a part of the screening process. This is another way to involve more of the corrections staff in supporting the program. Washington Department of Correction's (2016) policy requires that applicants for dog programs be screened by Mental Health staff for suitability and indicators that may preclude involvement in the program. Psychometric tools may be used to assess personality traits such as compassion and responsibility which are predictors of success in dog training (Britton and Button 2006). One advantage of administering psychological assessments for inmates prior to participation is that the same tests can be administered at the conclusion of the program to provide insight into the change process.

Criminal Record

Most dog programs also consider the inmate's crimes in the selection criteria. Interestingly, Furst (2006) found that nationally only 22.5% of programs reported that there are no crimes that make an inmate ineligible for participation. However, this number may be even higher because 18.3% of the respondents in Furst's (2006) research failed to respond to this question. Of the respondents who did answer this question, 59.2% stated that program eligibility is dependent upon the nature of the inmate's convictions. The most common types of crimes in Furst's (2006) survey that made inmates ineligible were crimes against animals (59.5%), sexual offenses (45.2%), and crimes against children (26.2%) with some programs listing more than one type of crime. In one program, the agreement between the group providing the dogs and the correctional facility was deliberately vague and excluded those who had committed "heinous" crimes. Those responsible for the program felt that this allowed them the latitude to reject an applicant who might meet other minimum criteria but simply did not seem like a good fit.

An inmate's record of violent crimes could preclude an inmate from being involved in dog programs (Achen 2012). However, some programs will allow inmates with violent histories to participate as long as the violence was not against vulnerable populations such as children, elderly, women or animals (National Broadcasting Company 2006). The Florida Department of Corrections specifies specific crime types such as crimes against animals (e.g., cruelty, neglect or abandonment, hoarding, or using animals for blood sports) and crimes related to pedophilia, rape, or paraphilia in their restrictions for dog training programming (Florida Department of Corrections 2018). Research has demonstrated an association with animal abuse and criminal activity and that the incidence of animal abuse documented during childhood is significantly higher among aggressive inmates as compared to other inmates and noninmates (Hoffer et al. 2018). Additionally, individuals who commit crimes against people, including violent crime and property crime, are more likely to abuse animals (Harkrader et al. 2004). The risk of potential abuse could be even greater for inmates with a history of family violence (Harkrader et al. 2004). In fact, there is a growing body of research, compiled by the American Humane Association, that is referred to as "the link"—the connection between violence perpetrated on animals and violent crimes against people (Arkow 2019). Therefore, it is imperative that the criminal history of the inmate be reviewed for signs of animal abuse, neglect, or evidence of cruelty as a way to protect the dogs from potential harm.

An additional criterion to consider when reviewing an inmate's criminal record is her or his potential risk of escape. Given the additional freedom and movement throughout the facility that involvement in a dog program may entail, correctional administrators may consider the security risks with involving inmates who have histories of escape or failure to appear in court. As mentioned in Chap. 6, dogs require access to outside areas for recreation as well as elimination of body waste. Although facilities must consider and minimize security risks with the implementation of dog training programs, correctional administrators may not want to risk the potential negative exposure of a security breach related to program activities.

One of the major debates has to do with inmates who are serving life sentences. While some partners who supply the dogs will agree to include a select few of these individuals, others insist on working with minimum security facilities only. Some groups consider that, particularly if an offense was committed early in life, an individual can mature, change, and become a very different person later on. Likewise, some groups representing the dogs prefer not to work with adolescent populations, preferring the maturity of adult offenders. Policies and procedures related to these issues need to be part of a memorandum of understanding (MOU) between and among the various partners. They may hold widely disparate views about which inmates to include. For example, the corrections partner might be particularly proud of the involvement of individuals with life sentences while the partner providing the dogs might see this as going overboard to help inmates. During a graduation speech, the founder of a group that trains guide dogs for the blind through a rigorous two-year program made the organization's position very clear: their priority is to produce an excellent service dog rather than rehabilitate an inmate.

It should be up to each facility to decide which inmate/volunteers will be allowed to participate in training programs based upon the crimes they have committed. However, correctional administrators should be very careful in selecting inmates to participate in training dogs. A dog in the hands of the wrong inmate could be detrimental to the training program and jeopardize the health, safety, and training progress of the dog.

Institutional Conduct

In addition to an inmate's criminal record, most dog programs also consider the inmate's conduct while in the prison environment. Many programs seek "model inmates" who have been exceptionally well-behaved during incarceration (Achen 2012). The most common eligibility criterion found in Furst's (2006) national study of prison animal programs, aside from criminal record, was behavioral (i.e., remaining free from disciplinary infractions). Of the prison animal programs noted in Furst's (2006) survey, 54.7% had behavioral criteria. In addition to infraction history, 34% of the programs in Furst's (2006) survey consider a participant's work or program history during the selection process.

Custody level is another consideration. It refers to an inmate's potential for escape, violence, or victimization by other inmates. Also included in an inmate's custody level could be the inmate's age, severity of current and past crimes, and institutional conduct. In one study, (26.4%) of programs considered the inmate's custody level in selection criteria (Furst 2006).

Although the categorization of institutional offenses varies from state to state, correctional departments typically separate offenses based upon their severity. Disciplinary infractions of a more serious nature such as assault, rioting, and possession of a weapon carry heavier penalties than consequences for offenses such as possession of contraband, disobeying an order, or failure to follow count procedures. For example, in Virginia disciplinary charges are divided into either 100 series infractions or 200 series infractions, with 100 series infraction being more serious in nature. Administrators of dog programs in correctional facilities tend to prefer inmates with less serious infractions and distinguish this in their criteria. An example of such criteria is that of the Animals Depending on Prison Time

(ADOPT) program at the Rockville Correctional Center in Indiana. The Indiana Department of Corrections has four classifications of disciplinary infractions (A, B, C, and D). Level A violations are of a more serious nature and the nature of the violation lessens with each category (levels C and D violations are less serious). Inmate participation criteria for the ADOPT program states that inmates must be free from Class A conduct reports for (1) year or any Class B conduct reports for (6) six months (Rockville Correctional Facility 2013). Additionally, inmates applying for the program should not have excessive Class C or D violations (Rockville Correctional Facility 2013).

Another issue that may be factored into criteria for inclusion in dog training is gang affiliation. Some institutions restrict inmates who are actively involved in a gang (or, in prison terms, a security threat group) from participating in their dog care or training program. This not surprising given the positive association between gang affiliation and prison misconduct (Gaes et al. 2002; Griffin and Hepburn 2006; Tewksbury et al. 2014). Given the behavioral issues presented by gang members, allowing gang inmates to participate in a dog training program may jeopardize program goals and place the dogs at risk. Conversely, the opportunity to participate in a dog program at a correctional facility often results in new housing arrangements that pull inmates out of the general population or "GP" and this might be an avenue for an inmate who is highly motivated to exit gang life to do so. As one inmate described in his dog training journal, his sense of obligation to a service dog he was training kept him out of trouble. When he happened to encounter one of his former gang buddies at the barber shop, he told him, "Nawh, man. I'm doing this now and I don't want to mess up. I don't do that stuff anymore."

As noted previously, participation in a dog program inside of a correctional facility typically is reserved for the most deserving inmates. Usually, those inmates seeking to be included must remain infraction free. Wait lists often are long. Most dog training programs require an inmate to sign a contract which clearly outlines their responsibilities and expectations as well as violations which may get them dismissed from the program. Box 7.1 is an example of the inmate criteria for Canine Partners for Life (CPL) was provided by Tonya Guy.

Box 7.1 Canine Partners for Life

Inmate Criteria

In the early years of Canine Partners for Life (CPL), all of our puppies were raised by volunteers in our local community. As CPL flourished and our program began to grow, we had a hard time finding enough community volunteers to meet the demands of our program. We had to think outside the box and with that, our Prison Puppy Raising Program began in 2001. Now, 18 years later, our Prison Puppy Raising Program is thriving! We have puppies being raised in 8 prisons throughout Pennsylvania and Maryland.

Most of our prisons raise between 4 and 6 puppies at a time which means 10–12 inmates are involved in the program at each facility. With such a small number of inmates participating, it is a competitive selection process. It is an honor to be chosen and inmates take this responsibility very seriously. They understand it is a privilege to participate; therefore, they are extremely dedicated and work hard to be successful.

We have specific criteria to determine which inmates are eligible for the program. Each prison must use our criteria when selecting inmates, however, the facilities are able to add additional requirements depending on their rules and regulations. If an inmate is interested in participating in the program, he/she must first submit an application. The Unit Manager or designee for the program will review the application to ensure the inmate meets CPL's following selection criteria:

1. Inmates whose crimes were against animals or children will not be considered
2. Inmates whose crimes were sexually predatory in nature will not be considered
3. Further offenses may be considered depending on program criteria
4. Must have been at the current facility for a minimum of 12 months
5. Must have a minimum of one year, preferably two, left to his/her minimum sentence or re-parole date;
6. Must be misconduct free for the last 12 months
7. Must have a stability score of A or B
8. Must be free from misconducts for assault or fighting for two years
9. Must be medically screened to determine that there is no medical condition that would preclude participation in the program (i.e., allergies, etc.)
10. Must be willing to change housing units if necessary
11. Must be willing to assume all care for the canine including, but not limited to, bathing, housing in his/her cell, clean up (including feces and vomit), grooming, etc.
12. Inmates wishing to participate in the program must be housed on a general population housing unit.

All of these requirements are important to CPL and to the success of the Prison Puppy Raising Program for a variety of reasons. As noted above, there are certain criminal offenses that will disqualify an inmate from the program because the safety of our dogs, staff, and volunteers is our top priority. We require inmates to have been at the current facility for a minimum of 12 months because that allows the staff at the prison the opportunity to evaluate each inmate and monitor their behavior for a length of time. The requirements against misconduct are necessary to ensure that everyone involved in the program has the ability to work cohesively in a group setting. Each inmate must also have a minimum of one year left on their sentence so that they are able to be properly trained by a CPL staff member or a prison liaison before receiving a puppy, and then can continually work with at least one puppy throughout its first year. Consistency is important.

Courtesy of Canine Partners for Life, Tonya Guy.

In fact, the mere possibility of being able to participate in a dog program can alter an inmate's behavior (Furst 2006). Therefore, dog programs not only impact the behavior of inmates participating, but also impact the behavior of inmates wishing to participate in the future. In some cases, prospective dog caregivers/trainers are housed with inmates who are actively working with the dogs as another tool for screening suitable candidates as well as a way to provide some training prior to admission to the program. Inmates participating in dog training programs experience increased pressure because they are monitored by both staff and other inmates (Britton and Button 2006). To illustrate, in a prison dog program that trained service dogs, a team of service dog providers would visit regularly to monitor the progress of the dogs. During class and in their dog training journals, the inmates described how they felt nervous, had a sleepless night the day before, and were embarrassed or disappointed if their dog did not perform as expected. They also mentioned that other inmates who had not experienced this would sometimes make comments about them "Just playing with puppies all day" when, in fact, they had been working diligently and felt the full weight of being evaluated as trainers and having their dogs evaluated as well. Dog training programs require an inmate's full attention, discipline, and commitment. However, inmates who are able to deal with such close scrutiny of being monitored and potentially having other inmates disrupt training are able to build positive character traits (Britton and Button 2006).

Becoming a member of a group of inmate/trainers can create a sense of belonging and participation in a different type of community within a correctional facility. *Photo Credit* Pattii Hubble

Given the fact that prison dog programs select the most promising prospects among the inmates for participation, empirical research regarding the effectiveness of these programs has been difficult (Furst 2006). The argument is that these programs show good results because they involve a carefully selected few. However, the patience and compassion required in order to be successful simply cannot be cultivated in some inmates. There is no disgrace in setting up a program to succeed at rehabilitation. Besides, there are other avenues for other inmates to make positive changes. They may be better suited to complete a repetitive task that does not require the skill set demanded of those who care for and train dogs. Correctional administrators have understandably been reluctant to include inmates who have lengthy records of behavioral maladjustment in prison dog programs. Placement of such inmates could be detrimental to program goals and could place the dogs at risk. PDPs offer inmates the opportunity to interact with a living being that has no interest in their criminal past (Aufderheide 2016). Interacting with dogs gives inmates an opportunity to reduce stress and help eliminate negative thinking (Harkrader et al. 2004). These programs have also shown to reduce inmate use of drugs and alcohol (Harkrader et al. 2004). Furthermore, prison dog programs facilitate interactions with civilians, staff members, and help reinforce law-abiding norms and values (Antonio and Klunk 2014).

Sentence Criteria

Dog programs in prison may also evaluate the length of time the inmate has remaining to serve in the selection process. Lengthier sentences allow inmates the opportunity to establish a bond with their dogs and give the inmate adequate time to complete training modules. Time remaining to serve is especially important for the training of service dogs because it takes a great deal of time to develop the necessary skills to train a puppy. This is particularly true when preparing leader dogs for the blind; programs such as Canine Partners for Life may be two years in length. In contrast, programs that help shelter dogs to become more adoptable through house training and basic obedience typically run for 12 weeks or less, so the same inmates could participate for several rotations of dog training (Harkrader et al. 2004). Even when every effort is made to plan for the same inmate or inmate team to work with a dog throughout the program, this can be subject to change. In one service dog program, new state legislation that reduced sentence time for juvenile offenders who had committed nonviolent offenses affected two of the inmate/trainers in the group. They were released earlier than anticipated so the other trainer in the pair assigned to each dog took over as primary trainer and a new program participant was assigned as the secondary trainer.

The inclusion of minimum sentences may exclude jails or pretrial populations who could be transferred or released at any moment (Cusack 2015). Some facilities also require inmates to be at their facility for a specified period of time prior to participation in a dog training program. This allows the correctional staff the ability to monitor the behavior and adjustment of the inmate prior to program participation. Additionally, the dogs may benefit from training with inmates who are stable and accustomed to the environment of the facility (Cusack 2015).

Education Criteria

Another criterion that may be considered in the selection of inmate dog trainers is education. For most programs, inmates must be able to understand written instructions and information to adequately train dogs. Thus, literacy levels enter into the selection process. This is especially true for programs that include some sort of testing for a handler/dog team (e.g., passing the American Kennel Club's Canine Good Citizen, a therapy dog test, or public access test) or that have partnered with a vocational or postsecondary education program offered at the facility (see Chap. 12).

An example of educational and vocational components being infused in dog training is in the Animal Depending on Prison Time (ADOPT) program. The ADOPT program has been implemented at the Madison Correctional Facility and Rockville Correctional Facility in Indiana. The ADOPT program takes dogs from local shelters and trains them for adoption. Inmates who participate in the ADOPT program may complete a Department of Labor apprenticeship. To complete the apprenticeship, inmates must complete 3600 hours of on-the-job training and 288 hours of related training on work readiness training in a two-year time frame. Inmates are required to sign an apprenticeship agreement and the agreement may be terminated by either the apprentice or sponsor during a 90-day probationary period. Upon completion of the program, the inmate has the option of leaving the program or remaining as a journey worker if a position is available.

It is known that inmates often have great deficits in education and vocational training. Approximately 64% of inmates have a high school diploma or credential (Rampey et al. 2016); however, while they remain stalled at the high school level, most of their cohorts "on the outside" are attending college. In 2016, the most recent year for which statistics are available, the Bureau of Labor Statistics reported that 69.7% of students who graduated high school in 2016 were enrolled in college (Thompson 2019). Given that many inmates' work history and skills are below the national average, the need for vocational programs is great (Lawrence et al. 2002). Inmate programming has not kept pace with the extraordinary number of inmates entering the correctional system. Correctional administrators acknowledge that educational programs make better use of inmates' time and often help to reinforce law-abiding values and norms (Antonio and Klunk 2014). Engaging in meaningful programming also gives inmates the opportunity to present themselves as positive role models to other inmates (Furst 2006).

In many instances, new handlers are matched with more experienced handlers to assess the new handler's suitability for the program while providing peer mentorship. Some programs offer "stackable" credentials (Rampey et al. 2016). In the Florida Department of Corrections, for example, it is possible for inmates to progress through a career ladder, commencing with the role of handler; next, to basic trainer; then, to intermediate trainer, and finally to advanced trainer (Florida Department of Corrections 2018). Each position within this hierarchy requires a minimum of 16 weeks of training. If an inmate completes the highest credential, he/she may remain in the program as a canine aide to maintain program consistency (Florida Department of Corrections 2018).

The establishment of progressive degrees of responsibility allows staff, inmates, and contractors to evaluate the inmate's progression in acquiring dog training skills and simultaneously assess the progress of the dog at each point. Such a hierarchy also allows inmates the opportunity to gain confidence in their degree of expertise as well as provides tangible markers of advancement. Establishment of a hierarchy also helps maintain program consistency as inmates are retained to serve as tutors or mentors who can support inexperienced dog handlers.

The addition of dog training programs has assisted in filling the void of quality programming in correctional facilities. When such programs include a cost-effective educational and/or vocational component, they not only positively impact the culture inside of the facility but also aid inmates in the transition to society by giving them practical work skills (see Chap. 12). Participation in educational programs also is a way of documenting progress to others and may serve as a reentry tool upon inmates' release.

Unsatisfactory Progress in the Program

Partly by virtue of the rigorous selection process, disciplinary infractions in prison dog programs are a relatively rare occurrence. Nevertheless, in many ways, the professionals in a prison dog program need to function as gatekeepers. Not only do they decide who gets admitted to the program, they also need to consider when disciplinary measures are warranted. The partners in the process need to agree, in advance of an incident, how to expel an inmate from the program. Although it is difficult to do, particularly when an inmate was considered to be a suitable candidate at the outset, inmates need to be notified about minor infractions, given sanctions for more serious issues, and dropped from the program for major violations of policies and rules. Those responsible for the programs must step in when an offender cannot or will not "do right by the dog." Questions to consider include:

1. *What types of behavior will result in a warning, a sanction, or outright dismissal from the program?* Practically everyone involved with prison dog programs would concur that abuse of an animal is grounds for being dismissed from the program. Many service dog providers view their animals as extremely valuable and will want to take swift action to identify another suitable trainer if the current one violates rules that will jeopardize the dogs' ability to fill the

service dog role. A good example is feeding the dogs human food. This is forbidden because service dogs will be permitted into restaurants and need to represent their service dog organizations well. Less severe but still a threat to the dog's progress is an inmate's resistance to implementing the dog training methods of the organization. Reputable dog trainers generally support the least intrusive, minimally aversive (acronym, LIMA) methods of dog training that rely on positive reinforcement to achieve behavioral change in dogs (International Association of Animal Behavior Consultants 2019). An inmate might be very skeptical of more positive training methods or refuse to comply with a professional dog trainer's instructions. In one dog training program, inmates were directed to use a higher-pitched, enthusiastic voice to signal that a dog had performed a command correctly but an inmate who prided himself on being "tough" could not bring himself to do this, even after it was discussed with him. Finally, the supervisors in the program "demoted" him but making his dog-training partner the primary for a while—something that got his attention and convinced him to change. At other times, it is a minor thing, such as using the word "down" to mean "off" when correcting a puppy for jumping up on people, and this can be addressed with a warning.

2. *What "counts" as evidence of having committed the offense?* In dog programs, the animals' behavior frequently is a clear indicator that something is not right. Training for staff that makes them aware of signs of stress in canines is important. Such behaviors as excessive lip licking, yawning, a tucked tail, or "whale eye" in which the whites of eyes are showing, are commonly seen in stressed out dogs. A good source for easy to understand visuals on this topic are the free posters originally developed by veterinarian Sophia Han (https://drsophiayin.com/blog/entry/free-downloads-posters-handouts-and-more/).

   Where shelter animals are concerned, it can be difficult to sort out the issues that a dog arrived with versus those that might be attributable to improper training methods, but unusual changes often are a clue. For instance, a dog that seems shy all of a sudden is communicating that there is a problem. All partners in the program need to share information as a way of documenting problems. Some issues can be identified by consulting records, such as observational notes gathered while working with the dog, class attendance records, a log of visits to other areas of the facility and inventories of materials and medications. Modern prisons and jails typically have sophisticated surveillance systems, so positioning cameras in a way that will reveal handlers' treatment of dogs is important. Areas such as the outdoor exercise yard for dogs may reveal some inappropriate training approaches that violate what is being taught during class. In light of the prison "code" of not informing on other offenders, there will need to be a confidential reporting system to let program supervisors know about serious infractions. It is important to encourage a spirit of asking for help rather than telling on one another, so some training on how to diplomatically share a concern with another trainer is warranted as well. Although most PDPs provide a clear statement about the rules, the penalties for particularly important offenses, and the grounds for dismissal from the program at the start of the program, these documents ought to be revisited from time to time.

3. *How will the problem be communicated to the inmate?* Policies and procedures need to spell out how unsatisfactory progress will be addressed. Suppose that one shelter dog bites another because an inmate failed to keep a dog leashed and at a distance from other new shelter arrivals. First of all, both the inmate's and the dog's intentions matter; so does the severity of the outcome. If the inmate was encouraging the dogs to fight, that is more serious than a lapse in judgment only. If the dog that bit was startled and the bite was a nip that did not break the skin, that is very different from a situation that required emergency veterinary treatment. Communicating about this incident with the inmate would involve, at the very least: (1) a dog bite policy that has been shared with all stakeholders, (2) the state laws pertaining to dog bite incidents, (3) the rules for dog handlers provided by the shelter, (4) an incident reporting form. An inmate should be notified in person and in writing that this was a serious mistake, one that jeopardized the safety of others. That communication should also make the consequences clear.

Conclusion

Usually when the instructor for the inmate/trainers' class would visit the prison, the staff would ask, "Do you want to see how the pups are doing?" and they would stop by the pod where the inmates training service dogs are housed. On one such occasion, an inmate who had not yet begun working with the dogs as a trainer had just finished wiping up the floor with a spray bottle of disinfectant and a cloth. He sighed and sank into a chair. One trainer demonstrated the commands that his 5-month old pup was learning. Afterwards, he put the pup in a sit so that the visitor could pet it. The puppy got excited and deposited a few drops of urine on the floor. With that, the inmate/trainer scooped the puppy up in his arms and said "Aww, you're a big boy now, you don't need to do that anymore." Meanwhile, the inmate who had just finished cleaning came over and calmly wiped up the accident.

This situation illustrates some of the traits that are sought in inmates who work with dog programs. They need to feel kindly toward dogs, tolerant of their inevitable mistakes, patient in caring for them, accepting of the responsibility for clean-up, able to control frustration, and resistant to the notion that a dog is trying to make them look bad.

As this chapter has detailed, prison dog programs are exceptionally diverse and demanding. Being among the few selected to participate and being entrusted with the care of another living being can be a form of affirmation for inmates. One woman said that she was motivated to apply for the dog program because of the looks on the inmate/trainers' faces; she wanted to look that way (Minton et al. 2015). An important guidepost for making choices about inmates is to consider what the best program participants have to say after they are given the opportunity to work with dogs in a corrections context. To illustrate, the Prison Greyhound program pairs inmates with former race track dogs to prepare the animals for life as family pets. As part of their evaluation process, inmate/trainers are asked to write answers to several questions about (1) how the program benefits them, (2) how it changes their day-to-day lives, and (3) what participation in the program means to them. Some of their responses were:

> …others see me helping and doing something positive. It shows them all that I have a caring heart. I'm given a chance to do something wonderful. Something meaningful. It means a bunch to me. It means the world to me. I love these dogs.

> 'Cause if it wasn't for these dogs, I wouldn't have the responsibility…the responsibility helps me stay out of trouble. It gives me something to look forward to every morning I wake up.

> it gives me a sense of purpose and I find that I'm happier when I'm able to help change these dogs' lives. It means that I'm playing a part in giving these dogs a new home and providing the family with a new family member and that means a lot.

> It allows me to remember my own dogs and how much I miss and need them in my life…It means I can do my time with love and caring in my life in a place where love and caring is hard to come by.

Looking at these outcomes for inmates offers direction to those responsible for beginning new programs and improving existing ones. Prison dog program staff and partners need to ask: Who, among the inmates, is most likely to respond in ways that help dogs to realize their full potential and benefit the people who are waiting to welcome those canine "graduates" into their families? Inmate/trainer screening and selection is an answer to this question.

References

Achen, P. (2012). Some Yacolt prison inmates given pet cats. *Seattle Times,* April 10. http://seattletimes.com/html/localnews/2017950824_apwacatsintheclink2ndldwritethru.htm.

Anonymous inmate handler. (2015). SCI Cambridge Springs. *All Paws on Deck, 2*(1), 23.

Antonio, M. E., & Klunk, F. R. (2014). Forty years after "what works?": Examining offender programming in Pennsylvania's board of probation & parole. *Corrections Today, 76*(6), 42–44.

Arkow, P. (2019). The "dark side" of the human-animal bond. In L. Kogan & C. Blazina (Eds.), *Clinician's guide to treating companion animal issues: Addressing human-animal interaction* (pp. 319–346). New York: Academic Press.

Aufderheide, C. (2016). *The application and effects of service dog training by inmates to self-perception and self-other overlap as a rehabilitative approach to incarceration.* (Unpublished Master's thesis). University of Oregon, Eugene, Oregon. Available: https://scholarsbank.uoregon.edu/xmlui/bitstream/handle/1794/20667/Aufderheide_oregon_0171N_11514.pdf?sequence=1&isAllowed=y.

Britton, D. M., & Button, A. (2006). Prison pups: Assessing the effects of dog training programs in correctional facilities. *Journal of Family Social Work, 9*(4), 79–95.

Cusack, C. M. (2015). *Animals and criminal justice.* New York, NY: Routledge.

Florida Department of Corrections. (2018, February 13). Service dog training and canine obedience training for canine adoptions, procedure 506.102.
Furst, G. (2006). Prison-based animal programs: A national survey. *The Prison Journal, 86*(4), 407–430.
Gaes, G., Wallace, S., Gilman, E., Klein-Saffran, J., & Suppa, S. (2002). The influence of prison gang affiliation on violence and other prison misconduct. *Prison Journal, 82,* 359–385.
Griffin, M. L., & Hepburn, J. R. (2006). The effect of gang affiliation on violent misconduct among inmates during the early years of confinement. *Criminal Justice and Behavior, 33*(4), 419–448.
Han, T. M., Flynn, E., Winchell, J., Gould, E., & Gandenberg, J. (2018). *Prison-based dog training programs: Standard Protocol.* Denver: Institute for Human-Animal Connections. https://animalstudiesrepository.org/cgi/viewcontent.cgi?article=1001&context=anitobe.
Harkrader, T., Burke, T. W., & Owen, S. S. (2004). Pound puppies: The rehabilitative uses of dogs in correctional facilities. *Corrections Today, 66*(2), 74–79.
Hoffer, T., Hargreaves-Cormany, H., Muirhead, Y., & Meloy, J. R. (2018). *Violence in animal cruelty offenders.* New York: Springer Briefs in Psychology and Behavioral Criminology.
International Association of Animal Behavior Consultants. (2019). *IAABC position statement on LIMA*. Retrieved March 3, 2019 form: https://m.iaabc.org/joint-standards-of-practice/.
Lawrence, S., Mears, D., Dubin, G., & Travis, J. (2002, May). *The practice and promise of prison programming.* Washington, DC: The Urban Institute.
Minton, C. A., Perez, P. R., & Miller, K. (2015). Voices from behind prison walls. *Society & Animals, 23,* 484–501. https://doi.org/10.1163/15685306-12341379.
Moneymaker, J., & Strimple, E. (1991). Animals and inmates: A sharing companionship behind bars. *Journal of Inmate Rehabilitation, 16*(3–4), 133–152.
National Broadcasting Company. (2006). *Prisoners rehabilitate death row dogs*. October 3. http://www.nbcnews.com/id/15014860/ns/health-pet_health/t/prisoners-rehabilitate-death-row-dogs/#.UjVEEMasim4.
Pendleton Correctional Facility. (2017, November 14). Indiana Canine Assistance Network "ICAN", Facility Directive 172.
Rampey, B. D., Keiper, S., Mohadjer, L., Krenzke, T., Li, J., Thornton, N., & Hogan, J. (2016). *Highlights from the U.S. PIAAC survey of incarcerated adults: Their skills, work experience, education, and training: Program for the international assessment of adult competencies: 2014 (NCES 2016-040).* U.S. Department of Education. Washington, DC: National Center for Education Statistics. Retrieved May 22, 2019 from http://nces.ed.gov/pubsearch.
Rockville Correctional Facility. (2013, December 1). ADOPT Apprenticeship Program, Facility Directive 14-01.
Tewksbury, R., Connor, D. P., & Denney, A. S. (2014). Disciplinary infractions behind bars: An exploration of importation and deprivation theories. *Criminal Justice Review, 39*(2), 201–218.
Thompson, V. (2019). *What percentage of students attend college after graduation?* Retrieved March 3, 2019 from: https://www.theclassroom.com/percentage-high-school-students-attend-college-after-graduation-1423.html.
Washington Department of Corrections. (2016, January 1). Inmate Dog/Cat Programs, Policy DOC 700.350.
Weiss, R. (2001). "Repatriating" low-wage work: The political economy of prison labor reprivatization in the postindustrial United States. *Criminology, 39,* 253–291.

Chapter 8
Designing and Delivering a Curriculum Matched to Program Goals

Mary Renck Jalongo

Introduction

A highly respected, thriving dog training club requested a presentation at their monthly meeting about the dog training program at the state correctional facility. The staff member who directed the prison program brought along one of the service dogs in training puppies, a six-month-old yellow Labrador retriever. Accompanying her was a retired professor who designed and was helping to teach courses for the inmates at the prison. Several members of the audience knew the latter as a fellow student in obedience classes with her dogs that were registered and insured with Alliance of Therapy Dogs. The presenter had said "As people who know dogs, you realize that one limitation of training in a correctional facility is that it is a very structured environment that would not provide the range of experiences a service dog needs. So, we take the dogs out of the facility to socialize them." One member of the audience said, "Who is **we**? *Do you mean the* **inmates** *are allowed to go out in the community?" After being reassured that this was not the case and that "we" referred to staff and volunteers, he said "Oh, OK. I would not be in favor of letting them out, that's for sure." The prison project director said, "All of you have dog training experience. Would you like to see what this pup can do?" With that, she placed the puppy on top of a large banquet table so that everyone could see. The puppy did a perfect sit, down, and stay. Placed back on the floor, the pup picked up his leash on command and brought it to her. Then the puppy not only did a perfect heel but when the leash got twisted around his leg, he responded to "fix it" by raising his leg to become disentangled. The group was wowed by the pup's performance. One expert trainer remarked, "I'm hugely impressed by anybody who can just get a Lab puppy not to pull on the leash!" Questions from the audience followed. A breeder wondered if they ever accepted a*

M. R. Jalongo (✉)
Emerita, Indiana University of Pennsylvania, Indiana, PA, USA
e-mail: mjalongo@comcast.net

M. R. Jalongo (ed.), *Prison Dog Programs*,
https://doi.org/10.1007/978-3-030-25618-0_8

donation of a dog that showed promise for service dog work (Answer: Not usually, this particular group has its own breeding program). A person with a difficult to train dog asked if a dog could be sent to the inmates for a sort of boot camp (Answer: No, this is a service dog training program only. The dogs live with teams of two trainer/inmates for 12–18 months.) A mother with a child who had multiple disabilities inquired about the process and costs associated with acquiring a service dog (Response: Copies of an informational brochure and the application form were shared.). Someone wondered what happened to dogs that don't make it as service dogs for various reasons (Answer: They might be used as emotional support animals, therapy dogs, retrained for a different purpose, or go to permanent homes as companion dogs. They are in high demand and there is a wait list because they are already trained.) One person approached the presenter afterwards and said, "You must be really brave. Aren't you worried they will (makes a gesture of grabbing around the neck from behind and slitting the throat) hurt you?"

As this experience out in the community suggests, there are echoes of the "get tough on crime" attitude yet some willingness to concede that the work being accomplished at the state correctional facility is exceptional, even in the opinion of expert dog trainers. When a front-page article about the program appeared in the online newspaper, some community members could sense the reciprocal benefits while others could not. One person wrote "Oh, sure—they commit a crime and then we give them a puppy to play with."

Public resistance to the idea of educating the incarcerated persists, perhaps because "the goals of prison and education are fundamentally different and even contradictory—prison is about punishment and education is about nurturance and learning" (Dick et al. 2016, p. 3). A major barrier to postsecondary education for inmates is the prevailing assumption that they are not worthy of an investment of time, effort, and money. There is an underlying fear that educating inmates represents a drain on taxpayers and a waste of resources that will go unappreciated and fail to yield results. Stated as a question, it is something such as "Why should the average person have to struggle to pay for higher education while these bad people get it for free?" Politicians, dependent on their voters for support, are generally reluctant to take on the challenge of changing public perceptions about postsecondary education for inmates and tend to pursue instead the more popular route of endorsing harsher sentences that supposedly improve public safety (Larkin 2016). Despite rhetoric about rehabilitation and successful re-entry into society only about 6% of inmates in the United States have access to educational programs beyond high school equivalency (Castro et al. 2016). "In prison, safety, security, cost and punishment come first, and then, almost as an afterthought, education and job training" (Dick et al. 2016, p. 37). Yet education is, based on decades of research in criminology, exactly what is needed. In fact, evidence-based and fiscally responsible decisions would dictate that postsecondary education should be a major emphasis in correctional facilities. To illustrate, Ohio spends $1950 annually to reimburse colleges for educating inmates while the average cost per year to incarcerate an individual is about $26,000 (Oakford et al. 2019). In their book, *Prison Education: Maximizing the Potential for Employment and Successful*

Community Reintegration, Leone and Wruble (2017) report that these programs have returned between $12 and $75 in benefits to the state for each dollar spent. Using a sophisticated statistical analysis of the results of thirty-seven years (1980–2017) of rigorous research on correctional education, one research team conducted a meta-analysis of 57 studies that used recidivism as an outcome and 21 that used employment as an outcome. They concluded that inmates participating in correctional education were 28% less likely to recidivate than those who did not participate in correctional education programs (Bozick et al. 2018). Granted, participation in programs that involve responsibility for canines is selective and, it has to be, given animal welfare considerations. Nevertheless, interviews conducted with participants suggest that even the cream of the inmate crop would not have progressed that far and fast in the absence of access to high-quality programming (see Chap. 1). Both from a more enlightened rehabilitative perspective on corrections and from a hard-line money-saving stance, postsecondary education for inmates makes sense, yet the general public is uniformed, misinformed, or simply unwilling to accept such ideas. In this chapter, we raise three key points about postsecondary education for offenders: (1) inmates represent a unique group of students, (2) a planned sequence for learning that is aligned with the philosophy and institutional missions is a key component, and (3) effective instructors who rely on evidence-based methods of teaching are essential.

Common Characteristics of Inmates as Learners

Taken as a group, inmates differ from the traditional college student in many important ways beyond the fact that they have been convicted of crimes. Aborn (2005), for example, uses the following statistics to explain the situation of female inmates:

> Every day our jails and prisons release approximately 177 women. On average they will be 35 years old, fewer than 44 will be married, and 118 will have minor children. Of those with children 26 will have an alcohol dependence problem and 37 will have a diagnosed mental illness. Seventy-four will not have finished high school, and more than half will be unemployed before their arrest. With little more than the proverbial bus ticket and pocket money, these women will leave prison and be told to stay out of trouble. Not surprisingly, the net result is that within three years of leaving prison, 101 will commit a new offense and 69 will go back to jail. (p. 1)

Given statistics such as these, not just any pre-existing program borrowed from a postsecondary institution will do; some caveats are in order. The process of planning education for inmates has to be tailored to their needs.

1. *Educational attainment*. Postsecondary education requires a high school diploma or its equivalent (the General Education Diploma or GED). If an institution does not have such a program, it may need to offer one to enable

more inmates to "stack" their credentials and eventually pursue higher/further education. Many inmates have academic challenges in literacy and mathematics; they also may have learning disabilities to contend with. In one major study, 4% of the prison population had earned an associate degree and 1% had earned a bachelor's degree. Among the general U.S. population, 9% hold an associate degree and 17% a baccalaureate (Vera Institute of Justice and Georgetown University Center on Poverty and Equality 2019). Where jobs in dog care and training are concerned, most can be pursued with practical work experience, evidence of training expertise, and, in the case of veterinary assistant or technician it frequently is a 2-year program. This makes these credentials more within reach of inmates.

2. *Mental health.* Taken as a group, the incarcerated have a higher incidence of mental health issues than the general population (Howells 2002). "The research literature continues to demonstrate a need for programs to provide offenders with opportunities to change behaviors and address the psychosocial problems resulting in (and then from) their incarceration" (Minton et al. 2015, p. 484). Dissertation research suggests that, overall, prisoners have higher levels of depression, anxiety and stress (Loe 2015; Swyers 2014; Zimmer 2013). Dogs, in particular, can evoke bonds that are similar to those experienced with a close family member or friend and therefore provide a sense of social support (Aufderheide 2016).
3. *Work history.* Inmates typically do not have jobs when they enter the penal system. In cognitive psychology, there is a concept called schema theory that is pertinent here. In a nutshell, schema theory argues that what learners already know is the chief determinant of what they can come to know; in other words, prior knowledge forms the foundation for learning. Given this limited prior work experience, they would have fewer skills to transfer and apply to a new role. This may be particularly true for academic tasks. Habits–such as submitting assignments in a timely fashion, completing a project with a small group, or using study skills—may be just as important to learn as the content. Before beginning to work with a dog program, inmates typically have a work history within the institution that can serve as a predictor of commitment. By working with dogs intensively during their incarceration, it is possible for inmates to build a skill set that can be applied not only to continue with the dog program but also to other roles in the community post release.
4. *Limited financial resources.* In the past, inmates were not eligible for Pell Grants for college students. Although there has been some effort recently to make exceptions to this rule on an experimental basis, the reality is that few inmates have the family support to pursue a traditional 4-year degree, even with access to low-interest loans. Eligibility for a Second Chance Pell Grant has several stipulations: (1) the inmate must be within five years of release, (2) be a minimum-risk or model prisoner, and (3) have a high school diploma or General Equivalency Development (GED) certificate (Gray 2018). In one study involving five different states almost none of the correctional facilities that began 4-year degree programs were able to sustain them due to high tuition

costs (Rampey et al. 2016). Most dog care and training programs in correctional facilities are linked with humane organizations, nonprofits, and volunteers. This makes them less costly and more sustainable.

5. *Motivation and interest to complete*. Unlike mandatory hard, physical labor used as a punishment, postsecondary education is completely voluntary. Alleviating boredom is a major motivation for enrolling in an educational program while incarcerated (Allred et al. 2013). Thus, the programs offered need to be appealing to inmates initially but also sufficiently interesting that they will persist until completion. Moreover, given the practice of transferring inmates from one institution to another, extended programs of study tend to be interrupted or even terminated when a similar program is not available at the next institution. One advantage of dog care and training programs is that many states now offer them at multiple institutions, making qualifications in this area more portable.
6. *Barriers to learning while incarcerated*. There are numerous obstacles presented to learning in a corrections context. A "realist model" of prison education recognizes that there are (1) *physical barriers* (e.g., lack of access to computers, the Internet, classroom space, and the disruptive force of institutional lockdowns); (2) *institutional barriers* (e.g., limited human, fiscal, and material resources); (3) *relational barriers* (e.g., interpersonal conflict and power imbalances between students and between students and staff) and (4) *psychological barriers* (e.g., living in a high stress environment away from friends and family while trying to develop critical thinking skills and learning complex post-secondary course content) (Fayter 2016; Petey 2016; Szifris et al. 2018). Prison culture often has a streak of anti-intellectualism in which the role of student is disparaged with the labels "college boy" or "college girl" viewed as an insult. With support, inmates can counteract these attitudes. For example, one inmate/student who paused at the doorway of the classroom with a notebook tucked under his arm, and said to another inmate who wanted to talk, "Sorry, man. I'll catch you later—I gotta go to class right now."
7. *Study preferences*. Most dog care and training program administrators recommend pulling their participants out of the general population (GP) so that they are in the company of others with similar educational goals. One good reason to do this is that these inmates will need access to the outdoors with their dogs. Another rationale is that it helps to prevent situations where inmates who are not in the program threaten or mistreat dogs to manipulate/intimidate trainers, incite misconduct, or get inmates ejected from the program because they are jealous of the privileges afforded to trainers. Furthermore, if inmates enroll in a postsecondary program it may be too noisy and chaotic for them to read, write, and study out in the general population. Offering a postsecondary program to offenders in a particular section or pod of the correctional facility also facilitates work accomplished with a partner or small group, which many adult learners prefer (Merriam and Bierema 2014). Inmates may be particularly attracted to collaborative work because it can shore up their real or perceived learning deficiencies.

8. *Self-efficacy*. Incarceration tends to undermine feelings of being able to respond to issues that surface in life and influence outcomes, often referred to as self-efficacy (Allred et al. 2013). One benefit of postsecondary education in a carceral setting is that it gives inmates a greater sense that their individual and group efforts have the power to effect social change (Allred et al. 2013). These feelings, sometimes referred to as agency, are reinforced by dog programs when inmates know, for example, that the timid shelter dog they worked with is now living happily in a home.
9. *Clear career pathways*. Decades ago, there was a segment on *60 Minutes* about a professor who taught a philosophy course to inmates. While it is important to respect the intelligence of the incarcerated, it is also questionable whether a course of this type has sufficient practical applicability and would support the employment objectives of some or most inmates. In one embarrassing example, inmates participated as volunteer firefighters only to later discover that they never would be hired as fire fighters because no applicants with a prior felony conviction were eligible. "An impediment to offender reintegration and rehabilitation is so-called collateral consequences—restrictions imposed by state and/or federal laws that apply to people who have been arrested, convicted, or incarcerated. Some laws limit formerly incarcerated individuals' eligibility for certain occupations and professional licensure and substantially restrict employment opportunities" (McCann et al. 2018). When educational programs are proposed in jails and prisons, linkages to gainful employment should be clear.

It is important to note that previous research suggests that merely keeping a pet (Katcher, Beck and Levine 1989) or brief visits from dogs (Conniff et al. 2005; Koda et al. 2015) may evoke positive feelings and elevate mood but they do not appear to exert much effect on the number and severity of incidents of misconduct on the part of inmates. This raises the question about whether the "dosage" of these interactions with dogs is sufficient to support positive behavioral change. In the absence of learning opportunities coupled with a planned curriculum and systematic instruction, the full benefits of bringing canines into a correctional facility may not be realized.

Understanding the Learning Process

Effective learning begins with a motivated individual. The learner must be engaged in the process in order for real learning to occur. Engagement has three different aspects:

1. *Interest* that refers to the individual's attention, concern, and curiosity about a particular topic or task.
2. *Concentration* that makes it possible to focus and filter out distractions.
3. *Enjoyment* that encourages the learner to try again, despite the initial awkwardness that frequently is associated with doing something new and to persist at a task long enough to master the requisite skills (Shernoff 2013).

It may well be the case that, for a person who cares about dogs, interest, concentration and enjoyment are exceptionally high.

The least efficient way of learning is through trial and error. In order to move beyond that, there are four different types of learning (Katz 1993). The basic level is knowledge—acquiring information. A second type of learning is skill—something that has to be developed through practice. In order to make enduring changes, however, two additional types of learning are necessary. One of them is dispositions, defined as customary, deeply engrained ways of approaching situations that advance learning. Where dog training is concerned, for example, an important disposition is patience with the animal rather than frustration or displays of anger. The fourth and final type of learning is feelings. Contrary to the right brain/left brain dichotomy, contemporary neuroscience supports the assertion that emotions play a major role in learning because we think deeply about things we care about (Immordino-Yang 2015). Many inmates have prior experiences of harsh criticism from family members, ridicule from peers, and adversarial interactions with authority figures. Invoking a feeling such as pride in the accomplishment of training a leader dog for the blind may be a relatively new experience that exerts a powerful influence on the person.

Cambourne's Conditions for Learning (2002) have been applied to a wide range of tasks for decades. As a first step, learners need to be engaged in the learning process. This means that they understand the purpose, see themselves as capable of success, and can act without fear of physical or psychological hurt if their attempts are not fully correct at first.

The seven conditions for learning follow.

1. *Immersion*. The context needs to surround the learner with the principles, practices, products and processes that support the learning endeavor. The Prison Pet Partnership Program that started it all in Gig Harbor, WA, for example, has a grooming salon operated by female inmates. A principle of a professional groomer would be to ensure the safety and health of the dog and the staff. A practice that supports this principle would be to require proof of current vaccinations on dogs being groomed and to have the dog's veterinarian's contact information in case of emergency. A groomer would need to become familiar with a wide range of grooming products, such as a soothing oatmeal bath for sensitive skin. A process that groomers would have to master is how to work with the fur or hair coat on various breeds. Immersion is a condition of learning because no one can become a skilled groomer through reading alone.

2. *Demonstration*. Learners need to interact with knowledgeable and enthusiastic role models. One key mechanism for learning is a demonstration—the opportunity to see how something is done properly. If, for example, an animal shelter suddenly gets an orphaned litter of puppies and enlists the help of the inmates, the puppy raisers will need to observe how to bottle feed a tiny puppy and show that they can do this correctly. They also will need to maintain a feeding schedule and keep notes on the puppies' progress that can be shared with veterinary staff.
3. *Expectation*. In effective learning experiences, the learner believes that, with hard work and practice, it is possible to succeed at the task. One way to communicate this is through success stories of dogs and inmates who have completed the program.
4. *Responsibility*. Learners need to take ownership of their own learning, to initiate activities, decide on a course of action, choose the necessary tools, set goals for themselves, and acquire skill in self-evaluation. For example, one of the instructors mentioned that, just because a service dog obeyed the inmate/trainer, that did not necessarily mean it would comply with the requests of the new owner. That is the reason for placement training in which the person with a disability and dog learn to work together as a team with the guidance of a professional dog trainer. The inmates were bothered by this, worrying that their dogs might not listen well to others. So, they had the idea of "trading dogs" from time to time to help their dogs be more versatile. One day when they had the multipurpose room for a sort of indoor recess for the pups, they set up a little obstacle/agility course using the available equipment and handlers worked with one another's dogs to put them through their paces.
5. *Guided Practice*. Most professional dog trainers recognize that it often is the owner, rather than the dog, that is most difficult to "train". This is where the learning condition of guided practice comes in. It means that, rather than leaving learners to their own devices, they are observed while they are performing the task and given corrective feedback as necessary. It is important for inmate/trainers to patiently make gentle corrections and set limits for puppies and dogs in training. Likewise, the professional dog trainers involved in the program need to use positive methods and to be firm about what behaviors will not be tolerated from the inmates.
6. *Approximations*. Contrary to simplistic ideas about learning, it is neither accomplished all at once nor does it progress in a neat, stair step fashion. Rather, if people learn from their mistakes, they try again after a less-than-perfect effort, change their behavior in a positive direction, and make progress toward their goal. One common issue with dogs is a tendency to dash through a doorway. Bolting out the door can result in injury to the animal as well as the owner, particularly if the owner is a young child, elderly, or has a disability. Inmate/trainers need to recognize that a dog might pause briefly in a doorway and that good behavior needs to be rewarded immediately. By gradually increasing the length of time the dog will pause they will achieve reliable control at the doorway.

7. *Response*. The feedback given to learners needs to be timely, constructive, relevant, and nonthreatening. New Hope Assistance Dogs, for example, visits State Correctional Institution Pine Grove on a monthly basis. At that time, each team of innate/trainers working with one of the puppies shows them the pup's progress. At one such session when the pups were 14 weeks old, one of the new handlers was worried that his pup had not learned the commands well enough. He explained that he had to discontinue the recommended practice of placing a portion of the dog's daily food intake in a treat pouch and using it as a training reward because the pup was having some digestive issues. He was worried that the pup had not performed well. The trainers reassured him that this was not the case. They reminded the men that their meeting created some new distractions—different people, new smells, and the furry cuffed and laced winter boots of two visitors. All of the young pups had demonstrated "watch me", "sit", "down" and a reasonably good "heel" so the service dog providers were well satisfied with the results. As they got ready to leave, one of the experienced dog trainers said, "If there's anything we aren't doing right or that you want us to start on, just tell us."

Using these conditions for learning as a foundation, the prison dog program can transition to developing a curriculum supported by effective instruction.

Curriculum and Instruction Basics

While there are many different theories and myriad models of curriculum and instruction, it is helpful to focus on the basics where dog care and training programs in correctional facilities are concerned. At its very essence, curriculum and instruction hinges on alignment among a few key components: (1) the underlying philosophy, (2) the Institutional mission, (3) the specific goals of the program, (4) a planned sequence of experiences for the learners, and (5) assessment of the outcomes. To illustrate, the remainder of this chapter will address each of these components.

The Underlying Philosophy

A prevailing public image of the incarcerated characterizes them as cruel, evil, indifferent to others' suffering and prone to violence. Surely there are some that fit that description. However, there are other people who have done far more harm to themselves or unintentional harm to others. Given the criteria that are in wide use to select inmates for these programs (e.g., no history of cruelty, abuse, neglect or violent crimes against people or animals), prison dog program participants are apt to be the latter rather than the former. Although many people would assume that the prison population would be the last place to attempt to develop traits such as compassion, empathy, altruism, and kindness that is exactly what needs to occur in highly effective programs. Inmates need humane education.

When most people hear the words "humane education," they immediately think about their local animal rescue and shelter organizations; however, this is just one part of the idea. World Animal Net (2012) defines humane education as "a process that encourages an understanding of the need for compassion and respect for people, animals and the environment and recognizes the interdependence of all living things". Modern concepts of humane education include broader humanistic, environmental, and social justice frameworks (Arbour et al. 2009) as well as guardianship of the earth, or sustainability. The Institute for Humane Education explains the concept as follows: "Humane education not only instills the desire and capacity to live with compassion, integrity, and wisdom, but as a process, it also provides the knowledge and tools to put our values into action in meaningful and far reaching ways." Founder Zoe Weil describes four key elements that comprise quality humane education. They are:

1. To provide students with accurate information about the pressing challenges of our time
2. To foster the 3 Cs of curiosity, creativity, and critical thinking
3. To nurture the 3 Rs of reverence, respect, and responsibility
4. To offer positive choices and the tools for problem solving

She goes on to say that humane education "expands the body of knowledge we consider important, offers the skill set to address entrenched and pervasive problems, and provides the ethical underpinnings that motivate us to do good in the world, to be of service…" (Weil 2013, p. 233).

Empathy is the cornerstone to humane education. Contemporary neuroscience suggests that the development of human empathy begins with an emotional response, requires an apprehension of emotions in others, and relies on efforts to control emotions; as such, it forges links among empathy, prosocial behavior, and regulation of aggression (Decety 2010). Puppies and dogs have the ability to evoke emotional responses from people. When a group of four Labrador retriever puppies arrived at one state prison, the service dog providers carried them through the facility to the inmate/trainers' pod and handed a puppy to each primary trainer. They held the squirming pups for a few moments but quickly decided to get down on the floor, play with them, and make positive comments about the pups' appearance and behavior. Likewise, when shelter dogs come into a facility, there is a "common ground" of being confined, rejected, and having an uncertain future. Programs that bring offenders together with dogs and puppies appear to be uniquely well suited to support the development of empathy (Seivert 2014).

The Mission of Each Partner Institution

Incarceration tends to exert a sort of gravitational pull in the direction of decline. There is plenty of bad company, lack of contact with the outside world, and limited opportunity to improve literacy skills. On all three counts, participation in a dog program can be uplifting. Dog programs often put inmates in the company of some exceptionally dedicated and altruistic individuals, such as animal rescuers, veterinary staff, service dog providers, program sponsors, community volunteers, and so forth. These interactions create a conduit for learning about important issues as well. Participation in a planned curriculum also boosts literacy skills. The inmate who previously kept his or her head down and kept quiet to avoid altercations is now encouraged to become a more skilled communicator in conversation, during class discussion, and through varied reading/writing tasks. Feelings of being disregarded, rejected, reviled can be counteracted by being entrusted with the care of another living creature and accomplishing a task that is important, both for the dog and the future owner. In the case of shelter dogs, an inmate/trainer may be literally saving the dog's life if euthanasia rates in overcrowded shelters are any indication. In the case of training a service dog for a veteran with PTSD, the inmate/trainer may be saving a person's life, if statistics on suicide in the military are any indication. There is little question that having a job involving dogs is regarded as important work within the prison culture or, as one inmate put it, "you have to be *really* good to get into that program."

Mission statements communicate values and goals to external constituencies (Evans et al. 2019). To illustrate, a service dog training program at State Correctional Institution (SCI) Pine Grove in Indiana, Pennsylvania the offers a Certificate of Completion in Humane Education and Dog Training represents a partnership among three institutions: (1) The Pennsylvania Department of Corrections, (2) Indiana University of Pennsylvania's noncredit courses for community members, and (3) New Hope Assistance Dogs. Their missions are:

- *Pennsylvania Department of Corrections* operates as one team, embraces diversity, and commits to enhancing public safety. We are proud of our reputation as leaders in the corrections field. Our mission is to reduce criminal behavior by providing individualized treatment and education to offenders, resulting in successful community reintegration through accountability and positive change.
- *The Office of Extended Studies at Indiana University of Pennsylvania's* mission is to support our community and provide the professional training and adult enrichment courses that you need .... We engage the local and regional community to provide adult noncredit education, training, and skill development courses.
- *New Hope Assistance Dogs, Inc.* is a charitable organization (501c3) dedicated to enable dogs to enhance the lives of individuals with disabilities and to educate the general public.

Mission statements matter because they are a touchstone that guides program development. Any policy or practice and any content, processes, or experiences that are inconsistent with the mission are out of bounds.

Content, Processes, and Relevant Work Experience

At its simplest, curriculum is a planned sequence of content and experiences consistent with a program's mission and matched to programmatic goals. Fundamentally, it is an answer to the question, "What should inmates know, understand and be able to do in order to successfully complete this dog program? One curricular strategy is referred to as "backward design," so named because planners begin with the outcome and match content and experiences to it (https://www.learning-theories.com/backward-design.html). If the hope is that some inmates would pursue work with dogs in the future as trainers, groomers, shelter personnel, and veterinary support staff, the planning begins by examining what is necessary to fulfill those roles. At the least, it would include understanding responsible dog care and mastery of reward-based dog training practices.

As a starting point for responsible dog care, share the American Kennel Club's Canine Good Citizen Program that requires dog owners to sign a Responsible Dog Care contract, which can be adapted for use with the inmate/trainers. Include topics that experienced instructors in courses for inmates recommend, such as dog fighting, puppy mills, animal cruelty around the world, animal testing, and animals harmed in the entertainment industry (Johnson and Bruneau 2016). It is also important to include dog laws governing such issues as licensing, cruel confinement, adequate shelter, leash laws, tethering regulations, and exposure to excessive heat/cold.

The curriculum that accompanies a dog training program needs to be dogcentric to a considerable extent. Enlightened, effective, humane, evidence-based methods of dog training are essential a prison dog project. Reward-based training has been shown to increase the bond between human and canine (Greenebaum 2010). Expert dog trainers also need to know how to find things out and how to seek out resources "such as veterinarians, trainers, and behaviorists" (Irvine 2004, p. 66). Greenebaum (2010) asserts that enlightened views of dog training are grounded in the development of meaningful, nonexploitive relationships with dogs and expanding knowledge about canine behavior, nutrition, health, history, breed characteristics, training, and the variety of things that enrich a dog's life. It also results in rapport with a dog based on an active interest in their emotions, communications, and cognition. This approach to training also includes different training tools, such as types of collars, that are permitted and ones that are banned from use by leading professional organizations. The Alliance of Therapy Dogs, for example, does not permit the use of choke, prong, or shock collars. All of these things need to be part of the curriculum.

Handlers need to have access to a variety of resource materials: "books, magazines, manuals, worksheets, handouts, or a video library that they can use when they are unable to receive direct support from a dog trainer" (Han et al. 2018, p. 36). Print copies of statements from groups such as the American Veterinary Medical Association or the American Humane Association can be printed out. If you include material on dog training, be certain to check with partners first to make sure that the advice does not conflict with their training philosophy and practices. Published documents of respected dog training organizations, such as the International Association of Animal Behavior Consultants (IAABC), the Association of Professional Dog Trainers (APDT), and the Certification Council for Professional Dog Trainers (CCPDT) are another type of material that is useful. Within your community, identify the "dog people" who subscribe to publications that would make good reading material for inmates. Back issues of *Whole Dog Journal*, *Dogwatch* (published by Cornell University Veterinary School) or breed-specific magazines, such as *Just Labs,* can be provided to inmates after the name and address of the recipient has been removed. For those programs that work with animal shelters, the Humane Society of the United States (HSUS) magazine, *Animal Sheltering* often has helpful articles. Putting the newsletters into 3-ring binders makes them easier to store and manage.

Instructors and Instruction in Postsecondary Education Programs

Where teaching inmates is concerned, not just any instructor will do. Consistent with the philosophy of humane education, teachers of inmates working in dog programs need to embody inquiry, introspection, and integrity; they need to model lifelong learning, self-reflection, and living according to one's values. A postsecondary institution may want to assign instructors based primarily on seniority considerations, with the least experienced faculty chosen for what they perceive as a more difficult assignment. Some possible instructors for postsecondary courses may be too biased, judgmental and/or fearful to function well inside a correctional facility. Others with very liberal views may be attracted to teaching "on the inside" primarily as a way to demonstrate that they are championing a marginalized group. Still others may be too naïve, impractical and easily manipulated—they can be susceptible to getting involved with inmates in an inappropriate way. Highly effective instructors for the incarcerated are: (1) ethical, principled individuals who can be trusted by staff, (2) people who have credibility and credentials from working directly with dogs beyond owning a family dog, (3) exemplary teachers of adult learners with both practical experience and subject matter competence matched to specific course content, (4) professionals with a strong commitment to furthering the education of all their students, and (5) responsible colleagues who have acquired the skills of collaboration and respect the work of those in the corrections field. Those seeking to teach inmates who are unaccustomed to the prison culture have many adjustments to make (Table 8.1).

Table 8.1 Adjustments to teaching in correctional facilities

Orientation. Most correctional facilities require volunteers to participate in some training prior to entering the facility. The orientation typically focuses on security issues and appropriate interactions with inmates. Such things as providing a driver's license to scan, leaving electronic devices behind, turning cars off with keys secured, signing in/out and so forth typically are addressed
Policies. Regular volunteers may be required to have an ID badge that is scanned in and uses their fingerprints. It is important to pay attention to the signage you encounter, such as: All visitors must report to the front desk immediately. No cellphones permitted. Do not use remote start on cars
Dress. Some institutions have a published dress code, so consult this first. Attire should be conservative, casual, and comfortable. Those entering go through a metal detector, so jewelry needs to be kept to a minimum. Shoes with steel shanks might need to be removed. Those with medical implants containing metal need a card from their surgeon like the ones used during security screenings at the airport
Technology. Computer use often is restricted to staff members' offices and kept locked inside, not just because of financial resources, but because of the potential for its misuse. Many modern correctional facilities have computerized systems of surveillance and lock down that could be interrupted by a virus on a USB, for example. Only professionally recorded DVDs may be permitted and there may not be a large monitor and player available to share them with a class
Security against contraband. Almost nothing can be carried in, so leave that water bottle behind. Books have to be searched first and no personal identification can appear anywhere in the book. Food items cannot be brought in. Any print materials you will use while teaching need to be searched, so provide extra time at the front entrance. Be considerate of the staff. There are peak times when people are checking in and checking out, so if you have a box of books to bring over and donate to the library, work around those times
Professional distance. The concept of distance maintained with inmates is both literal and figurative. No physical contact—even a handshake or a kindly touch on the shoulder—is permitted. A casual comment about physical appearance could be interpreted as favoritism or, worse yet, a sexual invitation or harassment. Focus on the learning and the dogs
Reciprocal Trust and Respect. The very nature of a correctional facility requires staff to be observant and cautious; this extends to volunteers as well. There are many instances where a volunteer is responsible—unintentionally or otherwise—for an incident. Staff members are constantly trying to avoid a bad situation from occurring on their watch. Instructors are guests and need to pay attention to what staff tell them to do
Inmate expectations. Postsecondary education frequently is a new experience for inmates. Inmates may have some biases, particularly about university professors, expecting them to be, as the British say, "posh" and ivory tower in their outlook. Instructors who avoid excessive jargon and emphasize the practical can bridge what offenders may initially see as a huge social divide

Key Principles of Effective Instruction

It is particularly important for instructors to capitalize on the findings from decades of research on learning. Many of these findings have been drawn from neuroscientific study of the human brain and implications for the classroom (Sousa 2010). In this section, each evidence-based precept of effective learning is accompanied by an example that was shared with inmates during the requisite 120 h of class time necessary to earn a Certificate of Completion in Humane Education and Dog Training from Indiana University of Pennsylvania.

1. **The brain responds to and recalls powerful visual images**. We anticipate that at least some of the inmates who participate in the dog program will seek to work with dogs in the future, perhaps in a dog rescue or shelter. Therefore, one of our instructors who volunteers at a shelter every week and manages their social media often brings in dramatic examples of dogs needing help. One that sparked outrage, both at the shelter (Four Footed Friends) and among the inmate/trainers was the plight of Wilma. The instructor had used a free photo editing program called PicMonkey to make a poster that showed the dog's condition, posted it on Facebook and Instagram, and published it in the newsletter.

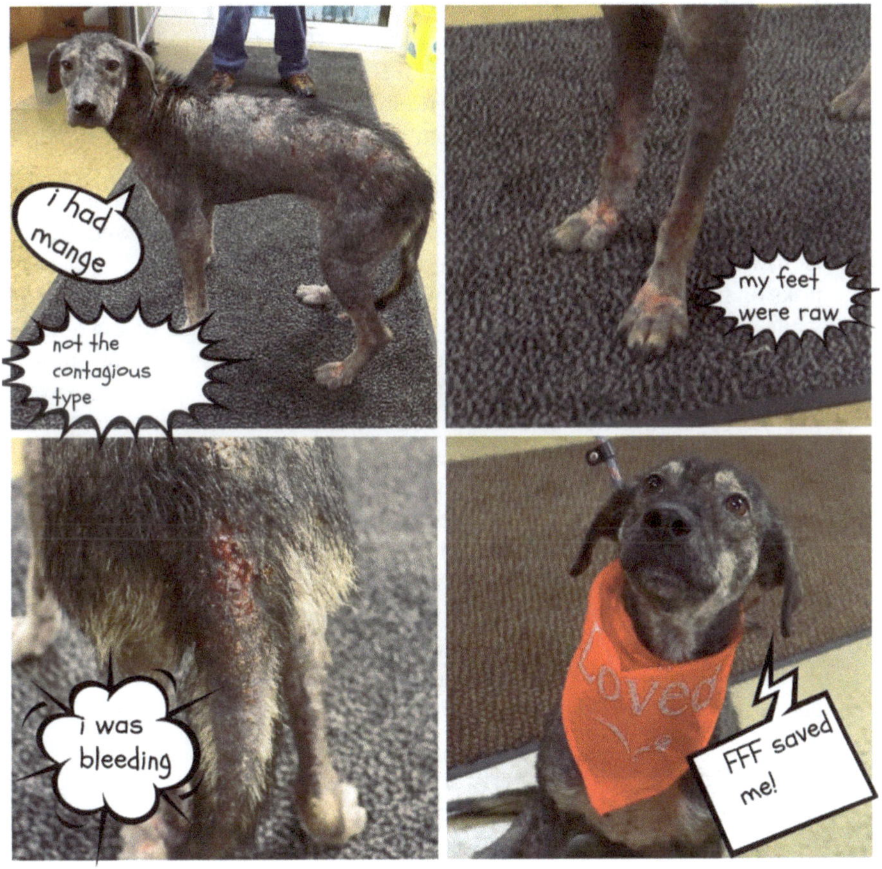

Wilma arrived at the local shelter in horrific condition. *Photo Credit* Mary Renck Jalongo

Wilma was easily the worst case of mange and secondary skin infection that anyone could recall. Almost every square inch of her body had hair loss and open sores. When she walked through the lobby of the shelter, she scattered droplets of blood everywhere. Wilma had been brought in by two people who claimed not to own her yet provided very different accounts of how she came into their possession. The dog was in absolute misery, yet sweet as she could be. It took months of veterinary treatment and medicated baths to restore her to health. Many community members followed her progress and some donated to her medical care. Wilma was adopted as soon as the veterinarian cleared her. Those images of the dog were unforgettable and led to a discussion about why some people become animal rescuers.

2. **Tap into prior learning**. Teaching is more than telling. Invite learners to draw upon their knowledge and experience with thought-provoking questions, such as: "What makes a dog smart? Are there different kinds of intelligence in dogs?" One of the corrections officers who stopped by to see what the inmates were learning in class mentioned the documentary *SEAL Dog* and Cairo, the Belgian Malinois who helped to capture Osama Bin Laden. The instructor had included a photograph of Cairo in the PowerPoint and another staff member remarked, "I'm probably unusual in that I watch the television series, *SEAL Team*, mainly because I want to see how they use Cerberus, their military dog, in their missions." From there, the group went into the latest research on canine cognition, including the work of researchers Adam Miklosi, Brian Hare and Alexandra Horowitz (2014). The inmates were eager to try out some of the dog intelligence tasks on the dogs that they were training, such as hiding an object under a pillow while the dog watches and observing whether or not their dog would try to search for it. Doing this brought questions to the next class, such as questioning the reliability of basing estimates of intelligence on a few specific tasks and the impressive intelligence in a guide dog for the blind, who would deliberately disobey a command to move forward if it sensed danger.
3. **Develop higher-order thinking skills**. Recognize that some of the inmates/students have endured insults to their intelligence and worry about their abilities as learners. The higher-order thinking skills, according to Bloom's Taxonomy, are: application, analysis, synthesis, and evaluation. It is important to design tasks that are not just busy work, assignments that challenge them intellectually. In our program, service dogs were being trained primarily to assist people with mobility issues, so the students were asked to think about service dogs to help people who are deaf through the written assignment in Box 8.1.

Box 8.1 Assistance Dogs for the Deaf

You have decided to work with a group that pulls dogs from shelters to be trained as hearing assistance dogs. Please write answers to the following questions:

1. What would you be looking for in terms of size, age, breed or mix, activity level, and temperament in the dogs?
2. How would you go about assessing a dog prior to beginning training?
3. What specific tasks/commands would these dogs need to learn? Are there particular sounds they would alert to?
4. What information would you want from people who are applying to get a hearing assistance dog?
5. What kinds of problems would you expect to come up in this type of program?
6. What process would you use to match hearing impaired people with a particular dog?
7. How would you ensure that the person and the dog are working well as a team?

4. **Recognize the role of emotions in learning**. Contrary to media portrayals, prison life can be a mind-numbing experience characterized by tedium. When postsecondary instructors first begin working with inmates, the tone can be emotionally flat. It can take a while before they make a comment, offer an opinion, share an experience, or ask a question. Negative emotions can "flood" the brain in such a way that logical thinking processes are derailed, such as when a person panics after reading the first question on an exam. Conversely, positive emotions make learning more efficient and enduring. Experts on college teaching assert that material that evokes strong emotional responses is an important way to energize the classroom (Cavanaugh 2016). A good source for true examples that support the philosophy of humane education is the publicity of various humane and service dog organizations. One particularly memorable story was that of Captain in Box 8.2.

Box 8.2 Captain's Rescue Story

His rescuer decided to name him Captain. He is a German shepherd/hound mix about 2 years old. Here is his story that his rescuers posted on Facebook:

"My husband went to work and he saw this dog close to the dirt road by fields. He thought it was a farm dog. He stopped but the dog ran. It was 15 degrees and raining ice and slush. Ten hours later, on his way back from work, the dog was still there. The dog was shaking, laying by a tree in melted snow. My husband gained the dog's trust. He knew some horrible person abandoned this dog because there was a frozen bowl of dog food beside him. Finally, after a few slim beef jerky sticks, my husband opened the truck and Captain climbed right in. He brought him home. We warmed him up, he ate/drank so fast. We found Four Footed Friends through our vet. FFF agreed to drive halfway to meet us around 8 pm (they're an hour away). All I keep thinking was this sweet dog was thrown into a field, freezing with a bowl of frozen food, staying there for over 10 h, WAITING FOR HIS OWNER DISGUSTING!"

Captain meets Lilac, a chow/golden/beagle mix pup, at the shelter.

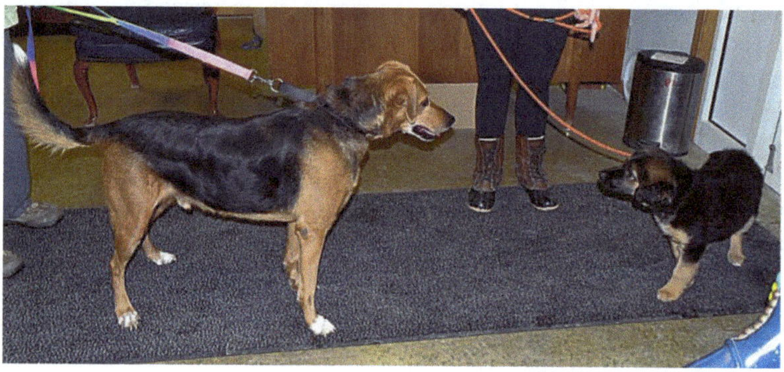

Photo Credit Mary Renck Jalongo

After Captain's story was publicized, several people were interested in adopting him. A family whose German shepherd dog had passed away recently came to meet him, fell in love immediately, and he found his forever home.

Bring Authenticity from the Outside Deliberately choose some controversies that hit close to home. One particularly successful class meeting began with an article about the problem of fake service dogs written by a person with a disability and a genuine service dog (http://servicedogcentral.org/content/On-the-Consequences-of-Fake-and-Undertrained-Service-Dogs). It described people who were purchasing equipment online and claiming that their pet dogs were service animals so that they could take them into stores, restaurants, and so forth. The students could hardly believe it and thought "there ought to be a law" against this practice because it undermined everything that real service dogs accomplished. One of the corrections staff went over to her office and printed off a copy of an ad where you could pay "just $69.95" (a $150 dollar value) and get a vest with the words "service dog" on it as well as ID cards that looked official. The instructor then shared this incident that occurred in the community:

A customer stops at a convenience store and notices a large German shepherd mix dog that is matted and muddy roaming around inside. The dog's owner glares at the customer and says, "I can tell by the look on your face that you don't like dogs. This is my comfort dog. I know the law. I'm allowed to have him here." The customer replies, "Actually, I love dogs but if it is your emotional support dog, it should be on a leash." The owner scoffs and says, "Oh, he's waaayyy past needing a leash." After calling the dog's name several times, it comes over to the owner, stands next to the cash register, and begins sniffing and slobbering on the candy bars on a display rack. With that, the customer responds, "What I really object to is you allowing your dog to lick the candy bar wrappers before people buy the candy."

This incident sparked a lively discussion and was followed up by the material in Box 8.3.

Box 8.3 How to Differentiate a Pet or Emotional Support Animal from a Trained Service Animal Under the American Disabilities Act

Many people say they derive emotional support from a pet's companionship. But ADI believes this relationship between an animal and an individual, standing alone, is not sufficient to cause an animal to be regarded as a service animal. If an individual with a mental, emotional or physiological disability wants access rights with an animal as an accommodation, this animal must be trained as required by the definition of a Service Animal published in the Code of Federal Regulations (CFR) in October 1991 by the U.S. Department of Justice.

The Americans with Disabilities Act (ADA) defines a Service Animal as a Guide Dog, Signal Dog or any other animal that is individually trained to perform tasks or to do work for the benefit of a disabled person. The U.S. Department of Justice illustrated what is meant by this training requirement, giving examples of tasks or work service animals are trained to perform, such as guiding the blind, alerting the deaf to specific sounds and pulling a wheelchair or providing balance support to individuals with a mobility impairment.

"Individual training" is the process of deliberately teaching the animal through the use of rewards and/or corrections to perform a task in response to a command or another stimulus such as the onset of a seizure. A "task" is a certain desired behavior or set of behaviors the animal is trained to perform whenever needed to assist the animal's partner in a way that mitigates his or her disabling condition.

If an animal has not been specifically trained to perform identifiable tasks to assist a disabled individual, it does not qualify under ADA as a service animal.

Source: Assistance Dogs International

During the class, international standards for service dogs (Box 8.4) were distributed:

Box 8.4 Behaviour and Training Standards for All Service Animals

Assistance Dogs International

For over 75 years, Assistance Dogs have worked successfully in public and won the public's acceptance by achieving high behavioral and training standards, that set them apart from pets and other animals. In order to assure the comfort and safety of people with disabilities and the general public, high behavioral and training standards must apply equally to all service animals. ADI believes that all service animals intended for use in public, regardless of species, should be required to meet the same standards required of dogs specifically trained to assist people with disabilities. Any animal that can meet the existing standards for behavior, training, cleanliness, and public appropriateness should be allowed to work in public when accompanied by the person for who's disability it was specifically trained. These standards include:

Public Appropriateness:

- Animal is clean and does not have a foul odor.
- Animal does not urinate or defecate in inappropriate locations.

Behavior:

- Animal does not annoy any member of the general public.
- Animal's conduct does not disrupt the normal course of business.
- Animal works without unnecessary vocalization.
- Animal shows no aggression toward people or other animals.
- Animal does not solicit or steal food or other items from the general public.

Training:

- Animal is specifically trained to perform more than one task to mitigate (lessen) the effects of its partner's disability; said disability being any condition as described by and covered under the ADA that substantially impairs one or more major life functions.
- Animal obeys the commands of its handler.
- Animal works calmly and quietly on a harness, leash, or other tether.

- Animal has been specifically trained to perform its duties in public and is accustomed to being out in public.
- Animal must be able to lie quietly beside the handler without blocking aisles, doorways, etc.
- Animal is trained to urinate or defecate on command.
- Animal stays within 24" of its handler at all times unless the nature of a trained task requires it to be working at a greater distance.

6. **Connect with the larger community**. Back on campus, in an information literacy course, students are given a choice of topics that would assist organizations out in the community. They work with the instructor, a university librarian, to locate authoritative resources that would support the efforts of their community partner. Several students, particularly those majoring in Criminology and Sociology, were interested in the service dog training program at the local state correctional facility. They were eager to learn more and make a contribution to the success of the program by assembling current evidence. Several students remarked that they: chose the topic because they love dogs, had not heard about this before, were familiar with the practice but wanted to learn more about how the program worked and what benefits might result. The students shared their library research with the prison dog staff.

Another link to the outside is television. Many times, inmates see news segments about dogs. During one of the classes, they talked about a rescue group in the area that was bringing Korean meat market dogs to the U.S., rehabilitating them, and putting them up for adoption. They were horrified that anyone would raise a dog for food and it led to a discussion about cultural differences as well as the possible dog training challenges with these animals.

7. **Respond to honest concerns on the inside**. During the orientation that instructors are required to complete before beginning to work with the inmates, they were cautioned about agreeing with an inmate's complaint about the correctional system or the staff. The reason for this is that they might be called upon to testify if an inmate filed a grievance. Nevertheless, there are skilful ways of responding to honest concerns. Interviews with inmates suggest that dealing with people who do not understand or support the prison dog program was the most stressful part of their inmate/trainer role (van Wormer, Kigerl and Hamilton 2015). During one class meeting, an inmate described how a corrections officer wanted to pet his dog and he said, "Nawh, man. He's working and should not be pet when he's got on his vest." but the CO took it as the

inmate just being difficult rather than adhering to the service dog provider's rules. In response, the instructor copied and distributed a one-page summary of appropriate behaviour with service dogs and their handlers or owners (Box 8.5). She also reported that it had been shared with the staff member responsible for professional development of the staff.

Box 8.5 Dos and Don'ts for Behavior Around a Service Dog Team

1. DO speak to the owner/handler rather than the dog.
   The service dog and her handler are a team. If you want to talk to them, always speak to the person first rather than automatically approaching the dog. Remember, the animal is working, and her human's life could depend on her staying focused on her job.
2. DON'T touch the dog without asking permission first.
   Touching or petting a working dog is a distraction and may prevent him from tending to his human partner. The dog may be in the process of completing a command or direction given by his human, and you don't want to interfere.
   Fortunately, most service dogs are trained to stay in work mode until they receive a release command from their handler. That's why many service dogs are able to ignore outside influences.
3. DO keep your own dog a distance away from a working dog
   If you happen to have your dog with you when you encounter a service dog team, don't allow your pet to approach them without first talking with the handler to see if it's permissible.
   Other animals are an obvious distraction to working dogs, and in a worst-case scenario, there could be an altercation between the two animals.
4. DON'T offer food to a service dog
   According to Canine Companions for Independence, "Food is the ultimate distraction to the working dog and can jeopardize the working assistance dog team."
   Not only are food and treats a potential distraction, but many service dogs are fed a specific diet and often on a specific schedule.
5. DO treat the owner/handler with sensitivity and respect
   Asking a service dog's handler personal questions about his or her disability is out of bounds. It's disrespectful and an intrusion of privacy.
   Assume the service dog team can handle things themselves. If you sense they could use your help, ask first. And don't take it personally if your offer is rejected, as there's usually a good reason.
6. DON'T assume a napping service dog is off duty
   All dogs nap, including working dogs. When her handler is sitting or standing for some length of time, it's perfectly natural and appropriate for a service dog to catch a few winks. She's still technically at work, however, so all dos and don'ts remain in effect.

7. DO inform the handler if a service dog approaches you
   If a working dog approaches you, sniffs or nudges you, etc., politely let the handler know. Resist the urge to respond to the dog — the handler will correct the dog.
8. DON'T assume service dogs never get to 'just be dogs'
   Working dogs typically get plenty of R and R and playtime. When they're home and out of their "work clothes," they're free to behave like any other dog. Since the jobs these wonderful animals do are often challenging and stressful, their handlers recognize they need plenty of downtime and exercise.
   Source: The Rules for Service Dogs: Don't Touch or Distract Them https://healthypets.mercola.com/sites/healthypets/archive/2016/01/23/behavior-around-service-dog-team.aspx

8. **Use the narrative mode**. The human brain "runs" on stories. We understand and remember material better when it is in story form. Highly effective professionals use cases to learn about their field; they also develop a repertoire of experiences, organized in story form, to guide their practice. In the media, compelling stories go viral. It is important for instructors of offenders in postsecondary education programs to use the power of narratives. For example, at one of the first class meetings, the inmates viewed the DVD "Dogs on the Inside" (http://www.dogsontheinside.com/) to learn about other inmates working with dogs. During a class on puppy mills, the instructor shared the story of Bill Smith of Main Line Animal Rescue who rented a billboard in Chicago with the message, "Oprah: Do a show on puppy mills. The dogs need you." His action persuaded Winfrey to expose cruelty in commercial dog breeding and pet store chains (https://www.oprah.com/oprahshow/investigating-puppy-mills/all#ixzz5fuLbJll4). While discussing dog fighting, students watched the DVD *The Champions* that documents the surprisingly successful efforts of rescue groups to rehabilitate the dogs seized by humane officers from Michael Vick's facility in Virginia. At a subsequent class, they learned that the Bad Newz Kennels had been repurposed to become the Good Newz Rehab Center for Chained and Penned Dogs by the organization Dogs Deserve Better.
9. **Design assessment tasks that rely on collaboration**. Contrary to the "lone scholar" perspective, learning is social and much of it is accomplished through interactions between those who are less knowledgeable/experienced and those who are more knowledgeable/competent (Bruner 1987). Research on adult learners suggests that they often prefer to work with peers on important projects (Merriam and Bierema 2014). This may be even more important for those who

doubt their abilities because they can work to one another's strengths and perhaps shore up any perceived difficulties. One group task that we tried was "18 months in the Life of a Service Dog Puppy". We used the brochure developed by Best Friends Animal Society to raise funds, "A Day at Dog Town" to illustrate the format. Groups of inmate trainers wrote a description of what the dogs were learning at each stage and the instructor added photographs, converting it to a brochure about the program on a Microsoft Word template that could be shared with corrections staff and community members.

10. **Invite Reflection**. Reflection is widely recognized a key to making positive changes in human behavior. Reflective discourse facilitates intentional dialogue with individuals and groups who participate freely and fully [e.g., open to new ideas, able to weigh evidence critically, willing to find understanding, have access to accurate information, not distorted by power (Mezirow 2012)]. One interesting activity was a discussion of "your ideal dog". It began with a Checklist for New Adopters (https://www.petfinder.com/pet-adoption/dog-adoption/pet-adoption-checklist/) designed to help people to be a bit less impulsive and think about matching their choice of dog to their lifestyles. Some of the students had become Labrador retriever enthusiasts after working with the service dog puppies. Others talked about the breeds they had owned in the past or the family dog they had to leave behind. One inmate who would be paroled soon wanted a Cane Corso. A young student said he would get one of those Caucasian Shepherds, originally used to hunt bears and now used in Russian prisons. He wanted to defy others' expectations and train it to be a gentle dog. One CO said she would love a Pomsky—a Pomeranian/Husky mix. The instructor said that her dream dog was a Borzoi, or a Russian Wolfhound that looks sort of like a giant greyhound with hair extensions.

    We asked inmates to revisit the essays that they wrote as part of the application process with: Read back over your application. What have you learned? How have your ideas developed? Have you been changed in any way by participation in the program? Try to frame your response along these lines: "I used to think…and now I think" (Elmore 2011). Reflection supports cognitive change and develops prosocial attitudes (Johnson and Bruneau 2016).

Outcomes: Toward Transformative Learning

Educational program outcomes are evidence of achievement of the goals by the learners, consistent with the mission. There can be no claim to program effectiveness in the absence of evidence of achieving important outcomes. This aspect is addressed in greater depth in Chaps. 9 and 10; however, it is important to consider a wide array of outcomes for all stakeholders: the inmates, the staff, the community partners, the people who give the dogs homes, and last—but certainly not least—the dogs themselves. Given that this chapter is on curriculum and instruction, the focus here will be on outcomes for the inmate/handlers as learners.

The goals of rehabilitation and successful reentry into society for offenders are, as with the goal of a democracy, so lofty that even approximations are cause for celebration. Getting close or getting there relies on transformative learning (Mczirow 2012). This well-respected learning theory in adult education occurs in the following progression:

1. Confront a disorienting dilemma
2. Conduct self-examination
3. Experience of new role, relationships, and actions
4. Plan a course of action
5. Acquire new knowledge and skills
6. Try on new roles/build confidence and competence
7. Gain a new perspective on one's life (Hoggan 2016).

In 2009, Hogle referred to dog care and training programs as a win-win—an often-quoted phrase. Hill (2016) reports that these programs now exist in all 50 states. More recently, Larkin (2016) has argued that prison dog programs can be seen as a "win-times-five":

> Inmates benefit because the animal-training instruction they receive, along with the experience they acquire training dogs in their care, provides them with a skill that they can use after their release. More importantly, the relationship that a prisoner builds with his dog teaches him the need to achieve a goal; the importance of discipline and patience, along with disutility of violence, in being successful; the value and sense of self-worth in empathizing and caring for another creature; and, perhaps for the first time, the emotional bond with another living creature that allows him to feel and express love. Dogs benefit because they escape their own death row and find their own "forever" homes. Prisons benefit because the close interaction between prisoners and dogs leads to a reduction in the number of infractions and amount of violence. Members of the community benefit by receiving a dog that can become a service dog or a treasured family member. And society benefits from a reduction in the recidivism rate of participating inmates. That is a "win-times-five" (unpaged).

References

Aborn, R. (2005, March 4). Time to end recidivism. *The Nation*, 1–2.

Allred, S. L., Harrison, L. D., & O'Connell, D. J. (2013). Self-efficacy: An important aspect of prison-based learning. *The Prison Journal, 93*(2), 211–233. https://doi.org/10.1177/0032885512472964.

Antonio, M. E., Davis, R. G., & Shutt, S. R. (2017). Dog training programs in Pennsylvania's department of corrections perceived effectiveness for inmates and staff. *Society & Animals, 25,* 475–489.

Arbour, R., Signal, T., & Taylor, N. (2009). Teaching kindness: The promise of humane education. *Society and Animals, 17*(2), 136–148.

Aufderheide, C. (2016). *The application and effects of service dog training by inmates to self-perception and self-other overlap as a rehabilitative approach to incarceration.* (Unpublished Master's thesis) University of Oregon, Eugene, Oregon.

Bozick, R., Steele, J., Davis, L., & Turner, S. (2018). Does providing inmates with education improve post release outcomes? A meta-analysis of correctional education programs in the United States. *Journal of Experimental Criminology, 14*(3), 389–428. https://doi.org/10.1007/s11292-018-9334-6.

Bruner, J. (1987). *Actual minds, possible worlds*. Boston: Harvard University Press.

Cambourne, B. (2002). The conditions of learning: Is learning natural? *The Reading Teacher, 55* (8), 758–762.

Castro, E. L., Brawn, M., Graves, D. E., Mayorga, O., Page, J. D., & Slater, A. (2016) Higher education in an era of mass incarceration: Possibility under constraint. *Journal of Critical Scholarship on Higher Education and Student Affairs,* 1(2). Retrieved February 20, 2019 from: https://ecommons.luc.edu/jcshesa/vol1/iss2/1.

Cavanaugh, S. R. (2016). *The spark of learning: Energizing the college classroom with the science of emotion.* Morgantown: West Virginia University Press.

Conniff, K. M., Scarlett, J. M., Goodman, S., & Appel, L. D. (2005). Effects of a pet visitation program on the behavior and emotional state of adjudicated female adolescents. *Anthrozoös, 18* (4), 379–395. https://doi.org/10.2752/089279305785593974.

DeLisle, S., & Ilte-Clark, C. (2011). *Humane education: A way to empower youth, enhance humane behaviors, and promote animal welfare*. Retrieved from http://www.atriskeducation.net/pdf/Silhouettes-2011-Fall-DeLisle-Humane.Education.pdf.

Decety, J. (2010). The neurodevelopment of empathy in humans. *Developmental Neuroscience, 32* (4), 257–267.

Dick, A. J., Rich, W., & Waters, T. (2016). *Prison vocational education and policy in the U.S.* New York: Springer.

Elmore, R. F. (2011). *I used to think…and now I think.* Cambridge, MA: Harvard University Press.

Evans, B. J., Marsciano, C. R., & Lennartz, C. J. (2019). Cracks in the bedrock of American democracy: Differences in civic engagement across institutions of higher education. *Educational Researcher, 48*(1), 38–44. https://doi.org/10.3102/0013189X18809053.

Fayter, R. (2016). Social justice praxis within the walls-to-bridges program: Pedagogy of the oppressed federally sentenced woman. *Journal of Prisoners on Prisons, 25*(2), 56–71.

Gray, K. (2018, December 27). A second chance: Second chance Pell students earn college degrees in prison. *Diverse Issues in Higher Education, 35*(24), Academic One File. Retrieved February 20, 2019 from: https://link.galegroup.com/apps/doc/A569456886/AONE?u=pl7321r&sid=AONE&xid=4609fcec.

Greenebaum, J. B. (2010). Training dogs and training humans: symbolic interaction and dog training *Anthrozoös, 23*(2). doi: http://dx.doi.org/10.2752/175303710X12682332909936.

Han, T. M., Flynn, E., Winchell, J., Gould, E., Gandenberger, J., Barattin, D., Tedeschi, P., & Morris, K. N. (2018). *Prison-based dog training programs: Standard protocol.* Denver: Institute for Human-Animal Connection. Retrieved February 28, 2019 from: https://animalstudiesrepository.org/cgi/viewcontent.cgi?article=1001&context=anitobe.

Hill, L. B. (2016). *Becoming the person your dog thinks you are: An assessment of Florida prison-based Dog Training Programs on prison misconduct, post-release employment and recidivism*. Tallahassee, FL: The Florida State University.

Hoggan, C. D. (2016). Transformative learning as a metatheory: Definition, criteria, and typology. *Adult Education Quarterly, 66*(1), https://doi.org/10.1177/0741713615611216.

Hogle, P. S. (2009). *Going to the Dogs: Prison-based training programs are win-win*. https://pamhogle.files.wordpress.com/2009/07/prison-based-dog-training.pdf.

Horowitz, A. (Ed.). (2014). *Domestic dog cognition and behavior: The scientific study of canis familiaris*. New York: Springer.

Howells, K. (2002). The psychological needs of women prisoners: Implications for rehabilitation and management. *Psychiatry, Psychology, and Law, 9*(1), 34–43.

Immordino-Yang, M. H. (2015). *Education, learning and the brain: Exploring the implications of affective neuroscience*. New York: W. W. Norton.

Irvine, L. (2004). *If you tame me: Understanding our connections with animals*. Philadelphia, PA: Temple University Press.

Johnson, A., & Bruneau, L. (2016). Healing bonds: Animal assisted interventions with adjudicated male youth. In C. Blazina and L. Kogan (Eds.), Men and their dogs: A new understanding of man's best friend (pp. 113–132). Switzerland: Springer International Publishing.

Larkin, P. J. (2016). *Prisoners, dogs, training, and rehabilitation*. The Heritage Foundation. Retrieved February 20, 2019 from: https://www.heritage.org/crime-and-justice/.../prisoners-dogs-training-and-rehabilitatio....

Leone, P. E. & Wruble, P. C. (2017). Prison education: Maximizing the potential for employment and successful community reintegration. *The Abell Report, 30*(6), https://www.abell.org/sites/default/files/files/Abell%20Prison%20Education%20Report%2072517%20final.pdf.

Loe, A. M. (2015). *Prison-based animal programs: A descriptive analysis*. Greeley, CO: University of Northern Colorado.

Mai, C., & Subramanian, R. (2017). *The price of prisons: Examining state spending trends, 2010–2015*. Vera Institute of Justice. 8 tbl.1 (2017), https://storage.goog.leapis.com/vera-web-assets/downloads/Publications/price-of-prisons-2015-state-spending-trends/legacy_downloads/the-price-of-prisons-2015-state-spending-trends.pdf.

McCann, W., Kowalski, M. A., Hemmens, C., & Stohr, M. K. (2018). An analysis of certificates of rehabilitation in the United States. Corrections, https://doi.org/10.1080/23774657.2018.1559002

Merriam, S. B., & Bierema, L. L. (2014). *Adult learning: Linking theory and practice*. San Francisco, CA: Jossey-Bass.

Mezirow, J. (2012). Learning to think like an adult: Core concepts of transformation theory. In E. W. Taylor, P. Cranton, & Associates. (Eds.), *The handbook of transformative learning: theory, research, and practice* (pp. 73–95). San Francisco: Jossey-Bass

Minton, C. A., Perez, P. R., & Miller, K. (2015). Voices from behind prison walls. *Society & Animals, 23,* 484–501. https://doi.org/10.1163/15685306-12341379.

Oakford, P., Brumfield, C., Goldvale, C., Tatum, L., di Zerega, M., & Patrick, F. (2019). *Investing in futures: Economic and fiscal benefits of postsecondary education in prison*. Retrieved February 20, 2019 from: http://www.georgetownpoverty.org/wp-content/uploads/2019/01/GCPI-ESOI-Investing-in-Futures-Report-FINAL-20190116.pdf.

Petey, (2016). Attempting to secure a university education while in prison. *Journal of Prisoners on Prisons, 25*(2), 72–79.

Rampey, B. D., Keiper, S., Mohadjer, L., Krenzke, T., Li, J., Thornton, N., & Hogan, J. (2016). *Highlights from the U.S. PIAAC survey of incarcerated adults: Their skills, work experience, education, and training: Program for the international assessment of adult competencies: 2014 (NCES 2016-040)*. Washington, DC: National Center for Education Statistics. Retrieved February 18, 2019 from http://nces.ed.gov/pubsearch.

Seivert, N. P. (2014). *Animal-assisted therapy for incarcerated youth: A randomized-controlled trial*. Wayne State University Theses. p 392. https://digitalcommons.wayne.edu/oa_theses/392.

Shernoff, D. J. (2013). *Optimal learning environments to promote student engagement*. New York: Springer.

Sousa, D. A. (2010). *Mind, brain, and education: Neuroscience implications for the classroom*. Bloomington, IN: Leading Edge/Solution Tree.

Swyers, K. N. (2014). *Prison-based animal programs (PAPs) and mental health outcome measures*. Portland, OR: Portland State University.

Szifris, K., Fox, C., & Bradbury, A. (2018). A realist model of prison education, growth, and desistance: A new theory. *Journal of Prison Education and Reentry, 5*(1), 41–62. https://doi.org/10.25771/qac7-9w77.

Turner, W. G. (2007). The experiences of offenders in a prison canine program. *Federal Probation, 71*(1), 38–43. Retrieved February 20, 2019 from https://www.uscourts.gov/sites/default/files/71_1_6_0.pdf.

Van Wormer, J., Kigerl, A., & Hamilton, Z. (3015). *Digging deeper: Exploring the value of prison-based dog handler programs*. Retrieved February 22, 2019 from: http://sustainabilityinprisons.org/wp-content/uploads/2015/04/WADOC-Dog-Program-Manuscript-for-WADOC.pdf.

Vera Institute of Justice and Georgetown University Center on Poverty and Inequality (2019, January). *Investing in futures: economic and fiscal benefits of postsecondary education in prison*.

Weil, Z. (2013). Epilogue: Humane education for a humane world. In M. R. Jalongo (Ed.), *Teaching compassion: Humane education in early childhood* (pp. 227–237). New York: Springer.

World Animal Net. (2012). *Definition of humane education*. Retrieved from www.worldanimal.net/resources/humane-education-resources.

Zimmer, R. M. (2013). *Partnering shelter dogs with prison inmates: An alternative strategy to reduce recidivism and teach social therapy*. Charles Town, WV: American Pubic University.

Chapter 9
Comprehensive Evaluation of Dog Training and Rehabilitation Initiatives in Correctional Facilities

Angela K. Fournier and Lori Winston

Introduction

Evaluation is a critical component of prison-based dog programs (PDPs). It is important for individual programs to understand whether the program is effective and, if so, how or why the program is effective. This information is critical to the success of individual programs, can guide development of future programs, and informs the work of key stakeholders (e.g., correctional facilities, animal-welfare organizations, researchers). This chapter discusses comprehensive PDP assessment, recommending evaluators (a) measure outcomes for all stakeholders (e.g., inmates, correctional staff, dogs, end-users), (b) examine underlying processes that may explain program outcomes, (c) assess for changes in the prison environment, and (d) apply rigorous assessment methods for the most accurate results. Throughout the chapter, points are illustrated by discussing findings from one PDP in particular—the Pen Pals program.

Example of a Comprehensive Evaluation: Pen Pals

A study was conducted to assess Pen Pals, a PDP in which shelter dogs are cared for and trained by inmates in prison for 8 weeks (FETCH a Cure 2018; Virginia Department of Corrections 2015). The inmates are educated in dog-training skills from a certified animal trainer and work in teams of four to care for and train a dog in basic obedience. The dogs are then adopted by individuals in the community.

A. K. Fournier (✉)
Department of Psychology, Bemidji State University, Bemidji, MN, USA
e-mail: afournier@bemidjistate.edu

L. Winston
Fetch Please Dog Training, LLC, Moses Lake, WA, USA

M. R. Jalongo (ed.), *Prison Dog Programs*,
https://doi.org/10.1007/978-3-030-25618-0_9

Programs like this are considered community-service programs, the most common type of PDP (Furst 2006). This particular institution was a minimum-security facility implementing the therapeutic community approach to corrections. A therapeutic community is a community-based residence within a correctional facility aimed at treating inmates with substance-use disorders (Lipton et al. 2002). Consistent with the therapeutic-community approach, the facility was limited to inmates with a history of substance-use disorders or legal charges related to alcohol or other drugs.

A wait-list control quasi-experiment was conducted to study the Pen Pals program. A total of 102 male inmates, ranging in age from 21 to 50 ($M_{age} = 32$), participated in the study. Participants had completed a mean of 11.9 years of education and were able to read at an 8th grade reading level or higher, as indicated by institutional intake assessment. With regard to race or ethnicity, 40.2% of the participants identified as White or Caucasian, 17.6% as Black or African American, 8.3% identified as Hispanic or Latinx, and 2.1% identified as Native American or American Indian. Of the 102 participants 24 began working in the Pen Pals program during the study, serving as the Treatment group. A matched-pairs design was used so that each member of the Treatment group was paired with an inmate still on the waiting list for Pen Pals, making up the Control group (n = 24). Thus, a total of 48 participants completed pretest and posttest measures. The aim of the research was to investigate (a) inmate outcomes regarding outlook and mood, social functioning, treatment progress, and perception of the prison environment; and (b) interactions between inmates and dogs as they related to underlying processes.

Summative Evaluation for All Stakeholders

Comprehensive PDP evaluation should measure program outcomes for all stakeholders. This includes the inmates, correctional staff and administrators, dogs, and program end-users (e.g., pet owners, service-dog recipients). Research on PDPs to date has focused primarily on inmates.

Inmates

The evidence base for inmate outcomes of PDPs is discussed in greater depth in other chapters. Therefore, we discuss it only briefly here. Individual studies suggest inmates benefit from a long list of outcomes, including improvements in psychosocial variables like self-esteem (e.g., Bustad 1990; Currie 2008), relationship variables such as communication skills (e.g., Turner 2007), and emotional well-being (e.g., Nef 2004). A survey of PDP programs indicated that administrators and staff perceive many benefits for inmates, with the most frequent being increased responsibility, job-skill development, improved patience/anger management, higher self-esteem, and greater capacity for empathy (Furst 2006). Cooke and Farrington (2016) conducted a systematic review on PDP outcomes for inmates. They found significant effects for internalizing outcomes (e.g., depression, self-efficacy) and externalizing outcomes (e.g., self-control, behavioral infractions, recidivism).

Given the variety of outcomes that have been measured to date, one might wonder which outcomes to measure for a given program. In addition to the empirical literature, evaluation should be guided by program objectives. What are the desired outcomes for the inmates? For example, if a PDP is being implemented to help inmates build interpersonal skills and reduce behavioral problems, the program evaluation should include reliable and valid measures of interpersonal skills and behavior problems. Unfortunately, the wide array of variables studied in the PDP literature may indicate a lack of clarity on just what the desired *inmate* objectives are. PDPs may be developed with identified objectives for the animals (i.e., dogs are prepared for adoption or service), with inmates working in service of those objectives (i.e., care for the dog and prepare it for adoption or service). It may be assumed the program will benefit the inmates, but the objectives guiding the program are to care for and train the dogs. This was the case with the Pen Pals program, complicating the process of identifying outcome variables in the study.

The objective of the Pen Pals program was to train shelter dogs and improve their adoption outlook and success. Coordinators at the dog shelter and the prison imagined there would be positive effects for the inmates, but no specific objectives were set prior to program implementation. The variables measured in our study were determined via a review of the literature on animal-assisted therapies and PDPs, discussions with staff at the prison and the shelter, and a focus group with inmates prior to the study. Anecdotal reports from the correctional staff suggested inmates were showing more positive behavior, had a more positive mood and outlook, and were getting along better. The inmates described the prison as a happier place with the dogs present and suggested it helped them move through the different levels of the prison's therapeutic community.

Based on this information, we measured optimism, mood state, social skills, treatment progress, and perceptions of the prison environment. We predicted that inmates in the Pen Pals program would show improvements in these variables from before beginning the program (pretest) to after working in the program for several weeks (posttest). Results were mixed, and are discussed throughout this chapter.

Treatment level[1] Treatment level was measured via participants' self-reported level in the prison therapeutic community. Treatment takes place in a series of four levels, with inmates entering treatment at Level I and advancing through Level IV when treatment goals for each level have been met. Figure 9.1 illustrates the mean treatment level at pretest and posttest, separated by group. You can see that mean treatment level was 1.8 at pretest for both groups, treatment level was higher at

[1]Findings on treatment level and social skills are discussed in detail elsewhere (Fournier et al. 2007) and reviewed briefly here.

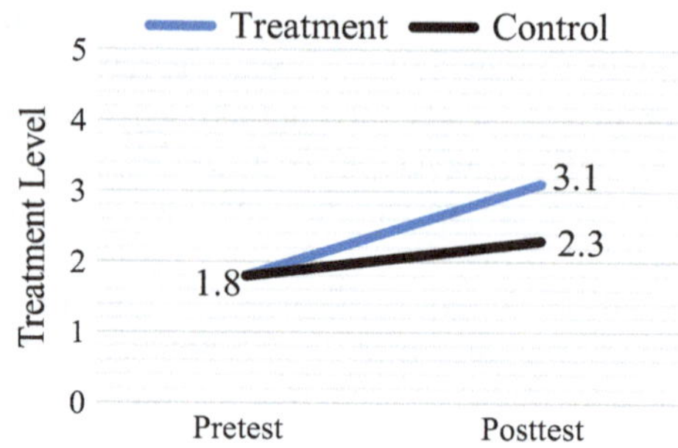

Fig. 9.1 Treatment level increased to a greater degree in the Treatment group

posttest for both groups, and posttest level was greater in the Treatment group ($M = 3.1$) than the Control group ($M = 2.3$), F (1, 44) = 6.50, $p < .05$.

Social Skills Social skills were assessed through pretest-posttest comparisons on the Social Skills Inventory (Riggio 1986), on which inmates answered questions on social and emotional communication skills. As you can see in Fig. 9.2, social sensitivity increased from pretest ($M = 35.9$) to posttest ($M = 39.4$) in the Treatment group, while it decreased from pretest ($M = 38.0$) to posttest ($M = 35.5$) in the Control group, F (1, 45) = 4.0, $p < .05$.

Optimism Optimism was measured with the Life Orientation Test—Revised (LOT-R). This is a 4-point rating scale designed to measure optimism based on the generalized outcome-expectancy model of motivation (Scheier et al. 1994). It assesses generalized expectancies for positive versus negative outcomes. Inmate participants completed the LOT-R at pretest and posttest. We predicted a group x phase interaction, such that optimism would increase from pretest to posttest for the Treatment group, but not in the Control group. An analysis of variance showed that optimism scores were higher overall in the Treatment group ($M = 15.4$) than the Control group ($M = 13.3$) regardless of phase, F (1, 46) = 4.5, $p < .05$); scores did not increase from pretest to posttest in either group. The lack of change is not so surprising, since the LOT-R is designed to measure *dispositional* optimism (Scheier and Carver 1985) rather than state optimism (Affleck et al. 2001), and thus may not

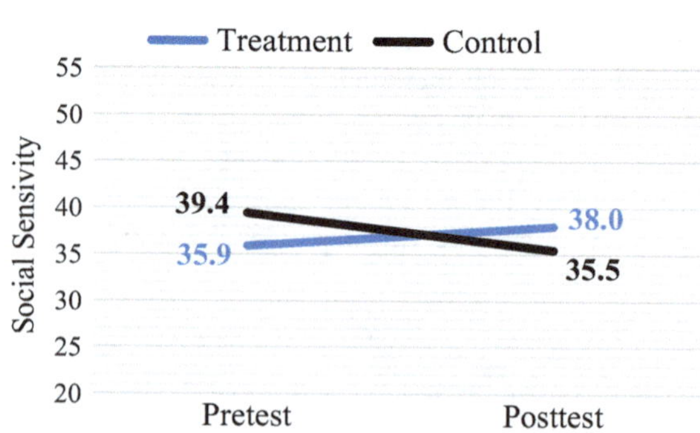

Fig. 9.2 Social sensitivity increased for inmates in the Pen Pals program, while it decreased for those on the waiting list

be adequate to detect small changes in positive outlook. While inmate outlook or positive thinking may change as the result of a PDP, one's *disposition* as optimistic versus pessimistic is less likely to be altered. The finding that optimism scores were higher in the Treatment group than the Control group is consistent with correlational studies on pet-ownership, suggesting pet-ownership is associated with higher psychological states such as self-esteem and personal control (e.g., Serpell 1990). In addition to the effects of PDPs on the inmates, it's important to understand how programs impact staff at the correctional facility.

Staff

The U.S. Bureau of Labor Statistics estimates that over 400,000 men and women work as correctional officers or jailers (2017). Research on PDP impact for correctional staff is limited, and discussions tend to focus on inmate-staff interactions. Humby and Barclay (2018) surveyed animal-welfare agencies and correctional staff involved in PDPs in Australia. Respondents reported improved relationships between inmates and staff; dogs gave them a common ground to discuss, helping to break down barriers. Others describe relationships between PDP inmates and staff as less contentious (Furst 2006). Britton and Button (2007) interviewed PDP inmates and staff and both reported improved relationships. Inmates described the dogs as a bridge between them and the staff; officers perceived the dogs as helping to soften their otherwise authoritarian stance.

Despite consistent reports of improved inmate-staff interaction, there are no data quantifying this effect. Research is necessary to better understand what, if anything, changes for staff when a PDP is implemented. In addition to positively impacting inmates, PDP outcomes for staff may buffer the effects of an otherwise stressful job. Correctional work can be stressful due to role challenges (e.g., role conflict, role ambiguity), danger on the job, harassment, and work-family conflict; over time these stressors put officers at-risk for distress and job burnout (Lambert et al. 2015). Should research show reliable, positive outcomes for staff, PDPs could be tested as an intervention to reduce work-related stress and strain.

Dogs PDP evaluation, particularly those aimed to train or socialize dogs, should include assessment of the dogs. Potential benefits to collecting quantitative data on the dogs' outcomes include but are not limited to: 1) providing inmates with objective evidence of their effectiveness as trainers, potentially creating an even greater impact on their self-improvement; and 2) potential increases in funding and community support with the presentation of empirical evidence of the dogs' improvement. The literature includes qualitative reports by inmates who notice improvements in the dogs and then perceive better outlook toward their own capacities to improve (Cooke and Farrington 2016). Empirical evidence is needed to confirm these reports, as research to date has focused on measuring human outcomes and we know very little about effects of the programs on the dogs.

The growing literature addressing PDP efficacy for inmates in PDPs fall short of defining how progress in the dogs is measured. According to the creator of the Ridge Dogs Program at Coyote Ridge Correctional Facility in Washington, a dog's progress can be evaluated by quantifying performance in learned behaviors with specific operational definitions[2] (K. Ellingson, personal communication, February 11 2019). Dog trainers can measure a dog's progress by noting varying elements of distance, duration and distraction. The closest thing to standardized, operational definitions of behaviors is provided by the American Kennel Club's (AKC) Canine Good Citizen (CGC) Program, which is discussed in Chap. 13. Though many PDPs will get participating dogs CGC tested, CGC certification measures behaviors that are more sophisticated than basic obedience training but less complex than those utilized by service animals. Further complicating matters, the training increments leading to and beyond CGC are not clearly defined by the AKC or consistently followed from program to program. The field needs a uniform standard for PDP dog assessment (e.g., Ridge Dogs Program). This would help to promote systematic evaluation of programs and encourage research on PDP outcomes for dogs.

End-Users Furst's national survey of prison administrators indicates that PDPs can be categorized into different typologies (2011). The most common PDP is aimed at rehabilitating shelter animals (i.e., community-service model), followed by programs aimed at socializing and training future service dogs. Both program types involve inmates providing a service, such as caring for and training dogs, which ultimately benefits the animal and another human. The end-users in community-service and service-dog socialization programs are the people with whom program dogs eventually live and/or serve. For example, when Pen Pals dogs completed the program, they left the prison and were adopted by community members as pets. The end-user was the adopting pet owner. For service-dog PDPs in which dogs are prepared for service work (e.g., guide dog, hearing dog), the end-user is the individual whom the dog will assist.

Comprehensive PDP evaluation should gather data from program end-users. At the time of this writing, there are no published studies on outcomes for PDP end-users. Similar to the irony of research focusing on inmate outcomes without clear inmate objectives, the ultimate objective of most PDPs is that the dogs end up as successful pets or service animals, yet we have not gathered data to determine whether that objective is being met. Research literature on service-dog use and effectiveness in general is limited, but may provide clues to PDP end-user evaluation.

Winkle et al. (2012) conducted a systematic review of the literature on the efficacy of service dogs for people with mobility-related physical disabilities. They found just 12 studies meeting inclusion criteria and all of them were limited by threats to internal validity. Still, the review can inform measure identification for

---

[2]For example, the handler asks the dog to maintain a down, stay. Measure distance from handler to dog and duration of time the dog maintains the down position.

PDP evaluation. Study outcomes were varied but centered around three types of effects—functional, social, and psychological. Functional effects included mobility assistance from the dog to increase daily functioning (e.g., retrieving items, opening doors). These effects were measured via reported functioning, need for help from others, and money or time spent on receiving assistance from other sources. Additional measures included sense of independence and effects for family members (e.g., decreased drain, increased peace of mind). Beyond improved functioning, social effects of service dogs included greater positive interaction with others and increased community participation, while psychological effects included improvements in psychosocial states such as self-esteem, locus of control, and affect. Each of these outcomes could be useful in evaluating PDPs, with functional effects as a primary measure and social and psychological outcomes as important secondary measures.

For PDPs aimed at producing adoptable pets, we can defer to the literature on successful pet adoption and risk factors for pet relinquishment. In each of these processes, the dog's behavior is key. Behavior problems are a top reason pet dogs are relinquished or rehomed (Gates et al. 2018) and behavioral interventions are key in reducing the number of homeless animals in shelters (Fournier and Geller 2004). In addition to basic obedience, PDPs promote healthy socialization of the dogs. Inmates are charged with exposing the animals to a variety of people, other dogs, and novel situations (Antonio et al. 2017). Taken together, measures for PDP adopters could include assessment of behavior related to obedience and healthy socialization.

Formative Evaluation to Examine Underlying Processes

In addition to determining *if* a PDP results in positive outcomes, it is important to examine *how* or *why* the program results in outcomes. The field of animal-assisted interventions needs a conceptual theory to explain how animals impact human health and well-being. Without a theory, research is guided by experience and piecemeal conclusions from individual studies. To date, the research on HAI in general is very broad, measuring physiology (e.g., Beetz et al. 2012); self-esteem, self-perception, and loneliness (Selby and Smith-Osborne 2013); as well as emotional and behavioral disorders (Wilkie et al. 2016). Regarding PDPs specifically, findings are reviewed throughout this book, revealing the broad array of outcomes that have been measured. The *phenomenon* of HAI within PDPs has been studied less.

At the most basic level, PDPs involve HAI—inmates interacting with dogs. In order to attribute PDP outcomes to inmate experiences with the animals, rather than other components of the program (e.g., increased attention from inmates or staff, education and training opportunities), evaluation should measure inmate-dog interaction, describing and quantifying HAI and its relationship with outcome variables.

Measuring HAI HAI in the Pen Pals program was measured with the Human-Animal Interaction Scale (HAIS). This is a self-report instrument completed by an individual after interacting with a non-human animal (e.g., animal-assisted therapy, animal-training session). Respondents rate the extent to which they or the animal engaged in various behaviors on a 5-point Likert scale, ranging from 0, indicating "not at all" to 4, indicating "a great deal." Research indicates the instrument has good reliability and validity (Fournier et al. 2016). The HAIS includes behaviors emitted from the human toward the animal (e.g., the human pets, talks to, or plays with the animal) and from the animal toward the human (e.g., the animal initiates interaction with, sniffs, or licks the human). Scores provide information on which individual behaviors occurred during inmate-dog interaction and how frequently they occurred. Figure 9.3 shows mean ratings on individual HAIS items for all Pen Pals participants who volunteered to participate (N = 102). They were asked to rate the amount they had experienced each interaction over the past week.

It is important to note these scores were taken at pretest. The participants had applied to join the Pen Pals program but had not yet been accepted. Thus, this represents interaction between general population inmates and the Pen Pals dogs. The graph illustrates a range of behaviors were reported, with some more frequent than others; petting, watching, and talking to the dogs were rated the highest. Behaviors on the graph are grouped into three categories, including passive interactions (i.e., watching or hearing the dogs), affiliative interactions (i.e., petting, talking to, playing with, holding, or hugging/kissing the dogs), and behaviors specific to caretaking or training (i.e., walking, feeding, grooming, or training the dogs).

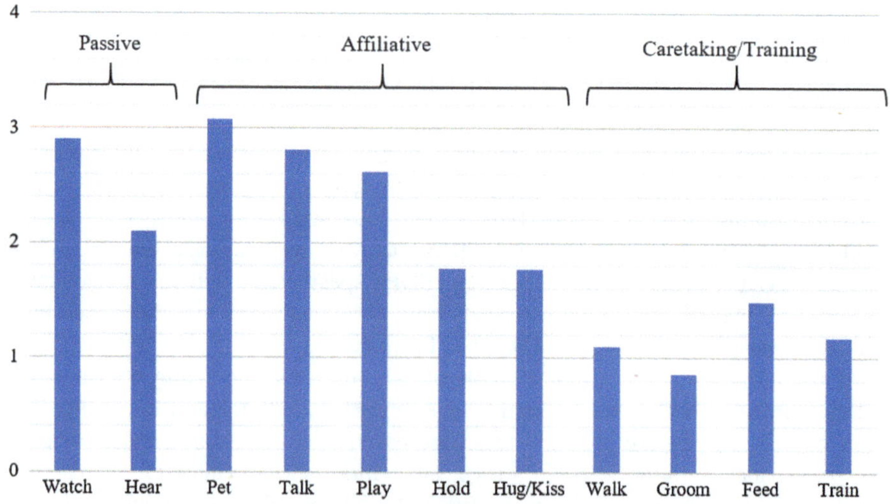

Fig. 9.3 Mean scores on the human–animal interaction scale. Interactions include passive (i.e., watch, hear), affiliative (pet, play), and caretaking or training (groom, train) behaviors

Note that these inmates, who were not in the PDP, reported experiencing HAI beyond mere passive exposure (i.e., seeing or hearing the program dogs). They reported a relatively high amount of affiliative behavior, including behaviors that could indicate a personal connection to the animal (i.e., holding, hugging or kissing a dog). Furthermore, the participants reported behaviors that might otherwise be reserved for those in the PDP (e.g., feeding, training). Although this sample of inmates had not yet begun the PDP, they had applied to participate in it. They may have been more interested in the dogs than the average inmate in the general population, seeking out HAI with program dogs. Therefore, these data are not a pure reflection of HAI in the general population. Still, they illustrate the *potential* for HAI among inmates outside of the program. This potential for HAI in the general population is an important component to PDP implementation and evaluation, highlighting the need to assess inmates *within* and *outside* the PDP. One potential outcome identified in this research is the opportunity for healthy expression of masculinity. Through interactions with the dogs, inmates can practice empathy, intimacy, self-reliance, and healthy relationship skills (Fournier 2016); which could be an important part of rehabilitation or transformation.

These data reflect HAI among inmates, but it is also important to understand HAI among correctional staff and administration. There were anecdotal reports from both staff and inmates that the correctional staff sought out the Pen Pals dogs, but data were not collected. Understanding how PDPs impact stakeholders requires going beyond description of inmate- or staff-dog interactions. Connecting HAI with outcomes can help us understand which interactions are most potent for rehabilitation and well-being.

Connecting HAI with Outcome Variables HAIS scores in the Pen Pals program were analyzed in the context of mood state; it was predicted that higher levels of HAI would be associated with lower levels of distress. Distress was measured with the brief form of the Profile of Mood States (POMS), which is a self-report adjective rating scale designed to assess transient, fluctuating affective states (McNair et al. 1971). HAI and distress were analyzed in two ways: (a) correlating scores for participants, separated by group at posttest and (b) graphing daily journal scores. Figure 9.4 shows the scatterplot between posttest distress and HAI (i.e., total HAIS scores), in the Treatment group. There was a significant negative correlation, such

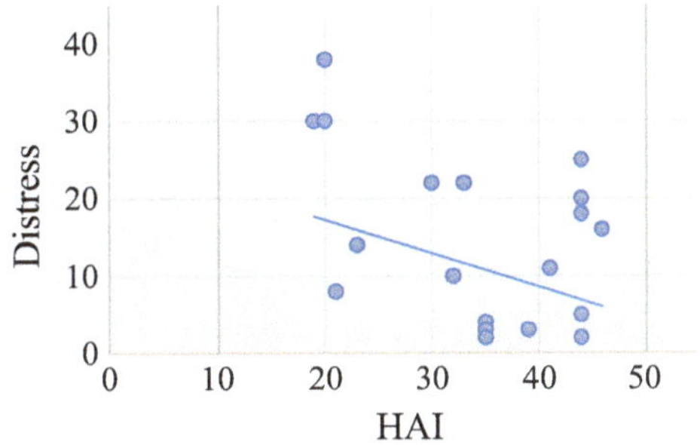

Fig. 9.4 Scatterplot showing association between reported HAI and distress at posttest for the Treatment group

that higher levels of HAI were associated with lower levels of distress, $r = -.439$, $p = .05$. This suggests an association between interaction with the dogs and subjective feelings of distress. The direction of the relationship cannot be determined from the data gathered. It is possible inmates experienced reduced distress because of HAI, or that they engaged in greater HAI because they felt less distressed, or these variables could have been associated with a third variable impacting their relationship. Still, this provides a potential method for studying PDPs.

A subset of 6 inmates (3 in the Treatment group and 3 in the Control group) agreed to complete daily journal entries for 14 consecutive days. Journals consisted of one POMS and one HAIS for each day; participants were instructed to complete the forms at the end of each day, reporting experienced HAI and distress. Journals began one week prior to beginning the Pen Pals program (i.e., pretest) and ended one week after beginning the program (i.e., posttest). Figure 9.5 displays the mean scores for the Treatment-group and Control-group participants, showing reported HAI and distress across the 14 days. Scores reflected variability in both constructs from day-to-day; ratings did not appear to change from pretest to posttest.

Note that HAI is higher in the Treatment group than the Control group. This is consistent with HAI data presented earlier. The graphs also show distress was relatively more variable in the Treatment group than the Control group. Treatment-group ratings included small increases and decreases in distress throughout the 14 days, whereas Control-group ratings remained low throughout. The variability could be related to HAI; caring for an animal, particularly an animal with behavior problems,

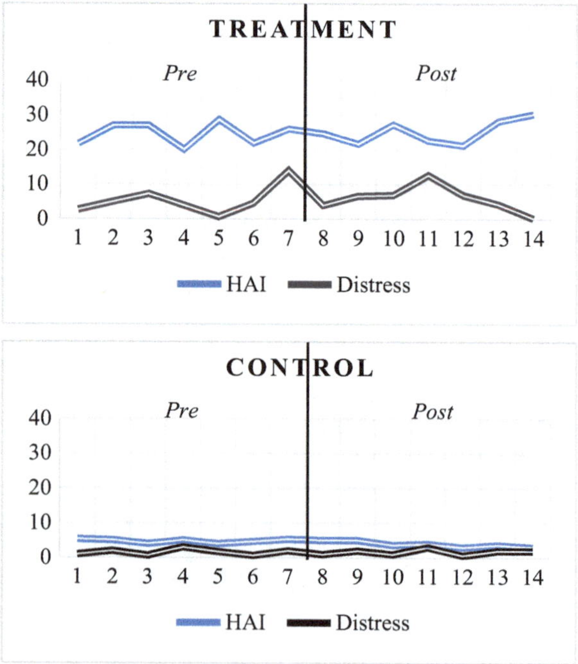

Fig. 9.5 Mean daily ratings in journals for the Treatment-group (top) and Control group (bottom), separated by phase

can be stressful (Sharkin and Ruff 2011). However, the fluctuation could also be from other program variables (e.g., increased responsibility, interaction with other program participants, difference in attention from staff) or factors unrelated to Pen Pals altogether. Although these data don't allow for definitive cause-and-effect conclusions, they provide a richer understanding of the HAI occurring on a daily basis and how it may or may not be related to outcomes.

HAI-Related Constructs Beyond measuring specific behaviors, important PDP processes may be illuminated through measurement of HAI-related variables. There is a growing collection of self-report instruments measuring these constructs. For example, attachment to pets can be measured via the Lexington Attachment to Pets Scale (Johnson et al. 1992) or the Short Attachment to Pets Scale (Marsa-Sambola et al. 2016). Attachment could be useful in assessing loss when a program dog leaves the facility. The bond between inmates and program dogs could be measured with the Companion-Animal Bonding Scale (Poresky et al. 1987) or the Companion-Animal Semantic Differential (Poresky et al. 1988). There are several instruments to measure attitude toward animals or pets, such as the Pet Attitude Scale (Templer et al. 2004). For a comprehensive list of measures assessing constructs related to the human-animal bond, see Anderson (2007).

Evaluation of the Prison Environment

Scholars began studying the social environment of institutional settings in the 1960s. Discussions centered around the influence of environmental factors on human behavior and functioning. Research then addressed the social environment in various institutions, including psychiatric treatment facilities (Moos and Houts 1968) and university dormitories (Gerst and Moos 1972). The literature soon expanded, addressing the environment in correctional institutions, its impact on inmate conduct and rehabilitation (e.g., Cressey 1961; Moos 1968), and development of measurement instruments (Wenk and Moos 1972). In 1989, Moos coined the term *social climate*, defined as the material, social, and emotional conditions of a given unit and the interaction between such factors.

Research on the effects of prison social climate for inmates has been mixed, complicated by measurement challenges. However, there is evidence associating environmental factors with positive results for inmates. For example, Wright (1993) found that institutions which provide greater support for self-advancement are associated with positive adjustment to the correctional institution, and institutions with more opportunities to build self-efficacy report fewer behavioral problems. More recently, Robinson et al. (2016) found that institutions where inmates perceive greater cohesion and safety and a more positive atmosphere had lower levels of aggression. Auty and Liebling (2019) studied moral and social climate in prison and its relationship to recidivism. They found that institutions allowing for higher moral quality of life have better outcomes for inmates upon release.

PDPs and Institutional Environment There is limited research to date on the effects of PDPs on the prison environment. Qualitative reports suggest programs create a more supportive environment and humanizing experience for inmates (Currie 2008). Others report PDPs help create a less stressful environment in general (Bachi 2013; Strimple 2003). Richardson-Taylor and Blanchette (2001) studied a PDP at a women's correctional facility. They assessed the prison environment, among other factors, via self-report measures and interviews. Inmates in the PDP reported a more positive perception of the facility than controls; staff reported a friendlier, more positive environment. Cooke and Farrington (2015) interviewed incarcerated women participating in a PDP. Respondents indicated the dog-training program improved their experience of imprisonment, including an increased sense of trust and security.

Taken together, the literature suggests prison social climate is an important factor in inmates' adjustment to incarceration, behavior while incarcerated, and outcomes upon release. The literature on PDPs and prison environment is limited, but suggests that programs may be impacting the institution's climate. Therefore, comprehensive PDP evaluation should include a measure of the prison environment. This could be done through qualitative methods, such as interviews or focus groups with inmates, staff, and administrators. There are also several self-report instruments for gathering quantitative data. Table 9.1 provides a list of instruments

Table 9.1 Measures of prison social climate

Instrument	Description
Correctional Institutions Environment Scale (Moos 1974, 1987)	Measures social climate of juvenile and adult correctional programs, as perceived by inmates and staff. Measures: involvement, support, expressiveness, autonomy, practical orientation, personal problem orientation, order and organization, clarity, staff control
Prison Preference Inventory (Toch 1992)	Measures inmate concerns regarding the prison environment. Measures: privacy, activity, support, freedom, safety, social stimulation, structure, and emotional feedback
Prison Environment Inventory (Wright 1985)	Measures social climate of correctional environments via contextual concerns of imprisoned inmates. Measures: Privacy, safety, structure, support, emotional feedback, social stimulation, activity, and freedom
Essen Climate Evaluation Schema (Schalast and Groenewald 2009)	Measures social climate within forensic psychiatric wards, has been adapted to prison environments. Measures hold and support, inmates' social cohesion and support, and experienced safety
Prison Group Climate Instrument (Van der Helm et al. 2011)	Measures group climate in youth and adult institutions where inmates reside in groups. Measures: Support, growth, repression, and atmosphere

that can be used to measure social climate in correctional institutions. For a more thorough review of measurement instruments used throughout the world, see Tonkin (2015).

Pen Pals and Social Climate The impact of the Pen Pals program on the institution's social climate was measured with the short form of the Correctional Institutions Environment Scale (Moos 1974, 1987). The Correctional Institutions Environment Scale (CIES) is a true-false measure designed to assess the social climate of juvenile and adult correctional programs, as perceived by inmates and staff. Inmate scores are separated into relationship, personal growth, and system maintenance dimensions. Each dimension is comprised of three scales for a total of nine scales. The nine scales are (a) involvement, (b) support, (c) expressiveness, (d) autonomy, (e) practical orientation, (f) personal problem orientation, (g) order and organization, (h) clarity, and (i) staff control (Moos 1974). The CIES is considered a valid measure for evaluating inmate and staff perceptions of the correctional environment and is considered particularly useful for following changes in a correctional program over time (Moos 1974).

The CIES was administered to Treatment- and Control-group participants at pretest and posttest. It was predicted that inmates' perceptions of the environment would become more positive from pretest to posttest in the Treatment group, but not change in the Control group. A multivariate analysis of variance showed scores were higher overall in the Treatment group than the Control group, $F\,(9, 38) = 3.1$, $p < .01$, but did not differ from pretest to posttest. Table 9.2 provides the mean scores for each of the nine CIES scales, separated by group and phase. Looking at the individual scales, Treatment-group participants scored higher on Support,

Table 9.2 Mean CIES scores, classified by group and phase (N = 24)

	Treatment		Control	
CIES Scale	Pretest	Posttest	Pretest	Posttest
Relationship				
Involvement	1.6 (1.2)	1.5 (1.3)	1.3 (1.2)	0.8 (0.7)
Support**	1.8 (1.2)	1.4 (1.2)	1.1 (1.2)	0.8 (0.7)
Expressiveness*	1.4 (1.2)	1.3 (1.2)	0.9 (1.1)	0.7 (0.8)
Personal growth				
Autonomy***	2.5 (1.1)	2.6 (0.9)	1.7 (0.8)	1.5 (1.1)
Practical orientation***	3.0 (1.0)	3.1 (0.9)	1.9 (1.6)	1.7 (1.6)
Personal problem orientation***	2.8 (1.3)	2.3 (1.2)	1.7 (1.1)	1.3 (0.9)
System maintenance				
Order and organization*	2.9 (1.1)	2.8 (0.9)	2.4 (1.0)	2.1 (1.0)
Clarity	1.7 (1.3)	1.3 (1.0)	1.4 (0.9)	1.4 (0.8)
Staff control	2.4 (1.0)	2.6 (0.9)	2.4 (0.9)	3.0 (0.8)

p-value reflect significant differences between the Treatment and Control Groups
$^*p < .05$, $^{**}p < .01$, $^{***}p < .001$

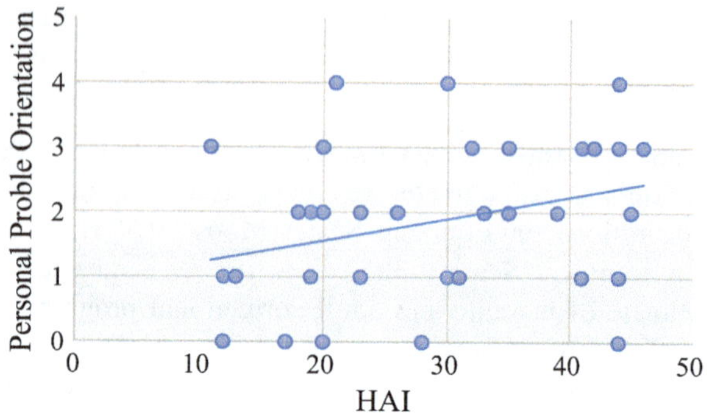

Fig. 9.6 Correlation between HAI and prison environment at posttest

Expressiveness, Autonomy, Practical Orientation, Personal Problem Orientation, and Order/Organization. These findings indicate participants in the Treatment group perceived (a) encouragement to be helpful and supportive of others and to have received more support, (b) help to express their feelings, (c) support to take initiative and leadership, (d) the environment as oriented towards preparing them for release, (e) encouragement to be concerned with and understand personal problems and feelings, and (f) the environment to put a greater emphasis on order and organization.

To explore the relationship between HAI and perceptions of the prison environment, Treatment and Control group scores were combined and correlation coefficients computed between CIES scale scores and HAI at posttest. The results indicated significant positive correlations between HAI and Autonomy ($r = .497$, $p < .001$), Practical Orientation ($r = .435$, $p = .002$), Personal Problem Orientation ($r = .346$, $p = .016$), and Order/Organization ($r = .304$, $p = .036$). As an example, Fig. 9.6 illustrates the correlation between HAI and Personal Problem Orientation scores. This subscale assesses the extent to which inmates feel they are encouraged to be concerned with their personal problems and feelings and to seek to understand them (Moos 1974). It should be noted that each of the subscales in the Personal Growth Dimension correlated with HAI. This suggests that interaction with the dogs is associated with inmates perceiving the prison as promoting personal growth. Similar to correlations between HAI and optimism or distress, we cannot infer causation. However, the results warrant further investigation of this kind. PDPs would benefit from measuring the prison's social climate as it relates to interactions with animals and other key components of the program.

Application of Rigorous Evaluation Methods

In addition to selecting appropriate constructs to measure—process and outcome variables—and deciding whom to assess—all stakeholders—it's important to develop an empirically-sound evaluation plan. Rigorous assessment requires using effective measurement instruments and following a design that allows for clear results. The literature on PDPs is growing but many studies have significant limitations, including small sample sizes, measures with limited reliability and/or validity, and poor generalizability (Cooke and Farrington 2016). There may be limitations inherent in evaluating PDPs, given the need for control in correctional facilities. Allison and Ramaswamy (2016) list institutional constraints that pose barriers to rigorous PDP evaluation and research, including limited resources, selection bias, and poor generalizability.

The Pen Pals program is a good example of a study design limited by the logistics of prison-based animal programs. Meta-analyses for animal-assisted programs in general (Anestis et al. 2014) and PDPs specifically (Cooke and Farrington 2016) indicate selection bias is a problem. Such was the case for the Pen Pals program. Inmates became involved in the program by first applying and then being selected by correctional staff. This is a common practice among PDPs (Furst 2011). It is likely the inmates who volunteered and were selected were different from inmates who did not volunteer and/or were not selected. Anecdotal reports from correctional staff indicated the inmates selected were the best of the best—men who showed exceptional behavior and had the best potential for successful rehabilitation. The consistent difference in scores between the Treatment group and the Control group, regardless of phase, may be an artifact of this selection bias. Inmates selected for the program were optimistic, less distressed, and perceived the prison environment as relatively positive. Scores were in the normal, non-clinical range at pretest. Furthermore, we did not find the predicted group x phase interaction on most outcome variables. The Treatment group did not improve from pretest to posttest above and beyond that of the Control group. This was likely due to a ceiling/floor effect. Pretest scores were already high (optimism, perception of the prison environment) or low (distress), precluding much improvement during the program.

A second key variable in the accuracy of evaluation is the timing of data collection and distinction between Treatment and Control groups, particularly for quantitative pre-post measures. Although it was not specifically predicted, there was an underlying assumption that HAI would increase significantly from Pretest to Posttest in the Treatment group but not in the Control group, or at least not to as great an extent. Based on the analyses, this underlying assumption was not met.

As Fig. 9.7 shows, participants in the Treatment group reported more HAI than the Control group, and participants reported more HAI at Posttest than Pretest.

Fig. 9.7 Reported HAI at pretest and posttest, separated by group

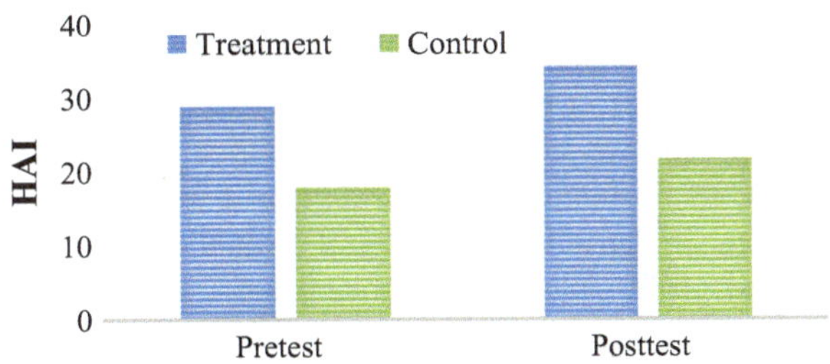

However, the increase from Pretest to Posttest was not different between the two groups. The mean HAIS scores at pretest suggests Treatment group participants interacted with the dogs prior to officially working in the HAI program. Thus, unfortunately, the research did not capture a true Pre-Post comparison with regard to HAI. It is possible some important effects of the PDP occurred before the study even began. For this reason, it is critical that PDP evaluations begin measuring dependent variables, ideally, before any dogs are placed in the prison.

Assessment, Evaluation, and Research

Assessment, evaluation, and research are three processes that involve gathering data to make decisions. The terms get used interchangeably at times, but each is a distinct process with unique objectives, carried out by trained professionals.

Assessment Assessment involves gathering data in order to make decisions (Huitt et al. 2001). With regard to correctional facilities, professionals within the institution (e.g., psychologists, social workers) might assess inmates to determine their individual needs for and progress toward rehabilitation. Assessment might be used to select which programs an inmate would benefit from and to measure readiness for release. Assessment requires specific skills (i.e., selection, administration, and scoring instruments; interpretation of findings) and should be conducted by professionals trained in measurement within their field.

Evaluation Evaluation involves gathering data to make judgments about value or worth. Data are gathered at the program or institutional level to determine whether a program is effective (Secolsky and Denison 2017). For example, a prison might gather data on the success rate for inmates who complete a skills-training program in order to determine whether the program should continue to be offered. This chapter has been addressing evaluation; suggestions are made to comprehensively evaluate the processes and outcomes of PDPs. Similar to assessment, evaluation should be conducted by professionals trained in measurement and program evaluation.

Research The process of research is quite different from assessment and evaluation, both in purpose and process. Research is the systematic investigation of empirical questions to create public knowledge (Zedeck 2014). Although research can involve gathering the same *kind* of data (e.g., self-report measure of optimism or prison social climate), the *objective* is to add to public knowledge and move science forward. In contrast to assessment and evaluation, in which data are gathered on the affected individual or group and shared with no one, research is conducted on citizens who volunteer to participate in research and findings are shared with the public. Similar to assessment and evaluation, research should only be conducted by trained professionals. Researchers are trained at the masters or doctoral level in research design, measurement, data analysis/interpretation, and ethics.

Research can involve control and manipulation of variables (e.g., inmates are randomly assigned to be in the PDP or traditional programming), leaving research subjects vulnerable to the researchers' actions. Thus, special permissions are required to conduct research. Prior to conducting a study, the plan must be reviewed for compliance with ethical guidelines. When research involves human subjects, it must be reviewed and approved by an institutional review board (IRB). This is a group of people who review the research plan within the context of ethical standards and laws. There are different levels of IRB review, depending on the risk associated with participation in the study. Studies involving more vulnerable populations, who lack the ability to fully consent to participate, require the highest level of review. This level of review—full review—is required for research involving children and vulnerable adults (e.g., prisoners, individuals with impaired decision-making capacity). Thus, research on PDPs require full IRB review. The Pen Pals research underwent full IRB review at the university where the researchers were located. Then the research plan went through a second full review by the department of corrections' IRB.

Research involving animals must be reviewed by an institutional animal care and use committee (IACUC). This committee looks at the research plan from the perspective of preventing harm to the animal(s) (National Association for Biomedical Research 2019). Research on PDPs may involve both human and animal subjects and thus may require approval from both an IRB and an IACUC. The Pen Pals program was not required to undergo IACUC review because (a) the research did not involve control or manipulation of the dogs, and (b) data were gathered on the inmates, not the dogs.

Collaborating for Success As we can see, gathering data on a PDP is complex. Depending on the objective, you may be interested in an assessment, a program evaluation, or a research study. Each of these requires special training. PDP coordinators will benefit from collaborating with professionals in the relevant field. Assessment may be conducted by trained professionals at the correctional facility or outside consultants (e.g., forensic clinical psychologist). This chapter has focused mostly on program evaluation. The suggestions for measurement of stakeholders and the environment should be conducted through collaboration with an expert in program evaluation. To contribute to science, PDPs should collaborate with researchers, particularly those who have done previous research in prisons or animal-assisted intervention in general, or PDPs specifically. To start, programs can contact researchers cited in the literature. In addition, some professional organizations specialize in human-animal scholarship and may be helpful in finding researchers with whom to partner. The International Society on Anthrozoology (ISAZ) is an organization for the scientific and scholarly study of human-animal interactions (ISAZ 2014). Within the field of psychology, Division 17 of the American Psychological Association has a Section 13 on Human-Animal Interaction: Research and Practice. This section is dedicated to professional and scholarly activities that advance the understanding of HAI as it relates to psychology (Human-Animal Interaction Section 2019).

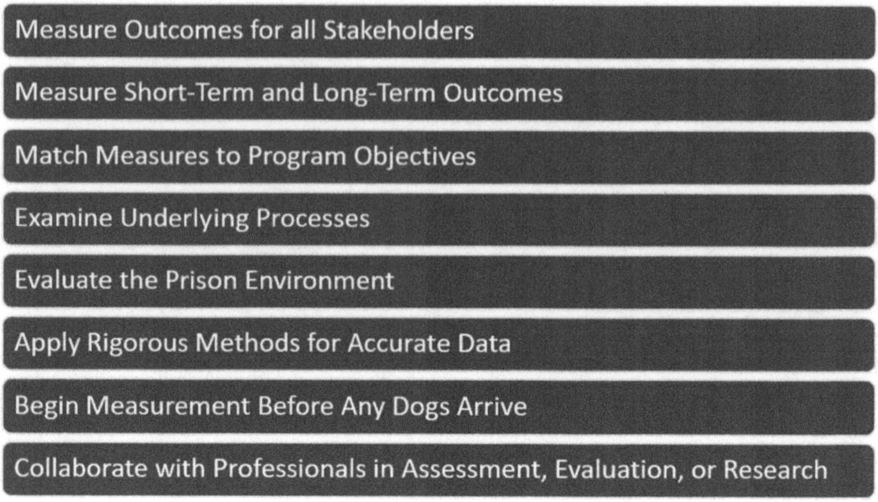

Fig. 9.8 Recommendations for comprehensive PDP evaluation

Summary

This chapter has provided suggestions for conducting comprehensive PDP evaluation. Rather than prescribing specific variables to measure or methods to follow, we suggest thoughtful planning of a rigorous evaluation plan incorporating the key components listed in Fig. 9.8. Despite anecdotal reports that PDPs impact the full spectrum of stakeholders (e.g., inmates, correctional staff, dogs, end-users), the literature to date focuses on inmates. Furthermore, studies on inmates are not linked to clear program objectives and are hampered by selection bias and nonexperimental methods. There will likely be constraints limiting the ideal evaluation. Nevertheless, evaluation should incorporate these suggestions to the greatest extent feasible. Gathering accurate data is imperative to drive ethical, effective decisions at the institution and program level. Rigorous, programmatic research is needed to inform the broad fields of corrections, animal welfare, and human-animal interaction.

References

Affleck, G., Tennen, H., & Apter, A. (2001). Optimism, pessimism, and daily life with chronic illness. In E. Chang (Ed.), *Optimism and pessimism: Implications for theory, research, and practice* (pp. 147–168). Washington, DC: American Psychological Association.

Allison, M., & Ramaswamy, M. (2016). Adapting animal-assisted therapy trials to prison-based animal programs. *Public Health Nursing, 33*(5), 472–480.

Anderson, D. C. (2007). *Assessing the human-animal bond: A compendium of actual measures*. West Lafayette, IN: Purdue University Press.

Anestis, M. D., Anestis, J. C., Zawilinski, L. L., Hopkins, T. A., & Lilienfeld, S. O. (2014). Equine-related treatments for mental disorders lack empirical support: A systematic review of empirical investigations. *Journal of Clinical Psychology, 70*(12), 1115–1132.

Antonio, M. E., Davis, R. G., & Shutt, S. R. (2017). Dog training programs in Pennsylvania's department of corrections: Perceived effectiveness for inmates and staff. *Society & Animals, 25* (5), 475–489.

Auty, K. M., & Liebling, A. (2019). Exploring the relationship between prison social climate and reoffending. *Justice Quarterly*, 1–24.

Bachi, K. (2013). Equine-facilitated prison-based programs within the context of prison-based animal programs: State of the science review. *Journal of Offender Rehabilitation, 52,* 46–74.

Beetz, A., Uvnäs-Moberg, K., Julius, H., & Kotrschal, K. (2012). Psychosocial and psychophysiological effects of human-animal interactions: The possible role of oxytocin. *Frontiers in Psychology, 3*(234), 1–15.

Britton, D. M., & Button, A. (2007). This isn't about us: Benefits of dog training programs in a women's prison. In S. L. Miller (Ed.), *Criminal justice and diversity: Voices from the field* (pp. 195–209). Boston, MA: Northeastern University Press.

Bureau of Labor Statistics. (May, 2017). *Occupational employment and wages: 33-3012 correctional officers and jailers*. Retrieved from: https://www.bls.gov/oes/2017/may/oes333012.htm.

Bustad, L. K. (1990). Prison programs involving animals. In L. K. Bustad (Ed.), *Compassion, our last great hope* (pp. 72–73). Renton, WA: Delta Society.

Cooke, B. J., & Farrington, D. P. (2015). The effects of dog-training programs: Experiences of incarcerated females. *Women & Criminal Justice, 25*(3), 201–214.

Cooke, B. J., & Farrington, D. P. (2016). The effectiveness of dog-training programs in prison: A systematic review and meta-analysis of the literature. *The Prison Journal, 96*(6), 854–876.

Cressey, D. R. (Ed.). (1961). *The prison: Studies in institutional organization and change*. New York: Holt, Rinehart and Winston.

Currie, N. S. (2008). *A case study of incarcerated males participating in a canine training program* (Unpublished doctoral dissertation). Department of Special Education, Counseling, and Student Affairs College of Education, Kansas State University, Manhattan, KS.

Deaton, C. (2005). Humanizing prisons with animals: A closer look at "cell dogs" and horse programs in correctional institutions. *Journal of Correctional Education, 56*(1), 46–62.

Ellingson, K. (2019, February 11). Coyote Ridge Dogs Program Interview. (L. Winston, Interviewer)

FETCH a Cure. (2018). *Pen pals*. Retrieved from: https://fetchacure.org/pen-pals/.

Fournier, A. K. (2016). Pen pals: An examination of human–animal interaction as an outlet for healthy masculinity in prison. In C. Blazina & L. R. Kogan (Eds.), *Men and their dogs* (pp. 175–194). Switzerland: Springer International Publishing.

Fournier, A. K., Berry, T. D., Letson, E., & Chanen, R. (2016). The human–animal interaction scale: Development and evaluation. *Anthrozoös, 29*(3), 455–467.

Fournier, A. K., & Geller, E. S. (2004). Behavior analysis of companion-animal overpopulation: A conceptualization of the problem and suggestions for intervention. *Behavior and Social Issues, 13*(1), 51–68.

Fournier, A. K., Geller, E. S., & Fortney, E. E. (2007). Human-animal interaction in a prison setting: Impact on criminal behavior, treatment progress, and social skills. *Behavior and Social Issues, 16*(1), 89–105.

Furst, G. (2006). Prison-based animal programs: A national survey. *The Prison Journal, 86*(4), 407–430.

Furst, G. (2011). *Animal programs in prison: A comprehensive assessment*. Boulder, CO: First Forum Press.

Gates, M., Zito, S., Thomas, J., & Dale, A. (2018). Post-adoption problem behaviours in adolescent and adult dogs rehomed through a New Zealand animal shelter. *Animals, 8*(93), 1–11.

Gerst, M., & Moos, R. H. (1972). The social ecology of university student residences. *Journal of Educational Psychology, 63*(6), 513–525.

Huitt, W., Hummel, J., & Kaeck, D. (2001). Assessment, measurement, evaluation, and research. *Educational Psychology Interactive*. Valdosta, GA: Valdosta State University. Retrieved from: http://www.edpsycinteractive.org/topics/intro/sciknow.html.

Human-Animal Interaction, Section 13 of Division 17. (2019). *HAI section home*. Retrieved from: https://www.apa-hai.org/human-animal-interaction/.

Humby, L., & Barclay, E. (2018). Pawsitive solutions: An overview of Prison Dog Programs in Australia. *The Prison Journal, 98*(5), 580–603.

International Society on Anthrozoology. (2014). *What is ISAZ?* Retrieved from: http://www.isaz.net/isaz/.

Johnson, T., Garrity, T., & Stallones, L. (1992). Psychometric evaluation of the Lexington Attachment to Pets Scale (LAPS). *Anthrozoös, 5*(3), 160–175.

Julius, H., Beetz, J. H. A., Kotrschal, K., Turner, D., & Uvnäs-Moberg, K. (2012). *Attachment to pets: An integrative view of human-animal relationships with implications for therapeutic practice*. Boston: Hogrefe Publishing.

Lambert, E. G., Hogan, N. L., Griffin, M. L., & Kelley, T. (2015). The correctional staff burnout literature. *Criminal Justice Studies, 28*(4), 397.

Lipton, D. S., Pearson, F. S., Cleland, C. M., & Yee, D. (2002). The effects of therapeutic communities and milieu therapy on recidivism. In J. McGuire (Ed.), *Offender rehabilitation and treatment: Effective programmes and policies to reduce re-offending* (pp. 39–77). West Sussex, London: Wiley.

Marsa-Sambola, F., Muldoon, J., Williams, J., Lawrence, A., Connor, M., & Currie, C. (2016). The short attachment to pets scale (SAPS) for children and young people: Development, psychometric qualities and demographic and health associations. *Child Indicators Research, 9*(1), 111–131.

McNair, D. M., Lorr, M., & Droppleman, L. F. (1971). *Manual for the profile of mood states (POMS)*. San Diego, CA: Educational and Industrial Testing Service.

Moos, R. H. (1968). The assessment of the social climates of correctional institutions. *Journal of Research in Crime & Delinquency, 5*, 174–188. https://doi.org/10.1177/002242786800500207.

Moos, R. H. (1974). *Evaluating correctional and community settings*. New York: Wiley.

Moos, R. H. (1987). *Correctional institutions environment scale* (2nd ed.). Redwood, CA: Mindgarden.

Moos, R. H. (1989). *Ward atmosphere scale manual*. Palo Alto, CA: Consulting Psychologists Press.

Moos, R. H., & Houts, P. S. (1968). Assessment of the social atmospheres of psychiatric wards. *Journal of Abnormal Psychology, 73*(6), 595–604.

National Association for Biomedical Research. *Functions of the IACUC*. Retrieved from: https://www.nabr.org/animal-welfare-2/animal-welfare-in-practice/functions-of-the-iacuc/.

Nef, N. (2004, October 6–9). *The cat programme, an animal-assisted therapy at Saxierriet prison for men: Its effects and results in a correctional establishment*. Paper presented at the 10th International Conference on Human-Animal Interactions, Glasgow, Scotland.

Poresky, R. H., Hendrix, C., Mosier, J. E., & Samuelson, M. L. (1987). The companion animal bonding scale: Internal reliability and construct validity. *Psychological Reports, 60*(3), 743–746.

Poresky, R. H., Hendrix, C., Mosier, J. E., & Samuelson, M. L. (1988). Young children's companion animal bonding and adults' pet attitudes: A retrospective study. *Psychological Reports, 62*(2), 419–425.

Richardson-Taylor, K., & Blanchette, K. (2001). *Results of an evaluation of the Pawsitive Directions Canine Program at Nova Institution for Women*. Ottawa, Ontario: Correctional Service of Canada.

Riggio, R. E. (1986). Assessment of basic social skills. *Journal of Personality and Social Psychology, 51*(3), 649–660.
Robinson, J., Craig, L. A., & Tonkin, M. (2016). Perceptions of social climate and aggressive behavior in forensic services: A systematic review. *Trauma, Violence, & Abuse, 19*(4), 391–405.
Schalast, N., & Groenewald, I. (2009). Ein Kurzfragebogen zur Einschätzung des sozialen Klimas im Strafvollzug [A short questionnaire to assess the social climate in prisons] (Erste Befunde auf Abteilungen des Regelvollzugs und der Sozialtherapie). In R. Haller & J. M. Jehle (Eds.), *Drogen – Sucht – Kriminalität* (pp. 329–352). Mönchengladbach, Germany: Forum.
Scheier, M. F., & Carver, C. S. (1985). Optimism, coping, and health: Assessment and implications of generalized outcome expectancies. *Health Psychology, 4*(3), 219.
Scheier, M. F., Carver, C. S., & Bridges, M. W. (1994). Distinguishing optimism from neuroticism (and trait anxiety, self-mastery, and self-esteem): A reevaluation of the Life Orientation Test. *Journal of Personality and Social Psychology, 67*(6), 1063.
Serpell, J. A. (1990). Evidence for long term effects of pet ownership on human health. *Pets, Benefits and Practice (Proceedings of Waltham Symposium), 20,* 1–7.
Sharkin, B. S., & Ruff, L. A. (2011). Broken bonds: Understanding the experience of pet relinquishment. In C. Blazina, G. Boyraz, & D. Shen-Miller (Eds.), *The psychology of the human-animal bond* (pp. 275–288). New York: Springer.
Secolsky, C., & Denison, D. B. (Eds.). (2017). *Handbook on measurement, assessment, and evaluation in higher education* (2nd ed.). New York: Routledge.
Selby, A., & Smith-Osborne, A. (2013). A systematic review of effectiveness of complementary and adjunct therapies and interventions involving equines. *Health Psychology, 32*(4), 418.
Strimple, E. O. (2003). A history of prison inmate-animal interaction programs. *American Behavioral Scientist, 47,* 70–78.
Templer, D., Arikawa, H., Canfield, M., Munsell, K., & Tangan, K. (2004). Modification of the pet attitude scale. *Society & Animals, 12*(2), 137–142.
Toch, H. (1992). *Living in prison: The ecology of survival.* Washington, DC: American Psychological Association.
Tonkin, M. (2015). A review of questionnaire measures for assessing the social climate in prisons and forensic psychiatric hospitals. *International Journal of Offender Therapy and Comparative Criminology, 60*(12), 1376–1405.
Turner, W. G. (2007). The experiences of offenders in a prison canine program. *Federal Probation, 71*(1), 38–43.
Van der Helm, P., Stams, G. J., & Van der Laan, P. (2011). Measuring group climate in prison. *The Prison Journal, 91*(2), 158–176.
Virginia Department of Corrections. (2015). *Pen pals.* Retrieved August 13, 2015 from: https://vadoc.virginia.gov/offenders/institutions/programs/penpals.shtm.
Wenk, E. A., & Moos, R. H. (1972). Social climates in prison: An attempt to conceptualize and measure environmental factors in total institutions. *Journal of Research in Crime and Delinquency, 9*(2), 134–148.
Wilkie, K. D., Germain, S., & Theule, J. (2016). Evaluating the efficacy of equine therapy among at-risk youth: A meta-analysis. *Anthrozoös, 29*(3), 377–393.
Winkle, M., Crowe, T. K., & Hendrix, I. (2012). Service dogs and people with physical disabilities partnerships: A systematic review. *Occupational Therapy International, 19*(1), 54–66.
Wright, K. N. (1985). Developing the prison environment inventory. *Journal of Research in Crime and Delinquency, 22*(3), 257–277.
Wright, K. N. (1993). Prison environment and behavioral outcomes. *Journal of Offender Rehabilitation, 20*(1–2), 93–114.
Zedeck, S. (Ed.). (2014). *APA dictionary of statistics and research methods.* Washington, DC: American Psychological Association.

Chapter 10
Evaluating Outcomes in a Prison-Based Canine Program: A Mixed-Method Analysis of New Leash on Life

James W. Conroy, Elizabeth C. Coppola, Charles S. Ferris, Nora L. Conroy, Steven J. Devlin and Julie A. Boc

Introduction

Recent decades have been met with a growing demand from government agencies and legislative bodies for rigorous social science research to inform decisions about policy options and tools. With the rising demand for accountability, policymakers and stakeholders want to know the extent to which interventions, programming, and services meet their intended purposes (McCall 2009). Further, elected officials, nonprofit funders, oversight agencies, and citizens have a growing interest in understanding the value provided to the public by the programs they fund via taxes and charitable contributions (Newcomer et al. 2010). Thus, program evaluation—the systematic method for collecting, analyzing, and using information to answer questions about a program (U.S. Department of Health and Human Services 2003)—is essential to understanding if, how, and why interventions, such as New Leash on Life (NLOL)—the prison dog program detailed in the present chapter—may mitigate complex problems in corrections such as recidivism and the challenges of successful reentry.

Interventions and the research programs used to evaluate them are typically justified in terms of their capacity to reflect society's public values, or the normative consensus regarding the rights, benefits, and prerogatives to which certain citizens should –or should not—be entitled (Bozeman 2007; Bozeman and Sarewitz 2011). The articulation of public values is pervasive in science policy-making, where policymakers draw from finite resources and choose to allocate public investments

J. W. Conroy · N. L. Conroy · S. J. Devlin · J. A. Boc
Center for Outcome Analysis, Havertown, PA, USA

E. C. Coppola (✉) · N. L. Conroy
Purdue University, West Lafayette, IN, USA
e-mail: ecoppola@purdue.edu

C. S. Ferris
Emory University, Atlanta, GA, USA

M. R. Jalongo (ed.), *Prison Dog Programs*,
https://doi.org/10.1007/978-3-030-25618-0_10

among competing scientific disciplines, projects, and programs (Bozeman and Sarewitz 2011). Nevertheless, the evidence base generated from empirical research is likely to have less standing and relevance on complex and value-laden issues due to their heightened vulnerability of being sidetracked by heated controversy, rhetoric, or politicization (Head 2010). Offender rehabilitation and reentry represents such an issue, as public values reflecting personal accountability and punishment are pervasive cultural narratives underlying governance in Western democracies (Day and Ward 2010). Thus, the pervasiveness of public values may undermine efforts to implement and fund certain interventions or programs designed to support inmates. With recidivism costing taxpayers an estimated $151,662 per recidivism event (Illinois Sentencing Policy Advisory Council 2018), one approach to appealing to public values in offender rehabilitation and reentry is demonstrating taxpayers' return on investment from such programming. This may be accomplished through a cost-benefit analysis, in which the expenses associated with participation in a prison animal programming (PAPs) are compared to the expenses associated with program implementation (Weisburd et al. 2017).

Although many policymakers and stakeholders have started moving beyond the "nothing works" doctrine (Cullen 2013), key gaps persist in the existing knowledge base regarding the economic benefits of offender rehabilitation and reentry programming (Weisburd et al. 2017). In the example of NLOL, although animal programs in correctional facilities provide many observable benefits to the community, such as saving shelter animals from euthanasia or training service animals, the impact of such programs on participants remains unclear (Mulcahy and McLaughlin 2013). Due to the salience of public values in the discourse on correctional issues, we contend that animal programs in corrections will continue to be privately funded, sporadic, "boutique" interventions until the cost-benefit science shows that these programs are "worth it" by demonstrating taxpayers' return on investment.

The evaluative studies described later in this chapter are based on the Philadelphia Prison System's decision to pilot test, and then expand, a "Prison-Based Animal Program" (Furst 2011). The program was initiated and conducted by a Pennsylvania non-profit organization, New Leash on Life USA. It was based on saving dogs condemned to euthanasia, training/retraining the dogs to make them suitable for adoption into loving families, and training prisoners to become fully competent trainers. The unusual leadership of this program, and the support it generated in correctional and philanthropic circles, created a rare opportunity for high quality scientific evaluation of the processes and outcomes of such a program. The study began with a qualitative analysis of the motivations, expectations, and experiences of the first six graduates and two of the involved correctional officers, and moved forward into quantitative analyses of perceived qualities of life among the same six inmates who participated during the qualitative phase.

Existing Research on PAPs

The modern history of PAPs can be traced back to 1975, when inmates at a forensic center were observed cooperating to protect and nurse an injured sparrow. The benefits of this first program were immediate and included an elimination of suicides and riots on the ward (Ormerod 2008). Later, in 1981, shelter animals were paired with inmates at Lorton Prison in a pet adoption program established by the People-Animals-Love group and, in the same year, Tacoma Community College permitted inmates to participate in the People Pet Partnership program through Tacoma Community College. Serving as an early prototype for NLOL, inmates in the People Pet Partnership program received classroom lessons and hands-on sessions with the goal of training shelter dogs for adoption (Furst 2006). Other attempts to catalogue the various programs exist and are largely focused on those in the U.S. (Furst 2006; Strimple 2003).

Anticipated Benefits of Prison Dog Programs (PDPs)

Benefits to dogs participating in PDPs are evident: many of these dogs would otherwise be put down and their continued life can be considered an immediate benefit without reference. However, studies have also shown that dogs trained in these programs display decreased aggression (Haynes 1991; Hennessy et al. 2006), are better trained than those trained outside of the prison environment (Harkrader et al. 2004), and experience reductions in salivary cortisol concentrations consistent with stress reduction (Koda et al. 2016).

Benefits accrue for the humans involved in such programs as well. Inmates, administrators, and correctional officers all demonstrate lower blood pressure and increased morale throughout the duration of animal programming at correctional facilities (Katcher et al. 1989; Harkrader et al. 2004). Past studies have also begun to document increases in various social skills, including an increased sense of responsibility, higher self-esteem, and more developed compassion for other humans (Harkrader et al. 2004; Furst 2006; Turner 2007). These observations have received support from biochemical research (Hennessy et al. 2006) and are consistent with findings in the broader human-animal interaction literature (Rodriguez Bryce Granger and O'Haire 2018). Moreover, participants in prison-based dog training programs accrue tangible vocational skills that facilitate their reentry into the community (Furst 2006; Harkrader et al. 2004).

PDPs may also yield broader benefits for society. While some studies found lower recidivism rates among populations that have been exposed to dog training programs in prison (Chianese 2009; Cooke 2014; Moneymaker and Strimple 1991; Merriam 2001; Strimple 2003; Turner 2007), these findings have been mixed with others that failed to produce significant findings (Cooke 2014). Large-scale replication, paired with the rigor of randomized controlled trials, may help rectify discrepancies in these findings. Nevertheless, these findings tentatively suggest that PDPs are a potential solution for promoting successful offender reentry (Cooke and Farrington 2016). Vulnerable segments of society also benefit from dog training programs groups, as many of them develop service animals for veterans with post-traumatic stress disorder and people with disabilities (Hershman 2008; Smith 2011).

Program Description

New Leash on Life USA (http://newleashonlife-usa.org/) was founded in 2010 primarily as a way to save dogs, particularly pit bulls, from destruction. By the time the first cohort of participants began training, New Leash on Life was also aimed strongly at benefiting the participating inmates by teaching them concrete skills that might heighten hope, build self-esteem, and potentially assist them in gaining employment post-release. According to the information on the group's website:

> New Leash on Life USA is a new generation prison dog-training program that saves the lives of shelter dogs by training and socializing them to enhance their adoptability while helping inmates learn to train and care for dogs.
>
> With New Leash on Life USA, dogs live in the cells with their inmate trainers 24/7, making New Leash dogs highly desirable for adoption and ensuring the long-term success for both humans and dogs.
>
> New Leash on Life USA provides:
>
> - Weekly sessions with professional trainers, animal behaviorists and veterinary technicians.
> - Job readiness and life skills courses to improve successful reentry and employability for inmates upon parole.
> - Scholarships for paroled inmates for additional training and education in the animal care field.

The program has been privately funded via donations from local philanthropic donations. The Philadelphia Prison System, including its commissioner, has been strongly supportive of NLOL from the beginning—a factor that the program's founders believe to have been crucial during early implementation.

NLOL's training agenda features a multi-pronged approach to prepare inmates and canines for life outside of prison. Inmates are required to attend two hours of classroom learning twice a week, where they learn about dogs including health, care, and training. Additionally, they receive two to three hours of hands on work with the dogs with an expert trainer twice a week, and attend weekly classes in life skills for post-release adaptation, provided by a private nonprofit agency with experience in correctional education. Finally, participants complete the Canine Good Citizen test through the American Kennel Club at the end of the 10 weeks, which serves as the criterion for both dog adoptability and participant receipt of a certificate.

The Present Studies

Both phases in the studies detailed below collected data from the same class of NLOL participants: the first phase administered qualitative interviews with six inmates and two correctional officers during the program, and the second phase collected quantitative data from five inmates after completion of the program.

This evaluation work was submitted for full Institutional Review Board (IRB) review by the City of Philadelphia's IRB, *Approval # 2011-34—New Leash on Life (NLOL): A Quantitative Program Evaluation of a Dog Training Program for Inmates*. Although coercion must be absent for valid consent, prisoners were offered significant benefits for participating. These benefits could be seen as related to basic human rights, such as freedom of movement, confinement regimens, and so forth. Both phases of the evaluation shared several additional common elements that are detailed below.

Inclusion Criteria for Participating Inmates

All participating inmates in either phase were in custody of the Alternative and Special Detentions (ASD) division of the Philadelphia Prison System, which was designed for low risk inmates who were judged likely to behave well and take educational and rehabilitative programs seriously. Inclusion criteria for inmates were therefore identical to the eligibility criteria for NLOL: candidates could have no history of harming animals or children and were not set to be discharged within the next 10 weeks in order to participate throughout the entire duration of the program.

Procedures

The program was a 10 week "live-in" design, in which five dogs rescued from imminent euthanasia were placed with 11 inmates of the Philadelphia city jail's ASD for 10 weeks. Participating inmates were trained in animal care generally, and training techniques specifically. Each dog completed the American Kennel Club's Canine Good Citizenship test at the end and participating inmates received a certificate of completion of the animal training curriculum.

Participants There were originally eight inmates enrolled in NLOL at the time of these studies.

Two of the eight original participants in NLOL committed an infraction that resulted in being sent to, and thus could not complete the program with their own class. Consequently, six males in the custody of the ASD division of the

Philadelphia Prison System and two corrections officers working on the same unit volunteered to participate in the first (qualitative) phase.

The sixth graduating member did not elect to engage in continued participation, meaning that five of the six graduating members of NLOL participated in the second (quantitative) phase.

First Phase: Qualitative Interviews

Methods

Materials Materials included a semi-structured interview with six guiding qualitative assessment questions. Inmates responded to the following questions:

- Why do you want to be (or why were you) involved in the NLOL program?
- What do you think you'll get (or what did you get) out of it?
- Do you think you will (or did) establish a connection with your dog?
- Do you think it will (or did) succeed and why?
- Do you think this program will be (was) good for anyone—participants, dogs, guards, managers, society?
- What do you think this will mean for you when you get out?

Procedures Both inmates and corrections officers were interviewed near the completion of the NLOL program. Instrument questions were read by interviewers with follow-up probing questions utilized as deemed appropriate. Interviews were recorded and then transcribed by a research team member.

Plans for Analysis The research team adopted a grounded theory approach (Glaser and Strauss 1967) by systematically reviewing and summarizing interviews and then reporting on findings. Interview transcripts were read and reviewed by the research team. Responses were condensed and re-categorized into four major themes: joining, gains, effect on relationships, and the future. Each interview was scanned for responses that fit the nature of these categories and a quotation file was manually synthesized.

Qualitative Results

After collecting data, transcribing, and reviewing the various accounts of the participants' experience with the program, our preliminary analysis identified four major recurring themes: (1) becoming motivated to join the program, (2) gaining valuable skills during the training process, (3) developing new relationships through their time with the dogs, and (4) looking to the future.

Theme 1: Motivations for Joining When questioned at the beginning of their involvement with the program, participants had a wide range of reasons for participating in the NLOL curriculum. The only recurring motivation for participants joining the program were variations of "Because I like dogs" (all 6) and "it sounded like a cool thing to try" (4 of the 6). However, the most interesting responses were the unorthodox ones. A few of the participants, it turned out, did not even want to be in the program.

> Honestly, I didn't want to join. They came around with papers saying, "Do you want to sign up for the New Leash on Life program?" I said "Yeah," so I signed it, but then they said, "You've got to move to D-block," and I was on B-block, but I didn't want to move over there so I didn't want to participate in the program, and Martin the guard told me "You ain't got no choice, now you in a hole."

This quote is drawn from the inmate who was later unanimously described by NLOL staff as the most successful member of the group. This participant was initially so uncooperative due to his generalized negative attitude about being what he viewed as his unjust conviction that there was serious discussion about removing him from the program. After successfully completing the program, this participant accepted a 30 day post-release internship at the Animal Care and Control Team facility, and then subsequently interviewed with a shelter for a paid job.

One of the great concerns in the early stages of the NLOL implementation was a spreading rumor that participants would be paroled upon graduation from the program. It is unclear exactly how this story was birthed, but it presented a potential danger in that the NLOL program had no authority over this aspect of inmate life. There was concern that members of the group would expect this benefit and would become confrontational if graduation prompted release did not become a reality.

> Cause it'll help me go home, yeah, and I was scared of the dogs so I thought this would be a good program. I thought it would be a good program to help me get over the fear of dogs.

This hurdle became a reality when after graduation members of the program were not all immediately released. Nevertheless, inmates and correctional officers still cited a myriad of benefits stemming from the implementation of this program.

Theme 2: Personal Benefits In response to the questions about what they thought they would gain from participation in the program, the most common answers involved training, responsibility, patience, and the chance to save dogs from euthanasia. Consistent with this theme, one participant remarked:

> I didn't really have expectations, all I want to do is save a dog's life, give him another chance.

Another participant illustrated how participation in NLOL fostered responsibility:

> So it just helped me prioritize, like I might not want to deal with him that day, but I got to deal with it, that's how I be with my son. Yeah, like he got to rely on me, he can't just get up and do what he want when he want to do it. That's how it is with your kid. So it just helped me just get my priorities together, and my responsibilities.

And yet another participant reflected a new sense of developing identity and purpose:

> Well, being in the streets I lost exactly who I was and started people pleasing, and then everybody, and trying to be the best at everything that I forgot who I was. By having Cash [the participant's assigned dog] with me for these past three months took me back.

Even the men who committed an infraction that got them removed from NLOL continued to feel caring, responsible, and affectionate toward their assigned dogs:

> I think it did [succeed] and then again it didn't because it did for some and it didn't for some, it's crazy because there were eight of us and now there's what six of us but they brought my celly [cellmate] back even though they kicked him out of the program already but he's still willing to help because that's how much he love Paris you feel what I'm saying?

The corrections officers commented, at times, on their observation of rather remarkable changes among the participants:

> I saw a big change in some of the inmates. A lot of the inmates that had that "I don't care" attitude started to appreciate a few things a little more. I saw them caring about something other than themselves and having to take care of something other than themselves…they were being a little more productive, sociable, and a lot calmer.

Overall, these qualitative findings illustrate some primary, personal benefits that inmates received from participating in the program.

Theme 3: Effects on Relationships and the Environment The presence of the dogs appeared to have an effect on the global prison environment. Participants described interactions between inmates and correction officers as being less tense:

> When it all started off there was a lot of, a little, a little tension on and off… but after a while everybody, I don't want to say everybody take a liking to each other but everybody understands each other now, and there hasn't been any crashing heads in like over a month. And everybody's just been uh, and everybody helped each other out, and the next dog and we all pulled through…

As evidenced by this participant's quote, the inmates were able to bond with both their dogs and each other once there was less tension. This participant observed a change in the way the inmates understood each other. A few participants reported that the experience of working with others was a change for them. Teamwork was a theme that emerged throughout the group's responses to many of the questions:

> Yeah it was different cause I ain't never been to work with nobody else so it was like a team thing, it was something new.

This program gave participants the opportunity to learn social skills through training the dogs. Another participant shared his reaction to witnessing his peers interact with the dogs:

> I saw them caring about something other than themselves, and having to take care of something other than themselves.

The implication behind this quotation is that these men tended to take care of number one, and spent little time or energy on others, human or animal. Many were surprised by the connection they formed with their dogs. One participant mentioned that even the correction officers and other inmates who were not in the program became attached to the dogs.

> The dogs not only helped the individuals that trained them get through their time, but a lot of the people that's living in the area, and on other blocks…Four dogs, the whole jail.

The interviews revealed a trend toward group bonding and mutual assistance to "do good time and get out." There were comments about teamwork that were surprising to the men themselves.

> It just, it brings, the atmosphere is a lot different with the dogs in the jail, cause people are a lot more at ease, then all tense and you know.

Similarly, another participant remarked:

> Yeah it was different cause I ain't never been to work with nobody else so it was like a team thing, it was something new

On cooperation and peaceful interaction, one inmate commented:

> Pretty much everybody in the program was kinda close, we grew a bond, I mean like everybody just really like clicked with each other.

There were comments about the corrections officers too:

> Yeah it did. The COs got attached to the dogs also the inmates that weren't involved in the program got attached to the dogs and stuff.

Improved attitude was also evident:

> The program] helped me, like, be more calmer, cause I knew I had stuff to work for.

One participant expressed a surprised "Yes" to the question "Did you think you established a connection with your dog?"

> Yes I did. No, I wasn't expecting it, it kind of surprised me. Once I got him, and then once they took him that one day, that's when I knew that I was attached.

Theme 4: Hope About the Future Another theme that emerged throughout the discussion was hope for the future. The inmates discussed a more positive future that they attributed to their participation in the program. Many participants referenced a future career in dog training. When further probed, participants described the job and self-regulatory skills that they expected to use in the future:

> Responsibility, patience, a lot of patience. It's just, I don't know, and I like to train the dogs, like I liked, yeah I can see me doing that like as a job.

This quote demonstrates how this program fostered a sense of job-readiness within the participants. Another participant described how he planned to use this training to his advantage:

> Yeah, it'll help me in the long run. Say I go to the SPCA…I'll be like I've got experience with dogs and I show them the paper that I graduate even if it's from jail, I show them that and they won't say nothing. I show them that paper, you never know and they, they hire me.

This participant felt confident that he would be able to get a job in the field of dog training after he was released. Having a sense that there will be job opportunities once they are released from jail can motivate the participants to seek them out. It gives them hope for a better future, rather than just returning them to the same situation they were in before they were incarcerated.

Another participant went into detail about their view on dog training. He describes the skills he acquired as a trade.

> I was taught how to groom a dog, and cut their nails, how to brush their teeth a certain way you know, and basically just the whole training process. At first it was a little complicated but as you go along with it, yeah it gets easier. Yeah, basically like a trade.

Even the correction officers who were interviewed described a better future for the inmates and the dogs.

> All the dogs passed. And we turned these guys into trainers, whether they know it or not, you know.

Second Phase: Quantitative Data

The second phase aimed to collect data on the self-perceptions of the participants about whether their life conditions and feelings improved during the NLOL. We anticipated that inmates would self-report improved perceptions in their quality of life as a consequence of participation in NLOL. We originally intended to conduct two waves of interviews, one prior to participation in NLOL (pre-test) and one after completing NLOL (post-test), but were unable to do so due to unexpected delays in the City of Philadelphia's Institutional Review Board (IRB) process. Since IRB approval was not obtained until near the end of the first NLOL cohort's program, the present study provides preliminary findings for a forthcoming planned pre- and post-test, in which recent graduates of NLOL reported on both their current quality of life in prison and were primed to recall their quality of life in prison prior to participation in NLOL.

Procedures

We conducted a post-only analysis of quality of prison life perceptions among participants in a recently initiated canine training program. Five dogs rescued from imminent euthanasia were placed with 11 inmates of the Philadelphia city jail's ASD for 10 weeks.

At the end of the 10 weeks, we asked participants to rate their qualities of life in the jail both "Then" (just before the program began) and "Now" (at the moment of the interview). This approach is called the "memory of change" method, and it is different from pre- and post-test approaches because it collects data concurrently from a single time point. The results were consistent, and their statistical significance fairly high.

Measures We designed a simple survey comprised of 38 questions about qualities of prison life. Responses ranged on a scale of 1 (*Very bad*) to 5 (*Very good*). Survey questions fit into five general categories: Feelings about self, emotions, relationships with staff, prison conditions, and relationships with other inmates.

Analytic Approach

Inferential statistics are intended to tell us whether what we see in a sample is likely to be true for the entire population. For this particular study, we have the entire population of NLOL participants, not a sample, and we do not claim to be generalizing to a larger group. Thus, the results can be represented in a graph because statistics are not strictly necessary for the present study.

As a formality, we compared mean "Now" and "Then" scores using the Student's t-test and the Wilcoxon Signed Ranks Test. The latter is designed for use with small numbers of cases in samples. We tested for statistical significance at the $p < .10$ level.

Quantitative Results

In the graph, the darker red colored bars on top show the "Then" ratings, representing inmates' memories of how things were before their dogs arrived, and the lighter colored blue bars at the bottom show the "Now" ratings, while near the end of their time working with the dogs (Fig. 10.1).

The top two bars of the graph show that the participants in the second NLOL cohort had strong positive feelings about themselves. Positive feelings about themselves increased from an average of 4.18 out of 5 points to 4.45. In fact, each of the "Now" lighter bars represents larger averages than the "Then" darker bars, showing that the participants' ratings about their lives improved across all five dimensions.

Statistical analysis with such small samples is challenged by the fact that it is very hard to achieve statistical significance with very small samples. We used both kinds of statistical tests for this situation, parametric and non-parametric, using the

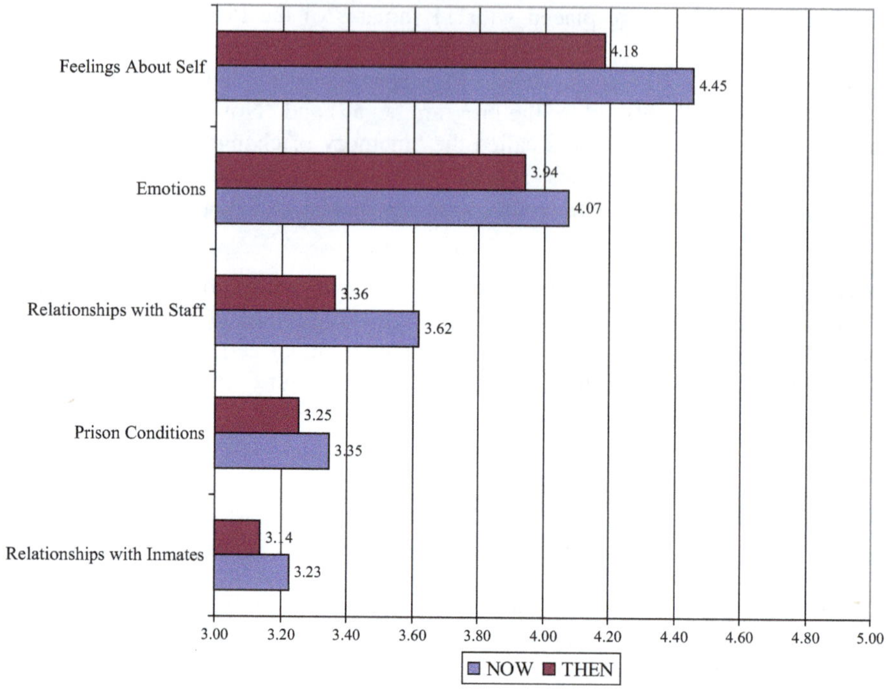

Fig. 10.1 Participants' self-reported ratings of their lives before and after participation in NLOL

Students' *t*-test and the Wilcoxon Signed Ranks Test, respectively. Both statistics showed that all five of the perceived changes reached significance at the $p < .10$ level.

We also combined all 38 items into one overall scale reflecting the prison experience before, and then with, the dogs. The average overall scale score increased from 3.65 to 3.83. This change was also significant ($p = .004$).

Discussion

These early findings from the evaluation of NLOL program showed that the participants reported themselves to be in better situations with the dogs. All five outcome areas significantly improved after participating in NLOL.

This study relied on retrospective reporting, which can be shaped by feelings and biases that develop during the program; the next test will include the "before and after" interview method. That method will give us the next level of scientific confidence.

The interviews with program stakeholders regarding program effects revealed further confirmation for many of the findings regarding psychosocial benefits previously reported. Supporting the work of Arkow (1998), most participants of both programs reported learning to get along with and trust each other as they worked together with shared responsibilities aimed at common goals. Similar to Moneymaker and Strimple (1991), most participants in NLOL reported having a more positive outlook on life since they began the program. These researchers and others, including Cushing et al. (1995) work on wild mustangs in prisons, also found evidence of participants experiencing improved self-worth and increased self-esteem. The majority of participants in the current study reported feeling more positive about themselves and feeling more worthwhile as a result of their work with the dogs. Increased self- confidence and patience, found in an evaluation of a wild mustang program (Lai 1998), was also reported in the current study. The results are also consistent with the findings of Cushing et al. (1995). As in their work, many of the current sample of participants noted that being entrusted with the dogs was significant or meaningful and contributed to their sense of accomplishment and of being able to take pride in their hard work.

The findings from the present study are consistent with those from a review of Scottish PAPs. According to Graham (2000) the programs were found to increase communication among inmates and between inmates and staff members. While a number of participants from both sites of the present study reported increased interactions with their fellow inmates, a nearly even number did not. Many did report more positive interactions with some staff members. The Scottish study found visitors stayed longer and many participants in the current study told of including the dogs on visits and in discussions during phone calls with family members. Also in concordance with Graham (2000) is the finding that the animals were associated with reduced levels of staff stress. Staff and administrators at both program sites reported the overall support of and enjoyment from the dogs.

The data support findings reported by Harbolt and Ward (1991) who examined a community service program with incarcerated older teenagers. Those researchers found that the youth demonstrated compassion, were dedicated to their responsibilities, and had gained experience giving and receiving positive regard. The participants in the current sample also consistently demonstrated compassion and dedication to their work. They also noted the therapeutic effects of having a dog with them inside prison.

The effect on vocational skills noted by Harkrader et al. (2004) and Lai (1998) was supported by the current research. Participants and stakeholders alike reported that the programs instilled a sense of responsibility in participants. Responsibility was also commonly reported in the national survey included in the present project. At the female facility, participants with at least a GED and 18 months left on their sentence are able to take a correspondence course in Veterinary Assistant paid for by the non-profit that administers the program. Administrators reported that five participants have taken advantage of the offer. Two participants reported currently pursuing the certification.

The sociological and more large-scale effects of PAPs reported in the literature (see Harkrader et al. 2004; Lai 1998) were found in the present examination. Positive community relations and positive press was reported as a benefit by administrators of both facilities. The sense of engaging in positive work and of serving the community was also raised by administrators from both facilities. NLOL reflected an independent and different social issue, the demand for the rescue of dogs that would have otherwise been destroyed at the male facility.

The academic literature lacks discussion of challenges to implementing PAPs. Administrators and staff members at both facilities acknowledged facing challenges to implementation. Concerns from union members, those allergic and fearful of dogs, and those who argued that "dogs just don't belong in prison" had to be addressed. Administrators and supportive staff members helped spread a positive message about the programs. Interviews from both sites indicated that today most staff members support the programs even while some refuse to be impressed by the lack of problems and relative success of the program. No one interviewed expressed concern that the programs might be in jeopardy because of these non-supporters.

Prior research has not considered the effects of these programs on non-participants nor how non-participants treat or regard those in PAPs. Participants at the facility occasionally mentioned being ridiculed or harassed by inmates not in the program. During interviews participants told of being taunted by those who see them as weak and needing a dog for protection. Some participants indicated that others see them as privileged.

Some of the findings from previously reported research were not addressed by the present investigation. Since the current study did not ask about illegal drug use prior to program participation, it is not known if participation positively impacted, or reduced, drug use. Hines (1983) reported that there was evidence of decreased suicide among PAP participants. The present study did ask about suicide ideation but respondents overwhelmingly reported the positive effect the dogs had on their mood.

Ultimately, our outcome studies will need to reveal how much impact the NLOL will have on the lives of the men after their release. At this stage, it is safe to say that inmates participating in NLOL reported having positive experiences with the program. The two largest changes they reported were in their feelings about themselves, including hope for their future, and their relationships with the corrections officers. These areas may be critical for successful completion of their sentence and later reintegration into society.

The qualitative interviews with the first class of NLOL participants were highly informative. The participants were universally positive about the program. Their comments to our structured interview questions tended to fall naturally into four themes:

(1) Why they got involved and what they expected to get out of it.
(2) Perceptions of what they actually got out of it.
(3) Effects on relationships and the environment in the jail.

(4) Hopes about how this might help them in their post-release re-entry life.

The interviews very strongly supported the inference that the program was valued and valuable. The participants were very glad to have had the chance to have a dog partner and to learn how to train an animal without force or punishment. They hoped their participation would help them get out sooner and stay out when they did leave.

Recommendations and Conclusions

Originally, we set out to follow the advice of Furst (2011) and designed an agenda of rigorous longitudinal studies. The phases envisioned were

1. Qualitative interviews with all participants
2. Post-Only Qualities of Life study, no control group
3. Pre-Post Qualities of Life study, no control group
4. Pre-Post Qualities of Life study with control group
5. Inside—incident reports analysis—Pre-Post with comparison group
6. Post-release follow up for recidivism analysis, with comparison group
7. Cost outcome analysis—projecting costs with and without lowered recidivism
8. Track succeeding cohorts, adding to the knowledge and data base, larger numbers

However, after the first two phases were completed, the funding for the evaluation ended. We use this experience as support for the contention that animal programs in corrections will continue to be privately funded, sporadic, "boutique" interventions until the cost-benefit science can be provided to demonstrate that these programs are "worth it" to the powers that be in the system.

Future Considerations

Despite their rapid expansion in the United States and abroad, PAPs vary drastically in design and few have been subject to research or evaluation, warranting the pressing need for more extensive research and a greater evidence base (Mulcahy and McLaughlin 2013). Given that several states now have prison dog programs or other types of animal care programs in nearly all of their correctional facilities, it would be possible to conduct multi-site studies with a consistent research protocol, thus strengthening confidence regarding how representative these findings are to the broader population. To date, much of the research has focused on recidivism and disciplinary behavior as outcomes, thus limiting the consideration of other potential benefits to participants. The studies detailed in this chapter indicate that NLOL promotes feelings of hope, prosocial interactions with others, positive emotions, and more positive feelings about the environment, which is significant given associations between many of these themes and positive change in offender outcomes (Huynh et al. 2015).

Future directions should aim to develop and evaluate theories and models seeking to help explain behavioral change in prison dog programs. Such efforts may help foster beneficial outcomes by identifying more effective ways that prison dog programs can yield positive results by influencing and changing inmates' behavior. For example, participation in PAPs may yield changes in factors such as mental health and psychosocial well-being, may be indirectly related to several post-release outcomes, such as reductions in recidivism and workforce success. In this hypothetical scenario, mental health and psychosocial well-being may serve as a mechanism of change, or a causal linkage between participation in prison dog programming and positive post-release outcomes (i.e., reduced recidivism and workforce success; Mulcahy and McLaughlin 2013). The identification of indirect effects, also known as mediators, is often a first step towards elucidating the underlying mechanisms of change. Mediators provide an explanation of a causal pathway in which participation in PAPs brings about change in participants' outcomes (MacKinnon 2008). Additional criteria for identifying potential mechanisms of change include: (1) determining their specificity between proposed causal pathways (whether a specific mediator, as opposed to multiple mediators, has a specific connection to the outcome), (2) assessing their sensitivity to the intervention, (3) examining temporal ordering (does participation in PAPs and putative mediators temporally precede the outcome?), (4) gathering evidence of dose-response relations (whether increased exposure to mediator is associated with a greater magnitude of change in the outcome), and (5) investigating their plausibility (Kazdin 2007). To effectively test putative mechanisms of change, careful consideration should be given to when they are measured in a longitudinal study.

The use of longitudinal research, in which individuals are repeatedly measured across time, is crucial to understanding change in intervention research because it permits the direct study of change across time (Fitzmaurice et al. 2011). Longitudinal approaches enable researchers to determine the duration of treatment effects—or, in the case of NLOL, how long inmates' gains in feelings of hope, prosocial interactions with others, positive emotions, and more positive feelings about the environment persist after completion of the program. The decision to measure variables of interest, such as putative mediators and outcomes, requires careful planning with regard to theory and hypotheses. For example, putative mediators should be measured at time points between the start and the end of the treatment, otherwise they will not have the opportunity to exhibit variability related to change in the outcome (Laurenceau et al. 2007).

Another consideration for future research is determining which subgroups of inmates benefit the most (or least) from PAPs. Such efforts may also elucidate whether certain inmates are more receptive to specific characteristics of PAPs (Gardner et al. 2010). For example, such approaches may identify that inmates participating in PAPs have better outcomes when they share the same race or ethnicity with PAP staff, which is consistent with findings in the broader literature on various types of interventions (Egalite et al. 2015; Griner and Smith 2006). Such findings may enhance inmates' outcomes with the targeted recruitment of PAP staff from relatable racial and ethnic backgrounds.

Finally, a cost-benefit analysis on PAPs is crucial to bridging the gap between basic social science research on correctional programming and policy analysis. Estimates from a cost-benefit analysis present an analysis of the degree to which the benefits of PAPs such as NLOL exceed associated expenses (Domínguez and Raphael 2015). These estimates also facilitate a comparative analysis of alternative policy options by enabling comparisons between NLOL and other programming designed to promote successful offender rehabilitation and reentry outcomes. An example of such an approach was conducted by the Washington State Institute for Public Policy's (WSIPP's) on crime prevention programming. First, WSIPP conducted a systematic review of experimental and quasi-experimental evaluations. Researchers used meta-analytical techniques to estimate program effectiveness and converted effect sizes into numbers of crimes saved. Second, they evaluated how these findings could be replicated after scaling up programming to statewide implementation. Third, they estimated program costs for program implementation at the state level. Fourth, they estimated monetary benefits of each program, including savings to the justice system and crime victims. Finally, they calculated a benefit-to-cost ratio and then compared programs in terms of to their likely economic efficiency in large-scale implementation in Washington State (Weisburd et al. 2017). Such approaches, when applied to PAP, would appeal to public values by enabling researchers to communicate about PAPs in terms of saving taxpayer dollars in expenses associated with recidivism and victimization.

References

Arkow, P. (1998). *Pet therapy: A study and resource guide for the use of companion animals in selected therapies* (8th ed.). Stratford, NJ: Author.

Bozeman, B. (2007). *Public values and public interest: Counter-balancing economic individualism*. Washington, DC: Georgetown University Press.

Bozeman, B., & Sarewitz, D. (2011). Public value mapping and science policy evaluation. *Minerva, 49,* 1–23. https://doi.org/10.1007/s11024-011-9161-7.

Chianese, N. M. (2009). *Girls, jails, and puppy dog tails: An evaluation of the New Leash on Life program* (Unpublished doctoral dissertation). California State University, Fullerton.

Cooke, B. J. (2014). *Bad to the bone? The effects of dog training programs on factors related to desistance* (Unpublished master's thesis). University of Cambridge, UK.

Cooke, B. J., & Farrington, D. P. (2016). The effectiveness of dog-training programs in prison: A systematic review and meta-analysis of the literature. *The Prison Journal, 96,* 854–876. https://doi.org/10.1177/0032885516671919.

Cullen, F. T. (2013). Rehabilitation: Beyond nothing works. *Crime and Justice, 42,* 299–376. https://doi.org/10.1086/670395.

Cushing, J. L., Williams, J. D., & Kronick, R. F. (1995). The wild mustang program: A case study in facilitated inmate therapy. *Journal of Offender Rehabilitation, 22,* 95–112. https://doi.org/10.1300/J076v22n03_08.

Day, A., & Ward, T. (2010). Offender rehabilitation as a value-laden process. *International Journal of Offender Therapy and Comparative Criminology, 54,* 289–306. https://doi.org/10.1177/0306624X09338284.

Domínguez, P., & Raphael, S. (2015). The role of the cost-of-crime literature in bridging the gap between social science research and policy making: Potentials and limitations. *Criminology & Public Policy, 14,* 589–632. https://doi.org/10.1111/1745-9133.12148.

Egalite, A. J., Kisida, B., & Winters, M. A. (2015). Representation in the classroom: The effect of own-race teachers on student achievement. *Economics of Education Review, 45,* 44–52. https://doi.org/10.1016/j.econedurev.2015.01.007.

Fitzmaurice, G. M., Laird, N. M., & Ware, J. H. (2011). *Applied longitudinal analysis* (2nd ed.). Hoboken: Wiley & Sons.

Furst, G. (2006). Prison-based animal programs: A national survey. *The Prison Journal, 86,* 407–430. https://doi.org/10.1177/0032885506293242.

Furst, G. (2011). *Animal programs in prison.* Boulder, CO: First Forum Press.

Gardner, F., Hutchings, J., Bywater, T., & Whitaker, C. (2010). Who benefits and how does it work? Moderators and mediators of outcome in an effectiveness trial of a parenting intervention. *Journal of Clinical Child & Adolescent Psychology, 39*(4), 568–580. https://doi.org/10.1080/15374416.2010.486315.

Glaser, B. G., & Strauss, A. L. (1967). *Discovery of grounded theory: Strategies for qualitative research.* New York: Aldine de Gruyter.

Graham, B. (2000). *Creature comfort: Animals that heal.* Amherst, NY: Prometheus Books.

Griner, D., & Smith, T. B. (2006). Culturally adapted mental health intervention: A meta-analytic review. *Psychotherapy: Theory, Research, Practice, Training, 43,* 531–548. https://doi.org/10.1037/0033-3204.43.4.531.

Harbolt, T., & Ward, T. (1991). Teaming incarcerated youth with shelter dogs for a second chance. *Society & Animals, 9,* 177–182. https://doi.org/10.1163/156853001753639279.

Harkrader, T. E., Burke, T. W., & Owen, S. S. (2004). Pound puppies: The rehabilitative uses of dogs in correctional facilities. *Corrections Today, 66,* 74–79.

Haynes, M. (1991). Pet therapy: Program lifts spirits, reduces violence in institution's mental health unit. *Corrections Today, 53,* 120–122.

Head, B. W. (2010). Reconsidering evidence-based policy: Key issues and challenges. *Policy and Society, 2,* 77–94. https://doi.org/10.1016/j.polsoc.2010.03.001.

Hennessy, M. B., Morris, A., & Linden, F. (2006). Evaluation of the effects of a socialization program in a prison on behavior and pituitary-adrenal hormone levels of shelter dogs. *Applied Animal Behaviour Science, 99,* 157–171. https://doi.org/10.1016/j.applanim.2005.09.011.

Hershman, C. L. (2008). Inaugural marine prison dog program assists wounded veterans. *Corrections Today, 70,* 46–48.

Hines, L. M. (1983). Pets in prison: A new partnership. *California Veterinarian, 5,* 7–11.

Huynh, K. H., Hall, B., Hurst, M. A., & Bikos, L. H. (2015). Evaluation of the positive re-entry in corrections program: A positive psychology intervention with prison inmates. *International Journal of Offender Therapy and Comparative Criminology, 59,* 1006–1023. https://doi.org/10.1177/0306624X14523385.

Illinois Sentencing Policy Advisory Council. (2018). *Illinois results first: The high cost of recidivism.* Retrieved from http://www.icjia.state.il.us/spac/pdf/Illinois_Result_First-The_High_Cost_of_Recidivism_2018.pdf.

Kazdin, A. E. (2007). Mediators and mechanisms of change in psychotherapy research. *Annual Review of Clinical Psychology, 3,* 1–27. https://doi.org/10.1146/annurev.clinpsy.3.022806.091432.

Katcher, A., Beck, A. M., & Levine, D. (1989). Evaluation of a pet program in prison: The PAL Project at Lorton. *Anthrozoös, 2,* 175–180.

Koda, N., Watanabe, G., Miyaji, Y., Kuniyoshi, M., Miyaji, C., & Hirata, T. (2016). Effects of a dog-assisted intervention assessed by salivary cortisol concentrations in inmates of a Japanese prison. *Asian Journal of Criminology, 11,* 309–319. https://doi.org/10.1007/s11417-016-9232-7

Lai, J. (1998, April). *Pet facilitated therapy in correctional institutions*. Paper prepared for Correctional Services of Canada by Office of the Deputy Commissioner for Women. Available at http://www.csc-scc.gc.ca.

Laurenceau, J. P., Hayes, A. M., & Feldman, G. C. (2007). Some methodological and statistical issues in the study of change processes in psychotherapy. *Clinical Psychology Review, 27,* 682–695. https://doi.org/10.1016/j.cpr.2007.01.007.

MacKinnon, D. P. (2008). *An introduction to statistical mediation analysis*. New York: Lawrence Erlbaum.

McCall, R. B. (2009). Evidence-based programming in the context of practice and policy and commentaries. *Social Policy Report, 23,* 1–20.

Merriam, S. (2001). *Discovering Project POOCH: A special program for violent incarcerated male juveniles*. (Unpublished doctoral dissertation). Pepperdine University, Malibu, California.

Moneymaker, J., & Strimple, E. (1991). Animals and inmates: A sharing companionship behind bars. *Journal of Offender Rehabilitation, 16,* 133–152.

Mulcahy, C., & McLaughlin, D. (2013). Is the tail wagging the dog? A review of the evidence for prison animal programs. *Australian Psychologist, 48,* 370–378. https://doi.org/10.1111/ap.12021.

Newcomer, K. E., Hatry, K. E., & Wholey, H. P. (2010). Planning and designing useful interventions. In J. S. Wholey, H. P. Hatry, & K. E. Newcomer (Eds.), *Handbook of practical program evaluation* (pp. 5–29). New York: Wiley.

New Leash on Life. Retrieved from http://newleashonlife-usa.org/about-us/.

Ormerod, E. (2008). Companion animals and offender rehabilitation: Experiences from a prison therapeutic community in Scotland. *Therapeutic Communities, 29,* 285–296.

Rodriguez, K. E., Bryce, C. I., Granger, D. A., & O'Haire, M. E. (2018). The effect of a service dog on salivary cortisol awakening response in a military population with posttraumatic stress disorder (PTSD). *Psychoneuroendocrinology, 98,* 202–210. https://doi.org/10.1016/j.psyneuen.2018.04.026.

Smith, M. D. (2011). From pound to prison … then paradise: The journey of a service animal. *All Hands, 1131,* 26–33.

Smith, T. B., & Griner, D. (2006). Culturally adapted mental health interventions: A meta-analytic review. *Psychotherapy: Theory, Research, Practice & Training, 43,* 531–548. https://doi.org/10.1037/0033-3204.43.4.531.

Strimple, E. O. (2003). A history of prison inmate-animal interaction programs. *American Behavioral Scientist, 47,* 70–78. https://doi.org/10.1177/0002764203255212.

Turner, W. G. (2007). The experiences of offenders in a canine prison program. *Federal Probation, 71,* 38–43.

U.S. Department of Health and Human Services, Administration for Children and Families, Administration on Children, Youth, and Families. (2003). *The program manager's guide to evaluation*. Washington, DC: Author.

Weisburd, D., Farrington, D. P., & Gill, C. (2017). What works in crime prevention and rehabilitation: An assessment of systematic reviews. *Criminology & Public Policy, 16,* 415–449. https://doi.org/10.1111/1745-9133.12298.

Chapter 11
Pursuing Certification, Licensure and Credentials as Re-entry Tools

Mary Renck Jalongo

Midway through a group of service dog trainer/inmates' required 120 h of class meeting time, the staff and instructor decided to share a presentation they had been doing for various community groups to explain the program. The PowerPoint was illustrated with beautiful photographs of dogs—both those they had trained in the previous two 12-month cycles and the puppies they were working with currently. For security reasons, the instructor could not bring a usb into the facility, so the slides had been printed out on 11 × 17 cardstock in full color. As each slide was shared, there were smiles of recognition as inmates identified each dog and commented on it. In some cases, there was a photo of the dog with the person with a disability who now owned it—something the trainers had not seen previously. Afterwards, one inmate said quietly, "It's good that someone is doing that—letting people know, I mean." Another inmate/trainer commented, "People think prison is like what they see on TV. They don't know that some *of us are trying to change." The instructor responded, "I can tell you that it wasn't easy to get this certificate program you are enrolled in approved at the university either. Some faculty and administrators expressed concern that the animals would be mistreated." One inmate said, "They think we would hurt a little puppy?!" The instructor said "I learned a long time ago that getting mad doesn't work when you are trying to get people to support you. So I just said that I was glad they were concerned about the dogs' welfare because it is so important to everyone associated with the project. I just assured them that inmates are carefully selected, work with the dogs is closely supervised by staff who completed service dog training, that the facility is video monitored, and that each dog's progress is evaluated regularly by professional service dog trainers. I won't lie to you. You have a lot to overcome where public*

M. R. Jalongo (✉)
Emerita, Indiana University of Pennsylvania, Indiana, PA, USA
e-mail: mjalongo@comcast.net

M. R. Jalongo (ed.), *Prison Dog Programs*,
https://doi.org/10.1007/978-3-030-25618-0_11

perception is concerned. But if you succeed at training a service dog, that is a huge achievement that no one can take away from you—most people can't even get their dog to stop pulling on the leash and you are teaching your dogs 60 different commands. Prove them wrong through your work—and remember, we are out there talking you up in the community, so don't let us down!"

As this experience illustrates, there are numerous barriers to offering postsecondary education in a correctional facility, not the least of which is public perception.

Mass Incarceration and Postsecondary Education

The general public is largely unaware of the mass incarceration issue in the United States. The U.S. has the highest incarceration rate of any county in the world, even when adjusting for population size (Woodredge and Smith 2018, p. xiii). Although the nation has just 5% of the world's population, it houses one-quarter of the world's prisoners. Since the 1970s, the U.S. prison population has grown by more than 700%. *The Oxford Handbook of Prison and Imprisonment* reports that there are approximately 2.4 million incarcerated people, and 95% of them are coming out at some time (Rampey et al. 2016). Given that an estimated 50–65% of inmates in state and federal prison have a traditional high school diploma or GED (Rampey et al. 2016), this represents a huge postsecondary education population at a time when the more traditional college student population continues to wane. Recent statistics reported by leading organizations in the field provide compelling evidence that educating inmates makes sense:

- 18 states spend more on prisons and jails than they do on their public colleges. Since 1986, state funding for prisons has increased 141%, compared to increases of 69% for K-12 education and 5.6% for higher education (Lumina Foundation 2016).
- In 2020, two-thirds of job postings will require some level of postsecondary education. Failing to educate inmates sets them up for failure when they exit the penal system (Oakford et al. 2019).
- Each year that an inmate is in prison represents a substantial financial investment of state correctional facilities. For example, average inmate costs the state of Ohio about $26,000 a year (Woodredge and Smith 2018).
- Over the years, the costs for housing a prisoner in California have risen significantly. Since 2005, the cost per prisoner per year has doubled and, according to an article in the Los Angeles Times, published June 4, 2017, it has risen to $75,000 per year per prisoner. That exceeds the cost of tuition for one year at Harvard University.
- When the price of long-term incarceration or execution is calculated, the costs are even more staggering. It costs $695,000 to keep an inmate in prison for 40 years and $740,000 to execute a prisoner in Texas (Oakford et al. 2019).

- In 2016, Maryland's Department of Public Safety and Correctional Services spent over $1 billion for prison operations. The state's recidivism rate was 40.5%, suggesting that many of those released were unprepared for the transition back to the community. Those who completed educational programs during incarceration had 43% lower rate of recidivism. Educational programs for inmates in Maryland return between $12 and $75 in benefits to the state for each dollar spent; for every dollar spent on education over a three-year period, $5 is saved—a 400% return on investment (Leone and Wruble 2017).

Statistics such as these suggest that making postsecondary education accessible and affordable for U.S. prisoners could save taxpayers millions of dollars (Berman 2019). Offering certificates and degrees to prisoners also may be one of the best first steps to helping them re-establish their lives and be less likely to reoffend in the future (Hopper 2013). Nevertheless, deeply engrained attitudes about the severe punishment for offenders persist. In many ways, "the goals of prison and education are fundamentally different and even contradictory—prison is about punishment and education is about nurturance and learning" (Dick et al. 2016, p. 3). As the tough on crime approach would have it, loss of freedom through incarceration is insufficient to deter crime and criminals deserve harsh punishment rather than educational opportunity. Those who advocate for the latter are seen as "bleeding hearts" with unrealistic expectations for inmates. When the first newspaper story about a service dog training program at a state correctional facility was posted, one of the comments was, "Oh sure, they committed a crime and now they get to play with puppies all day?" Yet research suggests that "In sum, prison and the severity of prison conditions does not appear to deter offenders from reoffending; indeed it may actually be criminogenic, exacerbating one's likelihood of returning to prison" (Bonta and Wormith 2018, p. 411).

Types of Postsecondary Programs for the Incarcerated

An inmate's mother and aunt arrived at the state correctional facility to visit with their family member. As they waited in line for security check with one of the volunteer instructors with the dog training program, they mentioned that it was their first time at the state prison. Just at that moment, a service dog puppy in training passed by, wearing a tiny red vest. The pup was going to one of the meeting rooms in the lobby area. Many of the employees, including the superintendent, had volunteered to take the puppies home with them on weekends to further the pups' socialization, so the service dog providers were conducting a training for them. The inmate's mother said "You mean you have a dog program here? My son would really want to do that, I think." The aunt agreed. "He's always been real good with animals."

Given that enrollment in educational programs is voluntary, whatever is offered needs to attract a sufficient number of participants to be sustainable. Generally speaking, people tend to invest in postsecondary education because they expect the benefits of a postsecondary courses, credentials, certifications, and degrees to outweigh the total costs of time, effort, and money (Paulsen and Smart 2001). Inmates appear to be even more practical in their educational aspirations because they are an exceptionally vulnerable student population. Taken as a group, they have: no control over their assignment to prison or cellmate(s), few financial resources nor access to grants, limited choices of postsecondary programs at a particular correctional facility, and uncertainty about whether their employment goals will materialize upon release. The majority want to pursue a program with clear pathways to employment, making programs that yield certificates and vocational types of credentials preferred. To illustrate, in a 2019 report published by the Vera Institute of Justice and Georgetown University Center on Poverty and Inequality, 18% of inmates wanted a GED, 29% of inmates wanted a certificate from a trade school or college, and 18% wanted a 2-year associate's degree. Only about 17% want a 4-year undergraduate degree. This means that almost half of them, 47%, are seeking some sort of postsecondary credential that can be earned in fewer than four years and that is clearly matched with a job. About 64% of the educational programs offered in corrections are delivered by the community college system, no doubt because the tuition is more affordable, the instructors have experience working with adult learners, and the programs offered tend to be more occupationally oriented. Although differences of opinion persist about vocational occupational programs versus degrees (e.g., liberal arts), one study of five different states' corrections programs found that none had succeeded in sustaining 4-year degree programs due to cost considerations (Davis et al. 2017, p. 9). Some of the interviewees in this study endorsed "stackable" credentials that build upon the previous work and are transferable—for example, a certificate of completion as a veterinary assistant while incarcerated that can transition to a veterinary technician program. Thus, while some may argue for the more traditional, baccalaureate degrees for inmates, there are various impediments to that goal—the high cost of college tuition, the duration of the program, and the fact that quite a few of the careers linked to these programs would be inaccessible to inmates with a prior felony conviction. Add to that the common practice of transferring inmates to other facilities for various reasons, and it makes a lengthy educational enterprise difficult to complete.

Deciding on an appropriate role for technology is another area of disagreement. There are numerous barriers to using technology in correctional facilities, including: security concerns, cost, and perceptions of policymakers, correctional officials, and the public that advanced technologies are not appropriate for incarcerated individuals (Davis et al. 2017). Yet without any opportunity to develop technology skills for instructional and vocational purposes, inmates operate at a huge disadvantage. Failing to equip them with some basic technology skills creates a nearly insurmountable obstacle to many types of employment for which they might otherwise be qualified.

Face-to-face versus a hybrid or online delivery system of courses is an issue as well. Although the latter might be more affordable or attractive to the postsecondary education provider, if the concomitant goals are to improve skill in verbal communication, foster prosocial behavior, and develop interpersonal skills, then opportunities for human interaction are important (Chen et al. 2008).

Table 11.1 highlights important issues to be considered when offering noncredit postsecondary education programs (Tolbert et al. 2016). We apply each of these precepts to dog care and training programs in correctional facilities.

As Table 11.1 suggests, offering a planned program in dog care and training to inmates in correctional facilities has much to recommend it. Increasingly, justice workers are exploring other settings for dog care and training programs, such as a military prison/brig (Hershman 2008), for adjudicated youth in detention (Syzmakski et al. 2018), with ex-offenders (Pastore-Klein 2017), or as part of required community service while under court supervision. In many situations, it is both a feasible and cost-effective intervention.

Table 11.1 Key program elements applied to prison dog programs

Program elements*	Application to dog care and training
Need	Nationally, 3.3 million dogs enter shelters and 670,000 are euthanized (American Society for the Protection of Animals 2017). Many times dogs are put down due to overcrowding rather than any serious health or behavioral issue with the dog. Trained dogs are viewed as far more adoptable. A leading reason for owner surrender is behavioral issues on the part of the dogs, such as separation anxiety. Nationally, the wait list time for service dogs is estimated to be 1–2 years. PDPs address community needs for trained family dogs and assistance dogs
Outcomes	Working with animals is a marketable skill set. According to The U.S. Bureau of Labor Statistics (BLS), job growth for animal care and service workers (e.g., shelter personnel, trainers, groomers, veterinary support staff) will increase about 20% between 2016–2026, a faster than average growth rate. Many people in these fields have great compassion for animals and may be more willing to offer second chances to inmates with documented skill in handling animals
Enrollment	In a national study the U. K., 81% of prisoner respondents reported that they enrolled in educational programs to occupy their time and relieve monotony; 69% said that it helped them to cope with prison (Taylor 2014). People who care about dogs find them captivating and see them as highly individual which makes them interesting. Dogs are exceptionally skilled in observing human behavior, being responsive to distress in humans, and demonstrating affection (Bradshaw 2011; Horowitz 2009). Dogs can not only be an antidote to boredom but also a support in coping with stress which encourages inmates to enroll in PDPs
Persistence	In order for educational programs to fulfill their promise, inmates need to complete them. Participants in dog care and training program have an exceptionally low incidence of disciplinary referrals and high completion rate

(continued)

Table 11.1 (continued)

Program elements*	Application to dog care and training
Offerings	Those who have amassed experience with dog care and training programs have a clear idea of what inmates need to know, understand and be capable of doing (see Chap. 8). These understandings can be used to develop course offerings tailored to the needs of the inmate/trainers
Cost	Dog care and training programs tend to be much more affordable than other types of postsecondary education programs due to reliance on volunteers and donations
Fidelity and quality	Rescues, shelters, humane organizations, service dog providers and specially trained corrections staff provide supervision and monitor quality. Progress of the dogs is evaluated regularly and effective supervision is facilitated by having a group of dogs at one location rather than placed with individual foster families
Facility obstacles	The most common facility obstacle is access to an outdoor exercise/elimination area for the dogs. Another obstacle is overcrowding and creating a designated area for those enrolled in the program. Usually, both can be addressed by administrators of the program, supported by donations/grants, and remain intact for future iterations of the program
Student obstacles	Most programs are noncredit and therefore do not require inmates to pay tuition. As with other adult/continuing education offerings, instructors for courses often are community members with extensive relevant work experience. Materials to deliver the program typically are supplied by the partners in animal rescue and training. This makes the programs within the financial means of the students
Economic value of program	Given the costs incurred in providing staff, space, food, and veterinary care, prompt, permanent adoptions can represent a major cost savings to the organization and, if the facility is tax-supported, the taxpayers. Where service dogs are concerned, the national average cost of a fully trained dog now exceeds $25,000. The typical client needing a service dog has a disability and often is the least able to pay. Training service dogs in prison makes them more affordable to clients. Costs for food, training equipment, and veterinary care are covered by the service dog provider or private donations and grants

Source for elements Tolbert et al. (2016)

Tangible Markers of Attainment in Prison Dog Programs

We live in a society that places a high value on credentials, certificates, licensure, and academic degrees. In the United States, approximately 71% of the U.S. born and 49% of undocumented immigrants between the ages of 18 and 24 years have enrolled in or attended college (Passel and Cohn 2016). Margaret diZerega, a project director at Vera Institute of Justice, reports that just 9% of incarcerated people received a certificate from a higher education institution while in prison during 2014—the latest year for which data are available. She goes on to state that

"People with conviction histories face a lot of barriers to employment and housing…Having a post-secondary credential is one way to demonstrate that this person has the skills and wants a life of economic opportunity like anyone else." (Berman 2019). It is important for inmates to thoughtfully consider what they can do upon release with a certificate, license, or degree not only in terms of earning a living wage but also in terms of becoming contributing members of their respective communities.

We need to examine how often participants decide to discontinue and how frequently inmates are dismissed from these programs because failure to complete has implications, not only for the inmate/trainers but also for the dogs. The potential exists to make an even greater contribution all around when success in these programs yields a credential conferred by people with no vested interest in the outcome. It is one thing for an inmate to say that he or she worked with dogs while incarcerated. A statement like this is less convincing to parole boards and prospective employers than saying, for example, "I successfully completed 4 courses, 120 h of class time and trained four service dogs. Three of them passed the Public Access test and one became an emotional support dog for a child on the Autism spectrum. I also earned a Certificate of Completion in Humane Education and Dog Training through the state university's College of Continuing Education."

If we can accept that one of the prime directives of a high-quality program is continuous improvement, then it makes sense to incorporate more tangible makers of success to incentivize program completion, recognize achievement, and document the expertise inmates have acquired through participation in PDPs. Where dog programs are concerned, there are at least four routes to creating markers of success in a program:

1. earning titles on the dogs trained,
2. gaining approval from the department of labor for the program to qualify as an internship for licensure,
3. partnering with a professional organization,
4. collaborating with vocational school or postsecondary institution to award a certificate to inmates, and
5. reducing the time remaining on sentences for exemplary work.

Earning Titles on the Dog

If a person applies to become a dog trainer or a tester/observer for the Alliance of Therapy Dogs, one of the questions is "What titles have you earned on your dog (s)?" For the uninitiated, this could include such things as obedience, conformation (show dog competition), agility, and so forth. Dog training programs are unique in the fact that they need to be evaluated, not only by the trainer's performance but also by the dog's (see Chap. 10). As is the case when preparing teachers to work with human students, effectiveness is evaluated by its secondary effects. For a shelter dog, did it get adopted and succeed as a family pet? For a service dog, information on successful placement with a client is essential: how did the dog fare as a support for a person with a disability? When an inmate is fired from the job of caring for and/or training a dog, we need to know why. We need to know the reasons why a service dog, for example, is pulled out of the program. Some issues are not in any way attributable to what a trainer does–such as health issues that make a dog unsuitable for extensive training (e.g., hip dysplasia or a heart murmur). Other issues may or may not be attributable to the quality of the training, such as being protective. The later might be more of a dispositional trait within the animal or it may have been shaped by inappropriate training strategies.

One title that could be earned is the American Kennel Club's Canine Good Citizen (https://images.akc.org/pdf/cgc/GK9GC1.pdf). Prison personnel would need to collaborate with a community member qualified to administer this test. The AKC describes the program's purpose as follows: "to teach good manners to dogs and responsible dog ownership to their owners". The basic tasks on the test are: (1) accepting a friendly stranger, (2) sitting politely for petting, (3) appearance/grooming and being handled, (4) walking on a loose lead, (5) walking through a crowd, (6) sit/down/stay on command, (7) coming when called, (8) reaction to another dog, (9) reaction to distraction, and (10) supervised brief separation from owner. There is also a Canine Good Citizen Advanced test. A video of the test being administered is at https://www.youtube.com/watch?v=Abt6h6MI0Kw.

As part of the test, the person responsible for the dog signs the Responsible Dog Owner's Pledge (images.akc.org/pdf/cgc/pledge.pdf). It would be appropriate for inmate/trainers to sign this pledge for a dog in their care. In some instances, insurance companies will lower the cost of homeowner's insurance for verification that a dog has earned the Canine Good Citizen title. If the new owner of an inmate trained dog wanted to pursue further training with the dog, he or she could complete the therapy dog test of a respected national organization, such as Alliance of Therapy Dogs, the Pet Partners Program of Delta Society, or Therapy Dogs International. These groups will register the handler/dog team and provide liability insurance coverage so that the owner can volunteer out in the community to visit schools, libraries, and health care facilities.

In addition to the CGC, after service dogs go to the service dog provider for advanced and placement training, the success of the dogs on the Public Access Test for service dogs would be another way of earning titles on the dogs.

Gaining Approval as an Internship from the Department of Labor

Much more than other students, those exiting the penal system can face a number of barriers to finding jobs or continuing their education.

> Reentry is a challenging time, as individuals must also try to find housing, employment, reunite with family and children, and deal with other personal issues, such as depression or substance abuse problems. Thus, many feel the pressure to work full-time while also going to school part-time or full-time. This can compete with their desire to continue their college education or other training out in the community. Balancing work, school, family, and other responsibilities can be a real challenge… This underscores the importance of setting up college programs that are part of a career pathway, that extend out into the community, and that help individuals make that transition upon release. (Davis et al. 2017, pp. 9, 24)

In collaboration with the Department of Labor, state and federal correctional facilities can establish internships and certificates that function as reentry tools. Loretto (2017) summarizes the general U.S. Department of Labor guidelines for internships as:

(1) Internships must be supervised with an on-the-job point of contact. The intern should know and understand how to contact the immediate supervisor and understand when and how job performance in the internship will be evaluated.
(2) Employers should schedule a minimum of three evaluations with their interns. Depending on the length of the experience, there should be one very soon after beginning, another at the midpoint, and a third at the conclusion of the experience.
(3) Interns should be learning about different aspects of the job so employers should consider ways to accomplish this during the internship experience.
(4) Those planning internships should consult the New Federal Guidelines on Internships to determine if interns should be paid.

One PDP with a longstanding internship program is Puppies for Parole (2019) in Missouri. This program that trains homeless dogs is funded entirely by private donations and donations from offender organizations. Since its inception in 2010, the program has collaborated with animal welfare groups to train over 5000 dogs that were subsequently adopted; some have been trained as assistance dogs. Prospective adopters can visit their website to see photographs of trained dogs available for adoption, narrow their search by various criteria, and submit an application. Qualified inmates enroll in an apprenticeship program through the U.S. Department of Labor. They complete formal training, individualized study, and practice their dog training skills to earn a certificate in animal handling that is recognized in all 50 states.

Partnering with a Professional Organization to Offer a Certificate

The Prison Pet Partnership (PPP) is the longest running prison dog program. It has been in existence since the early 1980s, led by Sister Pauline Quinn. In 1996, the program expanded to include grooming and boarding services at the Gig Harbor prison in the state of Washington. If offers a career ladder in which carefully selected and closely supervised inmates begin as kennel attendants after completing a 12-week course. Inmates with this skill set could pursue a certificate through the International Boarding and Pet Services Association. They socialize dogs, feed/ water, provide exercise, and clean animal waste in kennels and outside. If inmates are accepted into the grooming program they learn dog care skills such as clipping nails, cleaning ears, brushing teeth, and managing dogs who are fearful. From there, they can earn different levels of grooming certifications. Through a partnership with the International Professional Groomers' organization, inmates can earn a master groomer certificate. Grants and donations are used to offer scholarships and purchase a set of grooming tools for women who are being released from the facility. Other types of certification that inmate/trainers might pursue include canine cardiopulmonary resuscitation or CPR; more information is available through the American Red Cross app (https://www.redcross.org/take-a-class/first-aid/cat-dog-first-aid).

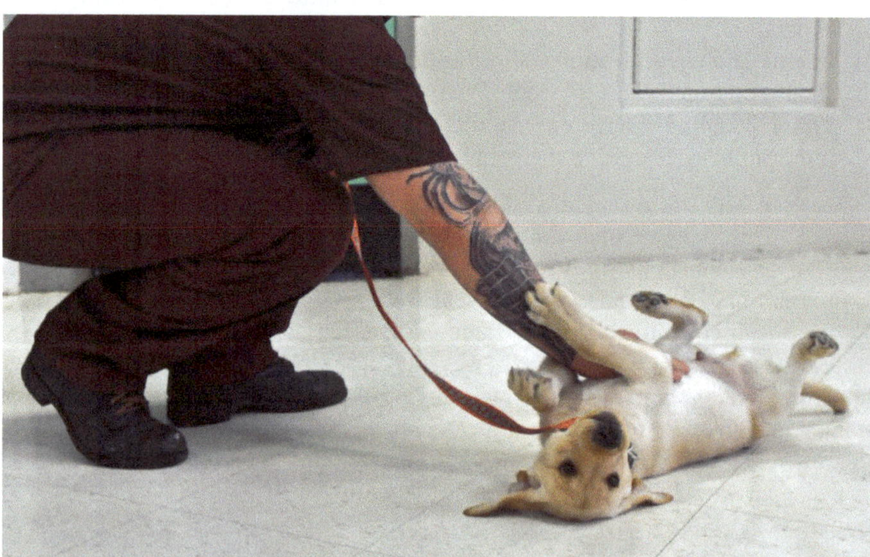

An inmate pauses to give a service dog puppy a much appreciated belly rub after a training session. The inmates also attended a class on dog massage presented by an expert dog trainer. *Photo credit* Jamie Empfield

Collaborating with Vocational School or Postsecondary Institution to Award a Certificate to Inmates

In a review of the literature on vocational education for inmates, Zoukis (2015) reports that 89% of inmates who return to prison are unemployed. Those who earn a vocational certificate while incarcerated have a 53% reduction in recidivism and are 28% more likely to be employed, leading him to conclude that a full course of training and earning a certificate or other qualification offers the greatest benefits. To that end, administrators of dog care and training programs should consider the local context and the educational institutions within a reasonable driving distance that offer vocational or postsecondary certificates.

State Correctional Institution (SCI) Pine Grove in the Pennsylvania Department of Corrections is in Indiana, Pennsylvania which is home to Indiana University of Pennsylvania IUP), the largest university in the Pennsylvania State System of Higher Education. In 2015, at the same time that several staff members at the facility were completing work as service dog trainers, they received a proposal from an IUP professor in Curriculum and Instruction. The document included a plan to work with IUP to offer a certificate of completion to the inmate/trainers. Collaboration among the corrections staff, service dog providers, and IUP's Office of Extended Studies resulted in the development of four courses that would constitute 120 contact hours during class. The four courses were: (1) Canine Wellness/ Dog Training in Correctional Facilities; (2) Training Dogs for Different Jobs; (3) Animal Rescue, Rehabilitation, and Shelters; and (4) Communication Skills and Working with the Public. Content in each course was developed using the recommendations of the most respected organizations in the field, such as the American Veterinary Medicine Association on canine health. Throughout all courses, there was emphasis on evidence-based information combined with the practical experience of the instructors. Table 11.2 is an example. It gleaned statistics from authoritative sources and combined them with stories of shelter dogs from the local no-kill shelter, Four Footed Friends. After successfully completing the coursework, training a service dog, and earning the recommendation of corrections staff, an inmate/trainer earned a Certificate of Completion in Humane Education and Dog Training from IUP. The Office of Extended Studies offers low-cost, noncredit education to adults in the community and agreed to charge a one time, $100 fee per inmate after successful program completion and prior to awarding the certificate. This was paid for the inmates by a donor.

Table 11.2 Questions about shelter dogs and adoption

Quest make a guess about the following statistics. The answers, based on research, are on the back of this page
1. What percentage of households are home to at least one dog?
2. How much does the average family spend on a dog per year?
3. How much money do all pet owners in the United States spend annually on their pets?
4. Approximately what percentage of dogs brought into shelters are placed in homes annually in the U.S.?
5. What percentage of respondents to surveys report adopting a homeless pet rather than purchasing one?
6. How many adopters out of every five would need to choose a shelter animal to seeking to practically eliminate the need to euthanize dogs?
7. What is the age of dogs most frequently surrendered to a shelter?
8. What percentage of dogs brought to the shelter have had no obedience training?
9. What percentage of families acquire their dogs from a shelter? From a breeder? From a pet store?
10. What percentage of owners cite behavioral problems in the dog as their reason for surrendering it to a shelter?
11. What percentage of parents cite the goal of "teaching children responsibility" as a major reason for acquiring a dog?
12. What percentage of pets in low-income or remote communities are not spayed or neutered? What percentage have never seen a veterinarian?
13. What percentage of households are home to more than one pet?

Three RTS (returned to shelter) dogs—Ben, Bruno and Barney

Adopted pronto—Xena, Toby, RJ and Blue. *Photo Credit* Mary Renck Jalongo

Answers from the Research

1. Depending on the survey conducted, about 40% of households have at least one dog https://www.animalsheltering.org/page/pets-by-the-numbers
2. About $1500 (2015–2016 American Pet Products Association [APPA] Survey).
3. Research conducted by the American Pet Products Association estimates the national expenditure at nearly 68 billion. In 1994, it was 17 billion.
4. Nationally, about half. Each year, 3.3 million dogs in the USA are brought to shelters. Only about 1.6 million of them are successfully placed in homes (ASPCA 2017).
5. Estimates vary widely, depending on the survey. The American Veterinary Medical Association (2017–2018) survey reported 28% while the American Pet Products Association (2017–2018) estimated it at 44% (Humane Society of the United States, 2018).
6. If just one of every five Americans seeking to add a dog to their family in the next year would adopt from a shelter or rescue, almost no healthy, treatable dogs would lose their lives in a shelter (Humane Society of the United States, 2018)
7. In a study of 12 shelters conducted by National Council on Pet Population Study and Policy (NCPPSP), 47.7% of the dogs returned to shelters are "teenagers" in dog years, ranging in age from about 6 months to 3 years. Most have been owned for less than a year prior to surrendering them and about 1/3 of them were acquired from a friend.
8. 97% of dogs at shelters have completed no obedience training (Kwan 2013).
9. According to the American Pet Products Association national survey, 34% of dogs are purchased from breeders, while 23% of dogs are adopted from shelters. Only 5% of dogs are now purchased as pets from a pet store, due mainly to public awareness of puppy mills.
10. Nearly half—47.7% of owners—say that they have surrendered the dog due to behavioral problems on the animal's part (ASPCA 2017).
11. Research conducted by the American Pet Products Association 2014–15 found that 60% of families acquired a dog "for the children" and that they regarded the family dog as an important way for children to learn responsibility.
12. 87% of pets in low-income or remote areas are not spayed/neutered and 77% have never seen a veterinarian (Humane Society of the United States 2018)
13. According to the American Veterinary Medical Association Sourcebook (2018) average number of dogs per household is 1.6, so families with multiple dogs are becoming the norm.

Reducing the Time Remaining on Sentences for Exemplary Work

In some prison systems, being a "model prisoner"–defined as complying with corrections officers, avoiding disciplinary referrals, complying with the rules, participating in community service or rehabilitation programs, and establishing an excellent work record–all help to build an inmate's case for parole. Some institutions have a mechanism to reduce time served, such as five fewer days of incarceration for every seven days without violating a rule (Miksen 2017). If there is a mechanism to reduce time served for good behavior, that same strategy can be applied specifically to success with a dog training program. Participation in a dog care and training program requires participants to do much more than log a specified number of hours sitting in class. These programs demand that inmate/trainers be "on call" at all times. Upon completion of the program, the dog becomes living, breathing, four-legged message about the inmates' skill as dog trainers that is sent out into the community.

A greyhound meets his handlers in the Prison Greyhounds program. *Photo credit* Mary Louden

Conclusion

When prison dog programs provide a strong educational component and tangible markers of achievement, they increase the power of the program to change lives. One inmate described how educational opportunities in conjunction with the prison dog program changed his goals.

> At the age of 17 I was convicted and incarcerated for murder and was sentenced to life without the possibility of parole. I've been incarcerated for almost 12 years now and up until I joined the FIDOS Program I've been lost and was on the verge of giving up hope. I was in and out of trouble constantly. I even joined a gang just to have some kind of meaning in my life. I didn't know what to do with myself. All of that changed once I became a dog handler. I know it might sound cheesy, but it's like someone flipped a switch and I can see everything so clearly.
>
> One of my first dogs was a Lhasa Apso. He was beaten and lit on fire inside of a dumpster, left for dead. When I got him you could still smell his burned skin. He had no name and he was from Philly, where I'm from. He was so small, scared and helpless. At that moment I knew I found my calling. Gizmo (that's the name I gave him) was able to fully recover and get adopted. After all he had been through he was still able to be a happy and friendly dog with so much love to give. Since Gizmo, I've trained 23 dogs; from a blind puppy to a two-year-old deaf dog.
>
> I am now certified in dog CPR and currently studying to become a veterinary assistant. Since I've become a part of the FIDOS Program I've been misconduct free and left the gang life for good. I would just like to say thank you to my grand mom who always believed in me and to all the people that's a part of the FIDOS Program who work so hard with the dogs. And, to all the people who adopted our dogs; you have given them a second chance at life and at happiness. (Felix 2017, p. 21)

Desistance from future criminal activity is a key concept in contemporary corrections (Kazemian and Maruna 2009; Rocque 2017). Both the quantitative data on disciplinary referrals from inmates and the self-report data gathered from inmates suggest that responsibility for a dog can be a powerful influence on desistance (Cooke and Farrington 2016; Furst 2007). Gove (1985) describes five internal transformations associated with desistance from crime:

1. A shift from self-absorption to concern for others
2. Increasing acceptance of societal values and behaving in socially appropriate ways
3. Increasing comfort with social relations
4. Increasing concern for others in their community
5. Increasing concern with the issue of the meaning of life.

Interview data with inmates involved in prison dog programs include statements about strong bonds and a sense of responsibility toward the animal that reduces impulsivity and causes them to think twice about jeopardizing their continuation with the dog and program. The following excerpts from interviews with inmates conducted by Minton et al. (2015) suggest that important changes take place for many participants in these programs.

> It enables me to see myself differently. I follow the rules; I hold myself to a higher standard. I have a title so I want to live up to that title of responsibility—people have entrusted it to me.
>
> It has made me realize that I have talents and abilities and a greater purpose. The people with disabilities are just as much prisoners as we are—they are prisoners of their disability. We help give them some freedom. It makes you feel like you are worth something. I had a childhood and a past where I didn't feel valuable and now it makes me feel valuable.
>
> The thing about the program is you have to envision yourself as if you had a disability, to consider the world from a disabled perspective. Then, you feel so good about what you're doing, the seriousness of it. You realize this dog will give something important to someone else. I now see myself more as a responsible and caring person. You have someone dependent on you and when they become healthy and happy, you say, O.K., I have accomplished something with my dog that's remarkable and you feel good about yourself.

At its finest, postsecondary education for inmates effects enduring, positive changes in prisoners. For some, it reclaims positive identities held prior to incarceration; for others, it forges new identities that "are associated with a sense of hope, progression and future-orientation" (Hughes 2009, p. 91). Education may therefore be a key way in which offenders put their period of incarceration to socially accepted and productive use rather than just marking time (Maruna 2001). In interviews with inmates, they often credited these substantive changes in their behavior to the generosity of some forgiving person or persons who could see beyond their mistakes, believe in them, and offer them an opportunity to redeem themselves in some way (Maruna 1997). "Education may provide an important means through which offenders construct 'redemption scripts', which are, in turn, an important forerunner to the development of a desistance identity" (Morrison and Bowman 2018, p. 97).

As a culture, we need to stop viewing education for inmates as a rare oasis of innovation found scattered across a barren landscape. Rather, education in prison should be regarded internationally as both a right and a privilege that saves money, unlocks potential, improves public safety, addresses the needs of a huge population of potential students, and contributes significantly to positive post-release outcomes (Coates 2016). As the Abell Report concluded, accomplishing important criminal justice reform goals will depend on a renaissance in postsecondary education for inmates (Leone and Wruble 2017).

References

American Veterinary Medical Association Sourcebook. (2017–2018). *U.S. pet ownership and demographics sourcebook 2012*. Available at https://www.avma.org/KB/Resources/Statistics/Pages/Market-research-statistics-US-Pet-Ownership-Demographics-Sourcebook.aspx.

American Society for the Prevention of Cruelty to Animals (ASPCA). (2017). *Pet statistics*. Retrieved April 27, 2017 from https://www.aspca.org/animal-homelessness/shelter-intake-and-surrender/pet-statistics.

Berman, J. (2019, January 16). Making college affordable for U.S. prisoners could save taxpayers millions of dollars. *Marketwatch*. Retrieved January 30, 2019 from: https://www.marketwatch.

com/story/making-college-affordable-for-us-prisoners-could-save-taxpayers-millions-of-dollars-2019-01-16.

Bonta, J., & Wormith, J. S. (2018). Adult offender cost and classification in custodial settings. In J. Woodredge & P. Smith, P. (Eds.), (2018). *The Oxford handbook of prison and imprisonment* (pp. 397–424). New York: Oxford University Press.

Bradshaw, J. (2011). *Dog sense: How the new science of dog behavior can make you a better friend to your pet*. New York: Basic Books.

Chen, P. S. D., Gonyea, R., & Kuh, G. (2008). Learning at a distance: Engaged or not? *Innovate: Journal of Online Education, 4*(3), 3. Retrieved February 24, 2019 from: https://nsuworks.nova.edu/cgi/viewcontent.cgi?referer=&httpsredir=1&article=1058&context=innovate.

Coates, S. (2016). *Unlocking potential: A review of education in prison*. London: Ministry of Justice.

Cooke, B. J., & Farrington, D. P. (2016). The effectiveness of dog-training programs in prison: A systematic review and meta-analysis of the literature. *Prison Journal, 96*(6), 854–876. https://doi.org/10.1177/0032885516671919.

Davis, L. M., Tolbert, M. A., & Mizel, M. (2017). *Working paper higher education in prison: Results from a national and regional landscape scan*. Santa Monica, CA: RAND Justice Infrastructure and Environment. https://careers.mygreatlakes.org/mglstatic/community/documents/RAND_Landscape_Scan_061517.pdf.

Dick, A. J., Rich, W., & Waters, T. (2016). *Prison vocational education and policy in the U.S.* New York: Springer.

Felix R. (2017). Inmate testimonials. *All Paws on Deck, 4*(1), 20–21. Retrieved June 1, 2019 from: https://www.cor.pa.gov/About%20Us/Newsroom/Pages/Newsletters.aspx.

Furst, G. (2007). Prison-based animal programs: Self-reported effects of participation and implications for desistance. *Prison Service Journal, 172,* 38–44.

Gove, W. (1985). The effect of age and gender on deviant behavior: A biopsychological perspective. In A. S. Rossi (Ed.), *Gender and the life course* (pp. 115–144). New York: Aldine.

Hershman, C. L. (2008). Inaugural marine prison dog program assists wounded veterans. *Corrections Today, 70*(6), 46–48.

Hill, L. B., Scaggs, S. J. A., & Bales, W. D. (2016). Assessing the statewide impact of the Specter Vocational Program on reentry outcomes: A propensity score matching analysis. *Journal of Offender Rehabilitation, 56*(1), 61–86. https://doi.org/10.1080/10509674.2016.1257535.

Hopper, J. D. (2013). Benefits of inmate employment programs: Evidence from the Prison Industry Enhancement Certification Program. *Journal of Business & Economics Research, 11*(5), 213–222.

Horowitz, A. (2009). *Inside of a dog: What dogs see, smell and know*. New York: Scribner.

Hughes, E. (2009). Thinking inside the box: Prisoner education learning identified, and the possibilities for change. In B. M. Veysey, J. Christian, & D. Martinez (Eds.), *How offenders transform their lives* (pp. 87–103). Cullompton, Devon: Willan Publishing.

Humane Society of the United States (2018). *Pets by the numbers*. Available at https://www.animalsheltering.org/page/pets-by-the-numbers.

Ingraham, C. (2016, July 7). The states that spend more money on prisoners than college students. *Washington Post.* Retrieved February 20, 2019 from: https://www.washingtonpost.com/news/wonk/wp/2016/07/07/the-states-that-spend-more-money-on-prisoners-than-college-students/?noredirect=on&utm_term=.ebe93d9af8bc.

Kazemian, L., & Maruna, S. (2009). Desistance from crime. In M. Krohn, A., Lizotte & G. Hall G. (Eds.), *Handbook on crime and deviance*. New York: Springer.

Kwan, J. Y. (2013). Owner attachment and problem behaviors related to relinquishment and training techniques of dogs. *Journal of Applied Animal Welfare Science, 16*(2), 168–183. http://dx.doi.org/10.1080/10888705.2013.768923.

Leone, P. E., & Wruble, P. C. (2017). Prison education: Maximizing the potential for employment and successful community reintegration. *The Abell Report, 30*(6). Retrieved February 24, 2019 from; https://www.abell.org/sites/default/files/files/Abell%20Prison%20Education%20Report%2072517%20final.pdf.

Loretto, P. (2017, August 17). *Get familiar with the new rules for working with interns*. https://www.thebalancecareers.com/new-department-of-labor-guidelines-on-internships-1986582es.

Lumina Foundation. (2016, Fall). Many barriers hinder efforts to develop talent among the incarcerated. *Focus*. Retrieved February 19, 2019 from: https://focus.luminafoundation.org/many-barriers-hinder-efforts-to-develop-talent-among-the-incarcerated/.

Maruna, S. (2001). *Making good: How ex-convicts reform and rebuild their lives*. Washington, DC: American Psychological Association.

Maruna, S. (2003). *Desistance and development: The psychosocial process of 'going straight'*. British Society of Criminology. Retrieved February 24, 2019 from: http://www.britsoccrim.org/volume2/003.pdf.

Maruna, S. (1997). 'Going straight': Desistance from crime and self-narratives of reform. *Narrative Study of Lives, 5*, 59–93.

Miksen, C. (2017, September 29). *How to reduce prison time*. Retrieved February 18, 208 from: https://classroom.synonym.com/how-to-reduce-prison-time-12081832.html.

Minton, C. A., Perez, P. R., & Miller, K. (2015). Voices from behind prison walls. *Society & Animals, 23*, 484–501. https://doi.org/10.1163/15685306-12341379.

Morrison, B., & Bowman, J. (2018). Education can be the key to success: How prison-based education can contribute to positive post-release outcomes. *Advancing Corrections, 6*, 95–106.

Oakford, P., Brumfield, C., Goldvale, C., Tatum, L., di Zerega, M., & Patrick, F. (2019). *Investing in futures: Economic and fiscal benefits of postsecondary education in prison*. Retrieved February 20, 2019 from: http://www.georgetownpoverty.org/wp-content/uploads/2019/01/GCPI-ESOI-Investing-in-Futures-Report-FINAL-20190116.pdf.

Passel, J. S., & Cohn, D. (2016, September). *Overall number of U.S. unauthorized immigrants holds steady since 2009*. Pew Research Center. Retrieved February 18, 2019 from: http://www.pewhispanic.org/2016/09/20/overall-number-of-u-s-unauthorized-immigrants-holds-steady-since-2009/.

Pastore-Klein, N. (2017). The District Court Re-Entry Project (DCREP): Connecting Baltimore City residents with job opportunities and educational training programs through the Judiciary. *University of Baltimore Law Review, 47*(1), article 4.

Paulsen, M. B. & Smart, J. C. (Eds.). (2001). *The finance of higher education: Theory, research, policy and practice*. New York: Agathon Press.

Puppies for Parole. (2019). Retrieved February 25, 2019 from: https://doc.mo.gov/programs/puppies-parole.

Rampey, B. D., Keiper, S., Mohadjer, L., Krenzke, T., Li, J., Thornton, N., & Hogan, J. (2016). *Highlights from the U.S. PIAAC Survey of incarcerated adults: Their skills, work experience, education, and training: Program for the international assessment of adult competencies: 2014 (NCES 2016-040)*. U.S. Department of Education. Washington, DC: National Center for Education Statistics. Retrieved February 19, 2019 from http://nces.ed.gov/pubsearch.

Rocque, M. (2017). *Desistance from crime: New advances in theory and practice*. New York: Palgrave/Macmillan.

Syzmakski, T., Casey, R. J., Johnson, A., Cano, A., Albright, D., & Seivert, N. P. (2018, December 11). *Dog training intervention shows social-cognitive change in the journals of incarcerated youth. Frontiers in Veterinary Science*. doi: http://dx.doi.org/10.3389/fvets.2018.00302.

Szifris, K., Fox, C., & Bradbury, A. (2018). A realist model of prison education, growth, and desistance: A new theory. *Journal of Prison Education and Reentry, 5*(1), 41–62. https://doi.org/10.25771/qac7-9w77.

Taylor, C. (2014). *PET brain cells* (3rd ed.). London, UK: Prisoners' Education Trust.

Tolbert, M., Foster, L. R., DeMichele, M., & Cataylo, S. (2016). *Nondegree credentials in correctional education: Status, challenges, and benefits*. Washington, DC: National Institute of Corrections. Retrieved February 20, 2019 from: https://files.eric.ed.gov/fulltext/ED571821.pdf.

Wooditch, A., Tang, L. L., & Taxman, F. S. (2014). Which criminogenic need changes are most important in promoting desistance from crime and substance use? *Criminal Justice and Behavior, 41*(3), 276–299.

Woodredge, J., & Smith, P. (Eds.). (2018). *The Oxford handbook of prison and imprisonment* (pp. 397–424). New York: Oxford University Press.

Zoukis, C. (2015, July 23). *Vocational training in prison: Helping offenders find skilled jobs and stay out of prison*. Retrieved February 28, 2019 from: https://prisoneducation.com/resources/prison-research-papers/vocational-training-in-prison/.

Chapter 12
Exploring Themes of Relinquishment and Loss

Mary Renck Jalongo and Mary-Ann Sontag-Bowman

Introduction: Loss in the Corrections Context

Incarceration is riddled with themes of loss—loss of freedom, loss of individuality, loss of status, and the absence of choices. In addition, there is the loss of relationships as inmates are abandoned by friends and family who move on, visit infrequently, or cut ties completely. Even if inmates succeed in maintaining positive relationships with family and friends on the outside, people they care about sometimes pass away during the incarcerated period, and the social support and rituals typically used to cope with such losses are inaccessible to them. Relationship losses are not just a feature of connections with those outside of the jail or prison. Inmates can and do form close bonds with other inmates who are transferred, exit the corrections system, or pass away. Indeed, incarcerated individuals live with constant loss and grief within a setting that offers little support and an ever-present fear of appearing weak and becoming a target. Therefore, inmates are correctly understood as a "vulnerable community" when it comes to loss and grief (Read et al. 2018).

Prison dog programs offer important prosocial benefits to inmates, but they also create yet another loss for a vulnerable population. Aufderheide (2016) reported that 92% of the 37 inmates interviewed from three prison dog programs shared that they found it difficult to part with the dogs at the conclusion of their time together. The relinquishment of a program dog must be understood as a potentially significant loss for inmates already awash in losses and grief, even though the loss is not death and the lost relationship is with a dog. As one inmate/handler remarked,

M. R. Jalongo (✉)
Emerita, Indiana University of Pennsylvania, Indiana, PA, USA
e-mail: mjalongo@comcast.net

M.-A. Sontag-Bowman
School of Social Work, University of Montana, Missoula, MT, USA

M. R. Jalongo (ed.), *Prison Dog Programs*,
https://doi.org/10.1007/978-3-030-25618-0_12

> How could you not miss them? You live with these guys in a bathroom. Your whole world exists around them. The dog comes first. I feel a sense of loss but you know they're going on to do a bigger thing. The next morning you get up to tend to the dog…but the dog is not there. (p. 79)

McKinney (2019) argues that we have a speciesist emotion culture that downplays the importance of the loss of a non-human animal. The insensitive comments so often made after a beloved dog is lost, rehomed, or dies—"It's just a dog" or "You can always get another one"—suggest that these bonds are relatively unimportant and that animals are interchangeable. Yet studies of people who have formed a strong bond with a dog make it clear that neither of these assumptions is true (Adrian and Stitt 2017; King and Werner 2011; Wrobel and Dye 2003). Many people rate their bond with their dog as closer than that with some family members (Cohen 2002; Meehan et al. 2017). Even if they do acquire another dog, each one is unique and irreplaceable. A handler who was facing the loss of the first dog she had ever trained in prison said:

> Tully is leaving for advanced training next week. I sat with him for a long time and talked with him and cried on him while holding him. I told him he is such a good boy, and how patient he was with me when I first got him. I'm going to miss the shit out of him. I love him so much and he's breaking my heart by leaving. (Aufderheide 2016, p. 79)

Giving up a dog after working with it intensively can also cause critical incidents that occurred during childhood to resurface. Children are oftentimes bonded to dogs in very special ways that adults do not recognize or fully appreciate (Jalongo 2018). When a child forms a bond with a dog and that bond is broken, it is a significant developmental event (Melson 2005). Children forced to give up a dog they are close to feel powerless, voiceless and frequently experience a deep, enduring emotional distress that can affect the parent-child relationship (Edwards et al. 2018). The reasons for that loss–old age, disease, accident, rehoming, or running off—are less important than the fact that a significant relationship with another being has been terminated.

During the class meeting of a service dog training program, the inmate/students/trainers were asked to create a personal timeline of memorable events involving animals—particularly dogs–throughout their lives. Joyful accounts of getting a first dog and the sorrow of losing one in some way were mentioned most frequently. As they discussed the timelines during class, one inmate/student commented that, when he was as a young child, his parents gave away his dog without any warning or explanation. He felt it was not the dog's fault because his little brother had been teasing the animal and it growled and snapped at the boy. Now in his 20's, this young man still disagreed with the way his parents had handled the situation. The other inmates/students appeared to want to support him, yet did not want to openly criticize his parents, so they shook their heads sadly. One inmate just said noncommittally, "*hmm hmm hmm*."

Relinquishment of program dogs and associated past loss experiences are not the only ways dogs are connected to loss and grief in incarcerated populations. A type of loss that tends to go unrecognized is the loss of a well-loved animal at home while an inmate is serving out a sentence. The message may come that the animal was taken to a shelter, got lost and was not recovered, or died from an accident, cruelty, illness or old age. When inmates believe they could have prevented the loss of the dog if had they been there, this can complicate grief by adding guilt, anger, and depression to the experience. Further, the inability to protect a dog amplifies awareness of the helplessness and lack of control that are inherent in the experience of incarceration.

One inmate wrote in his journal that he "just moped around all day" after he got the bad news from home that the dog he had raised from a puppy died. When the service dog puppy he would be working with over the next year arrived that same week, he took it as a sign that he was meant to be a dog trainer. He also formed a very strong bond with the puppy and found it difficult to watch it leave the facility for advanced training.

Although much of the literature on grief focuses on the death of an animal, the emotions associated with other ways of losing a dog are the same. Grief is a foundational emotion that reflects human selfhood and subjectivity (Brinkmann 2017). In a nationwide retrospective study conducted in Finland, adults were asked to write about the death of an animal during childhood. The researchers concluded that "there are special meanings involved in relations with animals in childhood" and that "the human-animal boundary does not appear clear-cut, but instead, mourning the loss of an animal bears similarities to mourning the death of a human. However, grief for a dead animal has been culturally forbidden, which is seen in parents' relative silence and the challenges faced in communicating the grief between parents and children" (Schuurman 2018, p. 2). Many mental health professionals refer to the widespread disregard for the experiences of a person who has lost an animal as disenfranchised grief because the loss often goes unrecognized as a legitimate reason for bereavement (Messam and Hart 2019).

> Although grief over the loss of a cherished pet may be as intense and even as lengthy as when a significant person in our life dies, our process of mourning is quite different. Many of the societal mechanisms of social and community support are absent when a pet dies. For example, few of us ask our employers for time off to grieve a beloved cat or dog because we fear doing so would paint us as overly sentimental, lacking in maturity, or emotionally weak. Since social support is a crucial ingredient in recovering from grief of all kinds, we are not only robbed of invaluable support systems when our pet dies, but our own perceptions of our emotional responses are likely to add an extra layer of distress. We may feel embarrassed and even ashamed about the severity of the heartbreak we feel and, consequently, hesitate to disclose our feelings to our loved ones. That additional emotional burden and sense of shame complicates the process of recovery, making it lengthier and more complex than it should be. (Winch 2018, unpaged)

One recurring theme in the literature on pet loss is that two key variables influence how well a person copes with the loss. Foremost is the closeness of the attachment and the amount of time invested in the relationship (Chur-Hansen 2010; Eckerd et al. 2016; Field et al. 2009). Two examples of human-canine bonds that often are particularly close are children on the autism spectrum who lose an emotional support dog (Carlisle et al. 2016) and owner/handlers who lose their therapy dog partners (Cohen 2015). In both cases, the loss can be acutely felt and difficult to manage because these animals were so fully enmeshed in the lives of the people who lost them.

The second strong influence on pet loss is the extent of a person's reliance on their dog for social support (Meehan et al. 2017). Both in the United States and internationally, a high percentage of people report viewing their dogs as members of the family. Italy, for example, is home to an estimated 60.5 million companion animals and 92% of Italians consider them to be family members (Testoni et al. 2019). In an interesting study of online dog obituaries, MacKay et al. (2016) found that dogs were described in child-like ways, viewed as part of the family, seen as capable of showing sympathy or gratitude, considered to possess a sense of humor, and believed to have an afterlife. People with fewer social supports in place are particularly vulnerable to intense feelings of grief over the loss of a dog. Specifically, the loss of a beloved dog may be especially difficult for individuals who live alone (Antonacopoulos and Pychyl 2010), those who lack empathy from close loved ones (Wong et al. 2017), people who are socially isolated and highly attached to the animal, and those with other recent, intense life stressors (Messam and Hart 2019).

An individual's reliance on a dog is not the only way that dogs provide social support. Dogs connect humans with each other helping to establish and facilitate relationships (Levinson and Mallon 1997). There is ample research evidence that people who are accompanied by a dog frequently are perceived as more approachable, friendly, and helpful, whether it is a college professor in his/her office (Wells and Perrine 2001), a person with a disability (Bould et al. 2018) or a mental health professional (MacNamarra et al. 2015). A woman who got her first dog later in life observed that her dog suddenly made her part of an entire community she did not know existed within her own neighborhood. Prison dogs are conduits to relationships that can and do serve important functions, including social support. The loss of a dog can mean the loss of other important social connections.

The growing awareness that emotional and social connections between dogs and their humans are significant and can create emotionally and socially challenging experiences for individuals has contributed to the emergence of a new field called veterinary social work (VSW). Veterinary social work is the intersection of veterinary medicine and social work. It focuses social work practice on four competency areas: "grief at the loss of an animal companion, compassion fatigue in the animal services fields, the connection between animal and human violence, and animal-assisted interventions" (Holcombe et al. 2015, p. 69).

The growing awareness that the human-animal bond has benefits yet, at the same time, places individuals at risk of experiencing emotions such as sadness, depression, and grief is especially relevant for incarcerated populations. Inmates often become highly attached to dogs they are assigned, have fewer social supports, and exist in a stressful, challenging social environment. It is not surprising that inmates may have a difficult time coping when a dog they have bonded with is lost to them, even though that loss is not related to death. Evidently, the reason for loss is less important than the loss itself. To illustrate, in a study conducted in the UK and Australia, one of the research questions had to do with ambiguous loss of a pet (e.g., getting lost and never being found) versus certain death of a pet (e.g., euthanasia when the dog had no hope of recovery). Interestingly, the former was not found to be more difficult than the latter and the research team concluded that there were no significant differences in grief reaction based on type of loss (Green et al. 2017). Dogs lost to inmates due to relinquishment are just as gone as if the dog had died, and grief must be anticipated.

For inmates who raise/train puppies, news that the adult service dog has "graduated" and passed the Public Access Test can foster feelings of pride and build resolve to train another dog. *Photo Credit* Lori Breece

The loss of a dog, just as with the loss of a human companion, is associated with a cascade of other losses that are likely to be especially acute in a correctional setting. Winch (2018) notes that "losing a pet can leave significant voids in our life that we need to fill: it can change our daily routines, causing ripple effects that go far beyond the loss of the actual animal. Caring for our pet creates responsibilities and a schedule around which we often craft our days" (unpaged). Consideration for the losses associated with relinquishment and the void created when a dog cared for and trained by inmate leaves should be a central feature of any prison dog program.

An administrator who championed the Certificate of Completion program at the university meets two dogs who will "graduate" early, thanks to the efforts of the inmate/trainers. *Photo Credit* Mary Renck Jalongo

Parting with Dogs in the Program

The success of any prison dog program relies on deeply felt, behaviorally healthy relationships between people and dogs: the inmates and the dogs in their care, the staff and others participating in the program, and the recipients of the dogs the inmates have prepared for life as family dogs or as working dogs. Loss is an unavoidable part of any strong emotional bond. As we form connections and build bonds with another, human or animal, we are also building the foundation for heartbreak and loss. The fact that loss is a predictable part of PDPs does not make it any easier to contend with. Therefore, prison dog programs are properly understood as the beginning of a loss and grief process for a vulnerable person in a largely unsupportive social context. Focusing only on the benefits of prison dog programs, without attention to the potentially turbulent and triggering processes of loss and grief associated with the experience, is both a disservice to the involved inmates and a missed therapeutic opportunity.

There is no accurate or quantifiable way to measure the strength and depth of connection in the relationships of others. Rather, individuals are the only experts in assessing how connected they are to another, and what the loss of that connection means to them. If an inmate has worked with an abused dog for three months and succeeded in teaching the dog to trust again, who can say that relinquishing this animal is less difficult than the inmate who trained a service dog puppy over 18 months? The nature of loss and grief depend on many different variables, both individual and social. What seems certain is that programs built on the formation of relationships also create loss and grief, even if the magnitude of the heartbreak cannot be quantified.

It may seem to those on the outside as though prison dog programs are nothing more than inmates having a good time with dogs, or as one inmate/trainer put it: "just playing with puppies all day." However, this perception is inaccurate and denigrates the contributions and sacrifices of the inmates. In a longitudinal study of guide dog puppy raisers outside of the corrections context, the researchers found that "participants reported more challenges than benefits in raising the puppies" and noted that "volunteering to be a guide dog puppy raiser may not be the pleasant experience that is anticipated when community members first offer their services" (Chur-Hansen et al. 2015, p. 1). One of the identified challenges was parting with a dog that had been in their lives for over a year—something that may be particularly difficult for inmates whose prior attachments to both dogs and people may have been disturbed.

Correctional facilities have strict rules that limit the way affection and connection can be expressed. Even inmates whose relationships with family and friends remain intact have limited avenues for the physical expressions of caring that are a natural component of the human experience. Dogs, however, are exempt from these restrictions and can—and do—physically demonstrate that the bonds people form with them are reciprocated via their extensive repertoire of prosocial behaviors (Topál et al. 1998). For example, although correctional facilities place restrictions on the kind and amount of physical contact between an inmate and a visiting family member, a dog can lean in and provide that physical contact so critical to human well-being. In addition, bonded dogs—unlike visitors—are nearly always available and responsive to human contact. There is evidence to suggest that the tactile stimulation of petting a dog's fur can have positive physiological and psychological effects (see Beetz et al. 2012 for a review). Therefore, it stands to reason that the absence of this interaction with a bonded animal can have an adverse effect. Relinquishment of a program dog can mean the loss of so many things to an inmate.

People who understand dogs immediately recognize that prison dog programs also represent loss. When community organizations request a presentation on prison dog programs, audience members often remark that it must be hard for inmates to give up a dog. These community members typically feel empathy for the inmates and appreciate the weight of the loss because they think about how it would affect them to lose a dog they care about. Yet, for many other people, the loss experienced by an inmate in a PDP is beneath consideration. This is both unfortunate and ill-informed. There is a biological basis for the feelings of loss that occur when an affectionate bond with a dog is severed by separation. Oxytocin, the hormone that is associated with positive mood, is disrupted when loss occurs. This disruption is associated with feelings of emotional disequilibrium and may increase the risk of the onset of stress-related disorders (Hurlemann and Scheele 2016). Consideration of potential emotional and physical consequences associated with disruption of the human-animal bond (Shear 2015) is critical for those charged with implementing prison dog programs.

Learning to say good-bye to a beloved dog and agreeing to try, once again, with another dog in need of support is an unselfish act. Rather than focusing on their own needs, inmates who navigate these separations successfully are realistic about the fact that they are in no position to be the dog's permanent guardian. They also consider the good life that the dog they were responsible for should have with a person or family and how the dog's presence in those people's lives will make a positive difference. All-in-all, it involves a sort of greater good thinking, as these written comments from inmate/handlers suggest:

> The thing that surprised me the most is that when I came to jail I lost almost everything and everyone in my life so I sort of became bitter. I lost feelings for the people I still have in my life, but when I wake up and I have a puppy looking at me like I am the greatest thing in the world, and that tail is moving a mile a minute, it makes you look at things a little differently, and when they finally get adopted and leave, a little piece of me leaves too, but I am happy knowing that I had a hand in finding that dog a home. (Anonymous inmate 2017, p. 17)

> When the dogs leave I'll be sad and happy at the same time. I'll be sad because I have been with this dog for 18 months and we built a bond together; and I'll be happy because I know the dog is going to get more training and go work with someone who needs him. I look at it like you send your kid off to college. You don't want them to go, but they're going to get better and learn more. (Inmate, SCI Pine Grove 2018, p. 11)

> Many of these dogs have had great struggles through their lives but yet still love the companionship and company of us unconditionally. I get great pleasure being able to wake up in the morning and have a happy dog ready to enjoy the day. The positive energy of

these dogs gives me happiness and comfort in being in the place I am in. These animals haven't given up despite all they have been through, so their strength gives me hope in knowing that I can also overcome my obstacles. So far I've had five dogs and four of them have been adopted to their new home. It is hard to watch them go but at the same time I know they now have a permanent home and it's partly due to the work I put in with them. (Robert 2018, p. 24)

In a qualitative study that explored how guardians cope with the loss of their animal companions, McKinney (2019) found that struggles in the process were widespread. Although this research explored grief associated with death of an animal, there are parallels with the situation of inmates in prison dog programs. According to McKinney (2019), the coping process of people whose beloved pet had died began with justifying grief to themselves and others. The focus then turned to acceptance that the animal had died "at the right time," and then to using rituals or spirituality to cope. The final stage was to agree to bring a new animal companion into their lives.

It is not unusual for inmates who work in prison dog programs to follow a similar progression. There is sadness when the dog leaves. One inmate commented that the way his dog poked his head out the crate and looked back at him before he was loaded into the van to return the shelter was so touching that he "would have cried" if the other guys had not been there. There are comments about the dogs being "ready" for the next phase, whether it is life in a home or going for more advanced training, and inmates express hope that all will be well. Rituals, such as looking at photos of dogs trained previously or reminiscing about their humorous quirks with the other trainers, are part of dealing with the separation. One inmate's writing captures the mixed emotions associated with prison dog programs:

A Life of Saving Lives

By: Gary B.

A tiny yellow Lab named Whitney came to SCI Somerset over a year ago with four other puppies. I instantly applied to be one of the very few chosen to be a handler in the new Canine Partners for Life puppy program. Once chosen I thought it would just be fun to work with dogs, but soon realized the transformation that a yellow ball of fur named Whitney would have on me.

At first I was guarded. I spent many years building my own wall to not let anyone or any emotions in. I was calloused and resentful, but that little, adorable ball of fur was persistent. It took only weeks for Whitney to crumble a wall that it took me many years to build, one tail wag and lick to the face at a time. Self-destruction was my answer for stress, now it's production. All the work involved in training a service dog pays for itself with tail wags and dog kisses. Looking at Whitney, I dread the day she leaves. My only consolation is I'm just one person that she will save in her life.

Inmates who are having a particularly difficult time relinquishing their canine companion may be ambivalent about whether or not to continue in the program. Indeed, feelings may be so painful for some that it is hard to imagine signing up for the multiplicity of losses again. Corrections staff who work successfully with these programs are sensitive to how difficult it can be when the dogs leave and respond appropriately to these feelings of grief. In many cases, the staff members have formed an attachment to the dogs in the program as well. This may be particularly true for service dog programs that keep the dogs for a year or more and involve taking the dogs out into the community or home for weekends with family members.

Tammy Delosh and Christina Smith are the program directors of a service dog training program at State Correctional Institution Pine Grove in Pennsylvania. Both of them have professional credentials as counselors. They described how they support inmate/trainers during loss as follows:

> The day that our service dog puppies leave is a difficult one for inmates and staff. All of us have been together for approximately a year and strong human-canine bonds were formed. After feelings are not quite so raw, we meet with the handlers as a group to get a sense of how they are coping. Some are excited to see the dogs move on to advanced training while others are upset to lose their friend. If the handlers prefer not to share their feelings in a group, we let them know that we are available to discuss the matter privately. During these individual meetings some of them cry because, chances are, they will never again see the dog that they love so much. This can be particularly difficult if it is their first year in the program; sometimes a handler did not expect to get so attached. Others accept the fact that the dogs are progressing to the next step in the career of becoming a service dog. When inmate/trainers continue to struggle with the loss, we suggest additional sources of support, such as opportunities to speak with Peer Specialists, Psychologists, or the Chaplain Department.
>
> As we wait for the next group of pups to arrive, we talk to the handlers informally and gauge how they are managing their loss. Some say that they are enjoying the break from training while others say they are bored. They make comments such as, "I really need a dog to train—I just don't know what to do with myself without one," or "Could they maybe bring over some shelter dogs for us to work with? I'd like to take on the challenge of working with an adult dog with behavior problems," or "What if you brought your puppy in? We could train it for you!" The absence of the dogs is also noticed by inmates that are not in the housing unit with the handlers. They ask questions such as: "Where are the dogs at?", "How come I haven't seen any dogs lately?", and "When are the dogs coming back?" The dogs are genuinely missed, not only by the handlers but across the institution.
>
> There is a definite change in demeanor after a group of dogs leaves. All of us, staff included, are worrying and wondering about how the dogs we invested so much care, time, and training into are doing. We eagerly await any news and immediately share updates on the dogs' progress with the inmate/trainers. These updates come in different forms–photographs posted on the service dog provider's Facebook page, a DVD of the service dogs' graduation ceremony, an email from the service dog partner, and perhaps a letter or even a visit from one of the recipients of a service dog. The handlers are overjoyed to find out that their hard work has helped someone out in the community. Afterwards, they will say with pride, "One of the dogs I trained was chosen to be the Service Dogs Program's ambassador dog!" or "The first dog I trained went to a child with autism," or "Now she is a service dog for a military veteran who is in a wheelchair."
>
> We try to keep the downtime between one group of dogs leaving and the next group of dogs arriving to a minimum. During that time, the inmates are constantly asking when the new dogs will get there and what kind of dogs we are getting. When we announce the day that the puppies will be delivered by the service dog group to the prison, the whole demeanor of the housing unit improves dramatically. After the pups arrive, it is a cause for celebration. Staff members stop by to see the dogs and speak with the handlers about their new "babies". Now the handlers' days (and sometimes, nights) are filled with caregiving and training. The puppies' endearing ways help to ease the sadness over the loss of the dogs that grew up and had to move on. Fond memories of all the dogs that preceded them are evoked as the handlers work with the tiny new puppies. The inmate/trainers accept their important responsibility and have a renewed sense of purpose. Now everyone is ready to start over and work hard so that these new arrivals fulfill their promise and become service dogs.

Sensitivity to the experience of loss is important but it is insufficient if a program hopes to achieve the full therapeutic potential of prison dog programs. The relinquishment of a program dog can be a non-threatening and effective avenue to explore the issues of loss and grief; it also can be an opportunity to learn better ways to manage and express emotions. Education and support can be utilized to normalize the grief experience, and coping resources can be explored and enhanced. Indeed, the loss of a program dog can serve as an important object lesson for an inmate, inviting processing of previous, current, and future loss experiences. To ignore this critical feature of a prison dog program is to miss a potentially transformative experience that could have lasting impact for an inmate.

Recommendations

After inmates put their hearts and minds to work to prepare a dog as a family or service animal, they need other people in the program to be respectful, compassionate, and thoughtful about ways to cope with the loss. At one state prison, a partnership with a service dog provider had ended and the trainers were dog-less for almost six months during the transition. Staff members were fully aware that the potential to change the lives of dogs and people was in a holding pattern, and it was a source of considerable frustration that they could not instantly implement a new program. The inmates made frequent inquiries about when they would have a dog to train again. On the first day that their new service dog partner visited, they had the foresight to bring along a beautiful young golden retriever/yellow Lab mix girl who would be going to a wounded military veteran the following week. As the group toured the prison with this dog, they encountered inmates who had trained service dogs previously. It was sad to see them performing other jobs, such as distributing exercise equipment at the gym, with none of the enthusiasm that had characterized their work with the dogs. When Izzy (short for Isadora) the service dog walked in, their entire demeanor changed. After they were reassured that she wasn't in vest/work mode, they eagerly interacted with her. Right before the Christmas holiday, word came through that the service dog providers could arrange to bring four puppies—all brothers from the same litter–to the facility. Although this would require a huge effort on the part of staff to get everything in place, those with primary responsibility for the program did it anyway, later referring to it as "the best Christmas gift, ever." The two women who manage this program both have a counseling background, so they are particularly perceptive about the feelings these programs evoke. Strategies that are available to everyone responsible for a PDP are described below.

Practice Consolation

The impact of losing a prison program dog often is more widespread than people might assume at first. Certainly, inmates who have invested so much time and effort into the dog will be affected but so too may any staff, volunteers, other inmates, and even visitors who have interacted over a period of time with the relinquished dog. Therefore, the correctional community needs to be thoughtful in understanding who might need consolation when a prison program dog departs from the facility.

When people are saddened by loss, caring individuals attempt to assuage their grief; this is referred to as consolation (Jedan et al. 2018). Different religious, cultural groups, and individual families have their own ways of consoling, and also in understanding, consolation efforts. Consolation requires more than a caring heart, however, because it is too easy to have the efforts at consoling reflect the one offering consolation rather than the one in need. Therefore, it is important to be both mindful and careful when offering consolation to someone experiencing loss. Otherwise, it can result in empty platitudes or remarks that the grieving person finds offensive, despite good intentions.

Common statements that can alienate rather than support include, "I know just how you feel" and "she is in a good/better place." Minimizing the loss ("It was just a dog") is never a good idea and neither is offering advice about how to feel or think about a loss. For example, people experiencing loss typically do not appreciate being told that they should think about the happy times or in some way try to see a bright side or silver lining. The reality is that grief is not a problem that anyone else can solve, and the goal of consolation should be to offer understanding and support—not solutions. This is best done by simply acknowledging the loss and expressing compassion for the impact. Many times, more listening and less talking is a better route to understanding.

Knowing that a dog they trained is loved and making a person's life better can be a source of consolation to inmate/trainers. *Photo Credit* Lori Breece

Normalize and Educate

The loss of a program dog presents opportunities to normalize the twin processes of loss and grief as well as to educate about effective ways to handle the experience.

These are lessons that can not only help in the current experience of loss and grief but also can support coping with future loss experiences. When inmates, staff, and volunteers understand normal grief and effective coping strategies, they can serve as resources to others undergoing loss experiences, thereby contributing to a more compassionate community environment.

There are various ways to deliver educational content about grief and coping. One simple way is to create handouts or other written content that are provided as a matter of routine before, during, and after the program dog relinquishment period. Important areas to include in written material are such things as the expected and normal impact of loss, the symptoms of grief (emotional, social, physical, spiritual and cognitive), and ideas for effective coping. Books, articles, speakers, videos, and podcasts can also be utilized to convey valuable perspectives and information about loss, grief, and effective coping. The opportunity to discuss and process educational content, finding and highlighting application to other losses, would be optimal.

Use Continuing Bonds Strategies

In the psychological literature, individuals who lost a pet tended to cope better through what is known as healthy "continuing bonds" (CB) practices (Packman et al. 2016). Continuing bond strategies provide ways to retain a connection with one who is gone, and are recommended when people are experiencing disenfranchised grief or are operating under social constraints (Bussolari et al. 2019); inmates could easily fall into both of these categories. Another part of CB is self-compassion, which refers to accepting that feelings of loss and grief are legitimate; educational content can assist with the promotion of self-compassion. Inmates who relinquish dogs can also benefit from activities and practices that commemorate and remember the dogs that have been so much a part of their lives (Habarth et al. 2017).

Some inmate/trainers engage in continuing bond strategies spontaneously and these should be supported. For example, inmates might tape a photo of each dog they have trained on the wall as one way to maintain bonds. An inmate mural painting crew at SCI Somerset in Pennsylvania, which is partnered with Canine Partners for Life, commemorated their "First Five" puppies by painting a portrait of each one onto the walls of the dayroom. Five of the artists were also dog trainers, which allowed them to beautifully capture the individual personalities of the dogs. Staff members were genuinely impressed by the quality of the work, and comments from visitors about the mural frequently evoke discussions of fond memories about each dog.

Work with Mental Health Professionals and Educate Staff

Companion animals are becoming increasingly important in society. Pets have been recognized for their vast contributions to human lives, including emotional support, social support, health benefits, and connection; these very things support prison dog programs. However, there is often too little recognition for the significant loss associated with losing a pet, which can contribute to bereaved pet owners feeling isolation and shame. Mental health professionals must be aware of this disenfranchised grief and creatively expand their services to provide support and advocacy for bereaved pet owners (Hess-Holden et al. 2017).

Most correctional facilities have mental health professionals who work with staff; however, it is not sufficient to relegate everything to them where prison dog programs are concerned. While it is important to make them aware when dogs that the inmates have trained are leaving, it is equally important for other staff members to be understanding about the sense of loss inmates feel when the dogs they have invested so much time and effort into have to be relinquished.

Get New Dogs Back in Quickly

A new dog cannot replace the relinquished dog but getting the next animal to the correctional facility soon after dogs have left can provide a focus and fill a void. However, it is important to understand that while the distraction of a new dog may well be useful in dealing with loss, it should never be the only intervention. Teaching and modeling distraction as a way to manage difficult emotions and experiences is a poor life skill lesson that tends to deny emotions and can result in maladaptive coping.

The VetDogs® program at State Correctional Institutions Dallas in Pennsylvania was scheduled to pick up two black Labs who had been trained at the facility. That very same day, they delivered four new puppies—as one staff member described them, "all blondes." Honoring the departure of the two dogs while also making the arrival of new dogs an important event for inmates, staff, and the community highlights the reality that both sorrows and joy can and do co-exist in our lives, and each deserves to be recognized.

Celebrating new dogs as a community event can be a way to gather in the pieces of broken hearts left in the wake of dog relinquishment. At State Correctional Institution (SCI) Retreat, the subject line of the Superintendent's e-mail to the staff read "The Puppies Are Coming!" The new recruits from the Luzerne County Society for the Prevention of Cruelty to Animals (SPCA) arrived with three dogs to find employees, a newspaper reporter and a photographer waiting for them. Dogs can and do serve as a sort of community glue, bringing people together for a common purpose, creating connections between people, and building cohesiveness among members of a group.

Seeing previously trained dogs successfully placed with their recipients can help inmate/handlers to cope with relinquishment. *Photo Credit* Lori Breece

Make Discussions About Loss Part of the Curriculum

"Do you think that a dog can save a person's life?" This question was posed to a group of experienced inmate/trainers. All said yes and gave examples—such as St. Bernard dogs that find people buried in the snow, military dogs that find an explosive device before it detonates, and a hero family dog that rouses the family from sleep after a house catches on fire. They also talked about less literal life-saving, such as a service dog for a military veteran that the person credits with preventing his or her suicide. Their instructor shared a personal experience and an unforgettable story that a perfect stranger shared with her.

> A Story of Loss
>
> Well before the start time of a session about companion animals in children's lives at an international conference, I sat down on a bench outside the meeting room where I would be speaking. A teacher who had signed up for the session joined me and we began to chat quietly. She asked if I thought that a dog could save a person's life and my response was, "Yes, I really do—both literally and figuratively."

> She went on to say that she was the mother of two preadolescent boys and a few years ago, her mother died suddenly. They were a close family and the loss was devastating, particularly for her father. Her parents had married as high school sweethearts and were inseparable. Within a few months of her mother's passing, her father died of no apparent illness, an outcome that everyone who knew the family attributed to a broken heart.
>
> The next year, the woman on the bench said that her husband—fit and in his 50 s—collapsed at work. She raced to the hospital to find that he had died of a brain aneurysm. Because she was without siblings, this sequence of events had wiped out all of her adult family members.
>
> Immobilized by grief, she sank into depression. Friends called but she did not answer the telephone. She felt uncomfortable leaving the house, panicked by crowds, and wanted to just stay in bed all day, yet knew that her teenage sons needed her. The family had two big, goofy Labrador retrievers that would come bounding into her room every morning, snuffle all around the bed, and plead with eyes and body posture for her to get up, go outside, and begin the day. "I truly believe that they saved my life," she said.
>
> Looking back on it, she now realized that she should have sought professional help. Yet just as the person is too physically ill to go to a doctor's appointment still may not be willing to summon an ambulance, she felt too emotionally depleted to seek out a therapist and, at the same time, unwilling to check herself into a psychiatric facility. Somehow, with the help of her dogs, she worked through her grief.

After this story was distributed in class, it spilled out into the corrections context. Inmate/trainers mentioned that they gave it to others to read or discussed it further with classmates. When the next class meeting convened, the men mentioned that they had watched the movie *A Dog's Purpose* and asked the instructor if she had seen it. When she said she had not, several made comments about how the film caused them to feel very emotional and warned her to "have tissues ready" if she decided to watch it. Several mentioned other movies about dogs that really "got to" them—*Marley, Eight Below, My Dog Skip*, and *Where the Red Fern Grows.* These movies and/or the books on which they were based can be made available to inmates and can serve as a resource for candid discussions about the legitimate grief associated with losing a dog.

Use Writing or Other Forms of Art to Encourage Expression

Vulnerability, weakness, and even emotion can be significant and dangerous liabilities in a prison and yet each person in a correctional facility harbors those very human qualities. Prison dog programs seek to engage with the humanity of inmates, and in doing so, leave them especially vulnerable during relinquishment of a dog. Art, including writing, can give voice to the Inside Self—that part of a human being who is weeping over the loss of a loved one.

Writing can be as a private as a journal or it can be shared in either individual or group sessions with inmates. Structuring writing with prompts or in response to specific content can both highlight "normal" (e.g., "Which of the symptoms of grief listed on the list are you experiencing?") and provide guidance to a loss-saturated mind. Poems, essays, letters, and stories are also ways that writing can be part of loss and grief support strategies. But words are not for everyone—music and other forms of art can also be supported and utilized to invite meaningful expressions of loss and grief.

Use Bibliotherapy

Bibliotherapy is a type of psychotherapy that relies on reader response to written material. The classic stages in therapy are identification (seeing a character as similar to oneself), catharsis, (responding and releasing emotions) and insight (applying the message and coping strategies to one's own life). Bibliotherapy has been used effectively with inmates (Pardini et al. 2014). Generally speaking, the goal is to encourage them to reflect on their situations, show them that they are not alone in experiencing powerful emotions, and support them in confronting/coping with the problem. Books provide ways to process an experience that may be less-threatening because the content is not immediately personal and provides permission to experience similar things. Further, books can be excellent ways to educate and normalize in a setting where open displays of emotion may well be viewed as weakness. Therefore, prison dog programs attuned to the impact of loss on inmates can consider utilizing bibliotherapy as one tool in their supportive repertoire.

Inmates can read or listen to targeted books with specific goals that can then be processed in journals and/or individual or group discussions. For example, one goal of bibliotherapy could be to educate about the experience of grief. Inmates could be asked to read the book and keep a list of signs and symptoms of grief that can be discussed and normalized later. Understanding normal grief is a powerful and useful intervention—people are able endure a lot if they know what to expect, and understand their signs and symptoms are normal.

Prison dog programs that utilize bibliotherapy as an intervention to address issues of loss and grief are not simply helping inmates cope with the loss of a relinquished dog. Effective coping of loss experiences is a critical life skill that may well have lasting impact for their future lives and relationships.

Write Narratives of Dogs' Achievements

Opportunities to tell the dog's story can be therapeutic (Bosticco and Thompson 2002; Remillard et al. 2017). Further, these stories can amplify and highlight successes, competence, and assist in creating meaning out of loss experiences. The opportunity to review shared achievements shines through in these dog descriptions written by inmates:

> Hello! My name is Martin. I am a two year old black Lab mix. I know the basic commands: sit, give paw, lay down and rollover. I really enjoy lots of love and belly rubs. I like playing

tug of war with my rope and will fetch it if you say "find rope." I also like playing ball and will fetch it back most of the time. I eat twice a day (7 am and 6 pm) and like some treats. I am very well housebroken and will let you know when I want out with a bark or a yip. I enjoy laying on the bed for naps and cuddle time. I love walks and sniff everything and mark my spot. I have a lot of energy and like to play. Do you want a loving, playful best friend? I do!!!! Come check me out. I'm waiting for you!

Hello everyone, my name is Charlie, I am a hound mix of about two years old. I love humans! I go wild for attention and affection, when I don't get it from you I let you know with a bark. I love having fun and exploring the wonderful scents of the land. I play great with my fellow dogs. I'm a master at the "tug" game, and I'm fast like a deer. I learned a lot of cool stuff since coming here to the CARE program: heel, sit stays, down stays, leash walking (although I've yet to master that one), crate, paw, show my belly, wait, eat, Shhhhh! (when I bark too much), break when playtime is over. I got all these on verbal cues, and my handlers are very proud of me, as well will you be. I want and need a forever home, I'll be happy and so will you. I'm a nice boy who's well behaved. I don't mess in the house, I listen well and I'm very loyal. All the things I think you'll want out of me. Oh yeah, I'm good looking too!

This 9 month old service dog in training has learned to sit quietly under the table at a restaurant. *Photo Credit* Mary Renck Jalongo

Provide Frequent Updates

It is gratifying for inmates and staff to reflect on the good work that is being done through prison dog programs. SCI Forest reported on several of its dogs for the state newsletter. A dog named Stark found his home with a female army veteran who took the time to write a letter of thanks. Archer, a black Lab puppy, went to a loving family and bonded with their son who had been significantly bullied. Bonzai, a little dog named after the hyena from *The Lion King*, became a companion dog for a child on the autism spectrum. Yellow Lab Simba became an assistance dog for a woman with multiple sclerosis. The future of Flower, a small Pomeranian mix, had not been decided when the newsletter was published. The plan was to try her as a working dog with victimized children and at a women's shelter. If that did not work out, a staff member was waiting in the wings to adopt her for his mother. Even newsbytes like these can be exhilarating for the people who invested so much thought, care, and time into the dog's training.

Inmates who work with prison program dogs are unlikely to see them again and do not have the option of contacting dogs' owners to find out how the animals are doing in their new roles. However, knowing their efforts have made a difference in the lives of both dogs and humans is a way for inmates to transform loss and sacrifice into something meaningful. Therefore, staff who work in prison dog programs must take the time to provide regular updates about the dogs' successes in their new lives. Many times, an inmate can be invited to write the report after basic details are shared. For example, an inmate Tom H. (2018) who works with rescue dogs wrote the following letter for the statewide newsletter:

> From Rescue Dog to Hero Dog
>
> Lilly, the border collie, came to the dog program here at SCI Frackville from Florida. For some unknown reason, nobody wanted her. She was a beautiful dog that was full of energy and with a nurturing personality. If you were to indicate any type of pain or sorrow, she would snuggle up to you and give you many kisses to make you feel better. Her intelligence was off the charts, that with her willingness to please, made her a joy to train. Lilly was adopted on October 26, 2018, to a large family. After less than a month with them, her smarts and heart came through and made her a hero in my eyes. One day, one of the children of her new family was terribly sick in her bed. With the mother in another part of the home, Lilly suddenly began barking. The mother thought that Lilly needed to be left out for a bathroom break, but when she got to Lilly, she continued to bark and led the mother to the sick child who was unconscious on the floor. This allowed the mother to get her child the help she needed before anything worse could happen. Lilly is a great example of why these programs are a good thing for more than just us inmates. If Lilly had not been brought to this program, she would have been put down and who knows what could have happened to her new family.

Effective training makes shelter dogs more adoptable. Families, particularly those with young children, want some reassurance that the dog will be nonaggressive. For PDPs that work with rescue and shelter dogs, staff members, their families, and their friends often become the adopters. The opportunity to meet the dog, coupled with the fact that it is already trained, make it highly adoptable. When dogs remain in the local community, it facilitates updates on the dog's progress or a scheduled reunion/visit.

An outcome that is very rare is an inmate becoming the recipient of a dog they worked with in a PDP. First of all, if it is a service dog training program, the person who gets the dog needs to have a professionally diagnosed disability. Even for shelter/rescue dogs, some programs have specific rules prohibiting dog adoptions by inmates and their families. Furthermore, the release time of a dog and trainer seldom coincide. Nevertheless, once in a great while, the stars align and a former inmate jumps at the chance to bring a much loved dog home to live with her or him on the outside. One such dog was Reggie, picked up in Philadelphia as a stray and enrolled in the HOPE program at SCI Camp Hill. The dog's appearance suggested that he might have been used as a bait dog, because he was covered in scars and scabs. In excerpts from a letter published in the state newsletter, Reggie's trainer Phillip (2018) wrote:

> Through the course of time, I was able to build a bond with Reggie that is indescribable. As Reggie learned through his training, I learned from Reggie as well. To be able to see Reggie grow and overcome so many obstacles through training, love, and the common bond we shared is great to see. To live in a prison cell with a dog isn't easy at times, but the end result was all worth it. I don't regret one moment of it. I will always have the everlasting memories of the time Reggie and I shared in prison. When my release neared, I couldn't bear to think about leaving Reggie behind. I was sick to my stomach the day that I left Reggie behind, and I actually cried because he became a part of my heart. I always told the HOPE program that I was going to adopt Reggie once I was released and that dream came true this past week. I was reunited with Reggie recently. I'm so happy that I was able to adopt him and give him a forever home that he's so much deserved. To be with Reggie on a daily basis is a constant reminder to me of where we came from and how far we've come and to never go back. I cannot thank the HOPE program enough for giving me the opportunity to adopt Reggie and being able to see him be a dog outside of the prison walls.... I can never thank you enough.

Ongoing communication about the new life of a valued dog amplifies the importance of inmate contributions and sacrifices, including the loss and grief experienced with relinquishment, and can temper the pain of separation from that dog.

Conclusion

United Disabilities Services Foundation (UDSF) in Lancaster, Pennsylvania has been partnered with several state and federal PDPs since 2014. Each year, they publish a calendar as a fundraiser. It features hockey players from the Hershey Bears and the UDSF service dogs. Like clockwork, a father calls to purchase a calendar because "my son is one of the trainers and his pups are in the calendar." The director of the Service Dogs Program observed that it is not only lives behind the razor wire that are being changed by these programs. Participation in the PDP has a profound effect on family, friends, and those who might have been embarrassed to be associated with an inmate previously. Feelings of pride and honor surface and, in the end, this benefits everyone associated with an effective PDP (Breece 2019, personal communication).

Prison dog programs create a multiplicity of opportunity and advantage for both humans and canines. Accessing a dog's deep capacity for acceptance, adoration, attention, forgiveness, and unconditional regard satisfies some of our greatest human needs, and this can be especially valuable for correctional facility inmates. However, by facilitating and supporting connection between dogs and inmates we are also creating the foundation for profound loss and deep grief.

The reality that prison dog programs create an emotional burden for a vulnerable population; however, this can be viewed as an opportunity for personal growth. Loss and grief are an ever-present feature of life, and especially for inmates who have already been stripped of so much. Therefore, relinquishment of a prison dog can serve to educate and support adaptive and functional ways of managing difficult emotions and experiences.

Creating benefit from the loss experience that is an inevitable part of prison dog programs begins with an understanding and acknowledgement that relationships between humans and animals can represent powerful and enduring connection. If a program is successful in creating a bonded relationship between a dog and inmates, relinquishment of a prison dog is properly understood as a significant loss which should be expected to generate a grief response. A proactive and thoughtful response to this completely normal and human experience of loss and grief allows prison dog programs to further their impact by using these experiences to promote and support functional, healthy coping, not only during incarceration but beyond.

References

Adrian, J. A. L., & Stitt, A. (2017). Pet loss, complicated grief, and post-traumatic stress disorder in Hawaii. *Anthrozoös, 30*(1), 123–133. https://doi.org/10.1080/08927936.2017.1270598.

Anonymous inmate. (2018). Inmate testimonials. *All Paws on Deck, 5*(1), 17. Retrieved February 1, 2019 from: https://www.cor.pa.gov/About%20Us/Newsroom/Pages/Newsletters.aspx.

Anonymous Inmate. (2018). SCI Pine Grove. *All Paws on Deck, 5*(1), 1. Retrieved February 1, 2019 from: https://www.cor.pa.gov/About%20Us/Newsroom/Pages/Newsletters.aspx.

Antonacopoulos, N. M., & Pychyl, T. A. (2010). An examination of the potential role of pet ownership, human social support and pet attachment in the psychological health of individuals living alone. *Anthrozoös, 23,* 37–54. https://doi.org/10.2752/175303710X12627079939143.

Aufderheide, C. (2016). *The application and effects of service dog training by inmates to self-perception and self-other overlap as a rehabilitative approach to incarceration.* (Unpublished Master's thesis), University of Oregon, Eugene, Oregon.

Beetz, A., Uvnas-Moberg, K., Julius, H., & Kotrschal, K. (2012). Psychosocial and psychophysiological effects of human-animal interactions: The possible role of oxytocin. *Frontiers in Psychology, 3,* Retrieved May 22, 2019 from: https://www.ncbi.nlm.nih.gov/pmc/articles/PMC3408111/.

Bosticco, C., & Thompson, C. L. (2002). Narratives and story telling in coping with grief and bereavement. *Western Journal of Nursing Research, 24*(6), 621–638. https://doi.org/10.1177/019394502320555386.

Bould, E., Bigby, C., Bennett, P. C., & Howell, T. J. (2018). "More people talk to you when you have a dog"—Dogs as catalysts for social inclusion of people with intellectual disabilities. *Journal of Intellectual Disability Research.* Retrieved May 22, 2019 from https://onlinelibrary.wiley.com/doi/full/10.1111/jir.12538.

Breece, L. (2019, May). Personal communication.

Brinkmann, S. (2017). The grieving animal: Grief as a foundational emotion. *Quarterly Journal of Experimental Psychology, 28*(2), https://doi.org/10.1177/0959354317747051.

Bussolari, C., Habarth, J. M., Phillips, S, Katz, R. & Packman, W. (2019, in press). Self-compassion, social constraints, and psychosocial outcomes in a pet bereavement sample. *OMEGA: Journal of Death and Dying.* https://doi.org/10.1177/0030222818814050.

Carlisle, G. K., Johnson, R. A., Mazurek, M., Bibbo, J. L., Tocco, F., & Cameron, G. T. (2016). Companion animals in families of children with autism spectrum disorder: Lessons learned from caregivers. *Journal of Family Social Work, 21*(4–5), 294–312.

Chur-Hansen, A., Werner, L., McGuiness, C. E., & Hazel, S. (2015). The experience of being a guide dog puppy raiser volunteer: A longitudinal qualitative collective case study. *Society & Animals, 5*(1), 1–12. https://doi.org/10.3390/ani5010001.

Chur-Hansen, A. (2010). Grief and bereavement issues and the loss of a companion animal: People living with a companion animal, owners of livestock, and animal support workers. *Clinical Psychologist, 14,* 14–21.

Cohen, S. P. (2002). Can pets function as family members? *Western Journal of Nursing Research, 24*(6), 621–638.

Cohen, S. P. (2015). Loss of a therapy animal: Assessment and healing. In A. H. Fine (Ed.), *Handbook on animal-assisted therapy* (4th ed., pp. 341–355). New York: Academic Press.

Eckerd, L. M., Barnett, J. E., Jett-Dias, Y., & Jett-Dias, L. (2016). Grief following pet and human loss: Closeness is key. *Death Studies, 40*(5), 275–282.

Edwards, M. E., Gringart, E., & Drake, D. (2018). "Getting rid of the dog": Adult recall of a childhood experience. *Society & Animals, 26*(4), https://doi.org/10.1163/15685306-12341545.

Field, N. P., Orsini, L., Gavish, R., & Packman, W. (2009). Role of attachment in response to pet loss. *Death Studies, 33,* 334–355. https://doi.org/10.1080/07481180802705783.

Green, C., Kangas, M., & Fairholm, I. (2017). Investigating the emotion regulation strategies implemented by adults grieving the death of a pet in Australia and the UK. *Journal of Loss and Trauma, 23*(6), 484–501.

Habarth, J., Bussolari, C., Gomez, R., Carmack, B. J., Ronen, R., Field, N. P., et al. (2017). Continuing bonds and psychosocial functioning in a recently bereaved pet loss sample. *Anthrozoös, 30*(4), 652–670. https://doi.org/10.1080/08927936.2017.1370242.

Hess-Holden, C. L., Monaghan, C. L., & Justice, C. A. (2017). Pet bereavement support groups: A guide for mental health professionals. *Journal of Creativity in Mental Health, 12*(4), 440–450. https://doi.org/10.1080/15401383.2017.1328291.

Holcombe, T. M., Strand, E. B., Nugent, W. R., & Ng, Z. Y. (2015). Veterinary social work: Practice within veterinary settings. *Journal of Human Behavior in the Social Environment, 26* (1), 69–80. https://doi.org/10.1080/10911359.2015.1059170.

Hurlemann, R. & Scheele, D. (2016). Dissecting the role of oxytocin in the formation and loss of social relationships. *Biological Psychiatry, 79*(3), 185–193. https://doi.org/10.1016/j.biopsych.2015.05.013

Jedan, C., Maddrell, A., & Venbrux, E. (2018). *Consolationscapes in the face of loss: Grief and consolation in space and time.* New York: Routledge.

Jalongo, M. R. (2018). *Children, dogs and education: Caring for, learning alongside, and gaining support from canine companions.* New York: Springer.

King, L. C., & Werner, P. D. (2011). Attachment, social support, and responses following the death of a companion animal. *OMEGA: Journal of Death and Dying, 64,* 119–141. https://doi.org/10.2190/om.64.2.b.

Levinson, B. M., & Mallon, G. P. (1997). *Pet-oriented child psychotherapy* (2nd ed.). Springfield, IL: Charles C. Thomas Publishers.

MacKay, J. R. D., Moore, J., & Huntingford, F. (2016). Characterizing the data in online companion-dog obituaries to assess their usefulness as a source of information about human–animal bonds. *Anthrozoös, 29*(3), 431–440. https://doi.org/10.1080/08927936.2016.1181374.

MacNamarra, M., Moga, J., & Pachel, S. (2015). What's love got to do with it? Selecting animals for animal-assisted interventions. In A. H. Fine (Ed.), *Handbook on animal-assisted therapy:*

Foundations and guidelines for animal-assisted interventions (4th ed., pp. 91–101). Waltham, MA: Academic Press.
McKinney, K. (2019, in press). Emotion work of coping with the death of a companion animal. *Society and Animals, 27*(1), https://doi.org/10.1163/15685306-12341586.
Meehan, M., Massavelli, B., & Pachana, N. (2017). Using attachment theory and social support theory to examine and measure pets as sources of social support and attachment figures. *Anthrozoös, 30*(2), 273–289. https://doi.org/10.1080/08927936.2017.1311050.
Melson, G. (2005). *Why the wild things are: Animals in the lives of children*. Boston: Harvard University Press.
Messam, L. M., & Hart, L. A. (2019). Persons experiencing prolonged grief after the loss of a pet. In L. R. Kogan & C. Blazina (Eds.), *Clinician's guide to treating companion animal issues: Addressing human-animal interaction* (pp. 267–280). New York: Academic Press. https://doi.org/10.1016/B978-0-12-812962-3.00015-0.
Packman, W., Bussolari, C., Katz, R., & Carmack, B. J. (2016). Continuing bonds research with animal companions: Implications for men grieving the loss of a dog. In C. Blazina & L. Kogan (Eds.), *Men and their dogs* (pp. 303–320). New York: Springer.
Pardini, J., Scogin, F., Schriver, J., Domino, M., Wilson, D., & LaRocca, M. (2014). Efficacy of cognitive bibliotherapy for the treatment of depression in jail and prison inmates. *Psychological Services, 11*(2), 141–152. https://doi.org/10.1037/a0033378.
Phillip, C. (2018). *All Paws on Deck, 5*(2), 2. Retrieved February 1, 2019 from: https://www.cor.pa.gov/About%20Us/Newsroom/Pages/Newsletters.aspx.
Read, S., Santazoglou, S., & Wrigley, A. (2018). *Loss, dying and bereavement in the criminal justice system*. New York: Routledge.
Remillard, L. W., Meehan, M., P., Kelton, D. F., & Coe, J. B. (2017). Exploring the grief experience among callers to a pet loss support hotline. *Anthrozoös, 30*(1), 149–161. https://doi.org/10.1080/08927936.2017.1270600.
Robert. (2018). SCI Fayette. *All Paws on Deck, 5*(1), 24. Retrieved February 1, 2019 from: https://www.cor.pa.gov/About%20Us/Newsroom/Pages/Newsletters.aspx.
Schuurman, N. (2018). Experiences of pet death in childhood memories. In A. Cutter-Mackenzie-Knowles, K. Malone, & E. B. Hacking (Eds.), *Research handbook on childhood nature* (pp. 1–12). New York: Springer.
Shear, M. K. (2015). Complicated grief. *New England Journal of Medicine, 372,* 153–160.
Testoni, I., De Cataldo, L., Ronconi, L., Colombo, E. S., Stefanini, C. Dal Zotto, B. & Zamperini, A. (2019, in press). Pet grief: Tools to assess owners' bereavement and veterinary communication skills. *Society and Animals, 9,* 67. https://doi.org/10.3390/ani9020067.
Tom, H. (2018). From rescue dog to hero dog, *All Paws on Deck, 5*(2), 4. Retrieved December 30, 2016 from: https://www.cor.pa.gov/About%20Us/Newsroom/Pages/Newsletters.aspx.
Topál, J., Miklósi, Á., Csányi, V., & Dóka, A. (1998). Attachment behavior in dogs (Canis familiaris): A new application of Ainsworth's (1969) Strange Situation Test. *Journal of Comparative Psychology, 112,* 3219–3229. https://doi.org/10.1037/0735-7036.112.3.219.
Wells, M., & Perrine, R. (2001). Pets go to college: The influence of pets on students' perceptions of faculty and their offices. *Anthrozoös, 14,* 161–168. https://doi.org/10.2752/089279301786999472.
Winch, G. (2018, May 22). Why we need to take pet loss seriously. *Scientific American*. Retrieved March 20, 2019 from: https://www.scientificamerican.com/article/why-we-need-to-take-pet-loss-seriously/.
Wong, P. W. C., Lau, K. C. T., Liu, L. L., Yuen, G. S. N., & Wing-Lok, P. (2017). Beyond recovery: Understanding post bereavement growth from companion animal loss. *Omega, 75* (2), 103–123. https://doi.org/10.1177/0030222815612603.
Wrobel, T. A., & Dye, A. L. (2003). Grieving pet death: Normative, gender, and attachment issues. OMEGA*: Journal of Death and Dying, 47*(4), 385–393.

Chapter 13
Making It Real: Neuroscience and the Narrative Mode in Prison Dog Programs

Mary Renck Jalongo

Introduction: Building a Case for Narratives

At the front gate, a volunteer and instructor in the postsecondary education program for inmate/trainers pauses for a routine security check and search of the course materials for that day. The prison staff member is interested in a PowerPoint on dogs' incredible sense of smell, says he definitely is a "dog person", and proudly reports that his daughter rescued a cat recently. The instructor says, "The guys are doing a great job of training and have been very respectful in class." The CO agrees that it is "a really good program", then grows very serious and says: "But don't ever trust them. Remember, inmates can be master manipulators and sometimes, it comes from the person you least expect."

Manipulation, deceit, pretense—they are an undeniable presence in corrections contexts. There are inmates who claim to be innocent or completely reformed when nothing could be further from the truth. There is plenty of acting tough while secretly feeling afraid. Being disingenuous is so prevalent that one major study of prison education described the dominant theme as "people in prison always lie" (Dick et al. 2016, p. 31). Narratives can be similarly suspect to those who insist on just the facts. The very word "story" can be used to refer to works of literary fiction or to imply disbelief as in "That's quite a story." Stories sometimes begin with a disclaimer that they represent a departure from the truth (e.g., "based on a true story"). Despite efforts to be completely accurate, witnesses to the same incident, such as an auto accident, provide different versions of what really happened. Even when describing a personal experience, issues with the veracity of stories persist. Namely, is this what actually happened or is it a person's "take" on the truth? As phenomenology would have it, Absolute Truth may not exist. The explanation for that view is that individual perceptions matter. In other words, reality is not all that

M. R. Jalongo (✉)
Emerita, Indiana University of Pennsylvania, Indiana, PA, USA
e-mail: mjalongo@comcast.net

M. R. Jalongo (ed.), *Prison Dog Programs*,
https://doi.org/10.1007/978-3-030-25618-0_13

objective; rather, it is filtered through humans' interpretive processes and influenced by our core values (Kaplan et al. 2017). Such ambiguity can be frustrating when law enforcement is attempting to "get to the bottom" of something and, at least for some, can result in general mistrust of any personal accounts of experience. However, as the next section details, the narrative mode—story—is one of the most powerful tools we have to communicate, shape, and transform the human experience. This chapter argues that it would be a major mistake to dismiss the many important functions that the narrative mode can serve in prison dog programs (PDPs).

For decades, the ability to use language was identified as the characteristic that distinguished human beings from nonhuman animals. As we learned more about the complex communication systems of other creatures, that line of demarcation began to blur. A growing group of experts from different fields now contend that one defining characteristic of human beings is the ability to use the narrative mode to describe past, present and future as well as to create imaginary worlds, as in works of fiction. We are the "storytelling animal" (Gottschall 2013) with an affinity for the narrative mode (Bruner 1990; 1991). A personal narrative is a first-person account of an experience told in story form (Merriam and Grenier 2019). The medium used to tell the story can take different forms and rely on spoken words (e.g., interviews), written words (e.g., a diary), images (e.g., a photo essay), or combinations thereof, as in a documentary film.

People remember and respond to inspiring true stories. Research on the human brain now provides a neuroscientific basis for this assertion. In fact, the field of neuroendocrinology has a whole new direction in research that studies connections between chemicals in the brain and prosocial behaviors such as compassion and empathy (Stevens and Woodruff 2018). A major focus in this line of inquiry is oxytocin. Oxytocin is a neurochemical that has been referred to as the "feel good" or "calm and connect" hormone. Some situations where it is activated are, for instance, when a mother holds her newborn child, when reuniting with a beloved family dog after a vacation, or when an inmate in the infirmary interacts with a therapy dog. Zak (2015), a prominent researcher in the field of neuroscience who is credited with identifying oxytocin, has published extensively on the topic of the brain's responses to stories. If a story "grabs us", it focuses our attention, elicits an emotional reaction, and the brain releases oxytocin "like turning on a garden hose" (Zak 2015, p. 2). He conducted a series of studies in which he used a video about a child with terminal cancer and public service announcements from the U.K. (so that the U.S. subjects weren't familiar with them already) to study how the subjects' brains responded to emotionally-charged messages versus other types of messages. The narrative mode is the most effective way of generating empathy (Steuber 2019). To illustrate, the American Society for the Prevention of Cruelty to Animals (ASPCA) commercial that featured Sarah McLachlan's song "Angel" has raised over 30 million dollars for the organization since it first aired in 2007. Powerful narratives not only have an immediate effect, causing us to "feel for" those in the story (compassion) but also appear to have a delayed effect, such as dramatically increasing the likelihood of making a donation (altruism) (Zak 2015). As just one

PDP example, after a woman in one community read about the prison dog program in the newspaper, she requested more information. Now almost 80, she did not own or use a computer, so a volunteer downloaded and printed out copies of the prison system's newsletter for her. This community member has a very long and distinguished history with dog rescue. After reading the newsletters, she remarked that several of the inmates' and dogs' stories had brought her to tears. Later, when the service dog provider set the sponsorship of a service dog puppy at $7000 each, her family decided to make a generous donation in support of the program. Compelling true stories can stir us to positive actions.

The Role of Narrative in Identity Work

Each of us has a concept of self; of who we think we are and what defines us as people. This can be thought of as three different selves (Higgins 1987). First is our real self, an answer to the "who-am-I question" (Bamberg 2011). Second is the "ought" self (what others expect from us) and third, our ideal self (the person we aspire to become). According to self-theory, the greater the incongruity between and among these selves, the greater the probability that we will be dissatisfied with our lives (Cherry 2018a, b). Offenders, in particular, are apt to have some major discrepancies in their "three selves" because society has judged them to be criminals. Many times, there are negative dimensions of self-concept in operation such as:

I am a slow learner and not very smart.

I am a terrible (child, sibling, spouse, parent, grandparent) who has become a burden on my family.

I am not really "good at" much of anything.

My psychological problems prevent me from being chosen as a friend by others.

I am filled with anger by my current situation and can't seem to get past that.

It takes a certain amount of self-compassion for people to avoid "giving up" on themselves and learn how to take care of themselves (Birkett and Sasaki 2018). Changes in self-concept are foundational to meaningful behavioral change. First-person narratives are an important way to chart the course of self-concept development. Autobiographical narratives supply a different answer to the "who-am-I" question, update comparisons between the different "selves", and describe the actions that were taken to effect positive changes (Munoz 2012). The following written by an anonymous dog handler (2017) offers an example:

> How many times have we heard the old saying, "Dog is a man's best friend?" I've never understood that. Mainly due to my minimum experience with dogs. As I sit here today, I can honestly say that it's true! Love, loyalty, acceptance, obedience, and many more, all are traits that I'm learning from a dog. I'm 35 years old and I'm learning from a dog…I'm now the handler of a miniature poodle named Pepper. Even his name is funny. Pepper wants to

> run and play. He's taken to me over these last 2 1/2 weeks. He's just a funny, little dog. Once you get to know him, you'll love him as well. So now that I've been given Pepper, he's entrusted me with his well being. Right now, Pepper and I are working on social skills. It's not easy, but he's getting better. At the same time, he's teaching me patience. Why not let Pepper or any other dog or pet teach you something? Why not return the favor of being a dog's best friend? It's more than giving a dog a second chance. It's more than just helping out. It's about showing our compassion as human beings. It's about giving that love to someone/something other than ourselves. Young, old, black, white, none of it matters. These dogs only ask to be loved and cared for, the rest will fall in place. To those that read this, I challenge you! I challenge you to care. I challenge you to show your compassion by reaching out and adopting! Allow your new best friend to meet his/her new best friend. I thank you for this opportunity. I thank you for all that you've done and will do. God Bless. (p. 11)

First-person accounts of experience are more than just heart-warming stories. There is growing evidence from the field of neuroscience that composing narratives about ourselves and responding to the narratives of others has the power to change how we think. One recent discovery that is especially relevant to identity work through story is the presence of the default mode network (DMN) in the human brain. The acronym OATS is used to explain it because it is the region of the brain primarily responsible for dealing with "Others and the Self" (Siegel 2017). It is the site that activates most strongly when people engage in social and emotional thought processes. Usually, this brain activity is recorded through functional magnetic resonance imaging (fMRI). The premise is that, when an area of the brain is active, it consumes more oxygen—which also increases blood flow to that area. An fMRI reveals where the activity occurs. The default mode network (DMN) "lights up" during mental processes such as introspection, autobiographical recall, social cognition, and moral sensitivity. Of particular interest to those in the mental health field is that the DMN appears to be disrupted in the brain scans of individuals exposed to chronic stress, or with conditions such as with autism, schizophrenia, and Alzheimer's. Following severe emotional trauma, the DMN can get "stuck" on particular narratives and replays them again and again, for example, during the flashbacks and night terrors sometimes associated with severe stress (Viard et al. 2019; Wang et al. 2019). The narrative metaphor each of us chooses is important because "Divining meaning in the world around us and integrating that into the stories we tell about who we are and what motivates us is essential to both our cognitive processing and overall well-being" (Roth 2019). The following life story from inmate Michael (2017) illustrates the process of charting changes in an autobiographical narrative, beginning in the past and projecting into the future:

> I have been in and out of prison my whole life and have always left here with a cold shoulder because of feeling like I again just wasted more years of my life. This time I feel good about myself and feel like I'm giving my best to help these rescue dogs to find their forever homes. In return I no longer feel like I'm wasting my years in prison. Now, I am learning what it feels like to do something positive and my life doesn't seem to be so bad anymore. I have also been able to have a very respectful and loving relationship with my family only because of the positive choices I choose to make today. These dogs have

> changed me in so many ways and taught me to love and care for someone other than myself. Thanks so much to all the rescue dogs who have made my life so much better…

Later on, at a graduation ceremony for the dogs, several program participants were moved 164 to tears when he said:

> I wanted to change the way I have been thinking and living for over 40 years. Here I am doing something I never thought I would be doing in prison. I'm loving and caring for these dogs seven days a week and the feeling is so rewarding having these dogs also love and care for me the same. Today I feel like I am somebody instead of just another inmate who is gonna fail. I will not fail. (p. 19)

Identity work should not be confused with glib protestations of innocence from an inmate. Confronting the self and making substantive changes frequently is a long, difficult, and—in some ways—painful process that leads to greater self-awareness and transformations in behavior. Desistance—an inmate's wherewithal that is summoned to prevent a return to criminal behavior—is the very essence of rehabilitation. One dominant theme in the desistance literature is that it requires a redefinition of a person's self-identity and narrative is the key tool in achieving that (Maruna 2001). Their stories are "redemption scripts" that chronicle change processes (Bullock et al. 2019). An inmate/handler described his bond with a greyhound wrote, wrote "Woolly taught me a lot about myself. It takes time, and not to give up, things can change, just like he did. I can change too. I'm very lucky to have had Woolly come into my life." As Langellier (2001) notes, personal narratives are "Embedded in the lives of the ordinary, the marginalized, and the muted"; through the narrative mode, people "make sense of experience, claim identities, and 'get a life' by telling and writing their stories" (p. 700). Autobiographical accounts told and written by inmates in dog care and training programs are a route to describing those meaningful and enduring changes.

Narratives as Teaching

In Jackson's (1990) classic qualitative study of teachers, he described the best in the field as tough-minded and tender-hearted—the very definition of so many people who are associated with prison dog programs. More recently, teachers who are highly effective with diverse student groups have been described as "warm demanders"—people who are kindly, encouraging, helpful, and are student advocates, yet hold them to high standards (Bondy and Ross 2008). In the no-nonsense world of postsecondary education for inmates, this admixture of teacher characteristics is especially important. Contemporary neuroscience supports the contention that social and emotional factors influence students' cognitive abilities and academic achievement much more than was previously assumed (Immordino-Yang 2016). Although it may seem odd at first, many highly respected experts in education advise teachers to conceptualize teaching as good stories to be told rather than sets of objectives to plow through (Egan 2019). Real stories of participants in prison dog programs are a major way of achieving this. The example that follows illustrates the thought process behind a class meeting conceptualized as a story.

A situation that instructors may encounter with adult populations is that some of the inmates selected to participate in the programs are seniors. The elderly who are incarcerated have been described as bearing a "double burden" because, in addition to being deprived of their liberty, they frequently do not have their needs for health and well-being met (Turner et al. 2018). Inmates convicted of "historic" crimes using new forensic technology may arrive at prison as seniors while others enter the system at a younger age but have such long sentences that they grow old while incarcerated. In the United Kingdom, senior inmates are the fastest-growing population (Turner et al. 2018).

When the prospect of working in a dog program is presented, seniors may worry that they are too old to be of use. They sometimes wonder about physical infirmities (e.g. "Can I handle an active, strong dog?"), loss of mental sharpness ("Will I be able to remember and learn the dog training skills?"), and stereotypic social attitudes ("Will these young kids think I'm losing it?"). In one group of inmate/handlers, for example, there were two white-haired men who were considerably older than anyone else. From time to time, comments and quips from the other handlers—particularly as they entered or exited the classroom–made reference to their advanced age. A 20-something inmate made a "go ahead of me" gesture and said, "Age before beauty". When an older inmate's knees were stiff from sitting, another inmate asked, "Do you need help getting up?" and at a later point, someone agreed with an older inmate saying "Sure thing, pops". None of this was said in a mean-spirited way, but it still conveyed an undercurrent of diminished capacity. Given that age is sometimes used as the basis for segregation in prison, intergenerational relationships can be more difficult to navigate (Filinson and Ciambrone 2019). Rather than confronting ageism head on, I planned a lesson around stories. It began with some information about Betty White.

> Betty White is an actress, now 97 years old, who is widely respected as a leading advocate for animals. You may recognize her name as one of the stars of the retro TV series, The Mary Tyler Moore Show and a bit more recently, The Golden Girls. Public documents list her net worth at 75 million dollars and she has championed and funded the cause of homeless animals for decades through a nonprofit called the Morris Animal Foundation. One favorite focus of her charitable work deals with the plight of senior pets at the shelter. First question: What are some reasons that an older dog would wind up at a shelter? Second question: Why do many people prefer a puppy or young dog?

The inmates generated lists of reasons, mentioning owner surrender reasons such as inability to pay for expensive medical treatment or parents preferring young animals in the hope that it would spare children from experiencing loss. The one reason they did not mention was the people who turn in dogs because they view them as objects; to them, it is like getting rid of an old sofa and replacing it with a new one. I had actually seen a family bring a dog that was 6 years old to the shelter because "it isn't playful enough with the kids anymore" and then inquire about adopting a puppy. For the inmate/trainers, subjecting a loyal, senior dog to the stress of a shelter seemed particularly harsh. From there, we went to "*As the old saying* goes, *'You can't teach an old dog new tricks?' Do you think that's accurate? Why or why not?*" and they were introduced to a shelter dog I knew.

Biscuit's Story

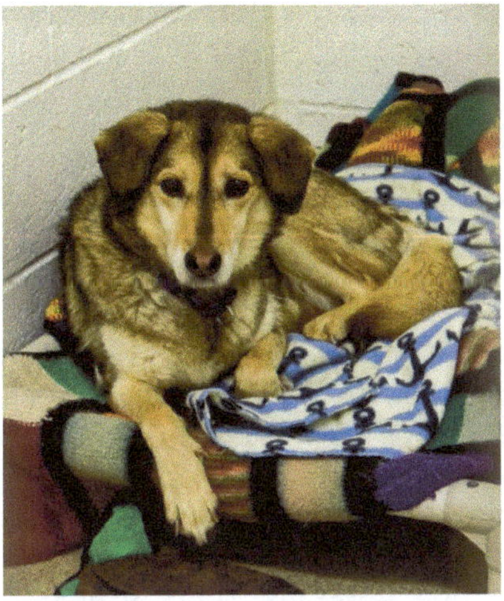

Biscuit was a 14-year-old beagle mix with hearing loss and some arthritis. Although she was exceptionally gentle and friendly, shelter personnel anticipated that it would be a challenge to find someone willing to adopt her. Just on the outskirts of town there is a motel that was converted into a small, private nursing home. The owner and manager of the personal care home visited the shelter and decided that Biscuit would be just perfect for what she had in mind. She wanted to adopt a dog who could accompany her to work each day. Surely the elderly residents would identify with this senior dog and many of them had the sad experience of giving up their own pets when their health failed. Giving them some canine company could really lift their spirits. Biscuit took to her new role immediately. Sounds that might have bothered a dog with good hearing such as alarms or loud voices did not affect her at all. She moved around at a pace that suited a nursing home and did not get underfoot. Within a short time, she seemed to instinctively know when to make a brief visit to a resident's patient's room, when to linger longer, and which rooms to pass by. After a video of Biscuit making her rounds was posted on the local newspaper's website in our small college town, it became the 4th most popular video of the year with over 40,000 downloads/views. The little beagle mix who had been passed over by so many potential adopters now had a whole group of people who appreciated her. Biscuit repaid that kindness by showing affection on a daily basis. She fulfilled her role for three years before passing on and the owner commemorated her with a fund raiser for the shelter.

Photo credits Megan Higgins Photography

The students were impressed by what Biscuit had accomplished late in life.

The next story was about a senior inmate/dog trainer at Graterford in Pennsylvania. There is a lake on the property and they have a problem with Canada geese. The inmates have trained several herding breed dogs to keep the geese from nesting and leaving their droppings everywhere. When the new superintendent arrived, she met Johnny Cash, an Australian cattle dog, so named because he was slated to go to Folsom Prison. It was love at first sight. She volunteered to take the dog home for the weekends and he fit in perfectly with her family. When it looked like Cash would go to another prison in the state system, she offered to bring him to work with her every day if she could be allowed to adopt him. While this process was under way Cash's trainer/handler, David (2016), who was 63 years old at the time, felt the pressure. He wrote this story for the newsletter:

> My thanks and gratitude to the Superintendent for trusting me with a member of her family, Cash. June 29, 2015 was the day that Cash was handed over to me by his last handler. The first couple of days I really had been second guessing my decision to take care of a dog and it just seemed like an overload of responsibility and to be honest Cash has been adopted by the superintendent and I really didn't want anything to happen to him. I had been hired and trained to work with Cash to eliminate the geese population here at Graterford Prison. What a new experience 'Wow' to watch him work was amazing to me. I had been doing everything with relating to his work as a good dog just as I had been trained to do. He responded day one to my commands and yes I was shocked because we had just become partners. Day after day we both looked forward to work (chasing geese). Watching him every day at his best made my responsibilities so much easier: baths, brushing and play-time. I came to enjoy doing all these things especially playtime. Cash is not a selfish dog he included me in his play and at the age of 63 he had a way to bring out the child in me. Over the months our partnership has grown way more than I had expected, he has a way of giving his unconditional love. Looking back I remember sending him to his kennel because of something he had done and boy I felt worse than he did. And since, I have never used his kennel as a punishment place, his kennel should be his safe place – some things are learned as we go along. Cash is not just a great working dog he has become my buddy, my pal, my friend. He has been helpful in replacing some of my good traits that I had cashed in during my addiction to drugs – sense of responsibility, commitment, caring, companionship,

> relationship, friendship, trust and teamwork. He has done more for me than I could ever do for him. The crazy part about our relationship is that I do a lot of talking to him, past, present and future stuff. He's a good listener and even if I'm having one of the bad days his response to me has been always the same, a face full of licks (kisses) kind of lets me know that I can start that bad over anytime I choose. Hopefully in six months I will be paroled and I am not looking forward to turning Cash over to a new handler, but I know I have to. In the few months that Cash and I have together nothing will change but me. That unconditional love works both ways now. Parting with him will surely be hurtful but it's another life experience. The things that were taught to me I will pass on to the new handler, when the time comes. What makes parting somewhat easier is that I know that Cash will be changing another man's life the way he has done for me and many thanks to the superintendent for allowing me this journey. (p. 17)

The narrative mode gets a message across in a way that has more impact than lecture. Stories are a superior method for arriving at new insights because they enable people to "stand in someone else's shoes" or "see through someone else's eyes"—the very essence of compassion and empathy (Hanne and Kaal 2019).

Stories of Practice

The word "mind" as it refers to human thought is surprisingly difficult to define; so much so that most people resort to comparing the human mind to a computer. A prominent researcher in neuroscience offers a definition that is a huge departure from mechanistic models: "The mind is an embodied and relational process that regulates the flow of energy and information" (Siegel 2012, p. 3). He goes on to say that the relationships we form with others and the neural networks in the brain interact to shape each person's mind and this defines who we are. In fact, there is an entire interdisciplinary field called interpersonal neurobiology (IPN) that studies the dynamic interaction between human relationships and neural networks in the brain. This same dynamic applies to professional development. "By organizing the self across past, present, and future, the integrating mind creates a sense of coherence and unity. Integration can be assessed by examining the structure of autobiographical narratives" (Siegel 2012, p. 14).

Professionals' autobiographical narratives are created over a lifetime; they also are revisited and revised as new insights come to light. They are a synthesis of more episodic stories of practice—individual incidents that we deem significant. There are "turning point" stories, events that forever change the course of our lives. There are stories in which it goes terribly wrong and ones in which everything falls into place. Professionals use these stories of practice to reflect on their lives. For example, Amanda McClung (2017) a Camp Hill psychological services associate, wrote this story of practice about her involvement with the dog training program.

> As a psychologist at the prison, I'm aware of many of the personal struggles the inmates on the specialized units endure on a daily basis. What I didn't expect was for some of those struggles to come to light when the dogs came on the housing unit. I was informed by several of the inmates that they missed their dogs/pets so much that they didn't even want

> to see the dogs. This prompted me as their psychologist to aid in getting the HOPE program more involved in the units. One specific inmate that shared these concerns with me is now interested in becoming a handler due to being exposed to the dogs on a weekly basis–more evidence that the HOPE program is an amazing asset to the Department of Corrections.
>
> As an employee, I also notice the difference in the overall demeanor of the inmates on the general population housing units. Walking through a housing unit on a daily basis is often intense and loud at times, specifically during day room. The inmates don't make much eye contact, appear very serious, and sometimes display an attitude, whether it be out of security or emotions. When the dogs are brought onto the block, the majority of the inmate population jumps at the opportunity to come out and see them. They are laughing, getting on the floor with the dogs, smiling, and acting care-free. I've heard inmates call the dogs pet-names such as "pretty girl" or "sweetie." They appear genuinely disappointed when their time is up with the dogs and they need to return to their cells. I'm often overwhelmed with questions about becoming a handler and moving to the block where the dogs are housed so they can see them more often. (p. 15)

When professionals read first-person accounts of what colleagues in other facilities are doing, it stimulates thinking and encourages them to try something new. Some programs permit dog trainer/handlers to bring dogs to the visitor's room and, after reading about this, others begin to consider how they might institute this practice at their facility. One prison started a "weaning program" in which mother dogs and their tiny puppies as young as 3 weeks of age were cared for by the inmates. A closet was converted into a nursery for the future service dogs and decorated accordingly. After the puppies were about 10 weeks old, they were already on site and ready to begin training. Such stories of practice can stimulate "outside the box" thinking. After many such stories of practice are generated, they become source material for describing an individual's trajectory of professional development. Collectively, these first-person accounts form an ongoing autobiographical account that is subject to revision as we learn and grow. Perhaps most important of all, these narratives highlight the ideals that motivated people to enter a profession in the first place.

Connecting with the Larger Community

A modern, high-quality correctional facility is already interdisciplinary, given that it involves professionals with backgrounds in criminology, psychology, sociology, counseling, health, education, and more. Highly effective PDPs rely on authentic collaborations with a whole new group of professionals, such as rescue/shelter personnel, veterinary staff, university faculty, expert dog trainers, and service dog providers. The best representatives of these occupations are compassionate, altruistic and committed to community service. When they form a partnership with like-minded staff members at a prison, their enthusiasm for the project and determination to succeed are a powerful catalyst for change. As one illustration of these fascinating interprofessional connections, consider just a sampling of dog training that occurs in Pennsylvania's State Correctional Institutions. Through their 24 prison dog programs, they have trained dogs for diverse roles such as: detecting explosives, locating invasive species (e.g., termites, bed bugs), identifying disease in small tissue samples, alerting/responding to seizures, serving as companions for children with Autism, supporting military veterans with PTSD, and providing balance/support when walking for people with mobility issues. After the dogs are placed with individuals and families, the network extends even further.

The typical offender has limited contact with anyone beyond the corrections context. Visits from friends and family often are infrequent or perhaps, nonexistent. For security reasons, the number of volunteers and community members coming in has to be controlled and carefully monitored. After a dog program has been instituted, the network of connections with adult role models expands. To illustrate, imagine the staff and inmate response to this letter that arrived in the mail from Laird (2016), the recipient of a service dog trained by inmates:

> An open letter to the prisoner that trained my service dog.
>
> I never would have imagined I would be writing this letter, but life doesn't always follow the rules. When I fell ill over three years ago, I had no idea that a stranger was going to impact my life in such a HUGE way. Without you, I wouldn't be who I am today. Because of your time, effort, love and compassion, I am forever in your debt…Your dedication and love for him shines daily through his skills and behavior. Every alert, every time he helps me take a step, I am grateful for you. You are living proof that mistakes do not define who you are. While you may have messed up in the past, you are giving back to humanity and have restored the well-being of a young woman who was so lost before her companion entered her life.
>
> Because of you and your hard work, I am able to live a *somewhat* normal life. I have been able to start college, volunteer daily and even apply for jobs I never imagined I would be able to have. I started a nonprofit when I was only 17 years old because of how much Jasper has helped my quality of life. I finally have independence—something that was stolen from me years ago as I fell unconscious multiple times daily. I never knew someone I have never met could play such an important role in my life. Never ever EVER question your worth, because you have helped change not only my world, but THE world. I know you miss him and I'm sure he misses you too, but when you think of his big brown eyes, his crooked teeth, his moans and groans, his love for water and snow, his paws that are too big for his body, think of me, the 15 year old girl whose life you changed forever. (p. 8)

Knowing the story of what happened to a dog that an inmate invested so much time in training is important but it is not always feasible for adopters and clients to actually make a return visit with the dog. Through first-person narratives, inmates see how their efforts have truly helped.

Film is another way to tell the story of a prison dog program. Several powerful documentaries that include interviews with inmates have been produced, including: "Paws in Prison: A Second Chance" that describes the program in Arkansas; "Saved by the Dogs: The Story of the Dog Men", that describes the four-year effort of one Oklahoma prison inmate to initiate a dog program; "Dogs on the Inside" (https://www.imdb.com/title/tt3393400/?ref_=ttpl_pl_tt) describes Project Good Dog, a shelter dog rehabilitation program in a Massachusetts prison, and "Saving

Castaways" (http://savingcastaways.com), that chronicles the efforts to rehabilitate puppy mill dogs through a partnership with a prison.

Dog Rescue, Rehoming and Success Stories

When our local shelter is looking for volunteers, these individuals often fit the description of "just can't get enough of successful rescue and adoption stories". For instance, the exceptionally dedicated college students who volunteer as "night walkers" to provide dogs with exercise outdoors generally are avid followers of the Facebook or Instagram page. The volunteers are overjoyed, particularly when a very difficult-to-adopt, long-term resident of the shelter gets a happy home (Jalongo, in press). Hearing that uplifting story and sharing it with others somehow makes it all worthwhile to trudge around in the dark in every kind of weather, picking up poop along the way. Participants in prison dog programs are no different in this regard; the successes of the dogs they've worked with can help to sustain motivation. There is no reason to deny or apologize for our attraction to success stories of the dogs who were cared for and trained by inmates. Dog rescue, rehabilitation, and training stories document the work that the inmates have achieved, remind everyone that it is possible to overcome obstacles, renew the resolve of participants in the program, and reveal what the dogs' new families have done to continue helping the animal.

One unforgettable dog was Sage, a dog who had experienced terrible abuse (Kelley 2018a, b). The Rottweiller was found wandering the streets after her previous owner struck her on the head and collapsed her skull, resulting in permanent blindness to her right eye. The owner poured acid on the dog's right side, leaving it scarred. After the court seized the dog, she was given to a rescue, received appropriate medical treatment, and was taken to SCI Coal Township for training. A corrections staff member wrote:

> Her new family changed her name to Sage, which means "wise through reflection and experience." It's a fitting name for a dog that has overcome many hurdles.
>
> Despite the horrors she endured with her previous owner, Sage continues to be very sweet and lovable. She has a bouncy personality and loves to play with her step-brothers, Duke and Hoss, both Rottweilers, who are compassionate therapy dogs. When she is not playing with her toys, going for walks or enjoying the beach on vacation, you'll find her sleeping with her brothers.
>
> As Sage became acclimated to her new family and home, she began therapy dog training. Eight months after her adoption, Sage passed her Therapy Dogs International (TDI) test, on the first try, with flying colors! She has been an official therapy dog since August 2017. Her friendly disposition and great temperament make her a great addition to her owner's TDI team. She's a real natural.
>
> Sage enjoys kids and has been involved with reading programs and afterschool programs at Shamokin Area School District. Sage gets along with all dogs, cats and even horses. Sage is a great example of a dog's ability to overcome significant abuse. She continues to do

wonderfully since being adopted and looks forward to all of her new adventures in her furever home. (Kelley 2018b, p. 7)

The most common reaction to a story such as this one is righteous indignation that anyone would be that cruel to a helpless animal. This points up another benefit of story: it can result in a shared point of view among people who might otherwise consider themselves to be very different.

The majority of prison dog programs in the nation are partnerships with humane organizations and shelters that help homeless and abused animals (see Chap. 3). At least some of the inmate participants are apt to pursue work with animals upon release, so dog rescue/rehoming/success stories are an important part of the inmate/trainer's education. These stories not only model empathy and altruism but also offer insight into what makes animal rescuers tick. Stories about overcoming terrible adversity also give inmate/trainers something interesting to talk about. During these discussions, the inmates/students often arrive at the conclusion that there should be better laws and stricter enforcement—a bit of irony that is not wasted on them, considering their current circumstances. In addition, humane officers can be the heroes in dog rescue stories providing a more positive perspective on law enforcement. I wrote the following example to use in class with inmate/trainers. In our service-dog training program, all of the dogs have been Labrador retriever puppies, so I thought these stories would strike a responsive chord.

Three Labs

As you know, now that I'm retired from the university, I volunteer at the local shelter three days a week and manage their Facebook page. Occasionally, there is a message in the inbox about reported abuse. An accusation of abuse isn't always as straightforward as it might seem; there are wide differences of opinion about what constitutes abuse and sometimes people are just trying to get somebody else into trouble for whatever reason. Recently, there were two messages—both involving black Labrador retrievers—that were unquestionably abuse and neglect.

The first message was from a woman who wanted to report dog abuse by her next-door neighbor. She said that she did not want to start a feud with this person, but she literally was losing sleep over the dog's suffering. Her husband told her not to confront the neighbor because "she's crazy", so the wife used her smartphone to secretly make a video from her second-floor window. The bird's eye view of the scene showed a small, makeshift kennel constructed out of wooden shipping pallets that were stood up on end and wired together. A woman appeared with a bowl of kibble and struggled to move one heavy pallet enough to squeeze through. Inside, an adult black Lab remained at a distance, watching her. The woman placed the bowl on the ground and started to leave but, as soon as the dog started to eat, she whirled around, picked up an empty aluminum dog dish, and began to beat the dog with all her might. The dog cried in pain and tried to get away, but she pursued it, continuing to hit it until was cowering in the corner. I was stunned. I advised the woman on how to contact the Dog Warden, urged her to share the video and concluded with "Thank you for helping this poor dog." The very next day, the Lab was seized and brought to the kennel. When it arrived, it was terrified and "hand shy" but not aggressive in any way. The dog appeared to be about five years old and had health issues associated with neglect—fleas, ticks, worms—but usually are relatively easy to remedy. After the story got around (unofficially, since it was an ongoing investigation), the dog was adopted instantly.

The second message about abuse came in late at night. It involved black two Labrador brothers that a man had purchased as puppies. When he got an offer to work out of state on construction, he asked his sister to look after the dogs for him. She drove to his home to take care of the dogs she had not seen for months and was appalled by what she found. Both of them were crammed into the same crate, standing in feces and urine, barely able to move. It was obvious that this was not a one-time arrangement, because the dogs had figured out a way to twist around and rest their heads on one another in order to fit. In addition, they were so skinny that every rib showed. She was ashamed and wrote, "I can't believe that anyone in my family would treat a dog like this." Several photos were attached to the message to show the dogs' terrible condition. As the mother of two young children with animals of her own, she could not keep the dogs herself. She had called her brother and persuaded him to let our no-kill shelter take them and find them good homes. On the day that the dogs arrived at the shelter, I saw the kennel manager outside hosing down a wire crate. She told me the dogs, now almost a year old, had been living in there, then raised her eyebrows and added emphatically, "Not one— BOTH *of them." The staff decided to name them Max and Mike. These two young dogs were very different from most owner surrenders I had seen during the past four years of volunteering. Rather than being sad and confused by kennel life, they were flat-out joyful. They ate heartily, learned to trust people, and played like crazy. It made everyone laugh to watch them race around in the shelter's big, fenced in area at full speed, tongues lolling out, and then shoot a quick look over their shoulders as if to say "Isn't this GREAT?!" Even though they had no training and were very puppyish in their behavior, both were quickly adopted into great homes.*

Ideally, the instructors who meet with the inmate/trainers on a regular basis should, from time to time, provide a print version of compelling rescue stories that include photographs. They can write the story themselves or borrow it from the organization's webpage or print materials. True dog rescue stories also can be found on social media and in newspapers and newsletters but it is best if the person sharing the story experienced it in some way so that questions that surface can be addressed.

Narrative Research

Many have contended that the experimental designs used in the medical field are the "gold standard" to which all fields must aspire in order to be welcomed into the scientific community. Yet if the experimental designs used in clinical trials to test drugs are the undisputed route to Truth, then why are drug commercials dominated by disclaimers and why do lawsuits surrounding various drugs that were tested experimentally proliferate? Few people realize that experimental designs were originally developed in agriculture. Their logic, applied to studies of crop yields, was a perfect fit. For example, a researcher could identify a tract of land, test the soil to make sure it was consistent, provide the same amounts of water, sunshine, and fertilizer but manipulate only one variable—the type of seed. Then, if one section had a better harvest than the others, the difference could be attributed to the seed alone—a clear cut route to cause and effect.

Applied to complex human behaviors, experimental designs fall short. Even when researchers do succeed in producing experimental design research—for example, in a laboratory setting—the downside is that the findings may not generalize to the "real world" because the environment was too controlled–a threat to validity called artificialism. The issues that are raised time and time again in research on prison dog programs—small sample sizes, selection bias—frequently point up the poor fit between the research questions and the research methods. Generally speaking, quantitative research deals with things that can be counted and not everything that matters can be readily quantified. To illustrate the difference, think about two concepts that are used in business–worth and value—and then apply it to dogs. Worth is monetary value that can be counted, as in "a fully trained service dog can cost between $15,000 and $50,000" (Block 2019) or a high price tag on a puppy sired by the best-in-show dog at Westminster. Value is more subjective. It refers to a person's perspective on the importance of something. So, a former stray that is beloved companion dog for a young child may have inestimable value to the family, yet not fetch a high price if advertised for sale. Who is to say, though, which of these dogs is "better" than the other? It depends.

Quantitative research tends to take the approach of a little bit of data across many instances, such as a national survey of prison superintendents. Its claims to rigor come from the sampling method and statistical analysis; its goal is to test a theory or hypothesis and generalize from a sample to the larger population. In quantitative methods, those who don't fit the normal curve are "outliers"; in qualitative research, the individual and the unusual case hold great interest. Conversely, qualitative research tends to rely on words as the primary data source and its goal is to describe, in considerable detail, the particular. The rigor of qualitative research comes from duration, depth, and multiple methods (e.g., observations collected over time, interviews, document analysis). Mixed-methods research tries to capitalize on "hybrid vigor" by combining quantitative and qualitative approaches—for example, interviewing people prior to developing a survey or following up a survey with interviews to further explore the reasons behind the answers given.

One approach to research is not superior to the other; it depends on the question. If we want to know "How many PDPs are there in the USA?" and "What kinds of programs predominate?" the answer can be reported in numbers and that certainly is worth knowing. If we want to know how an inmate has been changed by participation in a PDP, counting has its limitations. We can count using recidivism statistics but the criticism there is that exceptional inmates were chosen at outset (see Chap. 7), so they are not comparable to the general prison population. One way to address this issue statistically is to use a model for prediction, called propensity scoring (see Hill 2018). For all of these reasons, qualitative approaches that rely primarily on the words of the participants are an important part of research in corrections (Rennison and Hart 2018).

Narrative approaches are not appropriate for studies of large numbers of nameless and faceless subjects. When qualitative researchers want to understand human behavior, they go to the source and inmates surely are insiders in multiple senses of that word. Rather, the goal is to capture the perspectives of those who are living the experience. They immerse themselves in the culture (think Margaret Mead) rather than swoop in, administer a few tests or surveys, and go back to their offices to crunch the numbers. They conduct research *with*, rather than on people and refer to them as participants rather than subjects.

Narrative research is one of the five major qualitative research traditions (Creswell and Poth 2017) and recognized by the American Psychological Association as a primary method of conducting research (Bamberg 2012). In corrections contexts, narrative analysis is the particular type that is used most frequently. In narrative analysis, the researcher studies the content of first-person accounts that have been told or written and arrives at themes in the data (Fader 2013; Halsey 2006; King 2013; Leverentz 2014; Minke 2017: Ntinda 2019; Veysey et al. 2013). Of particular importance to research is that narrative analysis seeks the "emic" or insider's perspective. Narrative research has been used, for example, to study incarcerated mothers (Lockwood 2018), prison breaks (Bandyopadhyay 2018), and religious conversions of inmates (Kerley 2018). A major goal of qualitative research is "to give a voice to historically disenfranchised populations whose experiences may not be well-represented in the research literature" (Levitt et al. 2018, p. 28). For the qualitative researchers, the study of prison dog programs will need to go directly to the source—the various stakeholders—and rely on their self-narratives in order to better understand the complex processes at work.

Conclusion

Ultimately, "Stories organize and shape our experiences and also tell others about our lives, relationships, journeys, decisions, successes, and failures" (Patton 2015, p. 465).

Gottschall (2013) compares stories to a flight simulator that prepares pilots for difficult situations: they assist with navigating life's social problems. In fact, one of the widely endorsed interventions for use with children on the Autism spectrum is social stories that model interpersonal skills and provide a type of rehearsal for social interactions (Shelton and Jalongo 2017). Thus, when inmates hear or read other inmates' accounts of their experiences with dog care and training, these messages of transformation, renewal and redemption can encourage participants in prison dog programs to consider different possibilities for themselves. Former inmate Matt Kerr has been invited to numerous correctional facilities, both state and federal, to speak with offenders in PDPs (Graves 2016). He is a former inmate at State Correctional Facility (SCI) Mercer in the "Corrections Adoptive Rescue Endeavor" or CARE Program that rehabilitates shelter dogs. Upon his release, he started a dog training business called Matt's Mutts University. He is a respected member of his community and trains dogs for veterans with physical and psychological wounds. Kerr is what Maruna (2017) calls the "credible messenger." His message to inmates is that, if they put in the work, participation in the dog programs can be a route to successful change. These personal narratives encapsulate the desistance message, namely, that "people can change" (versus "once a criminal, always a criminal") (Maruna 2017). The narrative mode has a rightful place and makes important contributions to the individual identity work of inmates, effective in-class instruction, staff members' professional development, generating community support, documenting the outcomes of PDPs for the animals, and research conducted in correctional settings.

References

Anonymous inmate, Camp Hill. (2015). Inmate testimonials. *All Paws on Deck 2*(1), 11. Retrieved June 1, 2019 from: https://www.cor.pa.gov/About%20Us/Newsroom/Pages/Newsletters.aspx.

Bamberg, M. (2011). Who am I?–Narration and its contribution for self and identity. *Theory and Psychology, 21,* 3–24.

Bamberg, M. (2012). Narrative analysis. In H. Cooper (Ed.), *APA handbook of research methods in psychology* (Vol. 2, pp. 77–94), *Quantitative, qualitative, neuropsychological, and biological.* Washington, DC: American Psychological Association.

Bandyopadhyay, M. (2018). Prison escapes, everyday life and the state: Narratives of contiguity and disruption. In T. M. Martin & G. Chantraine (Eds.), *Prison breaks: Toward a sociology of escape* (pp. 33–59). New York: Springer/Palgrave Studies in Prison and Penology.

Birkett, M., & Sasaki, J. (2018). Why does it feel so good to care for others and myself? Neuroendocrinology and prosocial behavior. In. L. Stevens & C. C. Woodruff (Eds.), *The neuroscience of empathy, compassion, and self-compassion* (pp. 189–211). New York: Academic Press.

Block, E. (2019, February 26). *Does insurance cover a service dog*? Retrieved March 3, 2019 from: https://www.healthcare.com/blog/insurance-cover-service-dogs/.

Bondy, E., & Ross, D. D. (2008). The teacher as warm demander. *Educational Leadership, 66*(1), 54–58.

Bristol, M. (2013, April 26). *11 celebrities who speak for animals.* http://www.vetstreet.com/our-pet-experts/11-celebrities-who-speak-for-animals.

Bruner, J. (1990). *Acts of meaning*. Boston: Harvard University Press.

Bruner, J. S. (1991). The narrative construction of reality. *Critical Inquiry, 1,* 1–21. https://doi.org/10.1086/448619.

Bullock, K., Bunce, A., & McCarthy, D. (2019). Making good in uncompromising places: The development and cultivation of redemption scripts among long-term prisoners. *International Journal of Offender Therapy and Comparative Criminology, 63*(3), https://doi.org/10.1177/0306624X18800882.

Cherry, K. (2018a). What is self-awareness? *Very Well Mind*. Retrieved from https://www.verywellmind.com/what-is-self-awareness-2795023.

Cherry, K. (2018b). What is self-concept and how does it form? *Very Well Mind*. Retrieved from https://www.verywellmind.com/what-is-self-concept-2795865.

Creswell, J. W., & Poth, C. N. (2017). *Qualitative inquiry and research design: Choosing among five approaches* (4th ed.). Thousand Oaks: Sage.

David G. (2016). Inmate Testimonial. *All Paws on Deck, 3*(2), 17. Retrieved June 1, 2019 from: https://www.cor.pa.gov/About%20Us/Newsroom/Pages/Newsletters.aspx.

Dick, A. J., Rich, W., & Waters, T. (2016). *Prison vocational education and policy in the U. S.* New York: Springer.

Egan, K. (2019). Honouring the role of narrative and metaphor in education. In M. Hanne & A. A. Kahl (Eds.), *Narrative and metaphor in education: Looking both ways* (pp. 21–31). New York: Routledge.

Fader, J. J. (2013). *Falling back: incarceration and transitions to adulthood among urban youth.* New Brunswick, NJ: Rutgers University Press.

Filinson, R., & Ciambrone, D. (2019). "Trying to blend in, what else can we do?" Intergenerational relationships among aged inmates: Research. *Journal of Intergenerational Relationships, 17*(1), 74–92. https://doi.org/10.1080/15350770.2018.1500328.

Gibson, C. L., & Krohn, M. D. (Eds.). *Handbook of life-course criminology: Emerging trends and directions for future research.* New York: Springer.

Gottschall, J. (2013). *The storytelling animal: How stories make us human.* New York: Mariner Books.

Graves, L. (2016). *All Paws on Deck, 3*(2), 21. Retrieved June 1, 2019 from: https://www.cor.pa.gov/About%20Us/Newsroom/Pages/Newsletters.aspx.

Halsey, M. (2006). Negotiating conditional release: Juvenile narratives of repeat incarceration. *Punishment and Society, 8,* 147–181.

Higgins, E. T. (1987). Self-discrepancy: A theory relating self and affect. *Psychological Review, 94*(3), 319–340.

Hill, L. (2018). Becoming the person your dog thinks you are: An assessment of Floridaprison-based dog training programs on postrelease recidivism. *Corrections: Policy, Practice,and Research.* https://doi.org/10.1080/23774657.2018.1433564

Immordino-Yang, M. H. (2016). Emotion, sociality, and the brain's default mode network: Insights for educational practice and policy. *Policy Insights from the Behavioral and Brain Sciences*. Retrieved February 28, 2019 from https://doi.org/10.1177/2372732216656869.

Jackson, P. (1990). *Life in classrooms.* (re-issued edition). New York: Teachers College Press.

Jalongo, M. R. (Ed.), (in press). *The canine-campus connection: Roles for service, therapy and shelter dogs in college students' lives.* West Lafayette, IN: Purdue University Press.

Kaplan, J. T., Gimbel, S. I., Dehghani, M., Immordino-Yang, M. H., Sagae, K., Wong, J. D., et al. (2017). Processing narratives concerning protected values: A cross-cultural investigation of neural correlates. *Cerebral Cortex, 27*(2), 1428–1438. https://doi.org/10.1093/cercor/bhv325.

Kelley, T. (2018a). SCI Coal Township. Where are they now—Sage's story. *All Paws on Deck, 5* (1), 6. Retrieved June 1, 2019 from: https://www.cor.pa.gov/About%20Us/Newsroom/Pages/Newsletters.aspx.

Kelley, T. (2018b). Sage, 5-year-old Rottie, returns to FIDOS at SCI Coal Township. *All Paws on Deck, 5*(2), 7. Retrieved June 1, 2019 from: https://www.cor.pa.gov/About%20Us/Newsroom/Pages/Newsletters.aspx.

Kerley, K. R. (2018). *Finding freedom in confinement: The role of religion in prison life.* Santa Barbara, CA: ABC-CLIO.

King, S. (2013). Early desistance narratives: A qualitative analysis of probationers' transitions towards desistance. *Punishment and Society, 15*(2), 147–165.

Laird, K. (2016). SCI Smithfield. *All Paws on Deck, 3*(2), 8. Retrieved June 1, 2019 from: https://www.cor.pa.gov/About%20Us/Newsroom/Pages/Newsletters.aspx.

Langellier, K. M. (2001). Personal narrative. In M. Jolly (Ed.), *Encyclopedia of life writing: Autobiographical and biographical forms* (Vol. 2). London: Fitzroy Dearborn.

Leverentz, A. M. (2014). *The ex-prisoner's dilemma: How women negotiate competing narratives of reentry and desistance*. New Brunswick, NJ: Rutgers University Press.

Levitt, H. M., Bamberg, M., Creswell, J. W., Frost, D. M., Josselson, R., & Suárez-Orozco, C. (2018). Journal article reporting standards for qualitative primary, qualitative meta-analytic, and mixed methods research in psychology: The APA Publications and Communications Board task force report. *American Psychologist, 73*(1), 26–46.

Lockwood, K. (2018). Disrupted mothering: Narratives of mothers in prison. In T. Taylor & K. Bloch (Eds.), *Marginalized mothers, mothering from the margins* (pp. 157–173, Vol. 25). Bingley, UK: Emerald Publishing Limited.

Maruna, S. (2001). *Making good: How ex-convicts reform and rebuild their lives*. Washington, DC: American Psychological Association.

Maruna, S. (2017). Desistance as a social movement. *Irish Probation Journal, 14,* 5–20.

McClung, A. (2017). SCI Camp Hill. *All Paws on Deck, 4*(1), 15. Retrieved June 1, 2019 from: https://www.cor.pa.gov/About%20Us/Newsroom/Pages/Newsletters.aspx.

Merriam, S. B., & Grenier, R. S. (2019). *Qualitative research in practice: Examples for discussion and analysis*. New York: Wiley.

Michael H. (2017). SCI Benner Township. *All Paws on Deck, 4*(2), 19. Retrieved June 1, 2019 from: https://www.cor.pa.gov/About%20Us/Newsroom/Pages/Newsletters.aspx.

Minke, L. K. (2017). Normalization, social bonding, and emotional support—A dog's effect within a prison workshop for women. *Anthrozoös, 30*(3), 387–395. https://doi.org/10.1080/08927936.2017.1311065.

Munoz, L. (2012). Theories of self-concept maintenance. *Life Long Learning: Social Psychology*. Retrieved from https://lynnmunoz.wordpress.com/2012/11/22/theories-of-self-concept-maintenance/.

Neill, J. (2005). Definitions of various self constructs: Self-esteem, self-efficacy, self-confidence and self-concept. Retrieved March 19, 2019 from: http://www.wilderdom.com/self/.

Ntinda, K. (2019). Narrative research. In P. Liamputtong (Ed.), *Handbook of research methods in health and social sciences* (pp. 1–13). New York: Springer.

Patton, M. Q. (2015). *Qualitative research and evaluation methods: Integrating theory and practice* (4th ed.). Thousand Oaks: Sage.

Reissman, C. K. (2003). *Narrative analysis*. Retrieved February 1, 2019 from: http://www.mmcri.org/deptPages/core/downloads/Riessman_Narrative_Analysis.pdf.

Rennison, C. M., & Hart, T. C. (2018). *Research methods in criminal justice and criminology*. Thousand Oaks: Sage.

Roth, D. (2019, in press). Narrative metaphor: Integrating insights in cognitive science into a toolset for intentionally shaping vocational pursuits. *International Journal of Christianity and Education*. https://doi.org/10.1177/2056997118812897.

Shelton, T., & Jalongo, M. R. (2017). *Practical strategies for supporting young learners with autism spectrum disorders*. Lewisville, NC: Gryphon House.

Siegel, D. J. (2012). *The developing mind: how relationships and the brain interact to shape who we are* (2nd ed.). New York: Guilford Press.

Siegel, D. J. (2017). *Mind: A journey to the heart of being human*. New York: W. W. Norton.

Steuber, K. R. (2019). Understanding individual agency: How empathy and narrative competence cooperate. In D. Matravers & A. Waldow (Eds.), *Philosophical perspectives on empathy: Theoretical approaches and emerging challenges*. New York: Routledge.

Stevens, L., & Woodruff, C. C. (Eds.). (2018). *The neuroscience of empathy, compassion, and self-compassion*. New York: Academic Press.

Turner, M., Peacock, M., Payne, S., Fletcher, A., & Froggatt, K. (2018, September). Ageing and dying in the contemporary neoliberal prison system: Exploring the 'double burden' for older prisoners. *Social Science and Medicine*. http://dx.doi.org/10.1016/j.socscimed.2018.07.009.

Veysey, B. M., Martinez, D. J., & Christian, J. (2013). "Getting out": A summary of qualitative research on desistance across the life course. In C. L. Gibson & M. D. Krohn (Eds.), *Handbook of life-course criminology* (pp. 233–260). New York: Springer.

Viard, A., Mutlu, J., Chanraud, S. Guenole, F., Egler, P. Gerardin, P. Baleyte, J. Dayan, J. Eustache, F., & Guillery-Girard, B. (2019). Altered default mode network connectivity in adolescents with post-traumatic stress disorder. *NeuroImage: Clinical*. https://doi.org/10.1016/j.nicl.2019.101731.

Wang, H., Verkes, R., Roozendaal, B., & Hermans, E. J. (2019). Toward understanding developmental disruption of default mode network connectivity due to early life stress. *Biological Psychiatry, 4*(1), 5–7). doi:https://doi.org/10.1016/j.bpsc.2018.11.008.

Zak, P. J. (2015, February 2). Why inspiring stories make us react: The neuroscience of narrative. *Cerebrum, 2*. Retrieved February 28, 2019 from: http://neuroeconomicstudies.org/images/pdf-files/dana-org-Why-Inspiring-Stories-Make-Us-React-The-Neuroscience-of-Narrative-2.pdf.

Chapter 14
Celebrating the Achievements of Prison Dog Programs

Carmaleta Aufderheide and Mary Renck Jalongo

Introduction

Anthropomorphism cuts both ways. Where the human-canine bond is concerned, the word often is used to criticize people who attribute human capabilities to dogs. What is seldom considered is that treating dogs as if they were humans also imposes unnecessary limits on them when our own feeble senses—most especially, smell—are far outstripped by a dog's. Practically everyone now knows that a dog's sense of smell is superior to a human being's. Furthermore, the whole smelling apparatus of dogs is different—they have a separate nasal canal for breathing and for smelling. In addition, they can detect smells in miniscule amounts that are widely dispersed. Dogs can sort out many competing smells to focus on just one of them (Horowitz 2009). One illustration of this amazing ability occurred when the Federal Bureau of Investigation used a black Lab named Bear to locate a usb of child pornography in the apartment of Subway sandwich spokesperson, Jarrod Fogel. A search-and-rescue dog can follow a human vapor trail hours—even days—after a person has been there. Together, anthropomorphism and human arrogance say, in effect, "If a far superior being like me can't do this, then it just isn't possible" coupled with the attitude "The people reporting this canine ability are just fools who are crazy about dogs and are aren't thinking straight." Such attitudes that deny dogs their

Note: Content in this chapter is based on a thesis that included interviews with 37 inmates at three different institutions conducted by the first author, as noted throughout. Additional comments from inmates were originally published in the quarterly, online newsletter of the Pennsylvania Department of Corrections, All Paws on Deck.

C. Aufderheide
Insight Development Group, Restorative Justice Facilitator,
University of Oregon, Eugene, OR, USA

M. R. Jalongo (✉)
Emerita, Indiana University of Pennsylvania, Indiana, PA, USA
e-mail: mjalongo@comcast.net

M. R. Jalongo (ed.), *Prison Dog Programs*,
https://doi.org/10.1007/978-3-030-25618-0_14

due have been an anchor against progress in expanding roles for dogs as our working partners.

A case in point is the "cancer sniffing dog". It all began with owners reporting that their dogs seemed focused on a part of their bodies that later turned out to be cancerous. At first, others scoffed at these accounts. As more and more people dared to concur with these observations, it formulated a research question: Can dogs accurately detect the presence of cancer, presumably by smell? Rather than the research beginning with experimental design studies conducted in a laboratory setting, it began with many anecdotes. Empirical research had to "catch up" with what people had observed. Today, dogs with a particularly keen sense of smell and eagerness to work are being trained to detect disease in tissue, blood, and urine samples. Why do this? Don't we have scientific, medical tests that achieve this already? Actually, no, not as well. The In Situ Foundation reports three advantages to using specially trained dogs to detect different types of cancer. Dogs can: (1) identify cancer in smaller tissue samples, making the tests less invasive; (2) confirm its presence earlier than medical tests, making more immediate treatment possible; and (3) report fewer false positives, thereby sparing people unnecessary anguish as well as saving time and money. Of course, not every dog can perform this task equally well; it relies on a combination of exceptional physical abilities, appropriate training, and expert human handlers. Detecting cancer has tremendous significance for human health yet this valuable tool never would never have emerged without first acknowledging that a dog's abilities in some realms are far superior to our own. This breakthrough also required professionals who were willing to risk the ridicule of many of their peers in order to conduct the research. In fact, that is exactly what happened when psychologist Boris Levinson, widely regarded as a pioneer in the human-animal bond, presented his research on the positive effects of his dog's presence during sessions with clients at the American Psychological Association. He was derided for "going to the dogs" and most people thought it was ridiculous to incorporate a dog into mental health work (Coren 2013). Decades later, the practice is widely accepted and a whole new field, animal-assisted therapy (AAT), now exists (Chandler 2017; Parish-Plass 2013; Van Fleet and Faa-Thompson 2017). As this discussion has illustrated, the scientific method and first-person accounts of experiences do not stand in opposition to one another; rather, the relationship between the two is symbiotic. Despite its pretensions to complete objectivity, scientific inquiry often begins with a hunch that emanates from personal experience.

We would argue that a similar situation exists where the effects of prison dog programs on inmates, the correctional facility, the people who become the dog's permanent family, and the dogs themselves are concerned. There is extensive anecdotal information complemented by an emerging body of research. Qualitative research would take the stance that understanding a phenomenon requires the emic, or insider's point of view. In PDPs, that means turning to the inmates themselves. To illustrate, inmate/trainers from state prison Pine Grove complete the assignment in Box 15.1 in one of their classes:

Box 15.1 Writing Assignment
"We are who we are as much because of our relationships with non-human animals as because of the human ones, and we do ourselves a great disservice—and probably great harm—by denying or ignoring this" (Podberscek et al. 2000, p. 2).

Do you agree? Do you think that bonds with animals influence who we are and who we become? Has working in the service dog training program changed your ideas or others' ideas about who you are in any way? If so, how?

Two of their responses follow.

Brandon wrote: *Since I have begun training dogs I have become a much more patient individual and much more open to working with other people to serve a much better purpose. I have also learned that the world doesn't just revolve around me but I can do a lot of good by training these dogs. My favorite part of the program is seeing the dogs come from knowing nothing to knowing 59 commands and be very sharp with them. The bonds I have formed with my first 3 dogs has made me a lot less likely to engage in acts that may get me in trouble...It has changed my perception of myself that I can actually do something good in spite of my current situation. When others see me training the dog some people may think that I don't deserve to have a dog in prison, but these people don't understand why I train the dogs. I didn't sign up for a companion, I signed up to train the dogs to have an impact on other people's lives, especially people who have had a rough life...I no longer look at myself as the 17-year-old who made a mistake and got a lot of prison time. I'm now the 23-year-old man who trains dogs and changes people's lives for the better—good people, who deserve it.*

Inmate/trainer Jonathan wrote: *For me, this program is a God send. Not only do we teach and prepare the puppies to aid the people with disabilities, but the animals (without knowing) teaches us how to be patient with others. Although there was a lot of long nights when our pups were living in new environments. They were crying all night and going to the bathroom inside of their crates. At that point I was trying to figure out what was going on. I finally realized that what us handlers are doing is not for our personal enjoyment, but for the betterment of the puppy. And in the long run, this program is going to prepare many puppies to become good service dogs...As far as we (the handlers) are concerned, it gives us much gratification knowing that our pups passed all final testing and made the cut to be placed with a person and become a great service dog to that person.*

Many people who read these comments would argue that the punishments of these inmates do not sound sufficiently harsh. Shouldn't these offenders be suffering more, given the magnitude of their crimes and the fact that it is a maximum security facility? This is a contentious issue, both in the field of criminology and in cultures throughout the world. Namely, is the primary purpose of incarceration to punish or is it to promote positive change in prisoners?

Conflicting Views of Justice

Opinions on how best to hold people accountable for criminal activity run the gamut from cruel punishment to restitution/rehabilitation (Garland 2001; Phelps 2011). In the United States, fairness and consistency are basic tenets of the rule of law, yet these often give way to a "get tough" model that dominates public opinion (Armour 2012). Under the guise of public safety, politicians have argued that the only deterrent to crime is the "lock them up and throw away the key" approach. The result has been an exponential increase in the U.S. prison population. Whereas the criminal justice systems in many other developed countries tend to make a 20-year sentence with the opportunity for parole their maximum, the U.S. legal system is more likely to impose life sentences, often without the possibility of parole. The Sentencing Project (2018), an advocacy group that is opposed to these practices, offers the following statistics that challenge public perceptions:

> The United States is the world's leader in incarceration. There are 2.2 million people in the nation's prisons and jails—a 500% increase over the last 40 years. Changes in law and in policy, not changes in crime rates, explain most of this increase. The results are over-crowding in prisons and fiscal burdens on states, despite increasing evidence that large-scale incarceration is not an effective means of achieving public safety… The number of people serving life sentences continues to grow even while serious, violent crime has been declining for the past 20 years… The lifer population has nearly quintupled since 1984. One in nine people in prison is now serving a life sentence and nearly a third of lifers have been sentenced to life without parole. (p. 1)

A prevailing assumption is that only "bad people" become offenders and they need to be punished severely to deter them and others from committing crimes (Aronson et al. 2015). If society at large embraces the belief that inmates are irredeemable and incorrigible, it then follows that inmates are incapable of altruistic behavior of any kind (Gummerum and Hanoch 2012). Enlightened professionals in the corrections field frequently find themselves in a philosophy/reality conflict that makes it difficult to reconcile retributive justice (allocating proportionate punishment for a crime) with the ideal of rehabilitation (making restitution and preparing for re-entry into society). Justice workers carry the heavy emotional burden of holding offenders accountable for their criminal actions while, at the same time, striving to keep the hope of healing and rehabilitation alive.

Restorative justice shifts the emphasis toward repairing harm and rebuilding relationships among victims, offenders and communities (Consedine 1995; Kurki 2000; Van Ness and Strong 2002). Restorative justice recognizes not only how offenders harm their victims and communities but also themselves (Armour 2012; Dzur 2003). The premise here is that successful reintegration of an offender back into society is a two-way process; it not only requires effort on the part of the inmate in the form of desistance from crime and repentance for prior acts but also depends on community forgiveness and acceptance (Maruna 2011). Put into practice, restorative justice typically includes victim-offender mediation, family group conferencing, and victim-offender dialogue (Armour 2012; Zehr 2015). Yet, for a variety of reasons, this is difficult to orchestrate. Such initiatives would require—at the very least–skilled mediators on staff, victims and offenders willing to meet one another, a space in which to schedule the meetings, and heightened security measures.

Given the overcrowding and financial pressures on penal institutions, staff members with rehabilitative ideals have sought inexpensive, yet effective, interventions that use altruistic behavior as correctional treatment (Toch 2000). Prison dog programs are one possible route to practicing altruism. To illustrate, Humby and Barclay (2018) conducted a national survey of 23 different prison dog programs operating in six Australian states. They identified three barriers: (1) insufficient funding, (2) limited time to train the dogs, and (3) some staff resistance. Most of these programs followed a community service design and were administered by animal welfare organizations. Major benefits for inmates cited were: opportunities to train the dogs, give back to society, gain a sense of responsibility, improve self-confidence and social skills, and acquire vocational qualifications to improve job opportunities post-release. These survey findings are very consistent with other research of this type that has been discussed across all the chapters of this book. The various ways in which prison dog programs can support rehabilitation are highlighted in the section that follows. Each point is illustrated with the words of actual participants in PDPs.

Prison Dog Programs and Inmate Rehabilitation

Positive psychology is a branch in the field of psychology that has gained considerable attention in recent years. Rather than focusing on psychological issues, problems, and deviant behaviors, it studies the conditions that maximize human potential. One of the most prominent researchers in this field is Mihaly Csikszentmihaly. He has written extensively about the psychology of optimal experience, or flow. Csikszentmihaly (1990) contends that "The best moments in our lives are not the passive, receptive, relaxing times…The best moments usually occur if a person's body or mind is stretched to its limits in a voluntary effort to accomplish something difficult and worthwhile" (p. 3). Surely, that could be a description of the work that inmates undertake in prison dog programs: voluntary, challenging, and worthwhile. PDPs are consistent with the principles of positive psychology in at least six ways.

1. **Establishing reciprocal bonds between dogs and inmates**.

Although the original work on attachment behaviors focused exclusively on bonds between humans, particularly the mother-infant bond, the concept has been applied to the human-animal bond in recent years (Jalongo 2015). The classic attachment behaviors are: (1) seeking proximity, (2) resisting separation, and (3) relying on the person with whom the bond is formed as a "home base" who provides "emotional refueling" as needed. Where human beings are concerned, the formation of a stable and secure attachment to at least one primary caregiver is crucial as toddlers summon the confidence to take risks, explore their worlds, and develop optimally. The primary caregiver's sensitivity to the needs of the child greatly affects the strength of the bond. There is also some evidence that the quality of that first relationship influences bonds across the lifespan (Gilath et al. 2016). Histories of disrupted attachments with people occur at a considerably higher rate in inmates than in the general population, and this may be particularly true for women in prison (Minton et al. 2015; Saxena et al. 2014). For many individuals, bonds with dogs are highly valued forms of attachment. National survey data collected by the American Pet Products Association (2019) indicates that many people felt that they had stronger ties with their dog than with some family members. Likewise, Serpell (2017), a leader in human-animal bond research, has concluded that dogs can provide a unique form of social support to humans after a reciprocal bond is formed.

Inmate/handlers describe their bonds with dogs in ways that are very similar to how adults describe attachments with close family, friends, and spouses. Dogs can be a source of emotional support, comfort, and relief during times of need and stress (Allen et al. 2001; McCardle et al. 2011; Zilcha-Mano et al. 2012). An inmate who worked at an animal shelter housed at the correctional facility referred to visiting the dogs as "a haven" from prison life (Aufderheide 2016, p. 70). Research conducted in laboratory settings documents that dogs are particularly observant of their caregivers and responsive to their moods (Hare and Woods 2013; Mikosi 2016; Serpell 2017). One inmate/puppy raiser explained this as follows:

> When I'm aggravated for whatever reason small or big, I sit out back with him. We'll train and he'll look at me and act a certain way. I can't put my finger on what this way is but he's very attentive and he's tuned in in a different way. It's almost like he wants to ask me a question like…'Hey, man what's wrong with you?' It's the way they hold their body; the way their eye contact is. A service dog is always going to give you eye contact. I feel like when they're concerned their eye contact is more intense like they're really trying to ask you something with their eyes. I notice it. I tell him what's wrong with me. I use it as therapy. (Aufderheide 2016, p. 70)

Inmate/handlers also noted how their dogs attuned themselves to their caregivers. As one inmate described,

> These puppies know everything. They will act appropriately for what it is. If you're crying they'll put their head in your lap. If laughing, they'll cock their head. If you're withdrawn they'll paw at you. We've learned that it's ok to be sad and not perfect in front of the puppies. We didn't teach them to react this way…that's just a dog. (Aufderheide 2016, p. 71)

Bonds between humans and canines represent a unique form of attachment. *Photo Credit* Haley Romanko

2. **Forging new identities for offenders and canines.**

Bonds between humans and dogs shape new identities at both ends of the leash. Inmates begin to see themselves differently. In an interview study of inmates conducted by Minton et al. (2015), one woman addressed this with:

> So there's loss of identity, but the dog does give you identity. And becoming a dog trainer is a new, more positive identity…It enables me to see myself differently. I follow the rules; I hold myself to a higher standard. I have a title so I want to live up to that title of responsibility—people have entrusted it to me. (p. 492)

> I've spent 20 years existing. Now I'm actually doing something that has a positive impact on someone else. I can be identified for what I'm doing rather than where I am or what I did for 5 min to get to where I'm at. (Aufderheide 2016, p. 54)

Bonds with dogs also imbue the animals with new and unique identities. Many of the prison dog programs work with shelter dogs. Some of these dogs were never trained and have become unruly. Others were abandoned, neglected, abused, or traumatized. Still others have lost their homes due to owners' life changes, such as illness, geographic relocation, divorce, military deployment, mental health issues, or even death. As handlers in prison dog programs interact with rescued dogs and service dog puppies, they create identities for them. People speak for their dogs, an indication of "the intimacy of his or her relationship—the animal other is known so well that the owner can effectively discern what is 'on his or her mind'… it is also through the process of speaking for the dog that the owner actively constructs—both for him—or herself and for others—the identity of the animal" (Arluke and Sanders 1996, p. 67). One good example of forging an identity for a dog is a chocolate Labrador retriever named Rader. The inmate/trainers characterized him as follows:

"If Rader was a man, he'd be a blue-collar worker with his sleeves rolled up…Radar was like Norm [from the television program] *Cheers*. Big entrance and a steady presence. Take him for a walk and he would introduce you to the helicopter. As he searched for a spot to do his business when given the command, 'Better go now,' Rader would spin 360° several times and then settle into releasing his bowels. Grab a soccer ball and it's game time! Rader was obsessed with chasing and retrieving a soccer ball. No matter the distance and velocity, Rader wanted that soccer ball with his every breath and ounce of effort. Now ladies were really in for a treat! Rader was, and I'm certain still is, a ladies' man/dog. When he heard a soft female voice from a distance, let's just say, it was on! Rader was gallant and royal, ready to impress."

"From the beginning he was and is special. Rader's 'watch me' command was so good that he would just stare at you, watching you, paying attention to you, his friend, his pal. It's like he was saying to you, 'Tell me what you need me to do and I'll just do it'."

"I personally will always remember Rader in that when it was my turn to train a puppy, Rader took the puppy as his little brother. Watching Rader be so gentle with Trooper the puppy was everybody's "Awww" moment. Trooper would climb on top of Rader and he would just lay there. After a while, Rader would put his paw on Trooper, like letting him know that play time was over. Once Trooper was bigger, they would play like nonstop when they were in the yard…Rader's personality was and will always be something that I can look for in a dog from here on out."

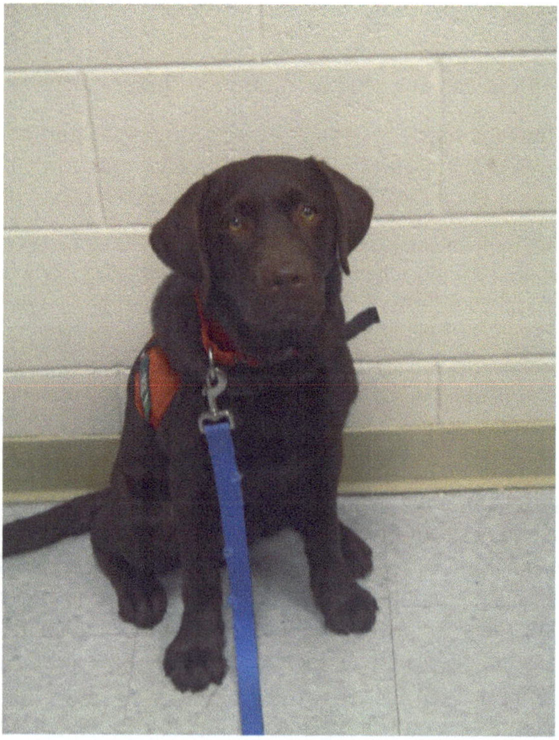

Rader, a United Disabilities Services Foundation dog, was trained by inmates at Moshannon Valley Correctional Center. He became a successful assistance dog for a child on the autism spectrum. *Photo credit* Lori Breece

There is also a mutual discovery of capabilities that occurs during effective and humane dog training. Each partner adapts as previously undiscovered talents surface in the trainer and the dog. Many inmates also credited their bonds with dogs as a route to shedding histories of being de-valued by others. The non-judgmental nature of the dogs was frequently cited as important to this process; as one inmate said, "Dogs don't judge and don't hold a grudge" (Aufderheide 2016, p. 57). An important part of that revision to self-concept has to do with meeting and accomplishing worthwhile goals. These improvements in behavioral choices helped to transform negative self-beliefs into optimistic self-beliefs:

> It's made me more confident in the things I'm doing. I don't feel like my attempts are futile. My confidence in training is helping my confidence in myself. When I first got into it that was a fear I had…I want to do this but I'm not sure I can do this. Working with a dog as a puppy and taking it when it knew nothing and seeing it learn something simple like its name, I realized I could do this. When I finished that first dog, I took a big jump in confidence because I could say…look what I did. (Aufderheide 2016, p. 75)

3. **Providing opportunities for healthy expression of emotions**.

Inmates are never alone in prison, yet their loneliness and isolation in prison life is evident. In interviews with 37 inmates at three institutions, there was frequent mention of the fact that all physical contact in prison is strictly prohibited, something that tends to increase feelings of loneliness and isolation during incarceration (Aufderheide 2016). Inmate handlers spoke about how working so closely with their dogs eased any loneliness they experienced; as one inmate put it, "with the dog nothing is said…but everything is said" (p. 65).

Inmates who don't present emotional detachment among other prisoners frequently risk becoming targets of ridicule and violence. Working with dogs allows handlers to express emotions without fear of retaliation or judgment. For example, when a group of eight inmates met the four, 12-week old service dog puppies they would be training the first time, the men stood against the wall, subdued and serious, awaiting instructions. The little Labs had other ideas about how to get acquainted. As the men attempted to cradle them in their arms, the pups were wiggling, vocalizing, and licking the men's faces. Within moments, all of the trainers adjourned to the floor, completely charmed by their puppies' exuberance, laughing as the pups tugged on a pants leg or chewed a shoelace, and scooping them up when the little yellow furballs wandered too far from the group.

Inmates in prison dog programs often remark that the dogs' unconditional acceptance introduces feelings of calm and contentment. They appreciate the freedom to give and receive affection as part of the behaviorally healthy relationship with their dogs. The dogs also introduced an element of forgiveness: they weren't concerned with their handlers' pasts and this allowed them to view themselves differently. Interacting with dogs also was a respite from the tensions of life in prison. The unfailing display of happiness from the dogs towards their handlers introduced a feeling that was rare in the corrections context: joy. Some observations about how the dogs contributed to inmate/handlers' well-being and helped them to manage powerful emotions are:

> I talk to the dog about what I'm going through…most everything I'm going through. It's just me and him a lot of the time and he's my outlet. He's helping me with that a lot. I'll go out and cradle the dog, and talk to the dog, and it don't feel so lonely anymore. I had a companion…a canine companion (p. 66).

> My anger has gone from being really high to really low. When I start to get angry I look into my dog's eyes and I just calm down. It's also helped with loneliness. This is a really lonely place but you're never alone when you have a dog (p. 66).

> When you're coming in (prison), you have a lot of different emotional feelings. A dog puts love back into your life. Dogs reinforce the element of love and helps with giving and receiving love not only for you but for anyone who comes in contact with the dog. I would say the dogs have helped me with sadness, grief, and depression (p. 66).

At times, the dogs were a buffer between the dog's caregiver/handler, other inmates, and staff. Many inmate/handlers reported taking cues from their dogs by observing the nonconfrontational way their dogs responded to people. Learning through and from their dogs was a recurring theme (Aufderheide 2016).

> I've noticed the most change with my anger. I was 22 years old with a brand-new life sentence. To say I was angry would be an understatement. Before the dog program I had grown up a little bit but didn't know how to put it into action…the dogs taught me how to do it. I closed myself off to the rest of the world. The dogs drew me out of that and taught me how to deal with them, which in turn taught me how to deal with people better (p. 66).

After one inmate/handler worked in the dog program, he later decided to volunteer to work with prison hospice.

> The dogs have helped me to care more. In this environment it's kind of difficult to care because you have so many offensive people doing offensive things. The animals helped me develop tolerance and that emotion to care for a person when they can't care for themselves. (p. 66).

Frederickson (2004) credits positive emotions with building physical, intellectual and social abilities. From this "broaden-and-build" point of view, positive emotions enable people to make more connections, expand their thought-action repertoires, enhance their skills and increase their resources (Table 15.1).

4. **Impelling meaningful changes in behavior**.

One way of thinking about change is a concept called "levels of use" (American Institutes for Research 2015). It outlines a sequence of adapting to an innovation. The concept here is that, as people become familiar with and involved in change, their perspectives change accordingly. Table 15.2 provides a description and example at each level for an inmate/trainer's participation in a prison dog program.

Table 15.1 Emotions as a tool for broadening and building human abilities

Emotion	Effects (Frederickson 2004)	Excerpts from inmate interviews (Aufderheide 2016)
Joy	Sparks the urge to play and create	"I think on a daily basis I'm happier that I have puppies in my life. They bring me such joy every day and it helps push out the sadness and broken heartedness I feel every day" (p. 69)
Interest	Sparks the urge to explore and discover	[The program] "has taught me I can go ask questions and that I don't have all the answers. That would have been impossible to say a while back" (p. 73)
Contentment	Sparks the urge to savor and integrate	"It's calming to hang out with my dog. He comes and just lays his head on me and rolls over and I'm at peace…just chilling" (p. 57)
Love	Promote positive emotions within safe, close relationships that result in social bonds	"All I've learned within this program has helped me become more confident, helped me grow, helped me cope with life within these walls. I had been emotionally closed off, but these dogs were the key to opening my heart to life again. I am relearning forgiveness, laughter, love, and joy. My responsibility to these dogs provides daily purpose for my life. I am able to contribute to society and feel that I am once again part of humanity" (p. 63)

Table 15.2 Inmate/trainers' levels of use of a prison dog program

Level	Typical statement
Nonuse	"I've seen the dogs in the visitor room and around the prison but don't know much about what trainers do."
Orientation	"I talked with someone who trained four service dogs and I'm going to attend an information meeting."
Preparation	"I applied to be assigned to the dorm with the program so that I can get a better idea of what is expected."
Mechanical use	"Now that I've been accepted into the program, most of my time is focused on keeping my head above water with all the new things I'm learning. We have to keep a dog trainer's daily log and keep notes on the dog's physical condition for the vet."
Routine use	"I did it! I successfully trained one dog. Now I feel like I have the basics and can work with another dog during the next cycle."
Refinement	"Last time around, I just 'went by the book' but now I have more than one way to teach a command, such as 'down'."
Integration	"Some people think our job is easy, but dog training isn't for everyone. You need a lot of patience and practice plus, I'm learning that every dog is different. One dog might be more food motivated and another, more play or praise motivated. If you are a really good trainer, you figure it out."
Renewal	"There is some pressure to have the dog you've trained perform and pass the tests. I'm now thinking that I might be able to work with dogs for a living when I get out, so I am making use of our library to find out more about behavior problems and training dogs for different purposes."

Source for stages: American Institutes for Research (2015)

5. **Increasing communication among various stakeholders.**

There is extensive research to suggest that dogs stimulate conversation, whether it is among residents of nursing homes (Borgi et al. 2018), college students preparing for exams (Barker et al. 2017), or inmates enrolled in education programs (Collica-Cox and Fagin 2018). The presence of dogs in correctional facilities is no exception. At Fort Dodge Correctional Facility, handlers frequently reported that other inmates—described as big, tough guys covered in tattoos—would approach them and ask to pet the dog. Likewise, Thomas H., a handler in the DAWGS Prison Program who had personally trained 18 dogs and interacted with nearly 100 of them, said "I have personally witnessed some of the hardest criminals who project the toughest attitudes turn into a kid who just got what he wanted for Christmas when they get a chance to interact with the dogs." Another inmate wrote, "My favorite memory is when an inmate was petting the dog and he told me 'I haven't pet a dog in 25 years.' Need I say more?"

Dixon Correctional Institution has an animal shelter on site. Unlike the service dog programs where the pups usually reside in the cells with the inmate/trainers, the dogs sleep in their kennels at night. Another difference in PDPs is the amount and kind of interaction with the public. Because the dogs at Pen Pals are being groomed for adoption, the inmates have frequent interactions with community members in search of a family dog. For service dog puppy raisers and trainers, there tends to be more interaction with service dog program staff who visit regularly and evaluate each pup's progress. Interactions with individuals who have disabilities and acquire the dogs occur primarily at a graduation type of event or during return visits to the facility. Despite the particulars, inmates have more interaction with people outside the immediate corrections context.

Many inmates described how the presence of dogs afforded more opportunities for positive interactions with staff as well. Individuals who may have been regarded previously as reserved, less approachable, or disapproving are sometimes seen in a different light after the dogs become part of the culture. Of course, not all staff members are enthused about dog programs but, as inmate Anthony described, there is buy-in from most: "Other staff around the institution have been very supportive of this program. About 80% of the staff love the dogs. I've heard a lot about their dogs and how they love to see the puppies around the institution. Everyone is so amazed at the puppies' progress and their skill level."

This photo collage of the prison pups at six months of age was shared with the inmate/handlers to show them how the dogs behaved during a demonstration at a local agility club. *Photo credit* Mary Renck Jalongo

Staff support of the program is not limited to corrections officers and other personnel responsible for working with offenders. Service dogs need to be "bomb proof" and well socialized to all types of experiences in order to be successful. One drawback on a correctional facility is that it cannot accomplish this adequately by limiting the dogs' experience to life on the "inside". Beth Linn, a records specialist at SCI Huntingdon in Pennsylvania, wrote about her volunteer efforts to help prepare guide dogs for the blind through Canine Partners for Life (CPL):

> At first, I just thought it would be fun to take the puppies out into the world and spend time with them. And it is! But it's so much more than that. Watching the puppies grow and learn under the guidance of their inmate handlers is amazing. So much is accomplished in such a relatively short period of time!
>
> As a staff volunteer, I've learned the importance of reinforcing what these puppies are learning when I take them out, whether it's just taking them back to my office for a few hours or home for a day or overnight visit. Taking them out into the "real world" is a vital part of their training, but only in conjunction with the skills they have already learned or are still learning. I've learned how important it is to be aware that, even though they are super

> cute puppies, they are being trained for an enormous responsibility; and we must always be respectful of that and only add to, not deter from, their training. Being exposed to many different settings, sounds, environments, people and places is crucial to the puppies' success as graduates of Canine Partners for Life (CPL).
>
> In addition, having the pleasure of spending time in the evenings or on weekends with the puppies has brought much joy to my family and me. My daughters love meeting the puppies, playing with them and taking them along on family outings. We also enjoy explaining the CPL program to people who come up to us and ask about the vest the puppies are wearing. Many people have approached us and inquired about the program and how to go about applying for the help of a service or companion dog. It's gratifying to know that, in addition to assisting with the puppies' training, we may also be helping to connect an individual with an organization that may possibly provide much needed assistance. And, of course, there's nothing like the playfulness, love, fun and joy that a puppy brings! I'm thrilled that SCI Huntingdon and CPL have partnered together. I have a profound respect for the work that the inmate handlers do every day to get these puppies ready for the next phase of their training. I understand that this 24-hour commitment on their part is not easy and not at all just fun and games. It takes a great deal of commitment, patience and hard work. And I'm grateful for the opportunity to be able to have even a small role in this extremely worthwhile and rewarding endeavor.

Investigating the ways that a PDP affects the entire culture of the correctional facility is an important area for future research.

6. **Participating in prosocial behavior**

Working with the dogs is a privilege that is reserved for a few carefully selected inmates. To illustrate, one state correctional facility houses approximately 1400 inmates yet only eight of them are directly responsible in training a service dog puppy each year. Interview data suggest that inmates are well aware of their special status within the institution and do not want to jeopardize it (Aufderheide 2016; Furst 2011; Minton et al. 2015). Part of restorative justice is a commitment on the part of the offender to resist lapsing back into damaging and destructive behaviors that hurt others and themselves. After inmate dog handlers bond with their dogs and start to view themselves differently, they often say that they are not willing to risk losing the opportunity to work with the dog by behaving as they tended to previously. Two inmate/handlers explained how work with the dogs prompted them to control impulses and engage in prosocial behavior:

> I definitely won't get mad at people anymore or try causing problems with other inmates or staff. It's having him (looks down at his dog) and not wanting to lose him that changes it. He makes me think ahead about consequences before I do stuff now. (p. 69)
>
> When I came inside, I was pretty angry. Over time, and when I got the dog, it changed me to do the right thing. With the dog I had to do what was expected of me. The dog helped keep me on the course to be the kind of person I should be. Having a dog kept me grounded to keep doing the right things. (p. 63)

Researchers from the University of Ottawa have proposed that the field of criminology can reduce recidivism through a model that emphasizes rehabilitation and reasoning (Tong and Farrington 2007). They describe the premise of their program, now supported by numerous evaluation studies (Antonowicz and Parker 2014), as follows:

> Antisocial individuals who are led to engage in prosocial roles as helpers for others may come to see themselves in a very different light...They begin to attribute to themselves positive, prosocial characteristics which were previously foreign to them. They also come to appreciate the value of prosocial behavior, to recognize the rewards it can bring them, and to acquire social skills which can serve as alternatives to their antisocial behavior. (Ross and Hilborn 2008, p. 198)

For many offenders, working with dogs is a way to exert a tangible, positive impact on the outside world that represents renewal and a form of redemption (Aufderheide 2016):

> I was a heroin junkie and been at the bottom. I feel better as a person from where I've been. I didn't care about nobody or nothing. I'd have to say this program has given me responsibility, compassion for other people, empathy, commitment, and a work ethic. You can apply this to anything. (p. 59)

> It shows me I'm kind, caring, and willing to do something for someone else. It gets you out of self. It showed me the soft side of me. I used to be a rough tough guy, had a temper problem and used to solve problems with violence. (p. 63)

> I'm able to provide a service animal to the community and make reparations. I can't change the past but can change somebody's future. (p. 59)

> It's shown me that regardless of what I've done in the past, I can do better and that I'm not defined by that crime". (p. 63)

Strategies for Celebrating Successes

After one person read about the service dog training program in the local prison, she remained unimpressed: "I mean, what else do they have to do all day? Wouldn't you expect results with all that time on their hands?" Not exactly. There are examples everywhere of people who have had a dog for many years and have never succeeded in teaching their pet the most basic "house manners." Surely, they had sufficient time to train the dog, yet it never happened. It is not unusual for these dogs to get turned in at the shelter when something as minor as installing new carpet occurs. So, obviously, time is not the only variable. Dogs are a living "report card" on the work achieved. They are walking, breathing messages about the trainers' competence. The remarkable achievement of preparing a great family dog or service dog cannot be denied. As an inmate who worked with a fearful shelter dog observed, "When you have a dog that's head shy and they make progress you just feel really good about that. When I get my dog to always get into the proper position and they follow commands correctly, it boosts my self-confidence and makes me feel a lot better about myself. It's like a proud parent watching their kids ride their bikes without their training wheels" (Aufderheide 2016, p. 75).

Corrections facilities frequently are places where there are few opportunities to do high-quality work, to be recognized for achievements, and to exert any control over the environment. Effective prison dog programs strive to counteract all three limitations by emphasizing the nature of the contributions made, instituting ways to celebrate achievements, and establishing traditions so that inmates can count on positive things happening in the future. The next section describes some of the practices, activities, and strategies that many PDPs have found to be successful in this regard.

Graduation Ceremonies

Many prison dog programs host events that celebrate the achievements of the handlers. Particularly for service dog training program in which the dogs are there for a year or more, graduation ceremonies that include a guest speaker, class valedictorian, dedicated volunteers who support the program, and community members who have made substantial donations of time and/or money typically are involved. Puppy Days is one such celebration.

Puppy Days at Fort Dodge Correctional Facility

Fort Dodge Correctional Facility (FDCF) is a medium security prison with a maximum capacity of 1183 male offenders located in Fort Dodge, Iowa. Inmates at FDCF live in double occupancy cells organized into seven housing units. This prison has one animal program affiliated with Leader Dog for The Blind (LDFB) based out of Rochester, Michigan. LDFB provides highly trained dogs to blind, visually impaired, and deaf-blind individuals empowering them with safe independent living and travel. FDCF is home to a large service dog puppy training program, with as many as 50 dogs in training at one time.

One of their traditions is Puppy Days, when Fort Dodge Correctional Facility welcomes community donors and sponsors of a Leader Dog for the Blind puppy inside prison for an afternoon of entertainment, fellowship, and the rare chance to see the product of their investments. The event is a team effort among prison staff, inmate handlers, and Leader Dog prison volunteers that showcases the puppy program, confirms sponsor commitments and represents what is possible when prisoners work with dogs. What follows are observations about one of these very special days:

The event began with an inmate-prepared lunch; afterwards, guests mingled with inmate handlers and their dogs. The opportunity to engage in casual conversation with guests is scarce and often stressful for inmate puppy raisers whose past relationship with the outside community is damaged. Each inmate/handler proudly introduced his dog to the guests while demonstrating commands mastered over several months of training. As the inmates waited for their turn, many could be observed playfully nuzzling puppies or petting the adult dogs in their care. The bonds between inmate handlers and their dogs were unmistakable. Dogs were attentive, focused, and affectionate towards their handlers leaving no doubt that they trusted and loved these men. To see an inmate handler reflexively swoop up a tired 10-week old puppy and kiss its head before a crowd of 300 people was a reminder of the importance of feeling connected to something in the absence of human contact. It was not clear if the guests recognized how difficult this type of interaction might be for inmates who have fallen out of favor with society. The dogs unknowingly served as a buffer between inmate handlers and their guests allowing for easy conversations centered on the dogs that added to each inmate's likeability. Guests witnessed the connection between inmates and their dogs and their ability to nurture something rather than take from it. The tone in the gym on this day resisted offender stereotypes and embraced the human potential for change.

As show time neared, anticipation filled the air. The crowd took their seats and quieted as the performance got underway. Inmate handlers with their dogs seamlessly demonstrated an impressive mastery of training commands fundamental for each dog's future success as a Leader Dog that elicited tears, laughter, applause, and "aww's" from the crowd. The dogs flawlessly executed complex commands such as remaining in a "down" while other dogs were cued to jump over them or as tennis balls rolled and bounced in front of them. The new puppies trotted alongside the dogs who would leave to pursue advanced training.

After giving the dogs a short break, speakers took center stage to share their experiences with the puppy program. First up, an inmate puppy raiser nearing his release from prison spoke from the heart about what a decade with this program had allowed him to accept within himself and his past while looking forward to a new life on the outside. Next, the CEO of Leader Dog shared how her initial reluctance to place a dog inside FDCF had been replaced by great enthusiasm after seeing the quality of preparation provided by the inmate/trainers. She read a letter written by a Leader Dog recipient whose dog got its start at FDCF that affirmed the value and long reach of this program. FDCF warden, J. McKinney, took center stage and expressed his commitment to the puppy raising program. He spoke about the ripple effect that the program continues to have on the handlers, prison culture, and outside community. Last up to speak was the Leader Dog prison puppy counselor who remarked that the daily commitment and ownership she sees from inmate handlers is the primary reason for her enduring dedication to the program.

Included among the guests in attendance was a former inmate puppy raiser released from Fort Dodge who has gone on to become a productive member of his community and who continues to raise puppies for Leader Dog on the outside. This former inmate's successful re-entry into his community demonstrated that working with dogs in prison has real application outside the razor wire.

As the visiting sponsors exited the facility, their comments reflected a renewed commitment to the program and greater understanding of its impact. A single afternoon at Fort Dodge Correctional Facility amply demonstrated that success, responsibility, forgiveness, and healing happen in different ways and are part of an effective prison dog program (Aufderheide 2016)

An inmate who participated in Puppy Days had this to say during an interview:

> Before (the dog program), I would never be in front of people. I would have thought Puppy Days was crazy. Now I've got no problem doing Puppy Days and talking to people I don't know. Also, now I'm an inside puppy counselor and have my own group of puppy raisers that I do classes for. That has been one of the hardest things I've ever had to do because I have to be the leader and explain things. I'm not a person that likes to be out front. Doing that has made me feel really good. Most days I feel more confident but I still get very nervous. It's forced me to improve myself. When I do get out (of prison), I'll hopefully be able to speak to other groups about the program. (Aufderheide 2016, p. 76)

Progress Reports and Reunions

Inmates eagerly await reports on their dogs' progress from humane organization personnel and service dog providers. The Pennsylvania Department of Corrections' newsletter about their prison dog programs, *All Paws on Deck*, has a regular feature, Where Are They Now? that gives an encouraging update about a dog that the inmates have worked with previously. For example:

> Atco is a yellow Labrador retriever who was at SCI Smithfield from 2008 to 2009. Atco was raised primarily by Glen and Mark. As a puppy Atco was a goofy puppy. He was very smart and picked up new commands quickly. Now Atco is living in Massachusetts matched with a lady who is full of enthusiasm and hope. Atco's recipient has had epilepsy since she was 14 years old. She uses Atco as her seizure alert dog. She has violent, partial complex seizures at least once or twice a week. Atco alerts to a seizure by lying his body over hers. He also pushes the 'life alert' button which notifies his recipient partner of the seizure. Atco also provides stability and balance when his recipient is feeling weak. Atco and his recipient volunteer at a local hospital at least three days a week and bring cheer to the patients.

When people with disabilities plan reunions between their service dogs and dogs' inmate/trainers, it often is a very emotional event. Video can document the story, such as a segment about a wounded warrior who brought his inmate-trained service dog back to the correctional facility that went viral after it appeared on *The Oprah Winfrey Show* (https://www.littlethings.com/veteran-service-dog-prison-reunion/).

True to their reputation for being loyal, the dogs immediately recognize the people who spent so much time with them and do not hold back on showing affection. Stories such as these are uplifting and can be used to help others understand what these programs do—and why. As one inmate observed:

> I had the privilege of seeing a couple of my dogs come back to prison for Puppy Days. To watch a dog I've raised come back that's a Leader Dog…that's just unreal. That feels rewarding to meet the person that received my dog and have them ask me if I want to pet my dog. To see the dog be focused as a working dog and remember me off harness…that's amazing. (Aufderheide 2016, pp. 54–55)

Involving Other Inmates

Accounts of how other inmates who are not caregivers/trainers of dogs, yet pitch into support the institution's efforts, are important ways of documenting institution-wide effects. For example, work crews of inmates supervised by staff have constructed outdoor kennels, built exercise yards or retrofitted an area of the prison to support the dog program. At one facility, a closet was transformed into a dog grooming area with the installation of a tub, hand-held faucet, and equipment. Other inmates painted, made shelves, decorated and made a sign for the door.

Inmates can participate in the program without necessarily having primary training responsibility for the dogs. In several of the correctional facilities in Pennsylvania, inmates who are dog-friendly live in the same pod as the service or shelter dog trainers to lend support as needed. Inmate Vic wrote about his experience for the state newsletter: "Wags Rescue has changed my life here at SCI Chester. Being a temporary 'foster pop' to four dogs since April has been dear to my heart. This opportunity has given me a second chance in life. This program gives me joy and happiness." One unique feature of Fort Dodge Correctional Facility is that older puppy handlers who have retired from training dogs for age-related reasons are given the opportunity to care for and keep a retired working dogs as companion animals. The retired Leader Dog and inmate/trainer reside together until the end of life for either the inmate, dog, or in the event of an inmate transfer to another correctional center.

Yet another way to involve inmates is a "Photo Day" in which they can opt to have their picture taken with a puppy or dog and send it home. This was something that got positive feedback from family members, particularly children. Hosting a Photo Day also afforded inmate/trainers with a memento of each dog they worked with and some decided to create a scrapbook with photographs of every dog they had trained. One of the counselors at a prison decided to work with the local schools, particularly the special education and life skills classes, and this ongoing partnership resulted in some local children who qualified for an assistance dog being paired with service dogs trained by the inmates.

Writing Stories of Change

Inmate/trainers can be invited to write or tell their stories about working with dogs by name or anonymously. Of course, the inmates' written consent would be necessary before sharing their stories in an in-house newsletter or on social media. One major obstacle with writing is that prior negative school experiences sometimes bubble up to the surface. Offenders may visualize poor grades on a report card, think about harshly critical comments written on past assignments, worry about spelling/grammar, and fear that they will judged as poor writers/thinkers. It is important to provide supports that minimize those worries and fears. Short, published stories told in clear prose, such as the six *Chicken Soup* books about dogs, are both easy to read and provide some helpful examples. The same strategy works when inmate/trainers are called upon to write an individual dog's story, such as an anonymous letter to service dog's new family, or a description of the dog that will be posted online and aid in the animal's adoption. Just as most people find it easier to follow a GPS than a map, good written examples help. Here is an essay written by service dog trainer/inmate Brandon:

> When I was first incarcerated I felt like my time in prison would be dim with little possibility of a better future when I got out. I didn't think that I would be able to do something or have an opportunity that would give me a chance to really better myself. I felt like there was one dreary road and that I was stuck on it. Once I signed up for the T.A.I.L.S. program and was given a chance to do something great, I realized how wrong I was. At first, I thought that I might be able to learn a couple of things and make myself look better in here. That was before I started learning not just about how to train a dog, but myself as well. Having to constantly work while putting my time, effort, and care into raising and training a puppy has given me, suprisingly, much more than I've put in. It has helped me feel more like a normal person and taught me how to put something else in front of myself. It has helped me feel like I actually worth it and I can be of use. I no longer have to chase things to make myself feel better because I feel great on my own. Respecting myself more as a man and knowing that

I can really do good things in my life is a direct result of all of the work I'm doing. The possibility of the dogs that I'm training have the chance of helping someone else live a better life is icing on the cake. Working with a dog and trying to teach him while he teaches me has given me peace and happiness. Nothing has given me those things before. With what I now know, I no longer feel like I'm stuck. If I put my full effort and mind to something I'll be able to accomplish it. Never before in my life would I have ever thought that a dog would of been able to teach me so much about life.

If examples from other inmates/trainers are used, it is best to select some from those who gave permission but have exited the system. This avoids making comparisons among those currently in the program. Inmates also need to know that it is not "cheating" to ask others to help by reading for them or offering help with mechanics and editing.

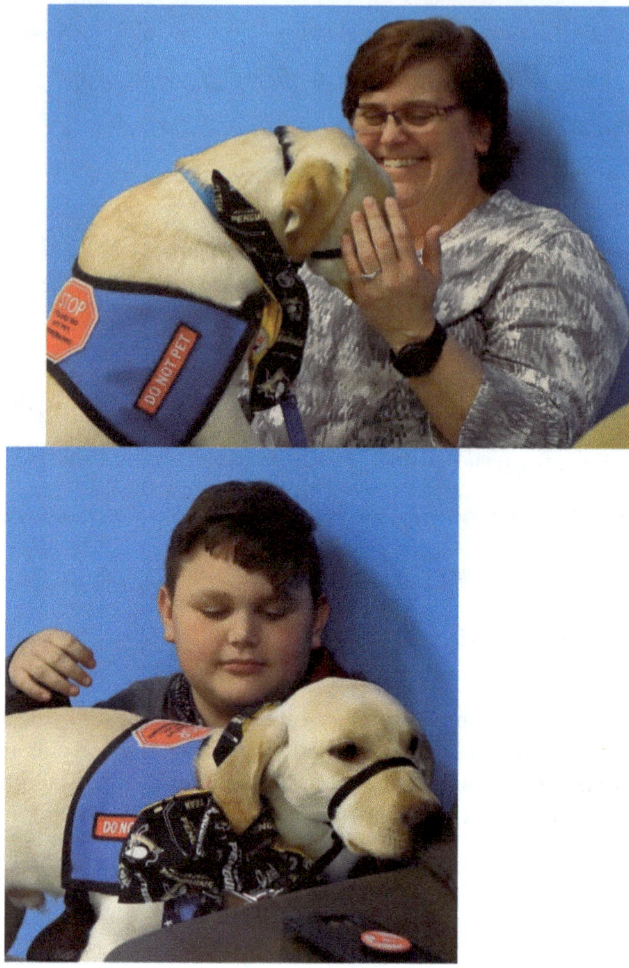

This prison administrator and her son take service dog puppies home over the weekend on a regular basis. During a presentation to a local dog training club, the 7-month-old pup retrieved a cell phone and credit card. *Credit* Mary Renck Jalongo

Policy Changes After dogs arrive at a correctional facility, new possibilities present themselves. For example, after one state prison decided to train a rehabilitated shelter dog as a therapy dog/mascot/facility dog, other correctional institutions in the state system followed. Now more of the inmates not directly involved in training dogs could interact with a dog, staff could plan to include the dog in various interventions, and the institution was never "dogless".

It is particularly important to share these ideas with others as a way to stimulate thinking and institute new practices that capitalize on the dogs' presence. One useful structure for reporting on these changes is: (1) what prompted the change,

(2) how changes were implemented, and (3) the consequences of the change. Policy changes can be initiated by the professionals associated with the program and written about from the perspective of the inmate/trainers responsible for implementing them, such as this account by Ronald (2017):

> I have been involved in the program for a little over two years. As of recently some things have changed, such as where I can take the dog and whom the dog can be around. For the most part, this is one form of change that we all welcomed.
>
> For a while, "handlers" were only allowed to take the dog to one or two places within the institution. Either out back or into the "dog yard," which is small fenced-in area located off of the main yard. Over the last few months things have really changed. I've been involved in a few self-help programs. Once I completed these programs, I became a co-facilitator. So I was given the opportunity to bring "Tiffany," a two year old all white Pit bull, with me to one of my groups.
>
> The response was unbelievable. Who would have thought that something as simple as allowing some of the guys in group to interact with a dog would have such an impact? I mean, we all know the stereotype that comes along with those that are incarcerated, big tough criminals. But when "Tiffany" came into that group, she's running around, licking people, jumping on the table, doing every single trick that she could think of. And the guys really responded. A few people I spoke with have told me that just being around the dog has given them hope. (There's that word again, H.O.P.E.) Others have told me that being around her reminds them that "it's not over, there is still life to go home to."
>
> Because of the positive response to me being allowed to bring "Tiffany" with me to one group, I am now allowed to take her into two. And again the response is wonderful. Who would have ever imagined that something that most people take for granted would serve to others a different point of view, a view of not what happened in the past, but a view of the future and what it brings, a view of HOPE… (p. 15)

Birthday Parties with a Purpose

Canine Partners for Life (CPL) designed a celebration and training opportunity for the dogs that coincided with the regular, bi-weekly visit from their CPL trainer. Two examples were:

- Retrieving a ball from a pool full of empty plastic bottles. Service dogs need to get comfortable walking on uneven or unusual surfaces (e.g., wheelchair lifts), unstable surfaces (e.g., a boat dock), or across items that may make noises (e.g., metal stairs).
- Opening presents. Dogs "unwrapped" a box without destroying it. Service dogs often assist with retrieving objects and need to learn how to do this gently. For instance, they learn how to pick up a credit card that has been dropped on the floor or from the ATM. CPL dogs learn the "go pay" command to help when making a store purchase. The dog delivers the cash or credit card to the cashier, retrieves the goods, and brings back the credit card or change (Stevens 2016).

These were just a few of the activities that the dogs performed while also enjoying a birthday party for two dogs that had reached their first birthday.

A service dog changes the life of the recipient. *Photo Credit* Lori Breece

Conclusion: Developing Empathy

Empathy, in some form, has been studied in psychology throughout the history of the field (Titchener 1911). Perhaps the most common understanding of the concept is that it involves "feeling for" someone else. Empathy is much more than that. It involves feelings, thinking, and—most important of all—actions (Day et al. 2010). In Davis' (1994) model of empathy, there are antecedents, followed by processes; both of these are followed by intrapersonal outcomes (within the individual) and interpersonal outcomes (in relationships with other people). There is an inverse relationship between empathy and aggression; people with high scores on measures of empathy typically have low scores on measures of aggressive behaviors (Lovett and Sheffield 2007). There is also some evidence that violent offenders often have empathy deficits, manifested as relative indifference to the harm they have caused and a tendency to misjudge the intentions of others as malevolent (Chambers et al. 2009).

Two persistent controversies about empathy have implications for prison dog programs. The first is whether or not empathy for an animal "transfers" to empathy for people, and vice versa (McPhedran 2009). Some people regard empathy for humans and nonhumans as interrelated while others see the two as entirely separate. Williams (2011) described these conflicting perspectives as follows:

> Several months ago, I sat in the community room at the denominational headquarters where I work listening to a heated discussion among my colleagues about a professional athlete who had recently completed a prison sentence for involvement in dog fighting. Although I had kept silent so far, preferring to listen, one colleague directed the following comments to me (no doubt because of my well-known interest in animals): "It depends on what touches your heart. For me, I care about people. I can't see how people can be so concerned about

> animals when so many children are suffering." I was shocked, not because I had not heard these sentiments before, but because in my job, I not only develop child advocacy resources but also provide the lone and frequently unpopular voice regularly insisting that any work we do in the area of domestic violence include rejection of corporal punishment of children… For me, compassion for children and compassion for animals flows from the same impulse—a concern for the vulnerable and a divine mandate both to care for those at risk in the world (human and other-than-human) and to advocate social change on their behalf. That the sufferings of animals and of humans are related in a variety of ways has long been an assumption of mine. That assumption, of course, is not universally held. Many people share my colleague's perspective that concern for animals and concern for humans are not only unrelated but also mutually exclusive interests, with compassion spent on the one requiring compassion robbed from the other. (p. 106)

The second ongoing debate is about whether empathy can be taught directly, for example, by having violent offenders read a letter from a victim, watch interviews with people harmed by a crime, or role play the perspective of the injured party. It may be the case that something more than observation or simulations is necessary. In fact, this is the conceptual underpinning of restorative justice. The Centre for Justice and Reconciliation is a program of the Prison Fellowship International. They define restorative justice as an approach "that emphasizes repairing the harm caused by criminal behavior. It is best accomplished through cooperative processes that allow all willing stakeholders to meet, although other approaches are available when that is impossible. This can lead to transformation of people, relationships and communities" It is founded on including all parties, encountering the other side, making amends for the harm, and reintegrating the parties into their communities.

Identification with another person is part of empathy. The person previously perceived as "other" now is seen as more alike than different from the self. This leads to engaging in prosocial behaviors that the person might naturally afford to themselves (Cialdini et al. 1997; Hodges et al. 2011; Myers and Hodges 2012).

In a similar fashion, a dog in an inmate's care may be regarded as "like me" in important ways. For instance, a timid shelter dog might be seen as "locked up and abandoned, neglected and abused, like me" while a lively puppy might be seen as "making mistakes and being impulsive, the way I have been". Thus, the identity of the dog can become integrated into the inmate's identity formation (Boya et al. 2012). Inmate Mark (2018) wrote, "When I look at the dogs in the program, I see myself when I came to prison, weary, rough and in need of rehabilitation. As I reside in a cage, so do the dogs we train. Just like my K9 friend, I am eager to get another chance beyond the cages. So I take pride in this program that I am providing that opportunity for the dogs so they don't end up in the pen again. It's a joy to experience personal accomplishment." (p. 11)

This supports the desire to take positive action on behalf of the animal. It may be the case that some individuals who have been repeatedly disappointed or damaged by other people are more accepting of animals because they are seen as innocent and guileless. Work with animals certainly has a long history as an intervention with troubled individuals (see Chap. 2).

The human-animal bond exerts a powerful influence on human emotions (Fine and Weaver 2018). There is very recent research focusing on the role of hormones in empathy, compassion, and self-compassion (Stevens and Woodruff 2018). It appears that the so called "calm and connect" hormone, oxytocin, is present in different species (Powell-Adam et al. 2019). Oxytocin levels are elevated in dogs bonded to their handlers as they participate together in animal-assisted activities (Wanser and Udell 2019). Based on clinical trials with humans, it also appears that these hormones are critical in the expression of prosocial behaviors such as empathy, compassion and possibly, self-compassion (Birkett and Sasaki 2018).

An inmate/trainer in the New Leash on Life prison dog program stated this more clearly as: "I read somewhere that when you offer yourself to others you get a 'helper's high'. Helping has a way of helping you. These dogs certainly have a way of helping us all."

Empathy and compassion are intertwined throughout highly effective prison dog programs, from start to finish. As this inmate has suggested, deciding to help others is a bold act. It requires courage to watch dearly loved dogs transition to their new lives, to take the risks associated with learning something new, to reconstruct self-concept, and to adopt a worldview that revolves around being of service to others.

References

Allen, K., Shykoff, B. E., & Izzo, J. L. (2001). Pet ownership, but not ACE inhibitor therapy, blunts home blood pressure responses to mental stress. *Hypertension, 38*(4), 815–820.

American Institutes for Research. (2015). *CBAM: The concerns-based adoption model*. Retrieved May 22, 2019 from: https://www.air.org/resource/cbam-concerns-based-adoption-model.

American Pet Products Association (APPA). (2019). *2019–2020 APPA national pet owners survey*. Retrieved May 20, 2019 from: https://www.americanpetproducts.org/pubs_survey.asp.

Antonowicz, D. H. & Parker, J. (2014) *Reducing recidivism: Evidence from 28 years of international evaluations of reasoning & rehabilitation programs*. http://archive.icpa.ca/tools/download/1937/Reasoning_and_Rehabilitation_Review.

Arluke, A., & Sanders, C. R. (1996). *Regarding animals*. Philadelphia, PA: Temple University Press.

Armour, M. (2012). Restorative justice: Some facts and history. *Tikkun, 27*(1), 25–65.

Aronson, E., Wilson, T. D., Akert, R. M., & Sommers, S. R. (2015). *Social psychology* (9th ed.). Boston: Pearson.

Aufderheide, C. (2016). *The application and effects of service dog training by inmates to self-perception and self-other overlap as a rehabilitative approach to incarceration*. (Unpublished Master's thesis), University of Oregon, Eugene, Oregon.

Barker, S. B., Barker, R. T., & Schubert, C. M. (2017). Therapy dogs on campus: A counseling outreach activity for college students preparing for final exams. *Journal of College Counseling, 20*(3), 278–288. https://doi.org/10.1002/jocc.12075.

Benson, E. (2003). *Rehabilitate or punish?* Retrieved May 14, 2019, from http://www.apa.org/monitor/julaug03/rehab.aspx.

Birkett, M., & Sasaki, J. (2018). Why does it feel so good to care for others and myself? Neuroendocrinology and prosocial behavior. In. L. Stevens & C. C. Woodruff (Eds.), *The neuroscience of empathy, compassion, and self-compassion* (pp. 189–211). New York: Academic Press.

Borgi, M., Collacchi, B., Giuliani, A., & Cirulli, F. (2018). Dog visiting programs for managing depressive symptoms in older adults: A meta-analysis. *The Gerontologist*. https://doi.org/10.1093/geront/gny149.

Boya, U. O., Dotson, M. J., & Hyatt, E. M. (2012). Dimensions of the dog-human relationship: A segmentation approach. *Journal of Targeting, Measurement and Analysis for Marketing, 20*(2), 133–143.

Cialdini, R., Brown, S. L., Lewis, B. P., Luce, C., & Neuberg, S. L. (1997). Reinterpreting the empathy-altruism relationship: When one into one equals oneness. *Journal of Personality and Social Psychology, 73*(3), 481–494.

Chambers, J. C., Ward, T., Eccleston, L., & Brown, (2009). The pathways model of assault: A qualitative analysis of the assault offender and offense. *Journal of Interpersonal Violence, 24*(9). https://doi.org/10.1177/0886260508323668.

Chandler, C. K. (2017). *Animal-assisted therapy in counseling* (3rd ed.). New York: Routledge.

Cognitive Centre of Canada. (2019). *Treatment of antisocial behavior*. Retrieved May 20, 2019 from: http://www.cognitivecentre.ca/publications.html.

Collica-Cox, K., & Fagin, B. (2018, May/June). Parenting, prison and pups with a purpose. *Corrections Today*, pp. 24–32.

Consedine, J. (1995). *Restorative justice: Healing the effects of crime*. Christchurch: Ploughshares.

Coren, S. (2013, February 11). How therapy dogs almost never came to exist. *Psychology Today*. https://www.psychologytoday.com/us/blog/canine-corner/201302/how-therapy-dogs-almost-never-came-exist.

Csikszentmihaly, M. (1990). *Flow: The psychology of optimal experience*. New York: Harper & Row.

Davis, M. H. (1994). *Empathy: A social psychological approach*. Boulder, CO: Westview.

Day, A., Casey, S., & Gerace, A. (2010). Interventions to improve empathy awareness in sexual and violent offenders: Conceptual, empirical, and clinical issues. *Aggression and Violent Behavior, 15*, 201–208.

Deaton, C. (2005). Humanizing prisons with animals: A closer look at "Cell Dogs" and horse programs in correctional institutions. *Journal of Correctional Education, 56*(1), 46–62.

Decker, J. D. (1987). *The shame-rage connection: Going from feeling defective and inadequate to becoming disrespectful and punishing*. http://www.angeresources.com.

Dzur, A. W. (2003). Civic implications of restorative justice theory: Citizen participation and criminal justice policy. *Policy Sciences, 36*(3/4), 279–306.

Fine, A. H., & Weaver, S. J. (2018). The human-animal bond and animal-assisted intervention. In M. van den Bosch & W. Bird (Eds.), (2018). *Oxford textbook of nature and public health: The role of nature in improving the health of a population* (pp. 132–138). New York: Oxford University Press.

Frederickson, B. L. (2004). The broaden-and-build theory of positive emotions. *Philosophy Transaction B, 359*(1449), 1367–1378. https://doi.org/10.1098/rstb.2004.1512.

Furst, G. (2011). *Animal programs in prison*. Boulder, CO: Lynne Rienner Publishers.

Garland, D. (2001). *Mass imprisonment: Social causes and consequences*. Thousand Oaks: Sage.

Gilath, O., Karantzas, G. C., & Fraley, R. C. (2016). *Adult attachment: A concise introduction to theory and research*. New York: Academic Press.

Gummerum, M., & Hanoch, Y. (2012). Altruism behind bars: Sharing, justice, perspective taking and empathy among inmates. *Social Justice Research, 25*(1), 61–78. Retrieved from http://doi.org/10.1007/s11211-012-0149-8.

Hare, B., & Woods, V. (2013). *The genius of dogs: How dogs are smarter than you think*. New York: Plume.

Hodges, S. D., Clark, B. A. M., & Myers, M. W. (2011). Better living through perspective taking. In R. Biswas-Diener (Ed.), *Positive psychology as social change* (pp. 193–218). New York: Springer.

Horowitz, A. (2009). *Inside of a dog: What dogs see, smell and know*. New York: Scribner.

Humby, L., & Barclay, E. (2018). Pawsitive solutions: An overview of prison dog programs in Australia. *The Prison Journal, 98*(5), 580–603. https://doi.org/10.1177/0032885518793951.

Jalongo, M. R. (2015). An attachment perspective on the child–dog bond: Interdisciplinary and international research findings. *Early Childhood Education Journal, 43*(5), 395–405.

James, J. (2018). What's happening in the community. *All Paws on Deck, 5*(1), 18. Retrieved June 1, 2019 from: https://www.cor.pa.gov/About%20Us/Newsroom/Pages/Newsletters.aspx.

Kurki, L. (2000). Restorative and community justice in the United States. *Crime and Justice, 27,* 235–303.

Lovett, B. J., & Sheffield, R. A. (2007). Affective empathy deficits in aggressive children and adolescents: A critical review. *Clinical Psychology Review, 27*(1), 1–13.

Mark S. (2018). Inmate testimonials. *All Paws on Deck, 5*(2), 11. Retrieved June 1, 2019 from: https://www.cor.pa.gov/About%20Us/Newsroom/Pages/Newsletters.aspx.

Maruna, S. (2011). Reentry as a rite of passage. *Punishment & Society, 13*(1), 3–28. https://doi.org/10.1177/1462474510385641.

McCardle, P., McCune, S., Griffin, J. A., Esposito, L., & Freund, L. (2011). *Animals in our lives: Human-animals interaction in family, community and therapeutic settings*. Baltimore: Paul H. Brooks.

McPhedran, S. (2009). A review of the evidence for associations between empathy, violence, and animal cruelty. *Aggression and Violent Behavior, 14,* 1–4.

Mikosi, A. (2016). *Dog behavior, evolution, and cognition* (2nd ed.). New York: Oxford University Press.

Minton, C. A., Perez, P. R., & Miller, K. (2015). Voices from behind prison walls. *Society & Animals, 23,* 484–501. https://doi.org/10.1163/15685306-12341379.

Myers, M. W., & Hodges, S. D. (2012). The structure of self-other overlap and its relationship to perspective taking. *Personal Relationships, 19*(4), 663–679. https://doi.org/10.1111/j.1475-6811.2011.01382.x.

Parish-Plass, N. (2013). *Animal assisted psychotherapy: Theory, issues and practice*. Lafayette, IN: Purdue University Press.

Phelps, M. (2011). Rehabilitation in the punitive era: The gap between rhetoric and reality in U.S. prison programs. *Law & Society Review, 45*(1), 33–68.

Podberscek, A. L., Paul, E. S., & Serpell, J. A. (Eds.). (2000). *Companion animals and us: Exploring the relationships between people and pets*. New York: Cambridge University Press.

Powell-Adam, L., Guastella, J., McGreevy, P., Bauman, A., Edwards, K. M., & Stamatakis, E. (2019). The physiological function of oxytocin in humans and its acute response to human-dog interactions: A review of the literature. *Journal of Veterinary Behavior, 30,* 25–32.

Ronald, B. (2017). Inmate testimonials. *All Paws on Deck, 4*(2), 13–15. Retrieved June 1, 2019 from: https://www.cor.pa.gov/About%20Us/Newsroom/Pages/Newsletters.aspx.

Ross, R. R., & Hilborn, J. (2008). *Rehabilitating rehabilitation: Neurocriminology for treatment of antisocial behavior*. Ottawa, Canada: Cognitive Centre of Canada.

Saxena, P., Messina, N. P., & Grella, C. E. (2014). Who benefits from gender-responsive treatment? Accounting for abuse history on longitudinal outcomes for women in prison. *Criminal Justice and Behavior, 41*(4), 417–432.

Serpell, J. (Ed.). (2017). *The domestic dog: Its evolution, behavior and interactions with people* (2nd ed.). New York: Cambridge University Press.

Stevens, E. (2016). SCI Muncy. *All Paws on Deck, 3*(2), 27. Retrieved June 1, 2019 from: https://www.cor.pa.gov/About%20Us/Newsroom/Pages/Newsletters.aspx.

Stevens, L., & Woodruff, C. C. (Eds.). (2018). *The neuroscience of empathy, compassion, and self-compassion*. New York: Academic Press.

The Centre for Justice and Reconciliation. (2019). *Restorative justice*. Retrieved May 20, 2019 from: http://restorativejustice.org/restorative-justice/about-restorative-justice/tutorial-intro-to-restorative-justice/lesson-1-what-is-restorative-justice/#sthash.x39KsWN4.dpbs.

The Sentencing Project. (2018). *Criminal justice facts*. Retrieved March 17, 2019 from: https://www.sentencingproject.org/criminal-justice-facts/.

Titchener, E. B. (1911). *A text-book of psychology*. New York: The Macmillan Company.
Toch, H. (2000). Altruistic activity as correctional treatment. *International Journal of Offender Therapy and Comparative Criminology, 44*(3), 270–278. https://doi.org/10.1177/0306624X0043002.
Tong, L. S. J., & Farrington, D. P. (2007). *Effectiveness of "reasoning and rehabilitation" in reducing reoffending*. Cambridge, UK: Cambridge University.
Van Fleet, R., & Faa-Thompson, T. (2017). *Animal-assisted play therapy*. Sarasota, FL: Professional Resource Press.
Van Ness, D., & Strong, K. H. (2002). *Restoring justice* (2nd ed.). Cincinnati, OH: Anderson Publishing.
Wanser, S. H., & Udell, M. A. R. (2019). Does attachment security to a human handler influence the behavior of dogs who engage in animal-assisted activities? *Applied Animal Behavior, 210,* 88–94.
Williams, C. C. (2011, Spring). The link between animal abuse and human violence [Book review]. *Journal of Animal Ethics, 1*(1), 106–108. https://doi.org/10.5406/janimalethics.1.1.0106.
Zehr, H. (2015). *The little book of restorative justice: Revised and updated.* New York: Simon & Schuster.
Zilcha-Mano, S., Mikulincer, M. & Shaver, P. R. (2012). Pets as safe havens and secure bases: The moderating role of pet attachment orientations. *Journal of Research in Personality, 4*(5), 571–580.

Appendix A
Dog Care and Training in Correctional Facilities: *Selected Programs*

Stephen S. Owen

Introduction

As illustrated throughout this book, there are many existing programs that provide dog training within correctional institutions, some of which are long-established. The successes and lessons learned from prior programs can help to shape the development of future programs. The purpose of this appendix is to provide a listing of diverse programs that may serve as useful examples.

Of course, programs are most effective when they strive for continuous improvement, so this list is a sampling of what was in effect at the time this book was published. Inclusion on this list should not be read to suggest that these are the only ways programs can be structured, or that the programs listed here must be adopted wholesale in other institutions without modification. Indeed, programs should be designed to fit the unique context of each institution and its partner agencies, program goals, and operational philosophy (see Appendix B for a concise overview of different purposes for programs). Those listed here may provide ideas for doing so.

Likewise, no negative connotation should be inferred toward programs that are not included on this list. Given that there are now prison dog programs operating in all 50 states (Hill 2016) and several other countries, this sampling of well-established programs is far from exhaustive. In selecting programs to include in this Appendix, contributors to this volume were asked to make recommendations. Beyond that, a search for additional programs was conducted based on four criteria: (1) availability of informative program websites that could serve as a resource to others; (2) visibility of the program in the media or publications; (3) diversity in program type, mission, institutions involved, and structure of the program; and (4) evidence of innovative approaches and accomplishments.

Stephen S. Owen
Department of Criminal Justice, Radford University, Radford, VA, USA
Email: ssowen@radford.edu

M. R. Jalongo (ed.), *Prison Dog Programs*,
https://doi.org/10.1007/978-3-030-25618-0

The sampling of programs below offers diversity in type of dog training provided, type of institution, inmate participants, and selected accomplishments. It is encouraging to see that there is in fact not one single model, but rather that there are multiple approaches to how programs may be structured (for guidance of program development, see also Han et al. 2018). And, for every program listed below, there are others that are equally strong. It would be virtually impossible to list all programs, so this list should be viewed simply as a starting point, and not an ending point, for researching current program offerings.

The information provided here is deliberately brief, listing the name of the program; the type or purpose of the program; a sampling of accomplishments; and a URL for each program's website. The listing of programs is alphabetical by title. Those who are seeking further information, whether for research purposes or to develop new programming, are encouraged to make contact with the programs below, and also to search for others that are appropriate for their needs. Readers are also encouraged to reach out to programs for further information, in the event that the program structure, content, or context have changed since this writing.

As already illustrated in this edited volume, prison dog programs in correctional facilities yield many positive outcomes and offer much potential in the area of correctional programming. No doubt the list of correctional institutions and community agencies participating in this dynamic field will continue to grow.

Overview of Selected Programs

Program Name: Canine Cellmates
Partners: Fulton County (Georgia) Sheriff's Department, Fulton County Jail, and Canine Cellmates.
Type or Purpose: Trains and socializes shelter dogs for public adoption; program operates in a local jail for adult male inmates.
Selected Accomplishments: Program was established in 2013; the program includes an aftercare component to assist inmates from the program who have been released, including assistance finding housing and employment, assistance with public transportation and purchasing basic necessities, and more; website includes numerous program testimonials in which adopters share stories of their new canine companions and their appreciation for the program.
Web Address: http://www.caninecellmates.org/home.html.

Program Name: Canines for Veterans
Partners: U.S Department of the Navy, U.S. Marine Corps, and Canines for Service.
Type or Purpose: Train shelter dogs to provide services to military veterans who are injured or who have post-traumatic stress disorder; program has alternated between two military correctional institutions, also known as "brigs," one of which was a jail

(where the program is housed as of this writing) and one of which was a prison, both for adult male military inmates.
Selected Accomplishments: Program was established in 2008; only program in a military brig to train dogs rescued from animal shelters as service dogs.
Web Address: https://www.caninesforservice.org/canines-for-veterans.

Program Name: CHAMP Prison Program
Partners: Missouri Department of Corrections, Puppies with Purpose, Humane Society of Missouri, and CHAMP Assistance Dogs (Canine Helpers Allow More Possibilities).
Type or Purpose: Program socializes and trains shelter dogs for public adoption and also trains service dogs; located in a multiple-security-level institution for adult female inmates.
Selected Accomplishments: Established in 2002; dogs spend up to two years with their trainers, who teach basic and advanced skills; program representatives spend one day a week working with inmate trainers and their dogs.
Web Address: https://www.champdogs.org/assistance-dog-program/prison.

Program Name: DAWGS in Prison
Partners: Florida Department of Corrections, St. Joseph Bay Humane Society, and and DAWGS in Prison (Delivering Adoptable Dogs With Good Sociability).
Type or Purpose: Socializing and training dogs for public adoption; located at a forest camp facility that is part of a larger correctional institution housing male offenders.
Selected Accomplishments: Established in 2009; over 50 classes of dogs have been trained and graduated from the program; in addition to in-state adoptions, program also transports dogs to locations on the east coast, outside of Florida, for adoption.
Web Address: http://www.dawgsinprison.com/index.cfm/m/1/Home/.

Program Name: Friends for Folks Dog Training Program
Partners: Oklahoma Department of Corrections, Second Chance Animal Rescue, local veterinary partners, local dog rescue organizations, and Friends for Folks.
Type or Purpose: Program trains abused and neglected dogs to serve as companion animals for senior citizens or as service dogs for persons with disabilities; current pet owners may also have their dog trained in a one-month program. The program is located in a multiple security level institution for adult male offenders.
Selected Accomplishments: Established in 1990; featured on Animal Planet; generally recognized as the second modern prison-based dog training program (the first was Prison Pet Partnership); subject of a documentary, *The Dogs of Lexington* (Lynch et al. 2013), nominated for an Emmy Award; influenced the development of the Guardian Angels dog training program at an Oklahoma women's prison.
Web Address: http://doc.ok.gov/friends-for-folks-dog-training-program-lexington-ar.

Program Name: GFNJ Prison Foster Program
Partners: New Jersey Department of Corrections and Greyhound Friends of New Jersey, Inc. (GFNJ).
Type or Purpose: Train former racing greyhounds to prepare them for public adoption; located in a prison for young adult male inmates, most of whom are between 18–30 years of age.
Selected Accomplishments: Program was established in 2002; over 800 greyhounds have been trained and adopted; inducted as an organizational member of the New Jersey Veterinary Medical Association Animal Hall of Fame; featured on the *About Greyhounds* podcast (episode 7).
Web Address: https://www.greyhoundfriendsnj.org/info/display?PageID=682.

Program Name: HOPE (Hounds of Prison Education)
Partners: Pennsylvania Department of Corrections and HOPE.
Type or Purpose: Socialize and train shelter dogs for public adoption; located at a classification center for male inmates (classification centers are facilities where inmates are held upon entering a state's correctional system, where risk and need assessments are conducted prior to assignment to another facility).
Selected Accomplishments: Established in 2005, the program has trained over 300 dogs; program maintains a dynamic website that includes blogs written by inmates about the dogs they are training; program also partners with numerous general and breed-specific rescue organizations; creatively structured sponsorship program.
Web Address: https://www.hopedogs.org/.

Program Name: Indiana Canine Assistance Network
Partners: Indiana Department of Corrections and Indiana Canine Assistance Network.
Type or Purpose: Train service dogs for children with disabilities, for children on the autism spectrum, and for persons with diabetes (in which dogs alert to low blood sugar); program operates at three state prisons including adult male and female inmates at multiple security levels.
Selected Accomplishments: Program originated in 2002; program originally was placed in a juvenile facility, but since has been relocated to adult institutions; over 200 dogs have been placed; large group of volunteer assistants to assist with program operations; includes opportunities to sponsor and name a dog in training; only Indiana service dog training provider with accreditation through Assistance Dogs International; featured in *Federal Probation* magazine (Turner 2007) and found to be associated with increased self-esteem and social skills for inmate participants, as well as positive effects on the institutional environment.
Web Address: https://www.icandog.org/about-ican/our-history/.

Program Name: Jail Dogs (Operation Second Chance)
Partners: Gwinnett (Georgia) County Sheriff's Department, Society of Humane Friends of Georgia, Top Dogg K9, and numerous corporate partners.
Type or Purpose: Socialize and train dogs from the county Animal Control office, for public adoption; recently also began training service dogs for military veterans. The program is located in a county jail with adult male inmates (there is a parallel program for cats located in an adult female housing unit in the jail).
Selected Accomplishments: Established in 2010; has successfully placed over 400 dogs for adoption; associated with reduced recidivism; privately funded, and includes an opportunity for private donors to sponsor a dog (or cat) in the program; featured in the book, *Troubled to Trained: All Dogs Need a Leader They Can Trust*, by Shane Hawkins (2017).
Web Address: https://www.jaildogs.org/who-we-are.html.

Program Name: MCSO Animal Safe Haven (MASH)
Partners: Maricopa County (Arizona) Sheriff's Office.
Type or Purpose: Care for dogs (and other animals) that have been abused and are being held as evidence in criminal cases; also, trains the animals in their care to be adopted by members of the public; some dogs that have been trained participate in visits to other jail housing units as therapy animals for inmate populations; the program is housed in a jail housing unit serving adult female inmates.
Selected Accomplishments: Program was established in 2000; only known program operated by a law enforcement agency with dogs from abuse cases.
Web Address: https://www.mcso.org/Mash.

Program Name: New Leash on Life USA
Partners: Philadelphia Department of Prisons and New Leash on Life USA.
Type or Purpose: Socializes and prepares for adoption shelter dogs that were previously identified as "unadoptable," who would otherwise potentially have been euthanized; housed in Philadelphia city jails and participants include adult male and female inmates.
Selected Accomplishments: Saving otherwise "condemned" dogs; fully funded by grants and donations; also provides job and life skills training; includes opportunity for internships and employment in animal service fields after release.
Web Address: https://newleashonlife-usa.org/.

Program Name: Paws Behind Bars Training Program
Partners: Kentucky Department of Corrections and Adopt Me! Bluegrass Pet Rescue.
Type or Purpose: Socialize and train shelter dogs for public adoption; located in an institution housing minimum and medium security adult male inmates.
Selected Accomplishments: Established in 2009; persons adopting dogs may meet with inmate trainers, inside the prison, to learn about their dog; dogs from the program have also been trained as emotional support and companion dogs for children with special needs.
Web Address: http://www.adoptmebluegrasspetrescue.com/programs.html.

Program Name: Paws for Life Prison Program
Partners: California Department of Corrections and Rehabilitation, Arizona Goldens LLC Service Dogs, and Paws for Life.
Type or Purpose: Training shelter dogs for adoption using the American Kennel Club's Canine Good Citizen certification, and continuing training for selected dogs to prepare them as service dogs for veterans with post-traumatic stress disorder; operates at multiple facilities, including a maximum-security prison and a medium-security prison, both housing adult male inmates.
Selected Accomplishments: Established in 2014; first such program to operate in a maximum-security setting; inmates constructed the dog run areas in the facility; over 90 inmates have participated and over 280 dogs have been trained; program inmates have more commuted life sentences than any other state program.
Web Address: https://pawsforlifek9.org/paws-for-life-prison-program/.

Program Name: Paws in Prison
Partners: Texas Department of Criminal Justice, multiple local animal shelters, Thunderpaws Canine Solutions, LLC, and Paws in Prison.
Type or Purpose: Socialize and train shelter dogs for public adoption; program operates in a minimum security private prison that houses adult male and female inmates.
Selected Accomplishments: Program is supported by its own nonprofit organization, the Friends of Paws in Prison, Inc.; courses at Texas Lutheran University have included service learning projects in conjunction with the program; program offers numerous fundraising activities, including a line of program-themed merchandise.
Web Address: http://www.pawsinprison.com/PIP_2-0/Home.html.

Program Name: Pawsitive Dogs
Partners: Washington Department of Corrections, Spokane Humane Society, and Diamonds in the Ruff.
Type or Purpose: Socialize and train shelter dogs for public adoption; program operates in a minimum/medium-security state prison housing adult male inmates.
Selected Accomplishments: Over 20 sessions have been completed and 150 dogs have been trained; fundraising strategies include sales from an art show featuring inmate artwork; dynamic social media (Facebook) presence.
Web Address: https://spokanehumanesociety.org/blog/pawsitive-dog-prison-training.

Program Name: Pen Pals Animal Shelter and Adoption Center
Partners: Louisiana Department of Corrections, Humane Society of the United States, and Louisiana State University School of Veterinary Medicine.
Type or Purpose: The Pen Pals, Inc., Dog and Cat Shelter and Adoption Center is a complete animal shelter located on prison grounds; program is located in a multiple security level state prison for adult male inmates.

Selected Accomplishments: The first shelter at the prison was developed in 2005 during Hurricane Katrina, to house animals rescued during the storm; a permanent shelter was subsequently constructed through a grant from the Humane Society of the United States, which can house over 200 animals (not limited to dogs); first program to place a complete animal shelter on prison grounds; featured in *Corrections Today* magazine (Smith and Unti 2016); veterinary students complete clinical training at the shelter; inmates are trained by veterinary school staff in animal care, and are certified as veterinary assistants; shelter animals are trained prior to adoption; over 600 dogs (and over 450 cats) have been adopted.
Web Address: https://doc.louisiana.gov/pen-pals-animal-shelter-and-other-dpsandc-canine-programs/.

Program Name: Prison Pet Partnership
Partners: Washington Department of Corrections and Prison Pet Partnership.
Type or Purpose: Program provides a number of services, to include training dogs as service animals for persons with disabilities, training dogs for public adoption, delivering obedience training for current pet owners, and providing boarding and grooming for dogs owned by local residents; program operates in a multiple security level state prison housing adult female inmates.
Selected Accomplishments: Initiated in 1981 by Sister Pauline Quinn of the Dominican Order in partnership with Dr. Leo Bustad of the Washington State University veterinary school; generally recognized as the first modern prison-based dog training program; 1986 finalist for recognition as Ford Foundation and John F. Kennedy School of Business "Innovations in State and Local Government" program; also includes vocational training for program participants; over 700 dogs have been successfully trained; includes an active community volunteer program.
Web Address: http://www.prisonpetpartnership.org/.

Program Name: Prison PUP Program (Massachusetts and Rhode Island)
Partners: Federal Bureau of Prisons, Massachusetts Department of Corrections, Rhode Island Department of Corrections, and NEADS (National Education for Assistance Dog Services).
Type or Purpose: Training service dogs for a variety of audiences, including persons with disabilities, persons with visual or auditory impairments, veterans, children with autism, and as therapy dogs; program operates in multiple minimum- and medium-security level facilities housing adult male and female inmates.
Selected Accomplishments: Almost all dogs placed by NEADS are trained in prisons; includes participation in institutions from multiple agencies, including state and federal prisons; a study of the program at one female institution (Drew et al., n. d.) found it to have beneficial impacts on inmates and the institution as a whole, while providing an effective means for training the dogs in the program.
Web Address: https://neads.org/training-placement/prison-pup-program/.

Program Name: Prison Pup Program (Virginia)
Partners: Virginia Department of Corrections and Saint Francis Service Dogs.
Type or Purpose: Training service dogs for persons with disabilities, medical needs, or emotional needs; located in a medium-security state prison housing adult male inmates.
Selected Accomplishments: Program has been in operation since 2002; featured in *Corrections Today* magazine (Harkrader et al. 2004); accredited by Assistance Dogs International (first accredited Virginia program).
Web Address: http://www.saintfrancisdogs.org/prisonpup.html.

Program Name: Prison Puppy Raising
Partners: Multiple state departments of corrections and Canine Companions for Independence.
Type or Purpose: Program trains service dogs; the dogs are trained at the prison for up to two years, followed by six months of training at a service dog school. The program is located in multiple correctional institutions.
Selected Accomplishments: Facilities in nine states host the program; each correctional institution has its own designated trainer to oversee the program's implementation at that facility; research at one facility found that the inmates were more successful than average in training delivery, and have lower recidivism than other inmates (see Von Lunen 2009).
Web Address: http://www.cci.org/get-involved/prison-puppy-raising.html.

Program Name: Prison Trained K-9 Companion Program (PTKCP)
Partners: Colorado Department of Corrections, multiple local animal shelters, and Colorado Correctional Industries.
Type or Purpose: Training shelter dogs for public adoption; current pet owners may also have their dogs trained through a 4-week initial training program and a 2-week (or more) refresher training program; the program is located in multiple facilities with multiple security levels housing adult male and female inmates.
Selected Accomplishments: Program established in 2002; over 8000 dogs trained; persons whose dogs have been trained may have free follow-up telephone consultation sessions; also sells dog houses, leashes, and children's books; program is financially self-supported through its fee structure.
Web Address: https://www.coloradoci.com/serviceproviders/puppy/index.html?p=aboutDogsDiv.

Program Name: Prisoners and Animals Working for Success (P.A.W.S.)
Partners: New Mexico Corrections Department, Animal Services Center of Mesilla Valley, and Action Programs for Animals.
Type or Purpose: Training shelter dogs for public adoption, including daily work and bi-weekly sessions supervised by a trainer; located in a medium-security state prison housing adult male inmates.

Selected Accomplishments: Established in 2015 through a collaboration between probation officer Renee Waskiewicz, who initiated the program, the unit manager and security supervisor for the housing unit, and a dog trainer; funded entirely through private resources, including donations and resources from non-profits.
Web Address: https://cd.nm.gov/apd/snmcf_paws.html.

Program Name: Project POOCH (Positive Opportunities Obvious Change with Hounds)
Partners: Oregon Youth Authority and Project POOCH, Inc.
Type or Purpose: Socialize and train shelter dogs for public adoption, through daily work with dogs in the program to meet the American Kennel Club's Canine Good Citizen Program; located in a juvenile correctional facility housing 15–24 year-old males.
Selected Accomplishments: Program was established in 1993; program participants assist in kennel operations and have the opportunity to receive certification in dog care services; the program is associated with very low recidivism (one study found 0%), positive behavior in the institution, and personal growth among participants (Merriam-Arduini 2000).
Web Address: https://www.pooch.org/.

Program Name: Puppies Behind Bars
Partners: New York Department of Corrections and Community Supervision, New Jersey Department of Corrections, and Puppies Behind Bars.
Type or Purpose: The program began by training puppies to qualify for guide dog school, after which they would be credentialed to serve as guide dogs for persons with visual impairments; the program now trains explosive detection dogs and service dogs for veterans suffering from post-traumatic stress disorder, traumatic brain injury, or other conditions; the program has been offered in prisons at multiple security levels housing adult male and female inmates.
Selected Accomplishments: Program has been in operation since 1997; operates in six correctional institutions with 140 inmate participants; has been prominently featured in national media, including the New York Times and Oprah Winfrey Show; over 700 dogs have been trained by the program; a documentary about the program titled *Prison Dogs* (Peltz and Gandbhir 2016) was produced and has been screened at numerous film festivals.
Web Address: https://puppiesbehindbars.com/.

Program Name: Puppies for Parole
Partners: Missouri Department of Corrections, numerous local animal shelters.
Type or Purpose: Socializing and training shelter dogs, some of whom are adopted by the public and some of whom go on to train as service dogs; located in multiple correctional institutions housing adult male and female inmates at multiple security levels.

Selected Accomplishments: Program was established in 2010; Over 5000 dogs have been trained and placed; inmate participants receive training, apprenticeship, and formal certification in animal services; program benefits include reduced recidivism for participants, greater employment for participants, and positive effects on institutions where the program operates; program is entirely privately funded.
Web Address: https://doc.mo.gov/programs/puppies-parole.

Program Name: Teacher's Pet: Dogs and Kids Learning Together
Partners: Multiple local juvenile correctional agencies and animal shelters, and Teacher's Pet.
Type or Purpose: Pairs at-risk youth in detention facilities with hard-to-adopt rescue dogs; program includes two hour sessions twice a week for 10 weeks. The program has been implemented in multiple juvenile detention facilities.
Selected Accomplishments: More than 2200 youth and 3200 dogs have participated in the program; program includes an educational component, including dog training, body language, and responsible pet ownership; program has developed a strong set of events to aid in fundraising.
Web Address: http://teacherspetmi.org/.

Conclusion

As illustrated by the small sampling of programs listed above, there is much variation in the mission, organization, and implementation of prison-based dog training programs. Also as illustrated by these 26 programs, the potential to yield positive outcomes is significant. With the potential to benefit inmate participants, the dogs they train, correctional institutions as a whole, and the communities where dogs are placed, it is likely that programs will continue to increase in number and type.

There are important lessons that can be drawn from the experience of other programs, so it is important for program planners and implementers—of both new and existing programs—to periodically survey the field in order to review trends, best practices, and new developments in program design. While the above list is a snapshot in time of selected programs, the field is dynamic, so vigilance for new information is always appropriate.

As the field of corrections seeks not only to rehabilitate, but also to restore and to promote a humanistic view of transforming corrections, prison-based dog training programs offer a unique option. It is worth study—academic and professional—of how they may do so, including—but certainly not limited to—a review of the programs noted above, and others like them.

References

Drew, J. D., Dearborn, C., Evans, M., Gagne, A., McBean, D., Saville, F., & Silliman, T. (n.d.). *The power of prison pups: The impact of the NEADS program on inmate dog trainers, MCI/Framingham, and the community*. Newton, MA: Lasell College. Available at https://neads.org/wp-content/uploads/2018/04/prison-pups-report-FINAL-ANSWER-3242014.pdf.

Han, T. M., Flynn, E., Winchell, J., Gould, E., Gandenberger, J., Barattin, D., Tedeschi, P., & Morris, K. N. (2018). *Prison-based dog training programs: Standard protocol*. Denver, CO: University of Denver Institute for Human- Animal Connection. Available at https://animalstudiesrepository.org/cgi/viewcontent.cgi?article=1001&context=anitobe.

Harkrader, T., Burke, T., & Owen, S. (2004, April). Pound puppies: The rehabilitative uses of dogs in correctional facilities. *Corrections Today*, pp. 74–79.

Hawkins, S. (2017). *Troubled to trained: All dogs need a leader they can trust*. Scotts Valley, CA: CreateSpace.

Hill, L. B. (2016). *Becoming the person your dog things you are: An assessment of Florida prison-based dog training programs on prison misconduct, post-release employment and recidivism* (Unpublished doctoral dissertation). Florida State University, Tallahassee, Florida.

Lynch, S. (Producer), Mellott, G. (Producer/Director), & Otto, J. (Producer). (2013). *The dogs of Lexington*. [Television broadcast]. USA: Oklahoma City Community College.

Merriam-Arduini, S. (2000). *Evaluation of an experimental program designed to have a positive effect on adjudicated violent, incarcerated male juveniles age 12–25 in the state of Oregon* (Unpublished doctoral dissertation). Pepperdine University, Malibu, CA.

Peltz, P. (Producer/Director) & Gandbhir, G. (Producer/Director). (2016). *Prison dogs* [Motion picture]. USA: G2P2 Films.

Smith, J. C., Unti, B. (2016, January/February). Second chances: Pen Pals Inc., the Dixon Correctional Institute and Louisiana's post-Katrina animal rescue legacy. *Corrections Today*, pp. 40–44.

Turner, W. (2007, June). The experiences of offenders in a prison canine program. *Federal Probation*. Available at https://www.uscourts.gov/sites/default/files/71_1_6_0.pdf.

Von Lunen, J. (2009, October 13). Future service dogs get their training by women inmates at Coffee Creek lockup. *The Oregonian*. Available at https://www.oregonlive.com/pets/2009/10/future_service_dogs_get_their.html.

Appendix B
Reasons to Bring Dogs into Correctional Facilities

The following table is intended to provide an overview of the purposes for bringing dogs into correctional institutions. As professionals consider what type of program would fit in a particular context, it is important to focus on the rationale, the type of dog involved, possible partners in the project, and the potential benefits.

Primary Purpose	Type of Dog	Typical Partners	Contributions
To make homeless and rescued dogs more adoptable and smooth the transition into a family, usually by teaching basic "house manners"	Family dog	Humane organizations, animal welfare groups, animal shelters, purebred rescue	Reduces overcrowding and euthanasia at shelters; increases successful adoptions by training dogs prior to placement
To socialize puppies and/or train assistance dogs for people with psychological and/or physical disabilities	Assistance dogs individually trained to perform tasks that help to mitigate a disability	Service dog providers, professional dog trainers, animal shelters and rescues, and reputable dog breeders	Increases the independence and social network of the recipient. Prepares more assistance dogs in a cost-effective manner
To train working dogs that support profess-sionals, particularly in the justice and mental health fields	Working dogs (e.g., search and rescue dogs, scent detection dogs). Visiting therapy dogs (e.g., courthouse dogs, dogs for domestic	Police officers, corrections officers, social workers, domestic violence shelter personnel. Therapy dog groups, dog training and obedience clubs	Promotes public safety and helps victims of crimes. Facilitates positive interactions between/among residents and staff, encourages residents

(continued)

M. R. Jalongo (ed.), *Prison Dog Programs*,
https://doi.org/10.1007/978-3-030-25618-0

(continued)

Primary Purpose	Type of Dog	Typical Partners	Contributions
	violence shelters) that usually are owned and trained by the handlers		to use available services and to participate in planned interventions
To raise litters of puppies under 12 weeks of age, orphaned or with their mothers, until the puppies are weaned	Family dogs or assistance dogs	Service dog providers or animal shelters/rescues	Saves the lives of orphaned pups. Supports assistance dog programs
To restore abused, neglected, ill or post-surgical dogs to health	Family dogs	Veterinary schools and animal welfare groups	Makes intensive care of dogs more affordable. Provides on-the-job training for inmates in veterinary medicine
To provide a constant dog presence at a correctional or justice institution and an ambassador for the dog program	Facility dog that is at the institution on a daily basis. It often is a dog that was exceptional in some way and/or represents the program well. May or may not have been trained by the inmates.	Resident dogs usually are owned/handled by administrators or mental health professionals	Gives inmates not directly involved with a dog program the documented physiological and psychological benefits of positive human-canine interaction. Dogs may be requested throughout the facility to reduce anxiety (e.g., during a dental appointment) and lift spirits (e.g., in hospice)
To support the larger community by operating a dog shelter/ kennel on site	Family dogs and assistance dogs	Local and county humane and animal welfare groups	Creates a safe haven for displaced, abandoned, neglected, stray, abused, and owner surrendered dogs. Operates a shelter in a cost-effective fashion
Rehabilitation of dogs with serious behavioral issues	Family dogs and sometimes assistance dogs	Animal rescue groups	Gives dogs with major issues access to trainers with an advanced level of

(continued)

(continued)

Primary Purpose	Type of Dog	Typical Partners	Contributions
			skill. Spares the dogs from extended sheltering that can exacerbate fear/aggression issues; reduces euthanasia rates

Index

M. R. Jalongo (ed.), *Prison Dog Programs*,
https://doi.org/10.1007/978-3-030-25618-0

Kolibri 360 GmbH
Ferdinand-Jühlke-Straße 7
99095 Erfurt, Deutschland
produktsicherheit@kolibri360.de